Letters from Prison

VOLUME I

747 *Letters*

COLUMBI

from Prison

VOLUME I

Antonio Gramsci

EDITED BY

Frank Rosengarten

TRANSLATED BY

Raymond Rosenthal

34475

UNIVERSITY PRESS • NEW YORK

COLUMBIA UNIVERSITY PRESS

New York   Chichester, West Sussex

Copyright © 1994 Columbia University Press

Library of Congress Cataloging-in-Publication Data

Gramsci, Antonio, 1891–1937.
   [Lettere dal carcere.   English]
   Letters from prison / Antonio Gramsci ; edited by Frank
Rosengarten ; translated by Raymond Rosenthal.
    p.   cm.
   ISBN 0-231-07558-8 (set)
   ISBN 0-231-07552-9 (v. 1)
   ISBN 0-231-07554-5 (v. 2)
   1. Gramsci, Antonio, 1891–1937—Correspondence.   2.
Communists—Italy—Correspondence.   I. Rosengarten,
Frank, 1927–
II. Title.
HX288.G69213   1994
335.43'092—dc20   93-737
                                           CIP

This edition of *Letters from Prison,* published under arrangement with the
Istituto Gramsci, is based on the Italian edition of 1965, published by
Giulio Einaudi and edited by Sergio Caprioglio and Elsa Fubini, and on
a subsequent Italian edition of 1988, published by *L'Unità* and edited by
Antonio Santucci, which in an appendix contains letters that were either
not yet found or not available for publication when the Einaudi edition
appeared.

All the letters and photographs published in this volume are by courtesy
of the Gramsci Institute Foundation in Rome. Permission to cite notes in
Lettere dal carcere (Einaudi, 1965), edited by Sergio Caprioglio and Elsa
Fubini, *Lettere dal carcere* (Einaudi, 1977), edited by Sebastiano Vassalli,
and in *Quaderni del carcere* (Einaudi, 1975), edited by Valentino
Gerratana, has also been granted by the Gramsci Foundation Institute.
The editor wishes to express his grateful acknowledgment to the
Gramsci Foundation Institute for permission to cite unpublished letters
from Tania Schucht to Antonio Gramsci and to Piero Sraffa.
Five footnotes appearing in *Letters from Prison* (Harper and Row, 1973)
are reprinted by permission of Georges Borchardt, Inc., on behalf of the
author; copyright © 1973 by Lynne Lawner.
Permission to cite footnote material from *Gramsci's Prison Letters,* edited
by Hamish Henderson and published in 1988 by Zwan Publications
(now Pluto Press), has been granted by Pluto Press.

Printed in the United States of America

c   10   9   8   7   6   5   4   3   2   1

Contents

Preface

The letters that Antonio Gramsci wrote during his years in prison, from 1926 to 1937, are almost all in the archives of the Gramsci Foundation Institute in Rome. The bulk of these letters was entrusted by the Gramsci family to Palmiro Togliatti and Felice Platone, who used them in their preparation of the first Italian edition of the *Letters from Prison*, published in 1947. In the following years, additional letters were donated to the Gramsci Institute by a few of their recipients and by other members of the Gramsci and Schucht families. In this way, the 218 letters of the 1947 edition were expanded to the 428 letters published in the 1965 edition, which was the first critical edition and the fruit of years of careful research done by Elsa Fubini and Sergio Caprioglio.

Since 1965 still other letters have been found or donated, some of which were published separately in various newspapers and magazines. In 1988, with the commendable intention of producing an edition of the prison letters that was within the reach of a mass audience, the Italian Communist party newspaper *L'Unità* published, as special supplements to its January 24, 1988, and February 14, 1988, issues, a two-volume, paperback edition of the 1965 *Letters*, plus an additional 28 letters that had come to light since 1965. These were edited by Antonio Santucci and introduced by Paolo Spriano and Valentino Gerratana.

The original letters are kept in a vault and cannot be handled, except a few at a time by scholars and others with a particular need to consult them. To avoid the risk of damaging the originals, I limited my consultation of them to a representative selection of forty letters. For the remaining majority of letters, I relied on photocopies of the originals.

Gramsci's precise, clear handwriting makes reading the letters a relatively simple task, although there are of course illegible words and phrases that, combined with sections of the letters deleted by prison censors, sometimes create problems in connecting one sentence with another. Even more remarkable than the handwriting is the almost total lack of erasures: what Gramsci had to say in his letters he had already, obviously, thought out in detail before putting pen to paper. In this way he made maximum use of the time allowed him for letter writing in prison. For the most part he used regular stationery, which he usually filled down to the last available square inch. But some letters are written on odd single sheets, and these are in varying states of preservation. Graphologists will find interesting two characteristics of Gramsci's handwriting. First, one notices the small size and clear, precise shape of the letters except for the capitals, which, especially in the case of *A*s, *T*s, *S*s and *F*s, are stately and somewhat ornate in appearance. The capital *S* looks like the symbol of the treble clef. Second, Gramsci's signature, whether Antonio or Nino, has a strong upward slant. No doubt these characteristics are due to early training in calligraphy, but for someone such as I, who has had to work with the letters of various figures in the Italian antiFascist movement, it is evident that not all Italians were faithful to their early training in penmanship. One needs paleographical skills to decipher most of them, suggesting that for Gramsci the appearance and easy legibility of a letter were important.

In order to give the reader a sense of Gramsci's *Letters from Prison* as part of a correspondence, I thought it desirable to include in this edition a sampling of the letters written to him by his wife, Giulia, and sister-in-law Tania Schucht. I have chosen letters in which the points of view and the writing style of Giulia and Tania give some sense of the personalities of these two exceptional women, ones that also facilitate an understanding of Gramsci's points of view and feelings at different moments of his years in prison. The letters from Giulia and Tania are to be found in footnotes.

The letters to Gramsci from his wife, sister-in-law, mother, and other family members and friends have been gathered over the years. Many of them were conserved by Tania Schucht and by Gramsci's younger brother Carlo, who were at his bedside at his death and who took it upon themselves to safeguard the record of Gramsci's life as a political prisoner. These letters were held by the Gramsci family and then bequeathed to the Gramsci Institute after the war.

This edition of Gramsci's *Letters from Prison* has a number of other features that should be noted. First, all the printed letters of the 1965 and 1988 Italian editions have been checked against the originals, and mistakes that were inevitably made in editing and printing the manuscripts have been corrected. These include wrong words, misspellings of words and proper names, paragraphs in incorrect order, errors in punctuation, incorrect dates of letters, and missing postscripts and sentences or in a few instances even paragraphs. Many of these mistakes had already been found by Elsa Fubini and Sergio Caprioglio but not yet been made known in a new Italian edition. In all, 117 of the printed letters were found to have mistakes of some sort, mostly minor, but in some cases of such a nature as to misrepresent Gramsci's intended meaning.

Second, this edition contains two groups of letters never before published *in book form* in any language, including Italian. (Some of these did appear previously in various magazines and newspapers.) The first consists of 20 letters that I came across in 1991 and 1992 while pursuing my research at the Gramsci Institute. That brought the total of personal letters to family and friends to 476. The second is a group of letters written to Mussolini and to various medical and prison authorities by Gramsci during his eleven-year prison ordeal. They concern matters that were of vital concern to Gramsci, who sought to avail himself of whatever opportunities the Italian criminal code allowed to political prisoners to obtain better treatment for his many illnesses and, above all, to read, study, and write in prison in as productive a manner as possible. With these, the total number of letters in this edition is 486. One of the 20 letters not yet published in book form has indeed never been published anywhere: it is a letter written from Milan's San Vittore prison to a Communist comrade, Virginio Borioni, on May 7, 1928. The letter, only a portion of which is legible, had lain all these years in a folder marked "Letters to Berti, to Bianco and others," the victim of an oversight that haunts the consciousness of all researchers who work with these kinds of materials. Third, the footnotes of this edition are based on a thorough review of existing documentation in preceding editions published in many different countries. Wherever existing notes were unclear or inaccurate, an attempt has been made to correct or to clarify them. Many new notes have been added. The more complete documentation and greater preciseness of this edition are not due to the superior sleuthing abilities of the editor but rather to the moment in which it appears. In the past four to five years our knowledge of Gramsci's prison experience, and of the contributions made by various people to his welfare and intellectual productivity in prison, has been vastly expanded. The authors and titles of these new books and articles are of course listed in the bibliography. I would also like to acknowledge here the work of John Cammett, Sergio Caprioglio, Giuseppe Fiori, Elsa Fubini, Valentino Gerratana, Aldo Natoli, Michele Pistillo, Jean-Pierre Potier, Mimma Paulesu Quercioli, Antonio Santucci, and Paolo Spriano.

This edition is based whenever possible on direct study of the originals and reproduces the original letter as it was written in most cases. In some instances, for reasons of intelligibility, changes have been made. For example, Gramsci's way of dating letters varied, from use of Roman numerals to Arabic numbers, and his paragraphing was often determined not by the normal concern for logical organization but rather by limitations of space and time. In these cases and a few others, I have taken the liberty of altering the original form of the letter.

Some of the photographs used in other editions of Gramsci's writings appear here as well, but there are some new ones that I think will enhance the reader's appreciation of the human and political significance of the letters. These were taken by Diego Zitelli.

This edition includes a bibliography of the most important critical writings on the letters, whether in the form of introductory essays or in separately published articles. There have been two earlier English-language editions—one with introduction, notes, and translation by Lynne Lawner published in 1973 by Harper and Row, the other translated in 1948–50 by Hamish Henderson but not published until 1974, in issues 25 and 26 of the *New Edinburgh Review*. The Henderson translation appeared in book form in 1988, published by Zwan Publications (now Pluto Press). The letters in the Lawner edition number 94, some of which are fragmentary; the Henderson edition has 219 letters, the same ones that were published in the first 1947 Italian edition.

Throughout the text three abbreviations—PCI (Italian Communist party), PSI (Italian Socialist party), and CI (Communist International)—are used.

The Columbia University Press edition of Gramsci's *Letters from Prison* aims to offer readers of English as complete and as reliably edited and documented a collection as possible, one that affords insight into the ideas and inner life of one of the most remarkable human beings of this century.

Acknowledgments

It is a pleasure for me to acknowledge my indebtedness to all of the people who have helped me bring this book to fruition.

The research I have done over the past decade on Gramsci's prison letters, beginning in the early 1980s and again, after a six-year interval, from 1989 to 1992, required access to the archival materials and library collections at the Gramsci Foundation Institute in Rome. From the outset of my work I received assistance, encouragement, and support from the entire staff of the Institute. Antonio Santucci, Elsa Fubini, Valentino Gerratana, and Giuseppe Vacca were always available to answer my questions, which were not only of a strictly scholarly nature but also involved difficult political issues. They willingly shared their expertise and their opinions with me, which I have taken into due account in the preparation of these volumes. Antonio Santucci and Elsa Fubini, together with Sergio Caprioglio, are among the best informed individuals in the world concerning Gramsci's prison letters and, indeed, concerning many other facets of the history of Italian communism. I could not have done my work without their cooperation and good will.

It is difficult for me to single out others at the Gramsci Institute whose help was important to me, since the entire staff was so generous with their time and advice. Nevertheless, I would like to thank in particular Marcello Forti and Fabrizio Zitelli, who share responsibility for protecting the manuscripts and other documents belonging to the Fondo Gramsci and assisting scholars who need to consult these materials; Patrizia Gabrielli and Chiara Daniele, professional archivists whose diligent labors made my work so much easier than it would have been without them; Dario Massimi, head of the Institute's book collection, who acquainted me with resources for the study of Italian political history of which I had been unaware; Lucio Conte, an efficient staff librarian with whom I had the pleasure of exchanging ideas on several occasions; and Arianna Pizzi and Germana Lotti, who informed me about many practical aspects of the Institute's activities and functions.

Gramsci's niece, Mimma Paulesu Quercioli, was my cordial and generous hostess at her apartment in Milan, where she and her husband house their extraordinary library. I am very grateful to her for shedding light on a number of knotty controversies concerning the Gramsci and the Schucht families. Her judicious views helped me to clarify my own. The friendship and professional cooperation offered to me by Giorgio Baratta have also been very important to me. In 1987 Giorgio was the animating force behind the creation of the International Gramsci Society, and he is today the person in Italy most involved on a grassroots level with every aspect of the task of preserving and diffusing Gramsci's legacy.

Among friends and colleagues who have provided me with supportive criticism and encouragement, I am pleased to express my gratitude to Joseph Buttigieg, John Cammett, George Bernstein, Renate Holub, Will Hartley, and David Forgacs. For many years now, I have exchanged ideas and discussed various "Gramsci projects" with Buttigieg and Cammett, both of whom have contributed in fundamental ways to Gramsci studies in this country: Joe with his excellent translation and editing of the *Prison Notebooks*, and John with his groundbreaking 1967 study of Gramsci and, more recently, with his *Bibliografia Gramsciana*. George Bernstein was among the founders of the Gramsci Study Circle of New York back in the mid–1980s, and since then he has continued to cultivate the study of Gramsci in an original and pedagogically useful manner. Renate Holub was good enough to read a first draft of the introduction to this edition of Gramsci's prison letters and to offer me some pertinent suggestions. Will Hartley was also among the early members of the Gramsci Study Circle. I assume he is aware of how much we all owe to him for the insights contained in his doctoral dissertation on Gramsci, completed some years ago at the University of Chicago.

David Forgacs was a reader and constructive critic of the first outline for this book. I have benefited from his ideas concerning the essential themes and problems to be highlighted in an English-language edition of Gramsci's prison letters.

For some of the facts and a good part of background information needed for the footnotes, I relied on the research skills of Marianela Belliard, Eric Canepa, and Rosanna Giammanco Frongia. They helped to fill in many troublesome empty spaces in my own research.

Finally, I would like to express my appreciation to Columbia University Press, especially to its director, John Moore, and senior editor Jennifer Crewe, as well as to my talented manuscript editor, Susan Heath. Their commitment to Gramsci studies in the United States has borne fruit in the first of a multivolume edition of the *Prison Notebooks* and in this two-volume edition of the *Letters from Prison*.

Gramsci's Correspondents and Members of the Gramsci and Schucht Families

Names marked with an asterisk are the correspondents. Unless otherwise indicated, the given names and nicknames of persons mentioned in the letters refer to correspondents and to members of the Gramsci and Schucht families.

The Gramsci family

Francesco ("Cicillo") Gramsci (1860–1937), Antonio's father, a native of Gaeta, of Albanian descent. He was employed in the Office of Land Registry in the town of Sòrgono. From 1898 to 1904, he spent close to five years in prison on charges of misuse of public funds. Two of his brothers, *Alfredo* and *Cesare*, are mentioned in Gramsci's letter of August 22, 1932, to his mother.

Giuseppina ("Peppina") Marcias Gramsci* (1861–1932), Gramsci's mother, a native Sardinian. She raised her seven children with only sporadic help from her husband, who worked irregularly after his release from prison. The daughter of a local tax collector, she was better educated and more culturally sophisticated than most women belonging to the petit bourgeois class of the island.

The following are Antonio Gramsci's six siblings.

Gennaro ("Nannaro") Gramsci (1884–1965), the eldest of the Gramsci children. He spent three years on the Austro-Italian front in World War I, was on the administrative staff of the newspaper *L'Ordine Nuovo* in 1921–1922, and fought with an anarchist unit in defense of the Republic in the Spanish Civil War. Bitterly disillusioned by his experiences in Spain, he was interned after the war, then made his way to France, where he worked for many years in a menial capacity and lost touch with his family. It was not until many years later that he became reconciled with his family and was able to overcome his intense hostility to the Communist party of Italy (PCI) that was a result of his experiences in Spain.

*Grazietta Gramsci** (1887–1962) had musical ability and extraordinary proficiency in the domestic arts. She raised Gennaro's daughter, *Edmea* (1920–), who married a physician and became an elementary school teacher.

Emma Gramsci (1889–1920) was employed as a bookkeeper for an industrial engineering firm and died of influenza in 1920.

Mario Gramsci (1893–1945), the sole Fascist member of the Gramsci family. He was secretary of the local Fascist federation in Ghilarza, then moved to Varese, where he lived with his wife and two children, *Gianfranco* and *Cesarina*. He fought in the Abyssinian War and, later, in North Africa.

*Teresina Gramsci Paulesu** (1895–1976) shared Antonio's intellectual interests and affinities. After her husband's death in 1941, she took his place as supervisor of the Ghilarza post office. She had four children: *Franco*, *Maria ("Mimma")*, *Luisa ("Diddi")*, and *Marco*. *Mimma* is the author and editor of important studies on Gramsci and on the Gramsci and Schucht families.

*Carlo Gramsci** (1897–1968) served as an army officer in World War I. He worked in an administrative capacity for a milk cooperative in Sardinia until 1931, when he obtained a position with the Snia Viscosa textile firm in Milan. He was very active in efforts to assist Gramsci in prison and to obtain his transfer from prison to the Cusumano clinic in Formia, in 1933.

The Schucht Family

Apollon Aleksandrovic Schucht (1860–1933) and *Julia ("Lula") Grigorievna Schucht* (1860s–1942), Gramsci's parents-in-law. Apollon was a Russian of German descent. A personal friend of Lenin, he was an anti-Czarist political émigré in Switzerland, France, and then in Rome, where he lived with his wife and six children from 1908 to

1917. From 1917, when he joined the Bolshevik party, to his death in 1933 he lived in Moscow, where he was employed as a librarian at the Electro-Technical Institute. *Lula* was the daughter of a Russian father, who was a well-known lawyer, and a Russian Jewish mother. Although not as politically engaged as her husband, she did occasional stints of administrative work for the Communist party in the early 1920s.

*Julca ("Giulia") Schucht** (1896–1980), Gramsci's wife. Born on September 19, 1896, in Geneva, *Giulia* became a professional violinist and taught violin in Ivanovo after World War I. She and Gramsci were married in 1923. Beginning in the early 1920s, she suffered from emotional and physical problems, caused almost certainly by a form of epilepsy, which required lengthy periods of rest and various forms of therapy. After World War II, she shared an apartment in Moscow and a dacha with her sister *Eugenia* until the latter's death in 1972. No longer able to care for herself, she spent the last eight years of her life at a home in Peredelkino reserved by the Central Committee of the Soviet Communist party for "old Bolsheviks."

The following are her five siblings.

Nadja ("Nadine") Schucht (1885–ca. 1918) had two children, *Oleg* and *Giuliano*.

*Tatiana ("Tania") Schucht** (1887–1943) was born in Samara (now Kuibyshev) during her father's exile to Siberia. She was sympathetic to the Socialist revolutionaries at the time of the Bolshevik Revolution but later gave critical support to the Soviet government. She lived in Rome independently from 1917 to 1938 when, after more than ten years of devoted assistance to Gramsci in prison, she returned to the Soviet Union. In 1941, after the German invasion of Russia, she escaped with her mother, *Lula*, and her sisters, *Giulia* and *Eugenia* to Frunze, the capital of Kirghizia in central Asia. She died in 1943, of pellagra.

Eugenia ("Genia") Schucht (1888–1972) was born in Tomsk, in Siberia. Prior to World War I, she earned a degree from the Academy of Fine Arts in Rome. Her friendship with Gramsci led to his meeting with *Giulia* in 1922. A dedicated Communist, in the early 1920s she was secretary to Lenin's wife, Nadyezhda Krupskaya, in the Commissariat of Public Education. She was one of two translators of the 1957 Russian-language edition of Gramsci's *Letters from Prison*.

Asja ("Anna") Schucht (1893–?), a violinist who married *Theodore Zabel*, a professional pianist with whom she had a son *Valja ("Volia")*.
Viktor ("Vittorio") Schucht (1899–?), also born in Geneva.

Antonio and Giulia Gramsci's Children

*Delio ("Delka") Gramsci** (1924–1981), Gramsci's eldest son, was a career officer in the Soviet Navy and taught mathematics at the Naval Academy in Leningrad.

*Giuliano ("Julik") Gramsci** (1926–) is a professional violinist and clarinetist, now retired. He resides in Moscow with his wife, *Zina*, a pianist, with whom he has two children, *Olga* and *Antonio*. In the 1930s *Delio* and *Giuliano* were given Italian lessons by the mother of a family friend, *Lisa Misiano*, who later became a professor at the University of Moscow and edited the first Russian-language editions of the *Prison Notebooks* and the *Letters from Prison*. But for *Giuliano*, who never saw his father, it was his mother's Italian violin even more than the Italian language that "represented the most important link with the culture of that far-off country, a link that will become stronger precisely through music." (*Lettere ai familiari*, p. xi)

Other Correspondents

*Clara Passarge** was the landlady at via Morgagni 45 in Rome, where Gramsci was living at the time of his arrest on the evening of November 8, 1926. She and her husband, *Giorgio*, were Germans who had settled in the Italian capital. They formed a close personal attachment to Gramsci.

*Giuseppe Berti** (1901–1979), was born in Naples. In 1921 he became the national secretary of the Italian Communist party's Youth Federation. After serving a period of police confinement and imprisonment, he fled to France and was active in the anti-Fascist movements in France, the Soviet Union, and the United States. After World War II, he was elected to the Chamber of Deputies and, in 1956, to the Senate.

*Virginio Borioni** (1903–1961) was born in Macerata. In November 1926 he was a young Communist student and was in prison with Gramsci in Regina Coeli in Rome. In early December of that year he was sent to the island of Ustica, where he again shared Gramsci's fate during the month prior to Gramsci's reassignment to prison in Milan. After World War II, he served as a Communist deputy in the first legislature of the Italian republic, from 1948 to 1953.

*Piero Sraffa** (1898–1983), the world-renowned economist, was born in Turin. In 1927, after teaching at the universities of Cagliari and Perugia, he took up a teaching post at Cambridge University, where he was invited by John Maynard Keynes to pursue his research on David Ricardo. His best-known works are a critical edition of Ricardo's *Collected Works* and *Production of Commodities by Means of Commodities* (1960), which "established Sraffa as a major figure in economic thought" (Bottomore, *A Dictionary of Marxist Thought*, p. 458). His material assistance to Gramsci and indirect correspondence with him through Tania were vital to Gramsci's survival and intellectual productivity in prison.

Introduction

Antonio Gramsci was widely known by people active in the anti-Fascist struggle before World War II, but it was not until the appearance in 1947 of his *Letters from Prison* that his name came to the attention of a mass public in Italy. Even more than the *Prison Notebooks*, which found their audience primarily in intellectual and university circles, the *Letters* were responsible for Gramsci's extraordinary posthumous popularity among millions of readers after the war. It was the *Letters* that marked the beginning of a process that eventually saw him emerge as a political thinker whose ideas were to leave their mark not only in postwar Europe and America but in many of the countries of the third world as well.

The impact in Italy of the 1947 edition of the *Letters* was immediate and prolonged. The politically mixed jury that in 1947 awarded the Viareggio prize for nonfiction to the *Lettere dal carcere* found common ground in recognizing their artistic value. The jury also agreed that in Gramsci they had discovered "a lucid affirmer and witness" of the human condition.[1] This intense response, which was reinforced by the subsequent homage paid to Gramsci by Italy's leading philosopher, Benedetto Croce, was the prelude to a long and varied publishing history. Within six years, the *Letters* had gone through nine Italian editions, and by the mid-1960s, up to the appearance of the first critical edition, they had been translated into fifteen languages.[2] Today, with numerous Italian editions aimed at different audiences, and with at least nineteen foreign language editions, the *Letters from Prison* have become at once a popular best-seller and a classic text for serious students of politics, philosophy, sociology, and other related fields.

As the expression of a man violently removed from the arena of political struggle in which he had been actively engaged since his teenage years in Sardinia in the first decade of this century, Gramsci's *Letters from Prison* are an excellent source of insight into both the physical and the psychological problems of prison life. In minute and meticulous detail, Gramsci composes in his letters a compendium of reflections on how he in particular and prisoners in general—especially political prisoners—contend with illness and the fear of death, with rules and regulations that efface all individuality, with prison censorship and the need for communication with the outside world. In so doing, he inadvertently paints a self-portrait that helps the reader to understand the personal qualities of a man who is still known by most people only as a great Marxist theorist and political leader. The *Letters from Prison* are an invaluable connecting thread joining Gramsci the thinker with Gramsci the individual human being. Through them, the reader can see how a man in prison reviews and reconstructs his life, tries to define his primary relationships, and struggles to maintain his sense of identity.

But the letters do not separate private concerns from issues of broad general interest. In many instances, they help the reader gain a precise understanding of the genesis and development of the intellectual projects Gramsci undertook in prison. For example, three letters to his sister-in-law, Tania Schucht, written on March 19, 1927, September 20, 1931, and May 2, 1932, offer insights respectively into Gramsci's way of relating culture and politics, his reading of Dante, and his theory of hegemony. In sum, the *Letters from Prison* are the best source for understanding the ways in which Gramsci's personal experiences from childhood to maturity conditioned and interacted with his development as a theorist of politics and culture. They allow the reader to feel the presence of the human being who, in the Notebooks and other writings, tends to detach himself from the various topics that occupied his attention. Whenever possible, Gramsci used his letters to probe moral, psychological, and philosophical questions. That he did so in such an original and stimulating manner is a tribute to his spiritual resilience, and is a reminder of the capacity for resistance that human beings possess when they understand why they are being persecuted and how thoughtful action might bring that persecution to an end.

Prior to his arrest by the Fascist political police on November 8, 1926, Gramsci had acquired a deserved reputation on the Italian national scene as a Marxist thinker and Communist party leader, and internationally as a follower and interpreter of Lenin and Italian delegate to the Comintern. From the outset of his journalistic and organizational work for the Italian Socialist party (PSI), Gramsci had consistently placed emphasis on the importance of mobilizing the Italian peasantry and working class in a unified struggle for a Socialist transformation of Italian society. This objective, allied with his great, although not uncritical, admiration for the Russian Bolshevik revolutionaries, led him to join forces with those members of the PSI who broke away from their party in January 1921 and founded the Communist party of Italy (PCI).

Gramsci's political life from 1921 to 1926 was eventful and productive. His editorship of the newspaper *L'Ordine Nuovo*, which had sponsored the Italian workers council movement; the year and a half he spent in Moscow, from May 1922 to November 1923, as an Italian delegate to the Communist International; and his election to the Chamber of Deputies in April 1924 were steps along the way to his being elected general secretary of the PCI, a position he held at the time of his arrest in 1926. During these years, on many occasions, he had warned his fellow Communists and members of other anti-Fascist parties that the Fascist regime, whose advent to power began with Benito Mussolini's assumption of the premiership at the end of October 1922, would probably not, as many thought, be a brief parenthesis in Italian political history. Gramsci's analysis of the forces at play in the early 1920s led him to the conclusion that either the Italian democratic and working-class parties would seize power in the name of the Italian people or the Fascist regime would unleash a massive counterrevolution whose final outcome would be a brutal dictatorship of the Right. This combination of shrewd analytical insight and revolutionary energy made Gramsci a prime target of the Fascist political police.

Gramsci's personal life during these "years of iron and fire," as he called them, was also filled with a series of significant experiences. Before his trip to Moscow in 1922, he had had several love affairs but none that could compare in intensity and devotion to the relationship he formed with a Russian woman named Julca Schucht, whom he met in the late summer of 1922, while convalescing from a nervous disorder at the sanatorium of the Silver Forest in Moscow. Their love, which blossomed immediately, was destined to be at once a source of happiness and hope for Gramsci in the difficult years that lay ahead and the cause of terrible suffering due in large part to conditions and circumstances over which neither he nor Julca (or Giulia, as he preferred to call her) could exercise any real control.

The tender love letters that Gramsci wrote to Giulia during the four years between their first meeting in 1922 and his arrest in November 1926 suggest that their relationship helped him overcome a lifelong fear that "there was an absolute impossibility, almost a fatal impossibility, that I could be loved."[3] Gramsci and Giulia had much in common. Both were dedicated Communists and in 1923 worked together on a number of projects in Ivanovo, where Giulia taught violin and did part-time secretarial work for the local section of the Communist party. Giulia had spent her teenage years in Italy and, like her parents and five siblings, spoke Italian quite well.[4] At the same time, she helped Gramsci in his study of Russian, in which he became fairly proficient. Although Gramsci did not share Giulia's ardent love of music, his letters make it clear that they talked at length about art and literature. With Giulia, Gramsci was able to enjoy conversations about his favorite verses from *The Divine Comedy*. A letter to Giulia sent from Rome to Moscow on October 6, 1924, two months after the birth of their first child, Delio, reveals that the famous verse from the Paolo and Francesca episode of the *Inferno*, "Amor, ch'a nullo amato amar perdona" ("Love, which permits no loved one not to love")[5] had formed the substance of long and impassioned talks between Gramsci and Giulia during the first tempestuous phase of their love affair.

But problems had arisen early on in their relationship, caused both by temperamental differences and by the life choices that each had made. The birth of their first child required that Giulia remain at home in Moscow with her parents and unmarried sister Eugenia, while Gramsci's political work demanded that he be away from Moscow, first in Vienna in 1923–24, then in Italy from 1924 to 1926. This meant that there were long periods when their only contact was epistolary. Both suffered: Gramsci from guilt that he was unable to be available to his wife and child, and Giulia from her loss of independence and from what appears to have been a lifelong sense of inferiority vis-à-vis her sister Eugenia. (Given the fact that Eugenia was on occasion hostile to Gramsci, whom she accused of "not being interested" in his family, and who was pictured by all of the Schuchts as someone whose imperious personality inhibited Giulia, it is ironic that she eventually became one of the two translators of the first Russian-language edition of Gramsci's *Letters from Prison*.)[6] On the one hand Giulia had great reserves of strength, as Gramsci himself recognized, one sign of which was her resolute refusal to accept any of the financial assistance that he offered her through a comrade living in Moscow, Vincenzo Bianco.[7] Yet she was unsure of herself and obsessively self-critical. Already in 1924, and in later years in exacerbated forms that were to cause Gramsci a great deal of anxiety in prison, Giulia suffered from an illness whose symptoms were depression, bouts of amnesia, and fainting spells. Many years of various types of therapy alleviated her symptoms but did not cure her illness. There is a consensus among her family members and people who visited her after World War II that Giulia suffered from a form of epilepsy characterized by fairly frequent "partial complex seizures," which sometimes cause loss of consciousness and are often associated with emotional difficulties.

In early August 1926 Giulia, then about to give birth to their second child, Giuliano, returned to the Soviet Union after having spent the previous nine months in Rome in order to be near her husband. During this period, since he was under constant police surveillance, Gramsci had remained in his own apartment on Via Morgagni while Giulia had shared an apartment with two of her sisters, Eugenia and Tania, the latter of whom had been living in Rome since 1908. Eugenia returned to the Soviet Union with Giulia, while Tania remained in Italy. This decision was a fateful one, because Gramsci's imminent arrest and subsequent lengthy prison term was to thrust Tania into a care-giving role that turned out to be of supreme importance to both of them.

Gramsci's prison ordeal began on the evening of November 8, 1926, when he was arrested at his apartment in Rome and put into solitary confinement at the Regina Coeli penitentiary from where, on

November 25, he was sent to relatively easy internment on the island of Ustica, off the coast of Sicily. As a parliamentary deputy, he ought to have been immune from arrest, but the Special Laws in Defense of the State, put into effect officially by the Fascist government on November 9, deprived him and hundreds of other anti-Fascist deputies of their parliamentary mandate and made any form of organized anti-Fascist activity illegal.

After six weeks at Ustica, Gramsci was transferred for judicial detention to the San Vittore prison in Milan, where he spent a year and a half waiting for evidence to be gathered against him by the investigative judges assigned to his case. During this period he was still free to communicate with his loved ones and comrades and to receive mail from friends as well as from family members.

Specific charges against Gramsci were not made and upheld by government authorities until his trial, together with thirty-two other leading Italian Communists (eight of whom were either in hiding or had fled the country), before the Special Tribunal in Defense of the State from May 28 to June 4, 1928. The trial was conducted according to military procedure: the president of the tribunal was a general, the jurymen were five colonels from the Fascist militia, and the court was guarded by a double cordon of militiamen. The accused had counsel provided by the court, but Gramsci, Umberto Terracini, and several others also spoke in their own defense. On the first day of proceedings there was a moment of high drama when, after being repeatedly interrupted by the president, General Alessandro Saporiti, Gramsci turned to the judges and said: "You will lead Italy to ruin and it will be up to us Communists to save her."

Long prison sentences were handed down to all the accused. On June 4, 1928, Gramsci and two of his comrades, Giovanni Roveda and Mauro Scoccimarro, were found guilty of "conspiratorial activity, instigation of civil war, justification of crime, and incitement to class hatred" and sentenced to twenty years, four months, and five days in prison.[8] The sentence was later reduced several times, as a result of amnesties and appeals. From June 4 to July 7, he waited at Regina Coeli prison in Rome, where on June 22 he was given a medical examination. On the basis of a diagnosis of chronic uremia, he was assigned to a special prison for the infirm and disabled in Turi, in the province of Bari, in Calabria.

On July 8, 1928, he left Rome and on July 19, after a horrendous train ride, arrived at the prison in Turi, where he became prisoner Number 7047. This was to remain his identification for over five years until November 19,1933, when, with the help of Tania and other friends and family members, he obtained a transfer, after a brief stay at the prison of Civitavecchia, to the Cusumano clinic in Formia, a resort town on the Mediterranean in south central Italy. He spent close to two years at Formia. In August 1935 he obtained another transfer, motivated by declining health, to the Quisisana Hospital in Rome. Still under strict police guard, he survived long enough to win his freedom on April 21, 1937. Six days later, in the early morning of April 27, he died of a cerebral hemorrhage at the age of forty-six. Tania was at his bedside when he died. She and his brother Carlo were present at his burial the following day.

Throughout his years in prison and in police custody at the clinics of Formia and Rome, Gramsci's physical and spiritual resources were put to the severest of tests. It is true that even during the worst years of physical suffering he retained his habitual poise and self-confidence. Alessandro Pertini, the future president of the Italian Republic who was imprisoned with Gramsci for more than a year at Turi in the early 1930s, recalls him as having had "the weak body of a pygmy and, on this body, the head of a Danton. He had steel blue eyes that, when fixed on an interlocutor, never relinquished their focus: from his eyes sprang all of the intelligence and genius of his brain."[9] But despite Gramsci's exceptional control of himself, his health, which had never been robust, underwent a gradual and painful deterioration that was compounded by the neglect and incompetence of prison doctors. His illnesses included uremia and circulatory disturbances, which weakened him to the point that he was often unable to stand up without assistance. These and other ailments, combined with infrequent and frustratingly vague letters from Giulia, often gave his prison experience a hellish aspect. As the years passed, he felt increasingly cut off from the outside world. That he was able finally to overcome periodic crises of alienation due mainly to his numerous physical afflictions, but also to fears that his links with family and friends had been irreparably severed, must be credited mainly to two people: his sister-in-law Tania Schucht, and his friend, the economist Piero Sraffa. Together Tania and Sraffa were the pillars of Gramsci's support system in prison. Their ministrations helped him to resist the brutalization of prison life and to continue his life-long work as a writer and thinker.

Tania was similar to Giulia in several ways. She resembled her sister physically, shared her political and artistic interests, and was high-strung and sensitive. She also had a strong sense of herself as a person committed to the ideal of service to others. In Tania's case, this commitment expressed itself almost to the point of self-abnegation, which has led some people who have studied her relationship with Gramsci to conclude that she unconsciously took on the traits of both wife and mother in her assiduous efforts on Gramsci's behalf.[10] Certainly she made Gramsci's survival and well-being in prison the central purpose of her life. But there is no reason to conclude from this that she had substituted herself for Giulia. In a letter to Gramsci written on February 8, 1929, for example, she assured him that "Giulia is certainly right when she says that she feels closer to you because I have been close to you." Tania was always as mindful of her responsibilities toward Giulia as toward Gramsci. She was in Italy at the time that the Fascist axe fell on Gramsci and felt an obligation to help him since she was aware of Giulia's problems and disabilities; there was really no one else close to him who could have assumed the responsibilities involved in attending to his needs. Moreover, like Giulia, although in a less doctrinaire manner, Tania identified herself with Gramsci's Communist ideals, and therefore did what she did for political as well as personal reasons.

However, there were also significant differences between Tania and Giulia that played a determining role in what each could do for Gramsci during his imprisonment. Tania held a doctorate in natural science from the University of Rome. She had lived alone in Italy for many years and was accustomed to faring for herself, with little help from friends and family, for prolonged periods of time. She was more practical and self-confident than Giulia. She had a circle of friends in Rome, mainly from the medical establishment, and seems to have led a rather interesting and varied life despite her repeated confession to Gramsci that she was unable to take anything for herself or "to open herself" to anyone, that she lived entirely through and for others. She had retained her Soviet citizenship, and since she had not completed her medical studies she made her living by translating, teaching, and doing secretarial work and correspondence for the Soviet Embassy and for the Soviet Trade Delegation in Rome. Like Giulia, she was hypochondriacal and rather sickly, but she had more resilient recuperative powers than Giulia and sprang back from periods of illness and withdrawal. Giulia's inability, or, as Gramsci thought, her unwillingness to fight her illness, to take charge of her life and be consistently attentive to her own and to his needs was what caused him the most suffering in prison.

Obviously, on the level of daily involvement in his life, there is no comparison between what Tania was able to do for Gramsci and what Giulia could do. But even considering the constraints on Giulia, it is disconcerting to consider the fact that throughout the years of his imprisonment she sent him at most forty or so letters, many of which were little more than short notes. Nor did she come to Italy to visit him. Apparently, her father, Apollon, and sister Eugenia did not think she was strong enough, psychologically and physically, to undertake such a trip, and she did not have the independence of will to reject their opinion. She probably also feared that if she were to become ill and have an epileptic attack during a visit with her husband, the effect on him would have been disastrous.

So in a sense a kind of substitution did take place between Giulia and Tania, although not the kind suggested by those who insist on a repressed amorous passion on Tania's part. More than half of the 476 prison letters[11] that Gramsci wrote to family and friends were written to Tania, and she wrote him a total of 652 letters and postcards from 1926 to 1935.[12] Letter writing was only one aspect of her commitment to Gramsci. She bought and mended clothing for him; sent him food packages and searched out the proper medicines for his various ailments; made innumerable appeals on his behalf to governmental authorities; visited him in prison from 1927 to 1933 and, after 1933, at the clinics of Formia and Rome; and kept in touch by letter with both the Gramsci family in Sardinia and the Schucht clan in Moscow, thus making herself the main link in a complex supportive network of human associations.

Gramsci's suffering with regard to Giulia seems to have been caused, therefore, by her elusiveness as a person and her vagueness and allusiveness as a correspondent. He yearned for concrete details of her life and that of his two sons, a desire that she could not satisfy.

Giulia left him in a permanent limbo of uncertainty concerning many aspects of her life and as a result made him feel powerless, a feeling that Gramsci hated and that he sometimes blamed on her. In regard to Tania, on the other hand, Gramsci's suffering, when not provoked by her occasional forgetfulness, was rooted in what often amounts to a conflict of wills. He was dependent on her, and as a result they often clashed about matters he felt should be decided entirely by him. Yet Tania was convinced that she had at all times to act not only according to Gramsci's wishes but on the basis of facts and circumstances of which she was aware and that he could not possibly know. This caused misunderstandings and resentments that on a number of occasions pushed Gramsci to the edge of breaking off their relationship. But Tania always persisted, and eventually he came to understand that, however justifiable some of his complaints might have been, she had acted in good faith and was an exceptionally trustworthy friend.

Friendship, together with political and moral solidarity, were in fact the basic reasons for Tania's many years of faithful service to Gramsci. Aldo Natoli, an appreciative and scholarly interpreter of the correspondence between Gramsci and Tania, has rightly emphasized that she "did not fulfill only the subaltern female role of help and consolation, but was able to be an educator of feelings and a bearer of hope."[13] Moreover, although it is true that Gramsci was not exempt from prejudicial sexist attitudes toward women (clearly revealed by several of his prison letters) and that Tania readily characterized herself as a person who could only find happiness "by living through and for others," it is also true that their relationship was at bottom a genuine friendship between two equal but very different persons.

Tania was the pivotal figure in Gramsci's life as a prisoner, but there was another person, the economist Piero Sraffa, whose efforts on Gramsci's behalf were also of crucial importance.[14] Sraffa, seven years younger than Gramsci, belonged to a wealthy and prominent Italian-Jewish family. His father, Angelo Sraffa, was a distinguished jurist who for many years was rector of the Università Bocconi in Milan, and an uncle on his mother's side, Mariano D'Amelio, was a senator and first president of the High Court of Appeal. In 1919, while completing his studies at the University of Turin, Piero was introduced to Gramsci by Professor Umberto Cosmo, whose courses on Italian literature Gramsci had attended a few years earlier. This meeting resulted in Sraffa's contributing several articles to the newspaper Gramsci had helped to found in Turin, *L'Ordine Nuovo*.

The acquaintance between Gramsci and Sraffa developed into a close friendship during 1925 and 1926, the years that Gramsci lived in Rome. Valentino Gerratana, editor of the *Prison Notebooks* and author of important essays on various aspects of Gramsci's life and thought, offers evidence to support the idea that it was Sraffa who, in the mid–1920s, encouraged Gramsci to rethink his position concerning the theory and the method of political struggle to be adopted by the PCI at that particular juncture.[15] In effect, Sraffa's cautious appraisal of the relations of force in Italy and in the world was similar to the analysis Gramsci himself was to make somewhat later, in prison, of the kind of transitional program that might lead eventually to the overthrow of fascism and to its replacement by a coalition of anti-Fascist forces led by the PCI.

After Gramsci's arrest in 1926, Sraffa did everything in his power to help his friend. His family's wealth and prestige, and his own growing renown as a scholar in the fields of economics and law, allowed him to accomplish many indispensable tasks for Gramsci. He published letters appealing for his release in various European newspapers; paid for medical and travel expenses in special efforts to cope with Gramsci's health crises; and above all allowed Gramsci to pursue his intellectual and political interests in prison by opening and maintaining an account for him at the Sperling & Kupfer bookstore in Milan. He visited Gramsci in prison on occasion and played an important role in securing Gramsci's transfer from Turi prison to the clinic at Formia in December 1933.

Beginning in 1928, after establishing contact with Tania, Sraffa became Gramsci's main link with the Italian Communist party. Although never a party member, Sraffa was sympathetic to the Party's goals and regarded himself as an independent Marxist thinker, as "a Communist without a Party," as Valentino Geratana aptly describes him in his introduction to *Lettere a Tania per Gramsci*, p. xxx. He was in touch with Palmiro Togliatti, Angelo Tasca, Camilla Ravera, and other Italian Communist leaders who had escaped to Paris and also to Moscow, where Saffra went from time to time to visit the Schucht family and to bring news of Gramsci to the Italian exile community in the Russian capital.

Despite prison walls and with Tania's help, Sraffa and Gramsci succeeded in maintaining their intellectual interaction. From 1928 to 1933, Tania acted as intermediary between the two men. By prearranged plan, she communicated Sraffa's thoughts to Gramsci in her own words, as if they were her own, in order to avoid arousing the suspicion of prison censors. Gramsci conveyed his ideas on particular topics, for example the neo-Hegelian philosophy of Benedetto Croce, by expounding them in letters to Tania, who copied and forwarded them to Sraffa. Indeed, many of Gramsci's letters on philosophical and historical questions, notably the series of letters in 1932 on Croce, were responses to letters from Sraffa as transcribed or rewritten by Tania. For this reason Valentino Gerratana entitled a collection of Sraffa's letters to Tania *Letters to Tania for Gramsci*.[16] By relying on Tania, who was in weekly contact with Gramsci either through letters or, in certain periods, through visits, Sraffa was able to act as an intermediary between Gramsci and the PCI leadership in exile. Her extensive and clandestinely delivered reports on Gramsci's situation in prison were relayed to PCI leaders by Sraffa, which meant that there was some intermittent contact between Gramsci and his comrades during most of the time he spent in prison. Tania was clever enough to find ways now and then of eluding the police surveillance to which she was subject from the beginning of her work for Gramsci.[17]

The conditions and rules under which Gramsci carried on his correspondence in prison varied considerably, as did the type of letters he sent to and received from friends and family members. While under police confinement on the island of Ustica (December 1926–January 1927), he was able to write at will, to whomever he wished, although of course his correspondence was subject to censorship. After his transfer to San Vittore prison in Milan (February 1927–May 1928), he was allowed to write two letters a week in his cell, to family members and to other approved individuals. In Turi (July 1928–November 1933), regulations and conditions were more stringent and censorship became more rigorous and intrusive. As a political prisoner who had been tried and convicted according to the procedures of a military tribunal, he was allowed to write only to family members. From July 1928 to July 1931 he could write once every fifteen days, thereafter once a week. At Turi, he wrote his letters in a large common room, at uncomfortable school desks, and was given an hour and a half of writing time. Extra letters were permitted at Christmas and Easter. At the clinic in Formia (December 1933–August 1935) and then at the Quisisana hospital in Rome (August 1935–April 1937), his letters were still censored but he could again write as often as he wished, to family members. At Formia, although under heavy police guard, he received weekly visits from Tania, who came from Rome by train to be with him on Sundays. This fact, and his deteriorating health, accounts for the relatively few letters from the years 1934 to 1937. These were all written to his wife and to his two sons.

Throughout his imprisonment, he was allowed to receive an unlimited number of letters from family members, although all of these letters were read by the censors and were sometimes confiscated. With the exception of Tania, who sent him over six hundred letters and postcards, his correspondents wrote to him rather irregularly. As already indicated, while the exact number of letters he received from Giulia is impossible to determine, it probably does not exceed forty. Tania received and transmitted most of the letters that Gramsci wrote to his wife in Moscow and that his wife sent to him. At Turi prison, since he could write only once every fifteen days, and then only once a week, Gramsci sometimes used the same piece of stationery to write two letters instead of one. One letter would be for Tania, the other for Giulia, or at times for his mother or siblings in Sardinia. This accounts for the fact that two letters sometimes have the same date.

Tania also carried on a correspondence with her family in Moscow[18] and with the Gramsci family in Sardinia. In this capacity, she felt that she had to practice a type of benign censorship of information and attitudes that the writers had themselves wished to convey. Indeed, the correspondence sometimes became an elaborate exercise in the arts of concealment and disclosure. Thus, for example, she chose not to inform Gramsci of his father-in-law's death in Moscow in 1933, fearing that such news would worsen his already precarious health; and she decided not to send Giulia Gramsci's proposal in 1932 that their marriage be terminated. She categorically rejected his request that she broach the subject with Giulia, arguing that his reason for proposing the divorce—that he would remain in prison for a long time and she was entitled to begin a new life for herself—was heartless and without foundation. These decisions were reached quite consciously by Tania as part of her work translating, transcribing, or summarizing for Gramsci many of the letters she received from Giulia and other members of the Schucht family, which were of course written in Russian. She also sent Gramsci's letters (except for passages she deemed it unwise to include) to her family in Moscow. These she did not have to translate, since all of the Schuchts had a good command of Italian. This abundant correspondence makes it clear that Tania did in fact remain in Italy, as she herself said, not only as a devoted sister-in-law, but also as a loving sister, daughter, and aunt.[19]

In addition to playing an indispensable part in Gramsci's personal correspondence, Tania was the key figure in official matters affecting his lot in prison. Almost all the letters and appeals written by the Schucht and Gramsci families to Italian prison and political authorities were conveyed through her. She was the bearer of these appeals to the various Ministries in Rome, and, with the help of Piero Sraffa, she made the approaches to individuals in Italian legal and medical circles whose interventions led to whatever concessions and advantages Gramsci was able to obtain in prison.

It is also probable that Tania's efforts had something to do with the fact that Gramsci enjoyed a somewhat greater measure of freedom than did most political prisoners in Fascist Italy to discuss other than family matters in his prison letters. She alludes to this in a letter of May 20, 1930, to her family in Moscow, where she notes that in one case, through her as intermediary, Gramsci had been able to communicate "with comrades who share his fate" as well as to receive certain Italian magazines and books not easily available to political prisoners.[20] The "case" to which Tania refers was doubtless Gramsci's letter of March 25, 1929, in which he asked Tania to transcribe and forward his recommendations for a program of study in philosophy to an imprisoned Communist comrade, Antonio Sanna, whose wife Malvina had recently sent Gramsci a postcard asking for such guidance on behalf of her husband.

Until her death in December 1932, Gramsci's mother Giuseppina (called "Peppina") wrote often to her son, but even to her Gramsci complained about a lack of continuous correspondence. He was a demanding correspondent, and it is always necessary to remember that prison censors and other authorities acted arbitrarily in many instances, resulting in interruptions in communication about which Gramsci knew nothing.

Gramsci's letters to his mother are among the most spontaneous and expressive he wrote in prison; they overflow with gratitude to her for the many sacrifices she had made for him and for her entire family throughout so many years of uninterrupted labors. The principal topic of his letters to Peppina was Sardinian folklore, about which she was very knowledgeable and to which he himself dedicated scholarly and politically motivated attention. Gramsci's father Francesco was of Albanian descent, but his mother was of pure Sardinian stock, and she took pride in the traditions and customs of her island.[21] A devoutly religious, intelligent and resourceful person, she was an important source of the emotional strength that sustained Antonio during a lifetime of privation and struggle. She was able to be helpful to him in prison, practically as well as emotionally. On several occasions, she wrote directly to Mussolini asking "The Head of Government" to prevent the breakdown of her son's health in prison. Noteworthy in this respect was her letter of August 25, 1928, which asked that Gramsci be removed from a cell that he was sharing with tubercular prisoners. In this instance, Mussolini responded favorably to her appeal.

In his letters to his mother, to his sisters Teresina and Grazietta, and to his younger brother Carlo, Gramsci often recalled episodes of his early years growing up in Sardinia. In these letters describing his adventurous life as a young boy and teenager, and in his recollections of family life, where his mother appears as a kind of beneficent guardian angel ever watchful over her brood of seven children, Gramsci's sense of humor and capacity for ironic detachment from even the most distressing of memories cannot help but capture the reader's imagination. Gramsci was capable of peppering his letters with sharp criticisms, but good humor and tenderness are more common in what he wrote to and about his mother and siblings. To Tania he confided in a letter of September 1, 1931, that one of his earliest memories was his brush with death at the age of four, when he fell from the arms of a servant, an accident to which his family attributed his deformity, a hunchback. "The doctor gave me up for dead," he wrote Tania, "and my mother kept a little casket that had been prepared for me, with a little outfit to bury me in, until 1914. An aunt of mine said I came back to life when she rubbed my feet with oil from a lamp devoted to the Madonna, so when I refused to perform religious rituals she reproached me bitterly, reminding me that I owed my life to the Virgin Mary, which impressed me very little, to tell the truth."

Gramsci's letters to his two sons, Delio and Giuliano, are also very touching and expressive. But it will be better to comment on them a little later, in relation to the theme of education that occupies such an important place in his correspondence. At this point it is necessary to look at the ways in which Gramsci conceived of the prison experience itself, an experience he was able to conceptualize remarkably well and one that he documented with meticulous attention to detail.

As a source for understanding everyday life in prison, Gramsci's letters are a mine of information. They are unflinchingly candid about the disease he called "prisonitis," characterized by numbness and torpor. They are richly informative about prison rules and regulations, which subject the prisoner to what he called "the monstrous machine" of routines that constantly threaten to rob the individual of his or her will and to destroy all initiative. They also provide a graphic record of what it means to suffer from chronic illnesses that under ordinary circumstances would be controllable or even curable but that, in prison, are perfunctorily and often incompetently treated. Gramsci tried to take control of his health by keeping fever charts and demanding proper treatment for his major illnesses and symptoms: uremia, poor circulation and hypertension, tubercular lesions in the right lung, gastroenterological disturbances, pyorrhea, and, in the seventh year of his imprisonment, culminating in the atrocious suffering of 1933, fainting spells, chest pains, dizziness, and hallucinations. Pyorrhea caused him to lose almost all of his teeth; the remaining few were too loose to be functional for chewing. For a man who enjoyed a hearty meal once in a while, being forced to be on a bland, mainly liquid diet was not the least of his prison miseries. It was not until March 1933, after repeated and ever more urgent appeals made by himself and by his brother Carlo, by Tania and by Sraffa, that he obtained a competent diagnosis and treatment plan from an outside physician, Doctor Uberto Arcangeli, who came from Rome to examine him at Turi.

In prison, Gramsci devoted himself to a study of canto 10 of

Dante's *Inferno*, in particular to an aspect of that canto that had long fascinated him: the representation of a historical character, Cavalcante de' Cavalcanti, whom many students of the *Divine Comedy* had tended to interpret together with another character, Farinata degli Uberti, as equally motivated by "political passions."[22] In his own original reading of this canto, and in his analysis of Cavalcante's role in it, Gramsci inadvertently reveals the two principal sides of his own situation in prison. He believed that almost everyone who had commented on canto 10 had missed the point that it contained "two dramas," the political drama tout court enacted by Farinata, and the much more tormented personal drama of Cavalcante. Gramsci observed that in Farinata Dante had created a character whose proud and disdainful bearing bespoke an unshakeable confidence in the justness of his political cause and party. But when depicting Cavalcante's anguished uncertainty about the fate of his son Guido, Dante was not at all concerned with politics. On the contrary, Gramsci insisted, Cavalcante's suffering was solely that of an aggrieved and heart-stricken father.

Farinata and Cavalcante symbolize the two main forces that ruled Gramsci's life as a prisoner. The prison letters express the political commitment of a man who had fought for a more just society in the name of principles that nothing, including death itself, could make him doubt or repudiate. But they also reveal the sufferings of a father and husband separated from his loved ones not only by prison walls but by insuperable problems in communication with his wife and by previous decisions on his part that now keep him from having the physical and emotional contact with his two sons for which he yearns.

The passages in Gramsci's letters that deal strictly with the political motivations of his life and with the political reasons for his imprisonment are characterized by a lucid coherence. That he had absolute confidence in his political beliefs and in his ability to withstand whatever methods his oppressors might devise to break his spirit is manifest, for example, in a letter to Tania of January 13, 1930, where he comments on the letters of Italian nineteenth-century patriots imprisoned by the Austrians during the culminating phase of the Risorgimento. One of these men, Silvio Spaventa, he found particularly admirable, observing that even if Spaventa's language reflected the somewhat flowery and "sentimental" style of a bygone era, the substance of his prison letters had lost nothing of their relevance for political prisoners in the twentieth century. He noted that Spaventa had set an example to follow in that he was among the minority of Italian nationalists who had refused to ask their oppressors for clemency. Indeed, Gramsci resisted all opportunities proffered to him to regain his freedom by asking Mussolini for clemency, understanding that such an action would have been seen as an implicit admission that, in some measure, he had recanted his views. Gramsci's close sense of identification with Spaventa is but one of various aspects of the prison letters that justify their categorization as worldly, historically conscious, and politically inspired communications, as well as personal and private expressions of love and anguish.

Two other letters show the strength of political and moral conviction that sustained Gramsci in prison. On May 10, 1928, three weeks prior to his trial before the Special Tribunal for the Defense of the State, he asked his mother "to understand completely, also emotionally, that I'm a political detainee and will be a political prisoner, that I have nothing now or in the future to be ashamed of in this situation. That, at bottom, I myself have in a certain sense asked for this detention and this sentence, because I've always refused to change my opinion, for which I would be willing to give my life and not just remain in prison." And in a letter to his brother Carlo, written on December 19, 1929, Gramsci compared the risks taken by a political revolutionary with those assumed by soldiers such as his older brother Gennaro, who had spent three years on the battlefield in World War I as part of a unit whose task was to lay and defuse land mines. "It seems to me, that under such conditions prolonged for years," Gramsci wrote, "and with such psychological experiences, a man should have reached the loftiest stage of stoic serenity and should have acquired such a profound conviction that man bears within himself the source of his own moral strength, that everything depends on him, on his energy, on his will, on the iron coherence of the aims that he sets for himself and the means he adopts to realize them, that he will never again despair and lapse into those vulgar, banal states of mind that are called pessimism and optimism. My state of mind synthesizes these two emotions and overcomes them: I'm a pessimist because of intelligence, but an optimist because of will."

Imprisonment was something Gramsci had anticipated and even, as he said, "asked for" as a consequence of political commitments accepted very early in his life. What he had not anticipated was the impact on his mind and spirit of prolonged separation from his wife and children. He had not prepared himself for the feeling of powerlessness that afflicted him during the periods, sometimes lasting for many months, when he received no direct news from his family. He realized with painful clarity that "iron coherence" would not give him the capacity to help his wife overcome her mental and emotional problems or help him shape the characters of his two sons. In this intimate realm Gramsci was compelled to recognize the limited relevance of his belief that "man bears within himself the source of his own moral strength, that everything depends on him, on his energy, on his will, on the iron coherence of the aims that he sets for himself and the means he adopts to realize them . . ."

Gramsci tried from time to time to expose his psychic wounds directly to Giulia, but as he became more deeply aware of her vulnerability he tended to think of Tania as the person to whom he could entrust his innermost feelings. In a letter to her of January 27, 1930, written from Turi prison, he said:

> I have an ample reserve of autonomous moral strength that is independent of the external environment; but can Giulia be an "external environment" for me? So it is not a question of my needing comfort, consolation etc. It is exactly the opposite that I would like: to be able to give a bit of strength to Giulia, who must struggle amid so many difficulties and who has been saddled with so many burdens because of our union. But I've been increasingly put in a position of not knowing, of being completely isolated from her life; therefore I am afraid for myself, of becoming ever more detached from her world, and of no longer understanding anything about it, of no longer feeling anything about it.

The failures and lapses in communication with Giulia were the principal aspect of that "other prison" about which Gramsci spoke in several of his letters to Tania, the prison of uncertainty and powerlessness to which he felt that his wife, and occasionally Tania too, had condemned him. His complaints about Tania's behavior, which were extremely harsh and unjust at times, were basically rooted in the same feeling of powerlessness that was so painful in regard to his wife. By taking initiatives that affected his life, without first obtaining his explicit approval, Tania, he thought, had unwittingly allied herself with his jailers, in that she, like the prison authorities, was "beginning not to recognize any will on my part, arranging my life at your whim and refusing to hear my opinion, after all I'm in prison, I know what it is, I bear its painful marks on my skin."

Terrible physical suffering, obsessive fears and insecurities, moments of alienation from Giulia and Tania, were part of Gramsci's prison experience. Despite this, he was able to draw on his intellectual and spiritual resources, and maintain his creative involvement in a remarkably broad spectrum of public issues. Nowhere is this capacity more in evidence than in his letters that deal with education and family life.

Gramsci took an active interest in the education of his two sons in the Soviet Union and of his nephews and nieces in Sardinia. During his years in prison, both countries were in the process of educational experimentation, which gave Gramsci the chance to comment, at times ironically, at times with explicit approval or disapproval, on the educational ideas and practices that were circulating in Soviet Russia and Fascist Italy. Underlying his observations was a set of assumptions about the learning process. He was opposed to the notion that children should be given a sense of their practical and career-oriented goals very early in life. What children needed above all, he thought, was the chance to explore their potential abilities in a variety of modes and areas of expression. Children also needed early training in intellectual rigor, lest the subsequent advent of adolescent rebelliousness occur prior to the formation of character and self-discipline. He took exception with what he viewed as his wife's excessively "Rousseauian" attitude towards personality development. He believed, he said, that parents and teachers ought not to shrink from exerting a shaping influence on young children, who need to acquire the strength to resist "the random and haphazard influences of the environment." Discovery and experimentation were cardinal elements of his philosophy of education. These concepts, he told his wife, were different from "spontaneist" and "libertarian" theories of education that eschewed conscious commitment to the ideological orientation of young people.

What Gramsci believed in and expressed a wish for in many of his prison letters was dialogue with others, the sense that there was an interlocutor with whom he could measure the soundness of his ideas. Closely linked to this was the habit of dialectical thinking, which was a method that had to be taught. It was precisely this kind of dialogical interaction that Gramsci craved from Giulia but that he rarely obtained from her. Tania, on the other hand, was a stimulating and at times tough-minded correspondent on questions of interpersonal ethics, and of course Piero Sraffa, who, as noted earlier, conveyed his ideas to Gramsci through Tania, "was one of the principal interlocutors of Gramsci's prison letters."[23] The two men managed to exchange ideas on such subjects as the philosophy of Benedetto Croce and the economic theories of David Ricardo and John Maynard Keynes.

Gramsci sought the same kind of dialogic relationship with his two sons, but their tender age during his years in prison, his failing health, and the fact that Delio and Giuliano did not know their father except through what Giulia and the Schuchts were able to tell them, made interactive communication exceedingly difficult. Yet despite these obstacles his letters to his sons offer more than conventional paternal guidance. They are filled with probing questions about his sons' schoolwork, their readings, their favorite hobbies and sports. At every opportunity, he urges them to think critically and to ask themselves not only what people believe but why they believe it and on what basis. He tries to instill in them a certain spirit of irreverence, and in some of his letters to Giulia he worries about a tendency to passivity in his sons. In the absence of an ongoing correspondence, he studied photographs that Giulia sent to him, scrutinizing the images of his sons with poignant attention to every small detail of their posture and facial expressions.

Gramsci's letters to his sons, and to Giulia, are especially noteworthy for the delicious anecdotes, fables, and apologues he recounts in them. His talent as a storyteller, which he doubtless inherited from his mother, is another distinctive feature of the prison letters, as is his ability to describe, in brief, pithy sentences, his attempts at various times to grow flowers and plants in the prison courtyard, to raise and train insects and birds that found their way into his cell, and to fashion useful things such as letter openers and soccer balls from materials available to him.

Equally striking are his concise and often acerbic comments on various writers and on questions of literary criticism. The range of Gramsci's readings in prison is astonishing, as evidenced in the *Prison Notebooks* but also in the letters, where he refers to, discusses, and periodically lists hundreds of books that prison regulations allowed him to read. He managed to keep abreast of current literary debates in Italy, economic developments in England and France, and theories of labor and factory organization in the United States. He also read or reread many of the classic works in nineteenth- and early twentieth-century sociology and political science. He trained himself to memorize long passages from his favorite Russian and German authors in order to fix the structures of the two languages in his mind, and also to sharpen his own attempts at translation, about which he offers a number of insightful judgments. In short, the *Letters from Prison* can also be read as fragments of a richly textured intellectual autobiography.

An aspect of Gramsci's prison experience that has stirred up heated controversy in recent years concerns his dissent from official political positions taken by the PCI. A few of the prison letters contain tantalizingly allusive passages that could be interpreted as having political as well as personal significance. More definite evidence of serious disagreements between Gramsci and the PCI can, however, be found in the testimony of men who shared Gramsci's fate as political prisoners at Turi, as well as that of PCI leaders during this period, especially the years 1930–1931.

Some scholars interested in Gramsci's relationship with the PCI during the prison years and in the meaning of his legacy for the subsequent fortunes of the Party in postwar Italy, have for example interpreted two passages from letters written on July 13 and August 3, 1931, as signs not only of dissidence on Gramsci's part, but of a real "rupture" in his relationship with the Party.[24] On July 13, 1931, he said to Tania that "it seems to me that every day a new thread is broken in my bonds with the world of the past and that it becomes ever more difficult to retie so many torn threads." On August 3, he elaborated in the following manner on what he had meant by a "breaking of threads" between himself and "the world of the past":

> [I]n the past this 'breaking of threads' almost filled me with pride, so much so that not only did I not try to avoid it, I even intentionally

fostered it. In reality at that time it was a matter of a succession of events necessary for the formation of my personality and the winning of my independence; this indeed could not have happened without breaking a certain number of threads, since it was imperative for me to change completely the basis on which my future life was to develop. That is not the case today, today more vital things are at stake; since there is no change in my cultural standpoint, I feel isolated on the very same ground that in itself should produce emotional ties.

These two passages, coming on top of a previous letter of June 16, 1930, alluding, as subsequent research has disclosed, to Gramsci's doubts about the way in which the PCI leadership had handled the expulsion from the Party's ranks of three men accused of Trotskyism, lend credibility to the thesis that there was serious dissension between him and the Party. The passages in question all belong to the period from June 1930 to August 1931, when we know from firsthand accounts that Gramsci clashed with the other Communist prisoners at Turi over a number of issues. During this period the PCI opted to endorse the new "class against class" line taken by the Communist International, which was based on the assumption that the capitalist world was in deep crisis and that the moment was ripe for a revolutionary seizure of power. Communists should therefore sever their ties with Socialist and social democratic parties, who were called "objectively social-Fascist."

In their recollections of the disputes that took place at Turi, Gramsci's fellow Communist prisoners at Turi agree that he found the idea of a sudden and decisive revolutionary seizure of power by the proletariat or even by a coalition of left forces to be nothing but "vacuous maximalism."[25] Instead of a revolutionary seizure of power, Gramsci thought there would be a fairly long "transitional democratic phase" during which it would be necessary for Communists to work together with bourgeois liberal, social democratic, and other non-Communist working-class and Catholic groupings within the confines of a pluralist parliamentary system. In the course of a series of discussions in prison, which at the time infuriated some of his prison mates, Gramsci presented the idea of a democratically elected Constituent Assembly as a workable replacement for fascism. In this connection, Gramsci even spoke of the need for a new Communist party, no longer tied in a doctrinaire fashion solely to the proletariat but one capable of taking the lead "in the political, cultural, and moral renewal of Italian society." One of his fellow prisoners, Alessandro Pertini, recalls that Gramsci was bitter about the rift between himself and his comrades. As a result, he turned to Pertini and to several anarchists for friendship and conversation and was criticized for this additional sign of heterodoxy.[26]

If it is true that Gramsci deviated from the Party line while in a Fascist prison, it nevertheless seems to me that to talk of a complete "rupture" with the Party goes beyond what the available evidence can bear. Despite the clashes in prison, the PCI never ceased to think of Gramsci as its leader and ideological standard-bearer. Efforts to alleviate his plight in prison were constant. Appeals for his release appeared regularly in Communist party newspapers. A clandestine network was created to funnel money to him. Party leaders in Moscow and Paris kept in touch with him indirectly through Piero Sraffa and Tania. Moreover, if one reads the testimony of the men at Turi carefully, one discovers that mixed in with memories of conflict and resentment are other memories in which Gramsci is remembered as a revered teacher and guide in prison. The same men who denounced him were at the same time his attentive and appreciative students at the series of discussions he led on such topics as the class character of fascism, the function of intellectuals, the southern question, and the motor forces of revolution in Italy. In sum, it seems to me that John Cammett is correct when he observes that, in the final analysis, "Gramsci may have moved away from the Party, but the Party did not move away from him."[27]

Gramsci's prison letters are a valuable contribution to the genre of prison literature, which has been vastly enriched by the victims of political persecution in the twentieth century. It is not difficult to find points of contact between his thoughts and sentiments as a political prisoner with those, for example, of Rosa Luxemburg in Germany at the time of World War I, of Dietrich Bonhoeffer in Nazi Germany, of Julian Besteiro in Spain under Franco, of Eugene Debs in early twentieth-century America, and, more recently, of Václav Havel in Communist Czechoslovakia.[28] In the Italian context, his letters invite comparison with those of nineteenth-century nationalist patriots such as Silvio Spaventa and more especially with those of other Italian anti-

Fascists imprisoned by the Fascist regime—not only Communists such as Umberto Terracini and Lea Betti Giaciglia but many others belonging to parties and movements ranging from the Italian Socialist party to the Justice and Freedom movement.[29] In this sense, Gramsci was not an isolated figure but rather part of a large and increasingly cohesive coalition of anti-Fascist groups intent on liberating and democratizing Italian society.

Unfortunately, this anti-Fascist unity was short-lived. The words of praise lavished on the *Letters from Prison* by the jury that awarded them the Viareggio prize for nonfiction in 1947 had by then already become suspect in some circles with the first ominous stirrings of the Cold War and the imminent collapse of the coalition of anti-Fascist forces that had contributed most to the restoration of Italian honor after more than two decades of militarism, imperialism, and pomposity. The jury's decision was one of several similar events of that moment. Another was the tribute paid to the *Letters* by Italy's leading philosopher, Benedetto Croce, to whose work Gramsci had dedicated years of impassioned critical study in prison. After observing that the *Letters from Prison* "belong also to those of other or of opposed political parties," Croce said that "as a man of thought Gramsci was one of us, one of those who in the first decades of this century in Italy devoted themselves to forming a philosophical and historical habit of mind adequate to the problems of the present."[30]

In one sense, Croce's response to the *Letters* amounts to a form of self-congratulation, since Gramsci, in his early years, even after he joined the Socialist party in 1913, was very much under Croce's influence. Yet there is more to Croce's response than self-praise. What he does, I think quite correctly, is to situate Gramsci's formative years in the political culture of Italy during the decade and a half prior to World War I, and in so doing to suggest the extent to which Gramsci had assimilated some of that culture's intellectual vitality, its restlessness, its impatience and dissatisfaction with ready-made philosophical formulas derived from positivism and a narrow, mechanistically construed Marxism. Another implication of what Croce had to say about Gramsci, one with which Croce himself would probably not have agreed, is that in Gramsci's thought, even as it appeared in fragmentary form in the prison letters, Italian Marxism, and therefore world Marxism, had won for itself a powerful exponent precisely because his thought was nourished and sustained by numerous intellectual currents.

The political ecumenism that still existed in Italy up to the late 1940s encouraged the emergence of an image of Gramsci that was to become more and more "national and popular" and less and less Marxist and revolutionary. This is the same image of Italy's leading Marxist thinker that is often projected today, in the early 1990s, by people anxious to appropriate his name and prestige for the causes of the "post-Communist" era. But the ecumenism of the 1940s was an outgrowth of the wartime grand alliance between left-wing, social democratic, and liberal anti-Fascist forces, which in turn reflected the military alliance between the western democracies and the Soviet Union. The "national popular" image of Gramsci today, on the other hand, reflects passions and controversies caused by retreat on the Left in the wake of the downfall of communism in Eastern Europe and the Soviet Union, which has given rise to an ideological sanitization of Gramsci designed to make him acceptable to the "post-Communist" Left in Italy.

Gramsci cannot be depoliticized in this manner except at the risk of removing from his thought precisely those elements that he derived from the Marxist tradition. This tradition insists that its adherents strive at all times to see their personal experiences, thoughts, and feelings, no matter how apparently detached from the field of worldly practice, as linked in the final analysis to a political and cultural project aimed at creating the bases for a Socialist society.

It is tempting to read Gramsci's *Letters from Prison* as exquisitely private communications and to place them in the category of autobiographical and confessional literature. Certainly many of the letters would justify such a categorization. But there are too many others that belie this restrictive definition. His letters do not privilege the personal over the political. Whenever possible, Gramsci used them to address problems of great public and historical significance. Indeed, as a Marxist thinker trained to historicize even the most intimate events, he paid the inevitable price of alienation from his loved ones, who did not always agree with his objectified interpretations of their problems. For example, Giulia reacted with some displeasure to his letter of December 30, 1929, written shortly after he learned that she had recently begun psychoanalytic therapy. "It is strange and interesting," Gramsci wrote, "that Freud's psychoanalysis should be creating, especially in Germany . . . tendencies similar to those that existed in France in the eighteenth century: it is forming a new type of 'noble savage' corrupted by society, that is to say, by history. This is the source of a new, very interesting form of intellectual disorder." He then quickly acknowledged that he could very well be wrong in this appraisal, but he let the judgment stand.

Gramsci was later to correct this objective response to his wife's therapy and, in fact, to see Freudianism as a way of valorizing the subject and "reinserting [it] into the social formation."[31] No doubt Gramsci's historically grounded interpretation of Giulia's illness was his way of protecting himself from a painful confrontation with the particularities of his relationship with her. This was not always the case in the prison letters, some of which are agonizingly personal and tormented. But in general, Gramsci's tendency was to try to objectify problems in order then to gain some control over them. To remain within the problem of Giulia's illness, and to deal with it constantly on its own existential terms, would have been strange and intolerable to him. In this sense, too, he was acting the part of a man trained to shape the world according to the dictates of conscious will. In this way he was able to maintain the integrity of a selfhood constructed arduously over decades, but at the same time, because of that very integrity, he was not always able to relate immediately and emotionally to his wife's condition.

It is my hope that readers of Gramsci's *Letters from Prison* will appreciate the qualities of mind that allowed him, often in the same letter, to move from preoccupation with the everyday necessities of creaturely existence to complex historical and philosophical problems. In the very first letter of this volume, for example, he asks his former landlady to pack the underwear he had left behind on the evening of his arrest, and then requests that she send him a German grammar, a book on linguistics, and a copy of the *Divine Comedy*. Such a juxtaposition of humdrum necessities and lofty intellectual concerns characterizes many of his prison letters.

Rarely has a man in prison been as afflicted by so much illness and torment as was Gramsci, and only rarely has a prisoner exercised his intellectual faculties with such constancy and imaginative élan.

---

1. The prize was given to Gramsci's sons, who had come to Rome for the occasion. The jury's statement is cited by Leonida Repaci in *Ricordo di Gramsci* (Rome: Macchia, 1948), pp. 7–8.

2. The 1947 "censored" edition of the *Letters from Prison* was translated into Hungarian (1949), Slovak (1949), Spanish (1950, Argentina), Slovene (1951), Hebrew (1953), English (translated 1948–50, pub. 1974), French (1953), Roumainian (1955), Croatian (1955), German (1956), Bulgarian (1956), Russian (1957), Albanian (1959), Polish (1961), Japanese (1962), Turkish (1966), and Portuguese (1966, Brazil). The 1965 critical edition was translated in its entirety or in part into French (1971), German (1972), English (1973), Hungarian (1974), Spanish (1975, Spain), Danish (1972), and Swedish (1981). The letters excluded from the 1947 edition by the book's two editors, Palmiro Togliatti and Felice Platone, turned out to be not only those that touched on "strictly family matters" whose publication would violate the rules of privacy but also many that were evidently considered politically dangerous at that time by the PCI leadership, such as the letters that referred to Gramsci's friendship with Amadeo Bordiga at Ustica and to his interest while in prison in the writings of Leon Trotsky.

3. From a letter to Giulia of February 13, 1923, in Santucci, *Lettere, 1908– 1926*, p. 108.

4. Giulia's father, Apollon, took his family into exile with him in the mid-1890s. After ten years in Switzerland and France, the family moved to Rome in 1908 and spent the next eight years there before returning to their homeland.

5. *Inferno*, 5:103; trans. John Ciardi, *The Inferno* (New Brunswick: Rutgers University Press, 1954), p. 61.

6. Eugenia Schucht was a dedicated member of the Communist party. During the 1930s, after the death of Apollon Schucht in 1933, she was effectively the head of the family. She was one of two translators of the 1957 Russian-language edition of Gramsci's prison letters. See *Izbrannye proizvedenija/Antonio Gramsci* (Moscow: Izdatel'stvo inostrannoj literatury, 1957), vol. 2: *Pisma iz tjurmy/Antonio Gramsci*, ed. K. F. Misiano, trans. T. S. Elocevskoj and E. A. Schucht.

7. From Vincenzo Bianco's testimony in *Gramsci vivo*, p. 36.

8. As cited by Domenico Zucaro, in *Vita del carcere di Antonio Gramsci*, p.

50. In *Il processone*, p. 198, Zucaro quotes the prosecuting attorney's charge against Gramsci and fourteen other Communists as that of having "planned and determined to commit—by means of the so-called revolutionary army composed principally of workers and peasants belonging to the Party, who were secretly and in part militarily organized for this purpose with weapons, munitions, and money coming even from abroad—acts aimed at provoking an armed uprising of the Kingdom against the powers of the State, in order violently to establish the Italian Republic of the Soviets."

9. From Pertini's testimony in *Gramsci vivo*, p. 211.

10. Adele Cambria, *Amore come rivoluzione*, p. 139.

11. I have arrived at this figure by adding the 428 letters in the 1965 Einaudi edition, the 28 new letters published by *L'Unità* in the 1988 two-volume edition, and the 20 letters that I found at the Gramsci Institute in 1991 and 1992 that had either never been published or that had been previously published but not in book form. However, on the assumption that Gramsci's correspondents lost or chose not to publish some of his letters, and from a reading of letters written to Gramsci in the first year or so of his confinement and imprisonment by fellow internees at Ustica, which refer to letters from Gramsci, a safe estimate of the total number of letters written by Gramsci in prison to family and friends would be closer to 550. Among the political internees at Ustica who wrote to Gramsci in 1927 and 1928, Augusto Nesti refers to "your letters that always bring pleasure to everyone"; Egle Gualdi writes "I am answering your letter a bit late"; Mario Lauriti says "Your letter of July 25 froze me in my tracks"; Cesare Marcucci says "You cannot imagine with how much pleasure we receive your letters"; Carlo Silvestri writes "Dear Gramsci, I have gotten your news . . . ;" and Pietro Ventura says "I was about to write to you to discuss your stubborn silence when I received your letter." These letters are in a folder at the Gramsci Institute marked "Correspondence with Gramsci," and were collected by Elsa Fubini and Antonio Santucci. In the hopes of finding some of the letters Gramsci wrote to these men, Elsa Fubini made an effort some years ago to determine whether any of them are still alive and, if not, to locate members of their families, but without success. Another such effort will be made in the near future.

12. Aldo Natoli, *Antigone e il prigioniero*, p. x.

13. *Ibid*, p. 58.

14. Sraffa's life and relationship with Gramsci are the subject of Jean Potier's biography, *Piero Sraffa*, Italian translation by Antonio Santucci (Rome: Editori Riuniti, 1990), of *Un économiste non conformiste—Piero Sraffa (1898–1983): Essai biographique* (Lyon: Presses Universitaires de Lyon, 1987).

15. The relationship and intellectual exchange between Gramsci and

Sraffa is discussed by Gerratana in his introduction to Piero Sraffa, *Lettere a Tania per Gramsci*, pp. xvi–xxi. Sraffa was the bearer of what amounts to Gramsci's political testament to the PCI. In a letter written to Paolo Spriano in December 1969, Sraffa recalled one of his last conversations with Gramsci at the Quisisana Clinic in Rome, in March of 1937. "I remember with certainty that one of the last times that I visited him at the Quisisana in Rome, Gramsci asked me to transmit his urgent recommendation that the policy position of the constituent assembly be adopted; I reported this in Paris, I don't recall whether to Grieco or to Donini—probably the former" (Spriano, "La morte di Gramsci"). A letter from Grieco to Togliatti of April 27, 1927, confirms the accuracy of Sraffa's memory.

16. Piero Sraffa, *Lettere a Tania per Gramsci*.

17. That Tania was in touch with the Party on Gramsci's behalf, and that she had full consciousness of her political responsibilities concerning his welfare in prison, is borne out by several lengthy reports she wrote for the PCI leadership and by many of the letters she wrote to Piero Sraffa and to her family in Moscow. On August 30, 1928, for example, she wrote to her family as follows: "Up to now comrades have always asked me to do everything possible for comrade Gramsci, to improve his condition and to maintain a constant contact. Therefore the reason for delaying my departure [for Moscow] is the necessity of organizing the existence of a prisoner, since—as you know—I am the only one to have meetings with him. I well know that Antonio will be happy when I am able to embrace all of you again, but for the moment he really needs my interventions and my presence, otherwise he would be completely isolated from the rest of the world." (*Lettere ai familiari*, p. 43).

Many of Tania's letters to Sraffa and to her family also reveal that she was under close police surveillance from 1926 to 1937, a fact of life that she accepted with good humor. In a letter sent from Turi to Sraffa on January 14, 1930, she wrote: "I saw Antonio once, he is well and speaks only and always of his children and Giulia. He wrote her a letter that he sent here and I promised to send it on, but I decided that it would be better to have it sent from a big city, inasmuch as the police are interested in me, they followed me from Rome to Bari and from Bari here, and every day a carabiniere comes [to my hotel room]. The hell with all of them! But on the whole I have to say that the carabinieri behave themselves well." As a consequence of her work for Gramsci, she was often interrogated and her apartments in Rome were searched. She moved at least six times during these years.

18. Tatiana Schucht, *Lettere ai familiari*.

19. For example, in a letter to Gramsci of January 29, 1930, Tania wrote: "I have remained in Italy in order that you not lose all contact with Giulia,

and I cannot believe that you want to say that you have not grasped this meaning of my work." (*Antigone e il prigioniero*, p. 213.)

20. *Lettere ai familiari*, p. 73.

21. A valuable source of information on Peppina Gramsci, and on Gramsci's siblings, is Quercioli, *Le donne di casa Gramsci*.

22. Gramsci's analysis of canto 10 is most fully developed in a letter to Tania of September 20, 1931, and in Antonio Gramsci, *Quaderni del carcere*, vol. 1, pp. 516–530. Two English translations of the pages from the Notebooks devoted to Canto 10 are by William Boelhower, in *Selections from Cultural Writings*, pp. 147–163, and by David Gorman, in *Critical Texts 2*, no. 2 (Autumn, 1984): 2–9. For an analysis of Gramsci's interpretation of Canto 10, see Frank Rosengarten, "Gramsci's 'Little Discovery': Gramsci's Interpretation of canto 10 of Dante's *Inferno*," *Boundary 2*, 14 no. 3 (Spring 1986): 71–90. Sebastiano Vassalli was the first to see the connection between Gramsci's analysis of Farinata and Cavalcante and the "two dramas" of Gramsci's own psychological situation in prison, in his introduction to the selected prison letters of Gramsci, *Lettere dal carcere*, ed. Caprioglio and Fubini, p. x.

23. Valentino Gerratana, introduction to *Lettere a Tania per Gramsci*, p. xxxvi.

24. One of the most articulate exponents of the "rupture" theory is Giuseppe Vacca, in his essay "1926, la rottura con il partito," in *Antonio Gramsci dopo la caduta di tutti i muri*, a thirty-two-page supplement to issue 12 of *L'Unità*, January 15, 1991, pp. 11–14.

25. One of the best sources for Gramsci's political ideas in prison and his disputes with some of his fellow Communist prisoners at Turi, is the testimony of Umberto Clementi, Giovanni Lai, Angelo Scucchia, Bruno Tosin, Alessandro Pertini, Gustavo Trombetti, and several others, in Quercioli, ed., *Gramsci vivo*, pp. 195–240. Also of great importance is the book *Memorie-in carcere con Gramsci* by Athos Lisa, which contains the report Lisa wrote for the PCI dated March 22, 1933, entitled "Rapporto sopra una discussione politica con il compagno—" [Report on a political discussion with comrade —]. (The name Gramsci is blotted out in the 1933 report.) In it Lisa says Gramsci outlined his ideas on the Constituent Assembly two and a half years earlier, somewhere between the late summer and fall of 1930. The report was reprinted in Lisa's *Memorie*.

26. Sandro Pertini, in Quercioli, ed., *Gramsci vivo*, pp. 210–214.

27. An opinion expressed to me in a private conversation, Fall 1991.

28. See Rosa Luxemburg, *Letters from Prison*; Dietrich Bonhoeffer, *Letters and Papers from Prison*; Julian Besteiro, *Cartas desde la Prisión*; Eugene Victor Debs, *Walls and Bars*, ed. Patrick Gorman (Chicago: Charles H. Kerr & Company, 1973); Václav Havel, *Letters to Olga* (New York: Knopf, 1988).

29. A good source for the prison letters of Italian anti-Fascists is Pajetta, ed., *Lettere di antifascisti dal carcere e dal confino*.

30. Croce's review of *Lettere dal carcere* appeared in *Quaderni della Critica*, 3, no. 8 (July 1947): 86. The review is discussed by Paolo Spriano in his introduction to his edition of *Lettere dal carcere*, p. xx.

31. Stone, "Italian Freud: Gramsci, Giulia Schucht, and Wild Analysis," p. 108.

The Letters

1926–30

1926

[undated]

Dear Signora,[1]

First of all, I want to apologize for the trouble and inconveniences[2] I have caused you, which in truth formed no part of our tenancy agreement. I feel fairly well and I'm calm and quiet.

I would be grateful if you'd prepare some of my underclothes and hand them over to a good woman called Marietta Bucciarelli, when she comes to ask for them on my behalf: I can't send you the woman's address because I've forgotten it.

I would like you to send me the following books: (1) the German grammar which was on the bookshelf near the entrance; (2) the *Breviario di linguistica* [A short treatise on linguistics] by Bertoni and Bartoli[3] which was in the wardrobe facing the bed; (3) I would be most grateful if you could send me an inexpensive *Divina Commedia*, because I had lent mine.

If the books have boards, you'll have to tear them off, taking care that the pages do not come apart.

I would like to have news about the child who fell ill with scarlet fever. Perhaps Marietta may know something about it.

If my stay in this place should last long, I think you should consider the room free and do as you wish with it.

You can pack the books and throw away the newspapers.

I apologize again, dear signora, and offer my regrets which are as deep as your kindness is great.

35

My regards to Signor Giorgio and to the young lady;[4] with heart-felt respect.

Antonio Gramsci

1. This undated letter to Gramsci's landlady in Rome, Clara Passarge, was written in mid-November, 1926, from Regina Coeli prison in Rome. It did not reach its destination because it was confiscated by the political police and attached to Gramsci's pretrial dossier.

2. The "trouble and inconveniences" are a reference to several police searches of his apartment in 1925 and 1926. On October 24, 1925, for example, police confiscated a large number of political and personal documents that were in his room on via Morgagni.

3. Giulio Bertoni (1878–1942), prolific philologist and coauthor, with Matteo Bartoli, of *Breviario di neolinguistica* [A short treatise on linguistics], 1925. Bartoli (1873–1946) was a professor of linguistics whose course Gramsci attended at the University of Turin.

4. The husband and daughter of Clara Passarge.

Rome, November 20, 1926

My dearest Julca,[1]

Do you remember one of your last letters? (At least it was the last letter I received and read). You wrote that the two of us were still young enough to hope that together we would be able to see our children grow up. You must now keep this vividly in mind whenever you think about me and associate me with the children. I am sure that you will be strong and brave, as you've always been. You will have to be these things even more so than in the past, so that the children grow up well and will in all ways be worthy of you. During these days I have thought about this a great deal. I've tried to imagine how all of your future life will unfold, because I certainly will not be receiving news from you for a long time; and I've thought again about the past, drawing from it reason for strength and immeasurable confidence. I am and I will be strong; I love you very much and I want to see Delio again and to see Giuliano.[2] I'm somewhat worried about the material situation: will your work be enough for everything? I think that it would be neither undignified nor too much for us to ask for some help. I would like to be able to convince you of this, so that you will listen to me and turn to my friends. This would make me feel more reassured and stronger, knowing that you are safe from distressing incidents. As you see, my responsibilities as a serious parent still torment me.

My dearest, I do not want to trouble you in any way: I'm a bit tired, because I sleep very little and so I cannot write everything that I would like to and how I would like to. I want to make you feel deeply all my love and trust. Embrace all of your family; I hug you and the children with the greatest tenderness.

Antonio

1. This is Gramsci's first letter to his wife after his imprisonment. The words "For Giulia" are written on the top of the first page. The letter was written from Regina Coeli prison in Rome, where he was kept in isolation for sixteen days, until his departure for Ustica by train on November 25. For the circumstances surrounding this letter and the following one to his mother, and Gramsci's state of mind just before writing them, see the last part of the letter to Giulia of January 13, 1931.

2. Gramsci says "I want to see Delio again and to see Giuliano" because he had spent many months with his elder son in 1926 (hence the words "to see again") but had never seen (and was never to see) his younger son Giuliano, who was born on August 30, 1926, after Gramsci's wife's return from Rome to the Soviet Union; this accounts for the verb "to see."

Rome, November 20, 1926

Dearest Mother,

I've thought about you a great deal during these days. I've thought about the new sorrow that I was going to cause you at your age and after all the suffering you've endured. You must be strong, despite everything, as I am strong and you must forgive me with all the tenderness of your immense love and goodness. Knowing that you are strong and patient at this moment of adversity will be a reason for fortitude for me too: think about it and when you write to me at the address I will send you, reassure me.

I'm tranquil and serene. Morally I was prepared for everything. Physically too I will try to overcome the difficulties that may await me and to keep my balance. You know my character and you know that at the bottom of it there is always a quantum of cheerful humor: this will help me live.

I had not yet written to you that another child was born to me: his name is Giuliano, and they tell me that he is strong and is developing well. However during these last weeks Delio had scarlet fever, it was a light case but at the moment I know nothing about his present condition: I know that he had already overcome the critical stage and that he was on the way to recovery. You mustn't worry about your grand-children: their mother has great fortitude and through her work she will bring them up very well.

Dearest mother, I don't have the strength to continue. I've written other letters, I've thought about many things, and not sleeping has tired me somewhat. Reassure everyone: tell everyone that they mustn't be ashamed of me and they must be superior to the petty, small-minded village morality. Tell Carlo that especially now he has the duty to be concerned with all of you, to be serious and hard work-ing. Grazietta and Teresina must be strong and serene, especially Ter-esina, if, as she has written me, she's going to have another child. Papa must be strong too. My dears, especially at this moment my heart weeps at the thought that I have not always been as affectionate and good toward all of you as I should have been and as all of you deserved. Love me nevertheless and think about me.

A kiss to all of you. And to you, dear mother, an embrace and an infinity of kisses.

Nino

P.S. An embrace for Paolo and may he always love and always be good to his dear Teresina.
And a kiss for Edmea and Franco.

Palermo, November 30, [1926]

Dear Signora,[1]

I've been in Palermo (in jail) for three days now. I left Rome on the morning of the twenty-fifth for Naples where I stayed for a few days and was devoured by insects. In a few days I will leave for the island of Ustica, to which I have been assigned for my *confino*. During my journey I was unable to send back the keys to the house: as soon as I arrive at Ustica I will forward them immediately and I'll send you the precise address and instructions for sending me or having sent to me the things that I'll be able to keep here and that may be useful to me. My health is fairly good: I'm a bit tired, that's all. Inform Maria[2] if she comes to see you and ask her to give my regards to all my relatives and friends who still remember me. Kind regards to Signor Giorgio and to the signorina.

Cordially

A. Gramsci

1. Clara Passarge.
2. Uncertain identification; possibly Marietta Bucciarelli. This letter, and the letters to Tania, January 19, 1927, January 20, 1927 and March 3, 1927 were unknown until the early 1970s, when Domenico David, who had in turn received them from Guglielmo Janna in the 1950s, gave them to the Gramsci Institute. The four letters were probably taken by Janna in 1927, when, as a turncoat Communist and Fascist informer, he had access to the archives of the political police in Rome. This is the version that seems most likely to Antonio Di Meo, who described the strange story of these four letters in "Quattro lettere inedite di Gramsci dal carcere," *Rinascita* (November 29, 1974): 26–27.

———

Ustica, December 9, 1926

Dearest Tatiana,

I arrived at Ustica on the seventh and on the eighth I received your letter of the third. In other letters I will describe for you all my impressions of the journey, as gradually the memories and various emotions will be arranged properly in my brain, and I will have rested from my exertions and lack of sleep. The journey, aside from the special conditions under which it took place—as you can understand, it is not very comfortable, even for a robust man, to travel for hour after hour on local trains and boat in handcuffs that are tied in turn to a chain that attaches you to the wrists of your travel companions— was very interesting and rich in the most varied motifs, running from the Shakespearian to the farcical. For example, I don't know whether I'll be able to reconstruct the nocturnal scene of our transit through Naples, huddled in a huge waiting room filled with phantasmagoric zoological specimens; I believe that only the grave diggers' scene in *Hamlet* could match it. The most difficult part of the trip was the crossing from Palermo to Ustica: we attempted it four times and three times we had to go back into the port of Palermo, because the boat could not ride out the storm. Despite all this, would you believe it, I've actually gained weight this last month. I myself am astonished at how well I feel and how hungry I am: I think that in a fortnight, after having rested and gotten enough sleep, I will be completely free from any trace of a migraine and will begin a totally new period in my molecular existence.

My impression of Ustica is excellent from every point of view. The island is large, about eight square kilometers and has a population of approximately 1,300 inhabitants, 600 of them common detainees, that is, criminals who are repeat offenders several times over. The locals are very courteous, everyone treats us most politely. We are kept strictly apart from the common detainees whose life I would be unable to describe to you in a few words: do you remember Kipling's short story "A Strange Ride" in the French volume of *The Man Who Would Be King*.[1] It immediately leaped to my mind so much that I felt I was living it. Up until now there are fifteen friends, among them Ortensia's husband whom I was very happy to meet.[2] Our life is very quiet: we keep busy exploring the island where one can take longish walks of about nine to ten kilometers, surrounded by pleasing landscapes and marine vistas, marvelous dawns and sunsets: every other day the steamer arrives, bringing news, newspapers, and new friends. We haven't all been assigned lodgings: I spent two nights in a large common room with the other friends; today I am already settled in a small hotel room and perhaps tomorrow or the day after tomorrow I will go to live in a small house that is being furnished for us. Ustica is much prettier than it looks in the picture postcards that I will send you: it is a small village of the Saracen type, picturesque and colorful. You cannot imagine how happy I am to stroll through the village and the island from end to end and to breathe the sea air after this month of transfers from one jail to another, but especially after the sixteen days at Regina Coeli, which I spent in the most complete isolation. I believe that I will become the Ustica champion in long distance stone-throwing, because I have already beaten all of my friends.

I'm writing to you helter-skelter, just as it comes to me, because I'm still a bit tired. Dearest Tatiana, you cannot imagine how moved I was when at Regina Coeli I saw your handwriting on the first bottle of coffee that I received and when I read Marietta's name; I literally became a child again. You see, at that time, knowing for certain that my letters would be read in accordance with prison regulations, I developed a kind of reticence, and I dared not write about certain emotions and when I tried to stifle them in order to adjust to the situation, I felt I was behaving like a sacristan. So I will confine myself to writing to you about my stay at R.C. only in response to your questions. I've received the woolen jacket, which has been most useful, and also the socks, etc. I would have suffered a great deal from the cold without them because I left wearing a light overcoat and often very early in the morning when we attempted the Palermo-Ustica crossing it was freezing cold. I received the small dishes that I was sorry to have to leave behind in Rome, because I had to put all my belongings in the pillowcase (that has given me inestimable service) and I was sure I would break them. I did not receive the Cirio preserves, nor the chocolate, nor the pound cake, all of which were not allowed: I saw them marked on the list, but with the notation that they could not pass; so I did not have the small glass for the coffee, but I took care of it by constructing a set of a half a dozen egg shells superbly mounted on pedestals of kneaded bread. I see that you were upset by the fact that the meals were almost always cold: no problem, because after the first few days I've always eaten at least twice as much as what I used to eat at the trattoria and I never experienced the slightest discomfort, whereas I heard that all my friends felt under the weather and made a great use and abuse of laxatives. I'm slowly becoming convinced that I'm much stronger than I could have ever thought, because, unlike everyone else, from all this I suffered only ordinary fatigue. I assure you that, save for a very few hours of intense gloom one evening when they turned off the lights in our cells, I've always been very cheerful; the sprite I bear within that helps me to grasp the comical and caricatural aspect of every scene has always been active and kept me in good spirits despite everything. I've been reading always, or almost always, illustrated magazines and sports papers and I am starting to build up a library. Here I have set myself this program: (1) to feel well in order to feel always better in health; (2) to study German and Russian with method and persistence; (3) to study economics and history. All of us together will follow a reasonable exercise program, etc., etc. Dearest Tatiana, if I didn't write to you earlier, you mustn't believe for even a minute that I forgot about you and did not think of you; your expression is absolutely correct, because everything I received and in which I saw the conspicuous sign of your dear hands was more than a greeting, it was also an affectionate caress. I would have liked to have Marietta's³ address; perhaps I might also want to write Nilde;⁴ what do you think? Will she remember me and be pleased by a word from me? To write and to receive letters have become some of the most intense moments of my life.

During these first days, until we are finally settled in, I must charge you with a number of tasks. I would like to have a travel bag that can be secured with a clasp or a lock: it is better than any suitcase or foot locker, in the not to be excluded possibility of further transfers among the islands or to the mainland. And so I will need all those small items, such as a safety razor with extra blades, nail scissors, nail file, etc., etc., that are always useful and are not sold here; I would also like a few tubes of aspirin in case the very strong winds here were to give me a toothache. With regard to the suit, the overcoat, and the underwear I left behind, I'm certain that you'll see to them. If you can, send me immediately the German and Russian grammars; the small German-Italian and Italian-German dictionary and a few books (*Max and Moritz*[5] [The Katzenjammer kids] and Vossler's history of Italian literature, if you can manage to track it down among the books). Send me also that huge tome of articles and studies on the Italian Risorgimento that is entitled, I think, *Storia politica del secolo XIX* [Political history of the nineteenth century] and a book with this title: R. Ciasca, *La formazione del programma dell'unità nazionale* [The development of the program of national unity] or something like that. At any rate, you look and decide on your own. This time, you write to Giulia: I'm unable to quell that feeling of reticence I mentioned before; I was very happy to hear the good news about Delio and Giuliano; I'm looking forward to the photographs. The address used by you is excellent, as you have seen: here the mail works quite simply, because I go to the window and ask for it the same as with poste restante and in Ustica there is only one post office. As for the telegrams I sent, I knew almost with certainty that the one from Rome announcing my departure would arrive with great delay, but I wanted to communicate the news and I did not exclude that it might be useful for a visit if the recipient knew that it was possible to come until eleven o'clock in the evening. Of the five men about to leave, only Molinelli,[6] who has traveled with me throughout, received a visit from his wife precisely at eleven o'clock: for the others nothing. Dearest Tatiana, I have written to you rather confusedly. I believe that today, the tenth, the steamer will not manage to get through because all night there was a very violent wind that didn't let me sleep, despite the softness of the bed and pillows to which I was no longer accustomed; it is a wind that penetrated all the chinks of the balcony, windows, and doors with very picturesque but irritating whistles and trumpetings. Write to Giulia and tell her that I really feel well, from all points of view, and that my stay here, which in any case I don't believe will be as long as the ordinance set down, will wrest from my body all my old ailments: perhaps I actually needed a period of absolute rest.

I embrace you tenderly, dearest, because with you I embrace all my dear ones.

Antonio

If Nilde would be pleased by a word from me, send me her address.

1. Gramsci refers to the story "The Strange Ride of Morrowbie Jukes," which he read in French translation. As indicated by Lawner (p. 64, *n*.1), the story "describes how, in India, men who are burned at the stake but are still alive are thrown into a pit. Kipling speaks of the dwelling place of the dead who are not dead but who are no longer alive."

2. Ortensia's husband is Amadeo Bordiga (1889–1970). Bordiga was born in Resina, a province of Naples. A civil engineer by profession, he was a founding member of the Communist party of Italy in 1921 and was the Party's first general secretary. He disagreed with the policy of the united front advocated by the Comintern in the early 1920s, and argued for the revolutionary overthrow of capitalism and liberal democracy. As indicated in this letter, he spent a period of internment with Gramsci on the island of Ustica in 1926 and early 1927. He was released in 1929 and withdrew from political activity. But in the following year, because of his "extremist" positions, he was expelled from the Italian Communist party. In 1934 he was living in Formia, not far from the Cusumano clinic where Gramsci was a patient under armed guard. After Gramsci obtained "conditional freedom," the two men met several times during Gramsci's brief outings with Tania, but they were unable to exchange any words because both were under police surveillance.

All of the passages in Gramsci's prison letters that refer to his friendship with Bordiga and to his interest in Trotsky were censored by omission from the first 1947 Italian edition and therefore did not appear in any of the subsequent editions in Italy and abroad published between 1947 and 1965. The 1965 edition prepared by Elsa Fubini and Sergio Caprioglio finally restored all of the previously excised passages. In the 1940s and 1950s the ideological struggle of the Cold War made it necessary for the PCI to treat the "left sectarian" politics of Bordiga and the anti-Stalinist politics of Trotskyism with contemptuous disregard.

3. Marietta Bucciarelli

4. Leonilde ("Nilde") Perilli befriended the entire Schucht family in Rome in the years 1910–1913 and became especially close with Tania and Eugenia. In the 1920s, she corresponded with the Schuchts, then living in Moscow, and was frequently asked to deliver messages to Tania, who for a while in those years had lost contact with her family. Tania subleased a room in her apartment for several years in the early 1930s. Nilde worked as a librarian and administrative assistant for Doctor Raffaele Bastianelli at the Rome General Hospital, and was a friend of Doctor Vittorio Puccinelli, director of the Quisisana Clinic, where Gramsci spent the last two years of his life. These contacts facilitated Tania's efforts to obtain competent medical assistance for Gramsci.

5. A story in verse by the German humorist and caricaturist Wilhelm Busch (1832–1908).

6. Guido Molinelli (1894–1963), a founding member of the PCI, later sentenced to fourteen years in prison but amnestied in 1932.

Ustica, December 11, 1926

My dear friend,[1]

I arrived at Ustica on December 7, after a somewhat uncomfortable (as you can understand) but very interesting journey. I'm in excellent health. My stay at Ustica will be pleasant enough from a purely animal standpoint, because the climate is excellent and I can take extremely salubrious walks: as for general comforts, you know that I'm not very demanding and can get by on very little. I'm a bit worried about the problem of boredom, which it will not be possible to solve simply with walks and the contacts with friends: up until now we are fourteen friends, among them Bordiga. I ask you to do me the kindness of sending me some books. I would like to have a good treatise on economics and finance for my studies: a fundamental book, I leave its choice to you. Whenever possible send me a few books and a few magazines of general culture that you think might interest me.[2] My dear friend, you are acquainted with my family situation and you know how difficult it is for me to receive books except from a few personal friends: believe me that I would not have dared trouble you in this way unless driven by the necessity of solving this problem of intellectual degradation that especially preoccupies me. I embrace you affectionately.

A. Gramsci

My address: A.G. Ustica (Palermo province)

1. Piero Sraffa.

2. In his reply to Gramsci of December 13, 1926, Sraffa told Gramsci that he had sent him a package of books and that he had already opened an account for him at the Sperling & Kupfer bookstore in Milan. (Gerratana, ed., *Lettere a Tania per Gramsci*, p. xxiii)

Ustica, December 17, 1926

My dear friend,[1]

I've received your letter of the thirteenth and I cordially thank you for your courtesy. My health is excellent; it is still warm here. I will write to you at length. I embrace you.

Antonio

1. Piero Sraffa

Ustica December 19, 1926

Dearest Tania,

I wrote a card on the eighteenth to inform you that I had received your certified letter of the fourteenth: before that I had written a long letter to the address of Signora Passarge that should have been delivered to you on the eleventh or twelfth. Let me summarize the main events through this entire time.

Having been arrested on the evening of the eighth at half past ten and immediately taken to jail, I departed from Rome very early in the morning of November 25. My stay at Regina Coeli was the worst of my detention: sixteen days of total isolation in a cell, under very strict discipline. I was able to obtain a room against payment only during the last days. I spent the first three days in a cell that was quite sunny during the day and was lit up at night; the bed however was very dirty; the sheets had already been used; they swarmed with the most varied insects: I was unable to get anything to read, not even the *Gazzetta dello Sport* [The sports gazette], because I had not put in a request for it in advance: I ate the prison soup, which was quite good. After that I was moved to another cell, darker in daytime and without illumination at night, but which had been disinfected with gasoline flames and its bed had freshly laundered sheets. I started to buy things at the prison commissary: candles for the night, milk for the morning, a soup with meat broth and a piece of boiled meat, cheese, wine, apples, cigarettes, newspapers, and illustrated magazines. I was moved from the regular cell to the paid room without warning, so that for a few days I was left without food, because the prison issues meals only to the inhabitants of the regular cells, while those in the paid rooms must "victualize" (a prison term) themselves at their own expense. For me the advantage of the paid room lay in the fact that a woolen mattress and a pillow *idem* was added to the straw pallet, and that the cell was furnished with a wash basin, a mug, and chair. I was also supposed to get a small table, a clothes rack, and a small cupboard, but the administration was short on "barrack fittings" (another prison term): I also received electric light but with no switch, so that all through the night I tossed and turned to protect my eyes from the glare. This is how our life went: at seven in the morning reveille and cleaning the room; around nine delivery of the milk, that became milk and coffee when I began to receive my food from the trattoria. The coffee was usually lukewarm when it arrived, the milk on the other hand was always cold, but I used it to make a big bowlful of sopped bread. Between nine and noon there came the exercise hour: one hour either from nine to ten or from ten to eleven or from eleven to twelve: they let us out one by one, forbidding us to speak or greet anyone at all, and we went into a courtyard divided into compartments with very high separating walls and an iron gate opening on to the rest of the yard. We were watched by a guard ensconced on a small balcony overlooking the compartments and by a second guard who walked back and forth in front of the gate; the yard was enclosed by very high walls and on one side it was dominated by the short smokestack of a small internal workshop; sometimes the air was smoke, once we were left for about half an hour under a downpour of rain. Approximately at noon lunch would arrive; the soup was again often lukewarm, the rest was always cold. At three we had cell inspection with the testing of the bars of the window grill; this inspection was repeated at ten in the evening and at three in the morning. I would sleep a bit between these two visits: once when awakened by the three o'clock visit I was unable to fall asleep again; but we were obliged to stay in bed from half past seven in the evening until dawn. The distraction came from the various voices and the snatches of conversation that it was sometimes possible to catch from the adjacent or opposite cells. I never incurred any punishment: Maffi[1] however was given three days on bread and water in the punishment cell. To tell the truth, I never felt ill; despite the fact that I never ate the entire meal, I still always ate with a better appetite than at the trattoria. I only had a wooden spoon; neither a fork nor a glass. A mug and a smaller mug of earthenware for water and for wine; a large earthenware bowl for the soup and another for the basin, before I was granted the paid room. On November 19 I was given notice of the ordinance that sentenced me to five years of internment[2] in a penal colony, without further explanation. During the following days the rumor reached me that I was to leave for Somalia. Only on the evening of the twenty-fourth and indirectly did I hear that I would serve the time of my internment on an Italian island: I was officially informed of the precise destination only when I got to Palermo: I could be going to Ustica but also to Favignana, Pantelleria, or Lampedusa; the Tremiti Islands were to be excluded, for in that case I would have had to travel from Caserta to Foggia. I left Rome on the morning of the twenty-fifth with the first local for Naples, where I arrived at approximately thirteen hours; my travel companions were Molinelli, Ferrari, Volpi, and Picelli, who had also been arrested on the eighth.[3] However Ferrari was detached from Caserta to be sent to the Tremiti: I say detached because even in the railroad car all of us were tied to a long chain. From Rome on I was always in company, which produced a notable change in my state of mind: we could talk and laugh, despite the fact that we were tied to the chain with both wrists clasped tightly by manacles and had to eat and smoke decked out so charmingly. And yet we were able to strike matches, eat, drink; our wrists swelled a bit, but we clearly felt how perfect the human machine is and how easily it adapts to the most unnatural circumstances. Within the limits of regulations, the carabinieri escorting us treated us with great correctness and courtesy. We stayed two nights in Naples, in the Carmine jail, still together, and we left again by boat on the evening of the twenty-seventh over a very calm sea. In Palermo we were given a small, very clean and airy dormitory, with a beautiful view of Mount Pellegrino; there we found other friends destined for the islands, the Maximalist Deputy Conca from Verona and Attorney Angeloni, a Republican from Perugia.[4] Others arrived afterward, among them Maffi who was being sent to Pantelleria and Bordiga slated for Ustica. I was scheduled to leave from Palermo on the second, instead I managed to depart only on the seventh; three attempts to cross failed due to a stormy sea. This was the worst phase of my journey. Just think: reveille at four in the morning, the formalities for the return of money and various other deposited objects, manacles and chain, a Black Maria at the harbor, down into a small boat to reach the steamer, up the ladder to get on board, up another ladder to get on deck, down another ladder to reach the third class section; all of this with shackled wrists and tied to a chain together with three others. At seven the steamer leaves, travels for an hour and a half leaping and swaying like a dolphin, then we turn about because the captain realizes that going ahead with the crossing is impossible. We negotiate the series of ladders, etc. in reverse, return to prison, are searched again and sent to the cells; meanwhile it's already noon, we haven't had the time to order our meal; we can't eat until five o'clock, and we hadn't eaten in the morning. All of this four times over with one day intervals. Four friends had already arrived in Ustica: Conca, Sbaraglini the former deputy from Perugia, and two from Aquila.[5] For several nights we slept in a dormitory: but now we are already settled in a house put at our disposal, six of us, myself, Bordiga, Conca, Sbaraglini, and the two from Aquila. The house is composed of one room on the ground floor where two men sleep: the ground floor also contains the kitchen, toilet, and a cubicle we are using as a common dressing room. On the second floor, four of us sleep in two rooms, three in a rather large room and one in a small walk-through room; above the large room there is an ample terrace that overlooks the inlet. We pay 100 lire a month for the house and two lire a day for the bed, bed linen, and other household equipment (two lire per person). During the first days we spent a lot for our meals; not less than two lire a day. Now we spend ten lire a day for board that includes lunch and dinner; we're organizing a communal mess that will perhaps allow us to live on the ten lire per diem assigned us by the government; there are already thirty of us political detainees, and perhaps a few more will arrive.

Our obligations are various and complex; the most conspicuous are not leaving the house before dawn and returning to it by eight in the evening; we cannot go beyond certain set limits that in a general way are represented by the perimeter of the town. However we have obtained permits that allow us to walk over the entire territory of the island on the condition that we return within the set limits by five in the afternoon. The total population is about 1,600 inhabitants, 600 of them detainees, that is, common criminals who have been sentenced several times. The local population is made up of Sicilians, very polite and hospitable; we are allowed to have relations with the locals. The detainees are subjected to a much more restrictive regime; the great majority, given the island's small size, cannot have any occupation and must live on the four lire per diem assigned by the government. You can imagine what happens: the *mazzetta* (the term used to signify the government allowance) is spent chiefly on wine; the meals are reduced to a bit of pasta with greens and a bit of bread; the lack of proper nutrition leads very quickly to the most depraved alcoholism. These detainees are shut up in certain special dormitories at five in the afternoon and they spend the entire night together (from five in the afternoon until seven in the morning), locked in from the outside: they play cards, sometimes they lose the *mazzetta* for several days and so are caught up in an everlasting infernal circle. From this standpoint it is truly a pity that we are forbidden to have any contact with creatures forced to live such an exceptional life: I think that it would be possible to make some unique psychological and folkloric observations. All that is elementary that survives in modern man irresistibly rises to the surface: these pulverized molecules come together in accordance with principles that correspond to essentials still existing in the most submerged folk strata.[6] There are four fundamental divisions: northerners, people from central Italy, southerners (including Sicily), and Sardinians. The Sardinians live totally apart from the rest. The northerners[7] evince a certain solidarity among themselves, but no organization, it would seem; for them it is a point of honor that they are thieves, pickpockets, swindlers but have never spilled blood. Among the people from central Italy, the Romans are the best organized; they will not even denounce the spies to people from the other regions, and keep their distrust to themselves. The southerners are highly organized, so it is said, but among them there are subdivisions: the Neapolitan State, the Apulian State, and the Sicilian State. For the Sicilian, the point of honor consists not in having stolen but only in having spilled blood. I owe all these observations to a detainee who was in the Palermo jail serving a sentence he had gotten during his detention and who was proud because, in accordance with a pre-established plan, he had inflicted a wound ten centimeters deep (actually measured, says he) on a boss who treated him badly: it was to be ten centimeters deep, and ten centimeters it was, not a millimeter more. This was the masterpiece that filled him with great pride. You must believe me when I say that my reference to Kipling's short story was not an exaggeration, though dictated by a first impression.

My financial situation in all this time has been excellent. When I was arrested I had 680 lire in my pocket, in Rome I saw another fifty lire credited to me. Expenses began to take an alarming form only after my departure from Rome. Especially in Palermo they skinned us alive: the *trattoria* owner charged thirty lire for a parcel containing: a portion of macaroni, half a liter of wine, a quarter of a chicken, fruit, which amounted to two meals. I arrived at Ustica with 250 lire, which lasted me for the first ten days, then I received: 100 lire of *mazzette* (ten lire a day), your 500 lire and the 374 lire of parliamentary indemnity for the days from the first to the ninth of November. So I am taken care of for quite a while, that is, I can buy a few coffees, smoke cigarettes, and see to the daily outlay for board and lodging that is now fourteen lire a day, but will be less after we organize the collective mess. So you mustn't worry about me: *I absolutely do not want* you to make *personal* sacrifices for me: if you can afford it, send your help to Giulia, whose needs are certainly greater than mine. Last time I neglected to tell you that as soon as I arrived in Ustica I found a letter in which I was given assurance that Giulia would receive help and that I shouldn't worry about this. I will turn to you to obtain certain things that I would otherwise be unable to procure: but in general I'm determined to arrange matters in such a way that I'll be able to live on the government *mazzetta*, because I believe that after a period of adjustment it will be possible. I must tell you another very important thing: our friend Sraffa has written me that he has opened an unlimited account on my behalf at a Milan bookshop,[8] from which I will be able to request newspapers, magazines, and books; in addition he has offered me any help I might want. As you see, I can look upon the future with sufficient serenity. If I have the assurance that Giulia and the children will not suffer any deprivation, I will really be untroubled; dear Tatiana, this is the single worry that has tormented me during this last period and not only after my arrest; I felt this storm coming, in an indistinct and instinctive way, which was therefore more tormenting. Do you remember, when you told me that our common friend mentioned my superstition? I've thought back on it several times, not in order to become more convinced that I was right and that I have exaggerated not out of superstition but due to lack of decisiveness and other scruples that I intellectually consider of an inferior order, but that I am unable to and will be unable to cast off. In truth, the analysis I made was correct, though I was unable to give an objective detailed demonstration of it.[9]

And so I've written to you with that abundance you wished, writing to you also about little things of slight importance. Are you satisfied? Do you know that I love you very much and that I'm very unhappy when I remember some trifling episodes in which, carelessly, I managed to hurt you? I want you to write to Giulia in my name too; I do not feel like sending you the drawings for Delio: I would have to accompany them with explanations and that displeases me enormously. I look forward to getting the photographs. Among the books to be sent me include the following: Hauser, *Les grandes puissances* [The great powers]; Mortara's *Le prospettive economiche del 1926* [Economic prospects for 1926]; the two Berlitz volumes—German and Russian. Among the things I would like—some soap, some after shave lotion, a toothbrush in a glass case, some toothpaste, some aspirin, and a clothes brush. Dearest Tatiana, I embrace you affectionately,

Antonio.

1. Fabrizio Maffi (1868–1955), a physician and ex-Socialist deputy. He joined the PCI in 1924. After the liberation in 1945, he was a deputy to the Constituent Assembly and later an honorary member of the Senate.

2. In Italy, police "internment," or internal exile, means detention in a penal colony or, as in this case, on an island or other place far from urban centers. It imposes restrictions on the movement and activities of the interned person, who must report regularly to the police.

3. On Molinelli, see letter to Tania, December 9, 1926, n. 6. The other men mentioned here are Enrico Ferrari (1897–1969), a labor organizer from Modena and former Communist deputy in 1921 and 1924; Giulio Volpi (1877–1947), first a Socialist, then a Communist lawyer and deputy from Rome; and Guido Picelli (1889–1937), secretary of the Federation of Proletarian Leagues in Parma and a former Communist deputy elected in 1924. In 1926 Picelli escaped to France from the island of Lipari. He died fighting for the Spanish Republic in the battle of Madrid.

4. Paolo Conca belonged to the "maximalist" or pro-Bolshevik revolutionary wing of the Italian Socialist party (PSI), which formed in 1919 under the leadership of Giacinto Menotti Serrati. It was the dominant group within the PSI from 1919 to the advent of Fascism. The term *maximalism* was first used in 1892, at the founding Congress of the PSI, to distinguish the "maximum" program for the conquest of power by the Socialists from

the gradualist and reformist "minimum" program. After World War I, in the wake of the Russian Revolution, maximalism implied a commitment to seizure of political power and the immediate institution of a Socialist republic and the dictatorship of the proletariat. Mario Angeloni (1882–1937) was a lawyer and member of the Italian Republican party that followed the Mazzinian tradition of militant revolutionary action against fascism. He was among the first Italian anti-Fascists to volunteer for combat in Spain, where he was killed in 1937.

5. Giuseppe Sbaraglini, former reformist "unitary" Socialist; the "two from Aquila" are Pietro Ventura and Ugo Sansone, both Communists.

6. Topic seven of the research program Gramsci outlined in 1929 in his prison notebooks was "The concept of folklore," a subject that long occupied his attention both as a professional politician and as a cultural historian. See especially sections 5 and 6 of Forgacs and Smith, eds., Selections from Cultural Writings, and section 11 of Forgacs, ed., A Gramsci Reader, for some of Gramsci's ideas on folklore as reflecting a "conception of life and the world," and as linked to "common sense."

7. The North-South question in Italian history was the subject of Gramsci's last important political essay before his imprisonment, the unfinished and then unpublished "Some Aspects of the Southern Question," published in Selections from Political Writings, 1921–1926 (London: Lawrence and Wishart, 1978), pp. 441–462.

8. The Sperling & Kupfer bookstore.

9. This allusive passage beginning "I felt the storm coming" almost certainly refers both to Gramsci's prediction as early as May 1920, of a possible Fascist conquest of power, and to the puzzling and never adequately explained lack of decisive action on his part to protect himself from arrest as the "storm" burst in 1926.

December 21, 1926

Dearest friend,[1]

I've received your letter of the thirteenth; however I've not yet received the books you listed. I thank you most cordially for your offer; I've already written to the Sperling bookshop and given them quite a large order, certain that I wasn't being indiscreet, for I know your kindness. Here in Ustica there are thirty of us political prisoners: we've already initiated a series of elementary and general culture courses for the various groups of prisoners; we will also begin a series of lectures. Bordiga directs the scientific section, while I have the historical-literary section; this is the reason I've ordered certain particular books. Let's hope that in this way we will spend our time without becoming completely brutalized and at the same time help our friends, who represent the entire gamut of political parties and cultural backgrounds. Here with me there are Schiavello and Fiorio[2] from Milan; among the Maximalists there is also the former deputy,

Conca, from Milan. Among the Unitarian Socialists there is Attorney Sbaraglini from Perugia and a magnificent Molinellese peasant type. There is a Republican from Massa and six Anarchists who have a complicated moral makeup; the rest are Communists, that is, the great majority. There are three or four who are illiterate, or almost; the education of the others varies, but the general average is very low. All of them, however, are very glad to have the school, which they attend with great assiduity and diligence.

Our financial situation is still good: they give us, the political prisoners, ten lire a day: the *mazzetta* of the common detainees at Ustica amounts to four lire a day, on the other islands, when there are possibilities for work, it is sometimes even less. We have the choice of living in private homes; six of us (I myself, Bordiga, Conca, Sbaraglini, and two others) live in a small house that costs us ninety lire a month each, all services included. We're planning to organize a collective mess, so as to be able to take care of our needs for board and lodging with the daily ten lire of the *mazzetta*. Of course the food is not at all varied: for example it is impossible to find eggs, and this annoys me a lot because I cannot eat the abundant meals based on fish and seafood. The regime by which we must abide consists in: reporting home by eight o'clock in the evening and not leaving the house before dawn; not going beyond the town limits without a special permit. The island is small (eight sq. km.) with a population of 1,600 inhabitants, approximately 600 of them common criminals: there is just one cluster of houses. The climate is excellent, it has not yet been cold; nevertheless the mail arrives irregularly because the steamer that makes the trip four times a week is not always able to overcome the wind and high seas. In order to reach Ustica we had to make four attempts to cross and this tired me more than the entire transfer from Rome to Palermo. But I've kept in excellent health, to the great surprise of my friends, who have suffered more than I: can you imagine, I've even gained a bit of weight. Recently, however, due to accumulated fatigue and the food that does not suit my habits and my constitution, I feel very weak and worn out. But I hope to adjust rapidly and get rid of all my past ailments once and for all.

I will write to you often if it pleases you, to give myself the illusion of still being in your enjoyable company. I greet you affectionately.

Antonio

1. Piero Sraffa
2. Ernesto Schiavello, a labor organizer from Milan, and Raffaele Fiorio.

December 27, 1926

Dearest Tania,

In a letter from Signor Passarge I have learned the reason, truly painful and irksome, due to which you received my first letter after a delay. I think that by now you must have also received my other letter, with all the detailed information on my mode of existence.

As you can well imagine, the news here is next to nil. Life goes by always the same; waiting for the steamer that brings news from the families and newspapers increasingly becomes the central problem owing to the bad weather and the forever imminent possibility that the crossing might fail. Bordiga's wife was supposed to arrive for the Christmas holidays: her first crossing failed after a very turbulent and painful attempt and Ortensia departed again for Naples without trying a second time. This has made everyone unhappy. Another disagreeable piece of news was the arrest and the removal to the local jail of the two former deputies, Damen[1] and Molinelli, while waiting for their respective transfers to Florence and Rome: Molinelli will perhaps leave as early as today, if the steamer arrives.

As for myself, nothing substantially new. I've already received a number of books from Sraffa, but I'm not as yet able to devote myself to any specific and methodical study. In particular I'm waiting for the grammars that I asked you for. Other books that I would like to receive from you are: a small parcel of Catholic Action[2] books that I had already gathered together on a small table in my room, though I don't know if they still are all in one place. Together with them send six volumes of Pietro Vigo's *Annali d'Italia* [Italian annals], Francesco Ercole's book on Machiavelli,[3] and three issues of F. Coppola's review *Politica* that contain articles also by the same Ercole: one of the issues of *Politica* is dated 1920. The other two are dated 1926 and contain a study on the "formation of cities in Italy"; if they have been lost, both or one of the two, you might buy them again for me. In general you should choose from among my books, which are not many, all the history volumes and send them to me methodically. Since it is not to be completely excluded that some day or other I might have the same fate as Molinelli I would be very grateful if you were to send me a spoon and fork of very hard wood and a celluloid soap container such as we are allowed to have with us in prison.

My health is reasonably good. I've begun to find very fresh eggs that I eat raw; from now on we'll also regularly receive beef and this will allow us to have more varied meals. The problem of sleep has yet to be resolved; I must sleep in the same room with two other friends, and this is the cause of many occasions for awakenings and insomnia. There may be a wonderful opportunity: to have a room to myself in a small villa that a friend who is waiting for his wife might rent: but since the small villa is located a few meters outside the legal limits of town, there are certain difficulties still to be overcome.

Dearest Tatiana, I want you to write at length to Giulia and convince her that I cannot write to her directly yet. I'm unable to overcome the state of mind that I've already described to you.[4] I will make another effort. Let me have news about yourself and send me the photographs. Has Giuliano already been photographed with Giulia and Delio? I embrace you affectionately.

Antonio.

1. Onorato Damen, one of nineteen Communists and "third-internationalist" Socialists elected on April 4, 1924, to the Italian Chamber of Deputies on the "Proletarian Unity" list.

2. The term *Catholic Action* was first employed by Pope Pius XI (1922–1938) to apply to the work of the Catholic laity. Under Fascism, Catholic Action was able to maintain a certain degree of independence, and, despite its conservative leadership, "harbored many anti-Fascists and served as the nucleus for the reemergence of the Christian Democrats in 1944." (Coppa, ed., *Dictionary of Modern Italian History*, pp. 6–7)

3. See letters to Tania, November 14, 1927, and March 14, 1932, n. 1, on Gramsci's view of Machiavelli.

4. A reference to the extreme emotional discomfort Gramsci experienced in expressing to his wife intimate feelings that would be scrutinized by censors and other government officials.

December 29, 1926

Dearest,[1]

I've received your telegram at this very moment. It is a quarter to ten. I'm not sure that the steamer will arrive. There was a tremendous rain storm all night long and it continues to rain: probably on the open sea the storm is still going on. I was very much concerned at not having received any more letters from you after the letter of the fourteenth: I thought that something unpleasant might have happened to you; the day before yesterday this gnawing thought became so strong that I decided to send you a telegram. Your reply has calmed me. I embrace you.

Antonio

I'm tearing up a note that I had already written to Signorina Nilde. At any rate, I believe it would be useful if you could send me Nilde's exact address and if you asked her for permission to write to her.

Yesterday the steamer did not come. Its arrival today is not certain either. I must trouble you some more. I would like to have a few tubes of aspirin; the aspirin I received has mysteriously disappeared. I would also like to receive a few cakes of toilet soap and disinfectant soap. I never do manage to make a definitive list of the small things that it is impossible to find here in Ustica. Greetings.

A.

1. Tania.

1927

January 2, 1927

Dearest friend,[1]

I've received the books that you mentioned in your penultimate letter and a first batch of the ones I ordered. So I have plenty to read for some time. I thank you for your great kindness, but I would not want to abuse it. Yet I assure you that quite frankly I will turn to you whenever I am in need of something. As you can imagine, there is no opportunity to spend much here, just the opposite; sometimes one can't spend one's money even when the purchase is necessary.

Life flows by without novelties or surprises; our only concern is the arrival of the steamer, which is not always able to make the four weekly crossings (Monday, Wednesday, Friday, Saturday) to the great disappointment of those of us who always anxiously wait for mail. There are already about sixty of us, thirty-six of whom are friends from various locations; the Romans are on the whole predominant. We have already started school,[2] divided into several courses: course one (first and second elementary grades), course two (third elementary), course three (fourth and fifth elementary), the complementary course, two courses of French (beginner and advanced), and a German course. The courses are set up in relation to the educational level of the students in those subjects that can be reduced to a certain exactly determinable set of notions (grammar and mathematics); therefore the students of the elementary courses for example attend the history and geography lessons of the complementary course. In short, we have tried to adjust the need for a gradual scholastic progression to the fact that the students, though sometimes semiliterate, are quite developed intellectually. The courses are followed with great diligence and attention. By means of the school, also frequented by a number of functionaries and inhabitants of the island, we have avoided the danger of demoralization that is very great. You cannot imagine to what a state of physical and moral degradation the common convicts have been reduced. For the sake of drink they would sell even their shirt; many of them have sold their shoes and jackets. A good number of them no longer dispose freely of the government *mazzetta*, which amounts to four lire daily, because they've pawned it with the money lenders. Usury is being repressed, but I don't believe it is possible to eliminate it, because the very convicts who are its victims will not report the usurers, except in very unusual cases. The interest on a ten lire loan is three lire a week. The interest is collected with an iron hand because the money lenders are surrounded by a small group of sycophants who for a glass of wine would disembowel their great grandfathers. The common convicts, save for rare exceptions, show us great respect and deference. The island population is most courteous. After all, our arrival has brought about a radical change in the place and will leave a deep mark. We are planning to install electricity, since among us political detainees there are technicians able to carry through such a project. The clock on the bell tower, which hasn't worked for six months, was repaired in two days: perhaps we shall revive the project of building a pier in the inlet where the steamer docks. Our relations with the authorities are most correct.

I would like to send you a few impressions gathered during my journey, especially in Palermo and Naples. I stayed in Palermo eight days: I attempted the crossing four times, and three times, after an hour and a half of being tossed on a stormy sea, I had to turn back. This was the worst part of my entire transfer, the one that tired me most. We had to get up at four in the morning, go to the port with manacles on our wrists; always bound and attached to the others with a chain, descend into a small boat, climb up and down several ladders on the steamer, where we remained bound by a single wrist, suffer from seasickness both because of the uncomfortable position (bound by one wrist and attached by half a meter of chain to the others and so unable to lie down) and because the steamer, which is very small and light, bounces about even when the sea is calm—only to turn back and resume the same story the following morning. In Palermo we had a small, very clean dormitory, prepared especially for us (deputies), because the jail is overcrowded and they avoided putting us in contact with the arrested Mafia men.[3] All through the journey we were treated with great correctness and even with courtesy.

I thank you for having taken the trouble to send me eggs. Now that the holidays are over, I should find very fresh ones right here. If you don't mind sending it to me, I'd really enjoy some Swiss condensed milk. I wouldn't know what to ask you for, even if I wanted to: here we lack a bit of everything and it is difficult to procure certain items; it usually involves long searches. There is no courier service with Palermo. I'd be grateful if you'd send me a bit of toilet and shaving soap and a few common medicinals that are always useful, such as Bayer aspirin (here the aspirin even drives the dogs crazy) and tincture of iodine, and a few compresses for headaches. Let me assure you once again that in case of need I will write to you: didn't you see how I took ample advantage of your book offer? Besides, I must confess that I am still somewhat dazed and have not completely finished getting my bearings in regard to many things. Write to me often: in my situation correspondence is my one true pleasure. Whenever you read an interesting book, such as the one by Lewinsohn,[4] send it to me. A fraternal embrace.

Antonio

Send me a small bottle of Cologne. I need it to disinfect myself after shaving.

1. Piero Sraffa.

2. As Gramsci says further on in this letter, the "school" was open to political prisoners and to other adult residents of the island. Ordinary criminals could not attend the courses, since the law forbade this kind of contact between them and the political prisoners.

3. Gramsci is probably alluding here to "small-fry Mafiosi," since the system of high-level collusion and collaboration between the big Mafia bosses and central Italian government authorities on the mainland came to a temporary end in the early years of Fascism. By destroying the parliamentary system, the Fascist regime "destroyed the political nexus between Mafia bosses in Sicily and the mainland political class in Rome." As a result, "the most powerful Mafia bosses were simply integrated into the hierarchical system of Mussolini's political machine," leaving the petty Mafiosi to the police. (Coppa, ed., *Dictionary of Modern Italian History*, p. 248).

4. Richard Lewinsohn, *Histoire de l'inflation: Le déplacement de la richesse en Europe, 1914–1925*, trans. Henri Simondet (Paris: Payot, 1926).

———————————

January 3, 1926[1]

Dearest Tania,

I've received your letter dated 28–29. I haven't been able to understand why you're so worried and nervous.[2] The hints contained in your letter are puzzling. Nothing the least worrisome has been written to me and to my friend. In short, I don't understand, but I am perturbed because I realize that you are very upset. You must let me know what this is all about, and clearly, starting with the understanding that I know nothing about the entire matter.

Dearest Tania, you absolutely must never lose your calm and tranquillity because of me. I assure you that I'm very well and that my existence runs along excellently. I've received many books from Milan and from this point of view too I'm well taken care of. I can read and study. What's more, we've organized a school of general culture; and I teach history and geography and attend the German course. I've subscribed to three daily newspapers and about fifteen periodicals; they've already begun to arrive. I should now receive a lot of books from Milan, because I've taken ample advantage of the account opened for me by my friend Sraffa, who has even added more books and magazines to the list I had sent to the bookshop that he patronizes. So, please don't worry if many of my books from Rome are delayed: I can still study and keep usefully occupied. In short, you must convince yourself that I don't lack for anything and you must avoid all agitation and nervousness. Our friend Sraffa writes to me insisting that I should turn to him also for financial help and for linens and foodstuffs: as a start, he's going to send me some Swiss condensed milk. I think I will have recourse to him in case of need, first because he's rich and helping me will not be a problem for him, and second because his offer is not purely one of courtesy or just talk; he has spontaneously sent me books worth about 1,000 lire. So you can put your mind at rest.

Dear Tatiana, I want you to write to me as often as you can. Getting mail is the most pleasurable gift any of us can receive. The two photographs have arrived: send me the others too and a photograph of yourself. I too have been very sad at not having been able to see and embrace you before my departure. I will tell you the whole story, which from the point of view of a jailbird would be a short novel. At eleven in the morning on November 24 I received the notice that I would leave on the twenty-sixth and that I was authorized to send a telegram: since I thought I noticed a certain embarrassment in the expression of the guard who gave me the news, I did not send the telegram immediately. Jail being a sort of sound box, in which over invisible and manifold conduits every cell receives the information that interests or might interest the various prisoners, I too made contact with these mysterious fluids and discovered that I was to leave on the morning of the twenty-fifth and not the twenty-sixth, that is, the very next day. Had I sent my telegram immediately I would have given the wrong information. I managed to obtain permission to leave the cell and seek out a superior who confirmed that I was to leave on the twenty-fifth: the guard, who was present, apologized for having deceived me, with the excuse that he had confused me with other people scheduled to leave. So the telegram left at two in the afternoon. I was certain that you would have come if you had received the communication, but I did not know whether you were aware that visits were allowed until eleven and I did not know whether you would be given permission. After seven, the hour at which one is regularly expected to go to bed, there began my struggle with the guard who was ordering me to lie down, while I wanted to remain ready to go downstairs at the first call. I managed to have my way, not only that, but at ten I was permitted to go downstairs to the office: I wanted to make sure there would be no more tricks to prevent a possible visit. It was raining very hard. At eleven I went to bed, but I was unable to sleep: at three in the morning I left, taking with me as a traveling bag the pillow case you had sent me and that served me perfectly all the way to Ustica: even handcuffed I could carry it quite comfortably while a suitcase continually banging against my legs would have been a great nuisance.

Dearest Tatiana, next time I will write a long letter for Giulia, I still don't feel up to it. Write to me immediately and send me the photographs; don't worry about anything else. I embrace you affectionately.

Antonio.

1. Gramsci's error: The year is 1927.
2. The reason Tania was concerned and worried was probably that she had already

heard about the possibility that the relatively easy conditions of internment at Ustica would soon come to an end, to be replaced by the much harsher restrictions of imprisonment in Milan. See Gramsci's letters to her of January 19 and 20, 1927.

January 7, 1927

Dearest Tania,

I've received your letter of January 4, a parcel containing toilet articles and a duffel bag and a second parcel containing the panettone that must however have arrived after great delay. I really can't accept your advice to . . . think up a few whims. Unfortunately in the conditions under which I live, whims spring up by themselves: it is incredible how men constrained by external forces to live in an exceptional and artificial way develop with particular alacrity all the negative aspects of their character! Especially intellectuals, or, more appropriately, that category of persons who in vulgar Italian are referred to as "*mezze calzette*,"[1] that is, "would be" intellectuals. The calmest, most serene and measured are the peasants; then come the factory workers, then the craftsmen, and after them the intellectuals, among whom there often arise sudden violent gusts of absurd and infantile madness. Of course I'm referring to the political prisoners, not the common convicts, whose life is primitive and elementary and in whom passions reach peaks of lunacy with fearful rapidity: in one month there have been five or six bloody crimes among the common prisoners.

Therefore I will not follow your advice to be whimsical. But you are right: at times I'm unwittingly unkind and I offend my friends without realizing it. This is due, I believe, to the fact that I've always lived in isolation, without a family, and that I have had to turn to strangers for my needs: so I've always been afraid of being a burden and importunate. But I never failed to recognize your affection and your goodness, I will turn to you whenever I have the need, with the commitment on your part that you will be extremely frank about what you can do and that you will not create useless and dangerous inconveniences for yourself. The ink you sent me is fine; and so are all the other things. I've received the photographs: Delio has had a great success and been much admired. Believe me when I say that I have discovered that I have a reserve of patience and strength that I did not know I possessed: only Bordiga can compete with me. We are the only ones who, during this entire period, have not had ailments of any kind, while the others, some more some less, have all had flu fevers and intestinal disorders due to the radical change in the food and the water, in which certain specimens of the Triton species visibly swim with magnificent agility. I have not yet begun any serious work,[2] even though I already have at my disposal quite a number of books; but I have begun the history lessons in the general culture course we have organized. So you mustn't worry about the urgent shipping of books.

I do however really need a bit of money. I thought I had enough for at least three months, but I had to spend some in order to help a number of prisoners who arrived here without resources and I had to advance money for the general expenses of the communal mess that will begin the day after tomorrow, the ninth. The period of unexpected expenses is over now: the communal mess will make it possible for us to avoid many small and large expenses that we had to carry until now in order to eat. You see that I tell you this quite frankly: I would need about 200 lire and I really don't feel like asking Sraffa who in fact just now is out of town.

Dearest Tania, I would really like to know that you are tranquil and that you are not suffering attacks of melancholy. But you must write to me all the same and confide in me: your letters give me great pleasure, for with each of them I feel close to you. Do you know that I received a card from Giulia with Delio's authentic signature. It seems incredible: the world is always smaller than we think. I will write to you again at length in preparation for the Monday mail, although it is quite possible that the steamer will not get here on Monday. Winter has begun on Ustica too. A very mild winter, because we can go out without hat or overcoat; but it rains often, and there are very violent winds that whip up the sea and prevent the crossing. But also what magnificent days! You can't imagine what colors the sea and sky manage to display on calm clear days.

Give my greetings to Giacomo[3] and his wife. I've made the acquaintance of Valentino's[4] friend, who is a very fine young man. I embrace you.

Antonio.

Send me a few issues of *Les Temps* and of the *Journal des Débats*; you can find them in the kiosk in the Treasury building.

The shoes that you describe for me will be good for next spring, I think. The shoes I was wearing when I left, despite the fact that they were coming apart (remember?) are holding up admirably.

Send me news about the small lemon tree: has it grown? how tall is it by now? is it healthy? I meant to write you about it, but then I decided not to, so as not to seem too . . . childish.

1. Literally "half stockings."

2. By "serious work" Gramsci was referring to the four subjects outlined in his letter to Tania, March 19, 1927, and to the systematic reading and note-taking that he began in Turi prison in February 1929.

3. Giacomo Bernolfo and his wife Margherita. See letters to Tania, June 15, 1931, n. 2 and April 4, 1932, n. 1 for two other references to Bernolfo.

4. Valentino Schreider, born in 1903, was the son of the Polish-Russian social-revolutionary Isaac Schreider, a friend of Tania's whom Gramsci had known in Rome in the years 1924–1926. Valentino served a five-year prison term because of his anti-Fascist activities.

———————

January 8, 1927

My dearest Julca,

I've received your letters of December 20 and 27 and the postcard of the twenty-eighth with Delio's authentic signature. I've tried to write to you several times: I never succeeded. From your letter I see that Tania has explained the reason, which is somewhat puerile, to be sure, but which has, nevertheless, been decisive up to now. I had planned to write a kind of diary for you, a series of vignettes about my life during this original and quite interesting period: I will undoubtedly do so. I want to try to give you all the elements that will enable you to picture my life as a whole and in its more notable details. You should do the same about yourself. I would so like to know what relationship is developing between Delio and Giuliano: how Delio conceives of and expresses his role as the older and more experienced brother.

Dearest Giulia, ask Bracco[1] from what source he got the news that I was not in good health. The fact is that I never imagined I had such a well supplied storehouse of physical strength and energy. Neither Bordiga or I have ever been sick at all since the moment of our arrest;

all the others, in one way or another, have at times suffered very serious crises of nerves, all of the same kind. In the jail at Palermo, Molinelli, in a single night, fainted three times while asleep, falling prey to convulsions that lasted as long as twenty minutes, and without our being able to get any help. Here on Ustica a friend from the Abruzzi, Ventura, who sleeps in the same room as I do, on many nights would wake up continually a prey to savage nightmares that made him scream and thrash about in a frightful manner. I've had no ailments, except for that of not getting enough sleep, which is not new and that moreover could not lead to the same consequences as before, considering the forced inactivity to which I was reduced; and yet my journey was full of discomforts and hardships because the stormy seas prevented us three times from completing the voyage to Ustica. I've become very proud of this capacity for physical endurance, which I did not suspect I had; that is why I mention it to you: it too represents a value in my present circumstances, and not one of the most contemptible.

I shall write to you at greater length and shall minutely describe my entire life. You too must write to me or ask Genia or mother to write me about the children's life and yours; I am sure that you are very busy and tired. I have the feeling that you are all very close to each other. I embrace you tenderly.

Antonio

1. A pseudonym of Ruggero Grieco.

———————————

January 15, 1927

Dearest Tania,

The last letter you sent me is dated January 4. You left me eleven days without news from you. In my present situation this worries me greatly. I believe it should be possible to bring our mutual needs into accord, with the commitment on your part to send me at least one postcard every three days. I've already begun to follow this system. When I don't have any subject for a letter, and for me this is the most common case, I will send you a card, so as not to miss out on any of the mail runs: life here flows by monotonous, uniform, without jolts. Perhaps I should describe for you some vignettes of peasant life, if I were in a sufficiently good mood. For example, I could describe the arrest of a pig, which was found grazing illegally along the streets of the village and was duly carted off to prison. This event amused me enormously, but I'm not sure that you or Giulia will believe me; perhaps Delka will believe me when he is a few years older and hears this story told together with others of the same kind (the story about the green eyeglasses, etc.) that are just as true and to be believed without a smirk. Also the way in which the pig was arrested amused me: it was grabbed by the hind legs and propelled forward like a wheelbarrow, while it squealed like a thing possessed. I have not been able to obtain precise information on how one determines the illegality of the grazing and trespass: I think that the sanitation guards are personally acquainted with all the village's livestock. Another detail that I never mentioned to you is that on the entire island I have yet to see any means of locomotion save the donkey, a magnificent animal indeed, of great stature and notable domesticity, which is an indication of the good disposition of the inhabitants: back in my town the donkeys are half wild and only allow their immediate owners to approach them. There's more about animals: yesterday I heard a wonderful story about horses told by an Arab who is interned here. The Arab spoke Italian in a rather outlandish manner and with many obscurities: but on the whole his tale was full of color and descriptive power. This, by a very strange association, reminds me that I've heard that it is very possible to find in Italy the famous Saracen maize[1]: some friends tell me that in the Veneto it is quite common and used to make polenta.

And thus I have depleted my stock of subjects worth recounting. I hope I've made you smile a little: it seems to me that your long silence must be interpreted as a consequence of melancholy and fatigue and that it was really necessary to make you smile. Dear Tania, you must write to me, because you are the only one from whom I receive letters: when I'm without your correspondence for such a long time I feel even more isolated, and it seems that all my relations with the world are severed. I embrace you affectionately.

Antonio

---

1. "Saracen maize" is buckwheat, "famous," perhaps, because it is mentioned in Alessandro Manzoni's novel *The Betrothed* (1827).

January 15, 1927

My dearest Julca,

Let me describe for you my daily life in its most essential outlines, so that you may follow it and every so often grasp some feature of it. As you know, since Tania must have already written this to you, I live together with four other friends, among them Engineer Bordiga from Naples, whose name you perhaps know. The other three are: a reformist former deputy from Perugia, Attorney Sbraglini, and two friends from the Abruzzo. Now I sleep in a room with one of these Abruzzesi, Piero Ventura; before this three of us slept here, because with us we had Paolo Conca, the Maximalist former deputy from Verona, a very engaging type of factory worker, who at night would not let us sleep because he was obsessed by thoughts of his wife, would sigh and pant, then he would turn on the light and smoke certain pestilential cigars. At last his wife has also come to Ustica to join her husband and Conca has left us, so there are five of us distributed in three bedrooms (this is the entire house): we have at our disposal a very beautiful terrace from which by day we admire the boundless sea and at night the magnificent sky. The sky free from all urban haziness allows us to enjoy these marvels with the greatest intensity. The colors of the sea's water and of the firmament are truly extraordinary in their variety and depth: I've seen unique rainbows.

In the morning, I'm usually the first to get up; Engineer Bordiga declares that at that moment my step has special characteristics, it is the step of a man who has not yet had his coffee and is waiting for it with a certain impatience. I myself make the coffee, when I've been unable to convince Bordiga to make it, in view of his outstanding culinary aptitude. Then our life begins: we go to school, as teachers or as pupils. If it is a mail day we go to the shore and anxiously wait for the arrival of the steamer: if because of bad weather the mail does not arrive, our day is ruined, for a sort of melancholy spreads over all our faces. At noon we eat: I participate in a communal mess and in fact today it is my turn to act as waiter and dishwasher: I don't know yet if I have to peel potatoes, prepare the lentils, or wash the salad before serving at table. My debut is looked forward to with great curiosity: several friends wanted to take my place for this service, but

I've been adamant in wanting to do my share. In the evening we must be back in our domiciles by eight. Sometimes there are inspections to ascertain whether we are really in the house. Unlike the common convicts we are not locked in from the outside. Another difference consists in the fact that we are free to stay out until eight and not just until five; we could obtain special evening permits if we needed them for anything. At home in the evening we play cards. I'd never played cards until now; Bordiga assures me that I have the stuff to become a good player at *scopone scientifico*.[1] I've already been able to rebuild something of a small library and I can read and study. The books and newspapers that arrive here for me have already brought about a certain struggle between me and Bordiga, who wrongly maintains that I'm very untidy; behind my back he creates disorder among my things, with the excuse of symmetry and architecture: but in reality I can no longer find anything in the symmetrical mess that he arranges for me.

Dearest Julca: write to me at length about your life and the life of the children. As soon as possible, send me Giuliano's photograph. Has Delka made much more progress? Did his hair grow back? Did his illness have any aftereffects? Write me a lot about Giuliano. And has Genia recovered? I give you a very tight embrace.

Antonio.

1. An Italian card game similar to cassino, in which each player wins cards by matching or combining cards exposed on the table with cards from his hand.

January 19, 1927

Dearest Tania,

On Monday, the seventeenth, the steamer did not arrive. I sent you a telegram, because when reading your letter of the eleventh I got the impression that you were more melancholy than usual and I did not want all communication between us to be cut off. I cannot understand why you are agitated and why you would think that I could possibly have left Ustica![1] The fact that one of my postcards bore a Palermo postmark could not mean anything: if, for any reason whatever, I should have to leave I would immediately inform you by telegram, or have you informed by a friend.

I thank you for the 500 lire you sent me; but that was too much. I absolutely don't want you to make so many sacrifices for me. I hope that this will tide me over for a few months and that I won't need to turn to anyone. The worst stage of internment, from a financial point of view, has passed: we've entered a period of stabilization, which will continue to consolidate, as gradually mess arrangements and supply services begin to function.

I would like to write to you at length, but it is already late. I will write at greater length next time. Meanwhile I would like to know that you are tranquil and serene. I embrace you affectionately.

Antonio

1. See letter to Tania, January 3, 1927, n. 2

January 20, 1927

Dear Tatiana,

I have at this very moment received orders to leave for my transfer to Milan. This is an ordinary transfer, that is, I will have to stop along the way, in the jails of Palermo, Naples, Rome, etc., unless I am able to convince them to grant me an extraordinary transfer that is more expeditious and less fraught with hardship. I will try to let you have this information by telegram. I believe that what is involved is a judicial procedure for one of the not so rare charges that result in a more or less brief acquittal. I send you my affectionate greetings.

Antonio

Milan, February 12, 1927

My dearest ones,[1]

I am writing to both of you so as to better utilize the few letters that I am allowed to write. I left Ustica on the morning of the twentieth,[2] suddenly. I barely had the time to dictate a short letter and have a telegram sent to warn you of this. I thought I would pass through Rome; instead, apparently due to a mistaken interpretation of the telegram that ordered my arrest, I was moved to Milan by ordinary rather than special transport: so my trip lasted nineteen days. At

Isernia I managed to send off a telegram that informed you of my change of itinerary. This journey has been for me a threefold or even fourfold test, from the moral point of view as well as and especially from the physical point of view. I don't want to describe it to you in detail as yet, because I do not want to alarm you or give you the impression that I've been worn to a rag. During these nineteen days, I have "resided" in the following jails: Palermo, Naples, Caianello, Isernia, Sulmona, Castellammare Adriatico, Ancona, Bologna; on the seventh, in the evening, I arrived in Milan. In Caianello and in Castellammare there are no jails; I "slept" in the detention cell of the carabinieri barracks; these were perhaps the two most horrific nights I've spent in my entire life. In Castellammare I caught a formidable cold that by now is almost gone.

During the Ustica–Palermo and Palermo–Naples crossings the sea was dreadful; but I did not get seasick. The Palermo–Naples voyage deserves to be described: I shall do this in another letter, when I will have thought back over all the details and will have refreshed my memory.

In general the trip has been for me a very long cinematic event: I've come to know and I've seen an infinity of types, from the most vulgar and repugnant to the oddest replete with interesting traits.

I've understood how difficult it is to know the true nature of men from outward signs; for example, in Ancona, a little jovial old man with the face of an honest provincial asked me to let him have my soup that I had decided not to eat; I did this gladly, struck by the serenity of his eyes and the natural modesty of his demeanor; I was immediately warned that he was a repulsive scoundrel: he had raped his daughter.

Let me give you an impression of my transfer as a whole. Just imagine that an immense worm slithers from Palermo to Milan, a worm that continually breaks up and comes together again, leaving part of its rings in each prison, reforming new ones, tossing the same parts to right and left and then reincorporating the extractions. This worm has lairs in each prison, which accumulate the dirt and misery of generations, clotting them together. You arrive tired, dirty, your wrists hurting because of the long hours in manacles, and on your face a long stubble, your hair disheveled, eyes sunk deep and glittering both from the excitation of strained fatigue and sleeplessness;

you fling yourself on the pallets that are who knows how old, fully dressed so as not to come into contact with the filth, wrapping your face and hands in your towels, covering yourself with the skimpy blankets just to avoid freezing. Then you leave again dirtier and wearier for the next transit, and your wrists are even more bruised because of the cold irons and the weight of the chains and the effort of carrying, thus decked out, your own luggage: but, let us be patient, now it is all over and I've already rested.[3]

I am here, in a good cell, warmed by the sun, covered by a heavy sweater that I immediately bought and at last I've driven the cold from my old bones.

In other letters I will describe some of my travel and chain companions: I have a series of them, rather interesting.

I was particularly struck by a lifer whom I met in Naples during the "exercise"; I found out only his name, Arturo, and these details: he is forty-six years old, has already served twenty-two years of his sentence, ten of them in isolation, and is a shoemaker.

He's a handsome, slim man, with fine, elegant features; he speaks with an astonishing precision, clarity and assurance. He does not have much culture, though he often quotes Nietzsche: for instance, he would say Dies irae, splitting the a-e. I saw him in Naples, serene, smiling, tranquil; his temples and ears were of a parchmentlike hue, his skin was yellowish, that is, almost tanned like leather. He left Naples two days before me. I saw him again in Ancona, when we arrived at the station in the rain: they had taken him up the Campobasso-Foggia line, I think, instead of the line between Caianello-Castellammare, because, being a lifer, during those transits he might have attempted to escape, even risking a bullet from the carabinieri. Having immediately recognized me, he greeted me. I saw him again at the registration office of the Ancona prison: they had left him in irons, because having reached his destination, he was going to his cell to be locked up and had to pass through several courtyards, all of them of course inside the prison walls. He had completely changed since Naples: he truly reminded me of Farinata:[4] his face was hard, angular, his eyes piercing and cold, his chest thrust out, his entire body as tense as a spring coiled and ready to snap: he shook my hand two or three times and then disappeared, swallowed up by the penitentiary.

Enough: as you see I have been chattering away like a silly woman. I want you to know that for now I am well, that I don't need anything, that I am tranquil and expect to receive news from you and the children. Does Delio remember me sometimes? You must send me Giuliano's photograph. I embrace you all tenderly.

Antonio.

1. This letter, written to both Tania and Giulia, did not reach its destination because it was confiscated and added to his pretrial dossier. The reason for its confiscation was its exact and "sincere" (meaning frank and explicit) description of prison life and of the horrendous train ride from Sicily to Milan. Gramsci arrived at the Milan prison on February 7, as he himself later told Tania, "after having been kept for fourteen hours in the bottom of the hold of the Palermo-Naples mail train tied to a criminal with epilepsy and on a chain a hand long, after having been kept in a dozen prisons, after having been dragged, in a feverish state, for twenty days, from one end of the peninsula to the other." See Gramsci's letter of October 26, 1931, for further reference to this episode. Gramsci was later to attribute most of his physical problems in prison to the effects of this horrible experience, especially the exposure to bitter cold inside box cars and prison cells in mid-winter. This is made apparent in one of Tania's still unpublished letters to Piero Sraffa, of May 4, 1933.

2. Not long after Gramsci was sent to police internment at Ustica, Judge Enrico Macis of the Military Tribunal of Milan, acting on instructions of the Special Tribunal in Defense of the State, reopened the inquiry into Gramsci's case and, on January 14, 1927, issued an order for his arrest. The minutes of three interrogations of Gramsci, conducted by Macis at the Milan prison, can be found in Zucaro, *Vita del carcere di Antonio Gramsci*, pp. 123–131.

3. The painful details of Gramsci's transfer, which took more than two weeks, were brought to public attention by Piero Sraffa in a letter that was published in the *Manchester Guardian* on October 24, 1927, p. 16. The English translation of Sraffa's letter, which was done by Maurice Dobb with the title "The Methods of Fascism—the Case of Antonio Gramsci," appears in *Lettere dal carcere*, ed. Caprioglio and Fubini, pp. 912–914. The letter was not signed by Sraffa. It is signed "An Italian in England." In general, Gramsci took a dim view of such attempts to publicize his case, since he felt they were ineffective and, moreover, tended to worsen his position vis-à-vis Fascist authorities.

4. The reference is to Farinata degli Uberti, a leader of the Florentine Ghibelline party, who appears in canto 10 of Dante's *Inferno*, as a man ruled by pride and seemingly indifferent to his fate as a heretic.

February 19, 1927

Dearest Tania,

It is a month and ten days since I've received news from you and I can't explain it. As I already wrote to you a week ago, at the time of my departure from Ustica the steamer had not yet docked for almost ten days: the steamer that took me to Palermo should have brought to Ustica at least a couple of your letters, that then ought to have been forwarded to me in Milan; instead, in the correspondence that was sent on from the island I haven't found anything from you. Dearest, if this is due to you and not (as is possible and probable) due to some administrative mixup, you must avoid keeping me on tenterhooks for so long a time: isolated as I am, every novelty and break in what is normal gives rise to gnawing and painful thoughts. Your last letters, which I received on Ustica, were really rather worrisome; what are these preoccupations about my health, which actually go so far as to make you physically ill? I assure you that I've always felt quite well and that I possess physical energies that are not easily depleted, despite my frail appearance. Do you think that having always lived an extremely sober and rigorous life means nothing? I realize now what it has meant never to have had serious illnesses and never to have inflicted a decisive wound to my organism; I can get horribly tired, that's true; but a bit of rest and nourishment allow me to rapidly regain my normal state. In short, I don't know what I must write you to keep you calm and healthy: must I resort to threats? I could stop writing, you know, so that you too will feel what it means to be completely without news.

I imagine you serious and gloomy without even a glimmer of a smile. I would like to cheer you up somehow. I will tell you a few little tales; what do you think of that? For example, as an intermezzo to the description of my journey through this vast and terrible world I want to tell you something about myself and my fame that is quite amusing. I'm not known outside a rather restricted circle; therefore my name is mangled in the most unlikely ways: Gramasci, Granusci, Gramisci, even Garamascon, with all the most bizarre in-betweens. In Palermo, while waiting for a baggage check, in the baggage room I met a group of workers from Turin on their way to internment, that is, internal banishment; with them there was a formidable, superindividualistic and anarchistic type known under the name of "Unico"[1] who refuses to entrust anyone, but especially the police and the authorities in general, with his personal data: "I am 'Unico' (the unique) and that's all," that was his answer. In the waiting crowd, among the common (Mafiosi) criminals, Unico recognized another fellow, a Sicilian (Unico was probably a Neapolitan or something of the sort) arrested for various motives, a combination of political and common delinquency, and then he proceeded to the introductions. When he introduced me the other fellow stared at me for a long time, then he asked: "Gramsci, Antonio?" Yes, Antonio! I answered. "That can't be," he retorted, "because Antonio Gramsci must be a giant and not such a tiny man."[2] He said nothing more, withdrew to a corner, sat down on an unmentionable contraption and stayed there, like Marius on the ruins of Carthage, meditating on his lost illusions. He painstakingly avoided speaking to me again during all the time we remained in the same room and did not say goodbye when we parted. Another similar episode happened to me later on, but, I believe, this was even more interesting and complex. We were on the point of leaving; the carabinieri escorting us had already put on our manacles and the chains; I had been bound in a new and most unpleasant way because the manacles held my wrists in a rigid position, for the wrist bone was pushed outside the iron and painfully scraped against it. The head of the escort, a gigantic sergeant, arrived and during the roll call stopped at my name and asked me whether I was a relative of the "famous deputy Gramsci."[3] I answered that I was that very man and he gave me a compassionate look, mumbling something incomprehensible. At all the stops I heard him talking about me, always describing me as the "famous deputy" to the clusters of people that would form around the police car (I must add that he had given orders to adjust my manacles so that they were less painful), so much so that, considering the general mood, I thought that on top of everything else some maniac might give me a whack with a club. At one point the sergeant who had been traveling in the second police car, moved into the one where I was and struck up a conversation. He was an extraordinarily interesting and bizarre type, full of "metaphysical needs" as Schopenhauer would say, but managed to satisfy them in the most outlandish and disorderly manner imaginable. He told me that he had always pictured my person as "Cyclopic"[4] and from that point of view he was very disappointed. He was reading a book by M. Mariani, L'equilibrio degli egoismi [The equilibrium of egotisms], and he had just finished reading a book by a certain Paolo Gilles, a confutation of Marxism.[5] I most certainly did not tell him that Gilles was a French anarchist devoid of all qualifications scientific or otherwise: I enjoyed hearing him speak with great enthusiasm about so many disparate and disconnected ideas and notions, as only an intelligent autodidact without discipline or method can speak. At a certain point he began to address me as "Maestro." I was most amused, as you can imagine. And so this is how I had a taste of my "fame." What do you think of it?

I'm almost out of paper. I meant to describe my life here in the minutest detail. I will do so schematically. In the morning I get up at half past six, a half hour before reveille. I make myself a very hot coffee (here in Milan we are allowed to use "Meta" fuel, which is very convenient and useful): I clean the cell and shave and wash. At half past seven I receive half a liter of milk that is still warm and drink it immediately. At eight I go for fresh air, that is, a walk, which lasts two hours. I take along a book, stroll, read, smoke a few cigarettes. At noon I receive my lunch from outside and in the same way I receive dinner in the evening: I never manage to eat everything, even though I eat more than in Rome. At seven in the evening I get into bed and read until about eleven o'clock. During the day I receive five daily newspapers: *Corriere, Stampa, Popolo d'Italia, Giornale d'Italia, Secolo*. I've subscribed to the library with a double subscription and I'm entitled to eight books a week. I also buy a few magazines and *Il Sole*, Milan's economic-financial paper. So I read all the time. I've already read Nansen's[6] *Voyages* and other books about which I shall talk to you some other time. I have not had ailments of any sort, except for feeling cold during the first few days. Write to me, my dear, and send me news of Giulia, Delio, Giuliano, Genia, and all the others: and your news, your news. I embrace you.

Antonio

My last letter and this one are without stamps because I forgot to buy any in time.

1. The name Unico, the Unique One, was probably taken from the title of a book by the anarchist philosopher Max Stirner, *Der Einzige und sein Eigentum* (H. G. Helms, 1845), known to many Italian anarchists in its 1902 Italian translation, *L'Unico e la sua proprietà*, trans. L. P. Zacchini.

2. Gramsci was a little less than five feet tall, weighed about 120 pounds, and was hunch-backed.

3. In the national elections of April 6, 1924, six weeks before his return to Italy from Vienna, Gramsci was elected to the Chamber of Deputies by an electoral constituency of the Veneto region. Parliamentary immunity from arrest allowed him to return to Italy in May.

4. Fascist propagandists created a special vocabulary for Mussolini and for friends and enemies of the regime. Thus Mussolini was a "titanic" figure, the regime's achievements were "granitelike," and leading opponents of fascism had personalities that were deformed, hence "cyclopic."

5. The references are to the writer Mario Mariani (1884–1951) and to the French philosopher Paul Gille (not Gilles). Gille's "confutation" of Marxism appeared in his introduction to *Esquisse d'une philosophie de la dignité humaine*, translated into Italian by L. Fabbri and published in Italy in 1926 with the title *Abbozzo di una filosofia della dignità umana*.

6. Fridtjof Nansen (1861–1930), Norwegian scientist and explorer.

February 26, 1927

Dearest Mother,

I've been in Milan in the San Vittore Detention Center[1] since February 7. I left Ustica on January 20 and here I've been given a letter of yours undated but that must be from the beginning of February. You mustn't worry about this change in my situation; it worsens only up to a certain point; there is only an increase in annoyances and vexations, nothing more. I don't even want to enter into the details of the charge brought against me, because even I have not yet been able to really understand it; in any case, what is at stake are the usual political questions owing to which I had already been saddled with the five years internment to Ustica. This calls for patience and I have tons, cartloads, housefuls of patience (do you remember what Carlo used to say when he was little and he was eating some tasty sweet? "I'd like to have a hundred housefuls of them"; I have *kentu domus e prus*[2] of patience).

But you too will have to have patience and kindness. Your letter, however, seems to show you in an altogether different state of mind. You write that you feel old, etc. Well, I'm sure that you're still very strong and resilient despite your age and the great sorrows and great labors that you've been forced to endure.

Corrias, corriazzu,[3] remember? I'm sure that we will all be together again, children, grandchildren, and perhaps, who knows, great-grandchildren, and we'll have a huge banquet with *kulurzones* and *pardulas* and *zippulas* and *pippias de zuccuru* and *figu sicada* (but none of those dried figs from the famous Aunt Maria from Tadasuni). Do you think that Delio will like the *pirichittus* and the *pippias de zuccuru*? I think he will and that he too will want to have a hundred housefuls of them; you wouldn't believe how much he resembles Mario and

Carlo as children, so far as I remember, especially Carlo, except for Carlo's nose, which at that time was barely formed.

Sometimes I think about all these things and I like to remember the scenes and events of my childhood: I find in them much sorrow and pain, that is true, but also something cheerful and beautiful. And besides you're always there, dear mother, and with your hands always busy for us, to alleviate our pains and extract something useful from everything. Do you remember my schemes to have good coffee without barley or other such rubbish? You see: when I think about all these things I also think that Edmea as a grown-up will not have such memories and this will have a great influence on her character, creating in her a certain softness and a certain sentimentality that are not to be recommended in these times of iron and fire in which we live. Since Edmea will also have to get ahead on her own, we must make sure that she's strengthened morally and prevent her from growing up surrounded only by the aspects of fossilized small-town life. I think that you ought to explain to her, with great tact, naturally, why Nannaro no longer pays much attention to her and seems to neglect her. You must explain to her that today her father cannot return from abroad and that this is due to the fact that Nannaro, like myself and many others, thought that the many Edmeas who live in this world should have a childhood better than the one we had and she herself is having. And you must tell her, without any subterfuge, that I'm in prison, for the same reason that her father is abroad. Certainly, you must take into account her age and her temperament and try not to sadden the poor little girl too much, but you must also tell her the truth and thus accumulate in her memories of strength, of courage, of resistance to the sorrows and mishaps of life.

Dearest mother, you mustn't worry about me and you mustn't think that I'm badly off. To the extent that this is possible I'm doing quite well. I have a paid-for cell, that has a reasonably good bed: I even have a mirror in which I can gaze at myself. I receive two meals a day from a trattoria; in the morning I drink half a liter of milk. I have at my disposal a small contraption to heat my food and make coffee. I read six newspapers a day and eight books a week, plus illustrated and humorous magazines. I have Macedonia cigarettes. In short, from a material standpoint I do not suffer any noticeable deprivation. True, I cannot write as much as I want to and I receive mail with great irregularity. I haven't had news from Giulia and the two boys for about a month and a half; so I cannot tell you anything about them. I know, however, that from a material standpoint they are secure and that Delio and Giuliano lack for nothing.

By the way, did you receive a beautiful photograph of Delio that was supposed to be sent to you? If you did receive it, write me your impressions.

Dearest mother, I promise to write you at least every three weeks and to keep you in good cheer; you too must write to me and make sure I receive the letters that Carlo, Grazietta, Teresina, Papa, and Paolo write to me and also from Edmea, who, I believe, must already have made progress and be able to put together a short letter; each letter I receive is a great consolation and a wonderful amusement for me.

I tenderly embrace everyone; and for you, dearest mother, an even more tender embrace.

Nino

My address now is: Judiciary House of Detention, Milan

1. The section of the Milan prison in which Gramsci was held was reserved for individuals in "detention," that is, persons charged with a crime whose case is under investigation by judicial authorities.
2. "A hundred houses and more," in Sardinian.
3. *Corriazzu* means "tough and leathery" in Sardinian, a word Gramsci associated with the surname of some of his mother's relatives, which was Corrias, and that connoted a quality that he prized in his mother. The meanings of the Sardinian gastronomic words in this paragraph are: *kurluzones*, almond-filled ravioli; *pardulas* and *zippulas*, types of cake; *pippias de zucurru*, doll-shaped cakes; *figu sigada*, dried figs; and *pirichittus*, round sugar candies.

February 26, 1927

Dearest Tania:

It's about a month and a half now that I have been without news about you, Giulia, and the children. I'm sure that you've written to me. I don't know to what I should attribute the fact that your letters do not reach me. One explanation might be found in this: that some of your letters were addressed (I don't know why) to the military jail and that on the envelopes I found written in pencil: "not here"; it is possible that due to this same reason some other letters may have been lost. But it seems impossible that "all" your letters went astray; I think that there might be some mysterious provision owing to which part of my correspondence is not delivered to me. I'm not even sure, therefore, that my letters are reaching you; if such is the case, and just to make sure, thinking that in your letters there might have been an even distant allusion to the regulation that concerns me, I beg you to avoid any such allusions, even the most vague and indirect, and confine yourself to family news.

Dearest Tania, if this letter reaches you, write to me immediately and tell me how you are and about Giulia and the children: please ignore the previous letters that you must certainly have written; repeat all the news. This is my only worry and it afflicts me to an extent that I cannot describe. Dearest Tania, I embrace you affectionately.

Antonio

My address: Judiciary House of Detention. This is the third letter I'm sending you from Milan.

March 12, 1927

Dearest Tania,

This week I've received your two cards of March 3 and 5. Finally! These are the only pieces of writing that I have received from you between the first days of January and today; I did not receive either the letters you mention or the overcoat. I was left absolutely without any news direct or indirect, and in fact I knew that the flu was going around. You haven't received all my letters either, or so it would appear from the cards. I wrote to you on the twelfth, nineteenth, and twenty-sixth of February, I did not write on March 5, and I had decided to stop writing into the void; to write like this gave me the same impression that I have on Sunday mornings, when they open the door a crack and from the end of the corridor I hear the indistinct and incomprehensible buzz of the mass.

I was expecting to receive some sort of very long letter from you; the expectancy of a prisoner, who has been deprived of news for such a long time and has not yet become used to it. Certainly with time I will become used to this too; perhaps it is the weakness of an "apprentice," a childishness, who knows.

I wrote you two long letters, in which I tried to give both you and Giulia at least some impression of the life I have lived during this recent time. It certainly is not superlatively interesting. The third letter was very brief; I wrote it thinking that for some reason of a superior order, the other two had been delayed. I also thought that you might be ill or had left Rome because of your work: in the last letter I received from you in Ustica you did mention something of the kind.

I don't know what answer to give you as regards Giulia's correspondence. I know nothing about my impending or far-off destination. As soon I arrived in Milan, they told me at the registration office that I would leave again for Rome; the pretrial judge, if I remember correctly, declared that no decision had been made on the matter. In sum, I know nothing definite. I would like to read Giulia's letters, but I would be very sorry if they were lost: could you send them registered? What particularly distresses me is the difficulty or impossibility of knowing with a certain amount of detail how the life of the children unfolds; and in the life of children it is the details that count. Perhaps this too is the weakness of an "apprentice," that one must shed. Who can tell! We shall see.

Dearest Tania, this long wait has truly wreaked havoc with me. Your two postcards, so short and dry, have added to this state of mind; but you mustn't take it in bad part if sometimes I write you maladroit things and perhaps even wound your feelings. Do not send this letter of mine to Giulia, who believes me to be much stronger than I am; I don't want to hurt her too much. You must forgive me if at times I make you suffer a bit and am such a nuisance and cause you so much trouble. Poor Tania, to think that you too had to fall into this pit of neurasthenics! And that I too should make you suffer and cause you so much trouble. Sometimes I think about this concatenation of events and I remember our first encounter, that left me with so many emotions! The world is truly vast and terrible![1]

I don't want to write you again as I am doing today. I will resume the story of my travel adventures and describe some of the types I've encountered. I still must tell you about my friend from Calabria, the peasant Salvatore Chiodo, who killed his wife, and about my protector, the peasant from Salerno, whose name I do not know, who killed his father-in-law and inherited his property (I've killed and I've inherited—this was his refrain) and about my second protector, the Neapolitan baker Gaetano Parise who killed his sister's seducer and about the Calabrian gang leader Domenico Vilella, sixteen years old, to whom I gave a pair of shoes and an undershirt (his feet without socks were stuck into two sewed-up rags and two pieces of cardboard and he had no underwear) who solemnly promised that he would never steal my chickens; and about the Neapolitan soldier, Scarpato, who told me the entire epic of Roland and Scalabrino and the *Reali di Francia* [Kings of France] and had a running dispute with a shoemaker from Messina as to whether the exploits of Ganellone di Maganza and those of Malagigi[2] could be the work of single individuals or were a historical *panachage*;[3] the fellow from Messina opted for *panachage*, Scarpato however was convinced that both Ganellone and Malagigi were also capable of other exploits; and this shoemaker from Messina recited for me all the adventures of Sinbad the Sailor in a Sicilian version, which he had heard from his grandfathers and refused to believe (I did not insist) that this was a tale from *A Thousand and One Nights*; and there was the poetry recital held in my honor by several Roman detainees, with the delivery of Pascarella's "Discovery of America"[4] and other poems in Roman dialect. In brief, I will try to cause you as little distress as possible and to amuse you a bit. Keep on being fond of me. I embrace you affectionately.

Antonio

Yesterday I had an audience with the warden to find out about the correspondence and overcoat. The man in charge of storage has assured me that the overcoat did not arrive. Since by now I wouldn't know what to do with it, if you trace it, hold on to it. You never wrote to me about the suit and shoes. The suit I'm wearing now is still holding up. On Ustica a friend gave me his shoes that are still good; those that I had brought with me from Rome were completely ruined and I gave them to the young Calabrian chicken and salami thief. As for underwear I am well provided: I don't need anything for the time being. Dearest, I embrace you again.

I've brought the photographs of Delio, Giulia, and those that were taken in Venice into my cell. They have been stamped. And so it seems to me that I've taken you all into prison with me and I'm very sorry about it; but there was no other way to have the photographs. Do you forgive me? Tell Giulia and Delio too about it: will he understand what "prison" means? As for this, I'll send you some thoughts I've had about this in my next.

1. "Vast and terrible world" is a phrase that Gramsci used very often in his letters to Giulia, both before and after his imprisonment, to convey a sense of the loneliness, hardships, and dangers that he and his wife would have to face as politically committed individuals. The phrase appears in four of his letters to his wife during the years 1924 to 1926. The fact that he also used it in his letters to Tania suggests that it was a way for him to express some deep and complex feelings about life. See also letters to Tania, February 20, 1928, and October 20, 1928.

2. Rolando, Ganellone, Malagigi are the names of characters in Italian chivalric and mock-heroic poems adapted from the French medieval originals, chiefly the *Chanson de Roland*. The *Reali di Francia* is an Italian chivalric epic written in the fourteenth century by Andrea da Barberino.

3. A mixing of different colors.

4. "The Discovery of America" is the best-known work by the Roman dialect poet Cesare Pascarella (1858–1940). It tells the story of Columbus's voyage and discovery as interpreted by a Roman *popolano* (a man of the popular classes) and is quite funny.

March 19, 1927[1]

Dearest Tania,

This week I received two postcards from you; one dated the ninth and the other the eleventh of March: but I have not received the letter that you mention. I thought I would receive your correspondence forwarded from Ustica: and indeed I did receive a parcel of books from the island and the clerk who handed it to me said that the parcel had contained a number of sealed letters and postcards that still had to go through the review office: I hope I'll get them in a few days.

Thank you for the news you've sent me about Giulia and the children; I'm unable to write directly to Giulia, as I'm waiting to receive some of her greatly delayed letters. I can imagine her mental and physical state, due to any number of reasons; this illness must have been very distressing. Poor Delio; from scarlet fever to the flu, in such a short time! I want you to write to grandma Lula and ask her to write me a long letter in Italian or French, as best she can (at any rate you could just send me the translation) and describe for me the life of the children in the minutest detail. I've really become convinced that grandmothers are better than mothers at describing children and their actions in a real and concrete way; they are more objective, and besides they have the experience of a whole lifelong development; it seems to me that the tenderness of grandmothers has greater substance than that of mothers (Giulia, however, mustn't be offended and consider me more wicked than I am!)

I really don't know what I ought to recommend to you for Giuliano; in this sphere I already failed once with Delio. Perhaps I would myself be able to put together something suitable for him, if I could be close to him. You decide, in accordance with your own taste, and choose something in my name. Recently I've made a papier-maché ball, which is now almost dry; I don't think that it will be possible to send it to you for Delio; besides, I still haven't been able to figure out how to varnish it, and without varnish any sort of dampness would cause it to fall apart.

My life still goes by always with the same monotony. Studying too is much more difficult than it might seem. I've received some books and I actually read a lot (more than a book a day, besides the newspapers), but this is not what I'm referring to, I'm talking about something else. I am obsessed (this is a phenomenon typical of people in jail, I think) by this idea: that I should do something *für ewig*, following a complex concept of Goethe's that as I remember tormented our Pascoli[2] a great deal. In short, in keeping with a preestablished program, I would like to concentrate intensely and systematically on some subject that would absorb and provide a center to my inner life. Up until now I've thought of four subjects, and this in itself is an indication that I'm unable to focus my thoughts, and they are: (1) a study of the formation of the public spirit in Italy during the past century; in other words, a study of Italian intellectuals, their origins, their groupings in accordance with cultural currents, and their various ways of thinking, etc., etc. A subject that is highly suggestive, which naturally I could only sketch in broad outline, considering the absolute impossibility of having at my disposal the immense volume of material that would be necessary. Do you remember my very hasty and quite superficial essay on southern Italy and on the importance of B. Croce? Well, I would like to fully develop in depth the thesis that I sketched out then, from a "disinterested," "*für ewig*" point of view.[3] (2) A study of comparative linguistics! Nothing less; but what could be more "disinterested" and *für ewig* than this? It would of course be a matter of dealing only with the methodological and purely theoretical part of the subject, which has never been dealt with completely and systematically from the new point of view of the neolinguists as opposed to the neogrammarians (this letter of mine, dear Tania, will horrify you!) A major intellectual "remorse" of my life is the deep sorrow that I caused my good professor Bartoli at the University of Turin, who was convinced that I was the archangel destined to put to definitive rout the neogrammarians, since he, belonging to the same generation and bound by a million academic ties to this mob of most infamous men, did not wish, in his pronouncements, to go beyond a certain limit set by convention and by deference to the old funerary monuments of erudition. (3) A study of Pirandello's theater and of the transformation of Italian theatrical taste that Pirandello represented and helped to form. Did you know that I discovered and contributed to the popularity of Pirandello's theater long before Adriano Tilgher? I wrote about Pirandello[4] from 1915 to 1920, enough to put together a book of 200 pages, and at the time my judgments were original and without precedent: Pirandello was either amiably tolerated or openly derided. (4) An essay on the serial novel and popular taste in literature. The idea came to me when reading the news about the death of Serafino Renzi, the actor-manager of an open-air theater company, the theatrical counterpart of the serial novel, and remembering what fun I had all the times I went to see him, because the performance was twofold: the suspense and unleashed passions, together with the intervention of the audience of ordinary folk, which was certainly not the least interesting part of the performance.

What do you say about all this? At bottom, if you examine them thoroughly, there is a certain homogeneity among these four subjects: the creative spirit of the people in its diverse stages and degrees of development is in equal measure at their base. Let me know your impressions; I have great faith in your common sense and in the soundness of your judgment. Have I bored you? You know, for me writing takes the place of our conversation: I really have the feeling that I'm talking to you when I write; the only problem is that everything is reduced to a monologue because your letters either don't reach me or do not fit in with the conversation I have started. So write to me and at length, letters and not just postcards; I will write you a letter every Saturday (I can write two of them a week) and will get everything off my chest. I will not resume the narration of my travel adventures and impressions, because I do not know whether they interest you; undoubtedly they have a personal value for me, inasmuch as they are linked to specific states of mind and also to specific sufferings; in order to make them interesting to others perhaps it would be necessary to present them in a literary form; but I must write straight off, in the short time that I am allowed to keep ink bottle and pen. By the way: is the little lemon tree still growing? You haven't mentioned it again. And how is my landlady, or did she die? I've always forgotten to ask you. At the beginning of January in Ustica I received a letter from Signor Passarge who was desperate and thought that his wife's death was imminent, then I no longer heard anything. Poor woman, I'm afraid that the scene of my arrest may have helped to accelerate her illness, because she liked me very much and looked so pale when they took me away. I embrace you, my dear, think fondly of me and write to me.

Antonio

1. This is the first of ten to fifteen letters in which there are passages that relate directly to themes that are central to Gramsci's interests in the *Prison Notebooks*. See especially the letter of August 8, 1927 to Berti, and letters to Tania, November 14, 1927, December 17, 1928, April 22, 1929, November 17, 1930, December 1, 1930, September 7, 1931, February 22, 1932, and May 2, 1932, for passages in the prison letters that illuminate various aspects of the notebooks.

2. The Italian poet Giovanni Pascoli (1855–1912) was obsessed by death and by the problems of historical memory and of Italian national literary tradition, of which he aspired to be "the prophet." In some harsh critical pages of the notebooks, Gramsci speaks of "the split within Pascoli's spirit: he wanted to be an epic poet and a popular bard while his temperament was rather 'intimist.'" See Antonio Gramsci, *Prison Notebooks*, ed. Joseph A. Buttigieg, 1:295–300. One of the poems in Pascoli's *Canti del Castelvecchio* is entitled "For always," about the impermanence of love and the finality of death, which in this poem is not interpreted from a Christian point of view.

3. Benedetto Croce (1866–1952) was one of Italy's leading intellectuals of the twentieth century and the author of numerous works of philosophy, history, and literary criticism. Among his best-known writings are the four volumes comprising his *Philosophy of the Spirit*; the *History of Italy from 1871 to 1915*; and *History as the Story of Liberty*. He was for Gramsci what Hegel had been for Marx, an exponent and systematizer of idealist thought in relation to whom Gramsci worked out the basic features of his own historical-materialist conception of life. Croce's influence on Gramsci's early writings is evident. His ideas are a constant point of reference for Gramsci in his prison writings. After a brief period of support for Fascism, Croce turned against Mussolini's regime, and became an important voice among the liberal-democratic groups that opposed Fascism.

Gramsci did not really aspire to achieve the kind of serene and "olympian" detachment from immediate concerns that some people associate with such figures as Goethe and

Croce. What he wished to achieve in prison, and encapsulated in the Goethean phrase "für ewig," (for always, for eternity), was a more comprehensive, more "disinterested" frame of reference for his studies than his earlier political and journalistic writing could have afforded. The reference to his "very rapid and superficial writing on southern Italy and on the importance of Croce" is to *Some Aspects of the Southern Question*, available in English translation in Antonio Gramsci, *Selections from Political Writings, 1921–1926* , ed. and trans. Quintin Hoare (New York: International Publishers, 1978), pp. 441–462.

4. For English translations of Gramsci's early writings on Pirandello and some of the pages in the notebooks devoted to the Italian playwright, see Antonio Gramsci, *Selections from Cultural Writings*, ed. Forgacs and Smith.

March 26, 1927

Dearest Tania,

This week I have received neither postcards nor letters from you; instead, your letter of January 17 (together with Giulia's letter of the tenth) has been delivered to me, sent on from Ustica. So, in a certain sense and up to a certain point, I've been reasonably satisfied; I've again seen Giulia's handwriting (but how little this girl does write and how well she knows how to justify herself, blaming it on the racket the children make around her!) and I have diligently memorized your letter. In which I began to find several errors (I also study these small things, you know, and I've had the impression that this letter of yours was not thought in Italian, but hastily and badly translated and this means you were tired and unwell and thought about me only in a complicated, roundabout way; perhaps you had already received the news about Giulia's and the children's influenzas), among other errors an unforgivable confusion between St. Anthony of Padua, whose feast falls in the month of June, and the St. Anthony commonly referred to as St. Anthony of the Pig, who is in fact my saint, because I was born on January 22, and by whom I set much store for many reasons of a magical character.[1] Your letter made me think back to my life in Ustica, which you certainly imagined very differently from what it was;[2] in the future I will perhaps resume the narration of my life during that time, and then I'll give you a picture of it; today I have no wish to do so and I feel a bit tired. I asked them to send me from Ustica the small grammars and the *Faust*; the method is good, but it requires a teacher's assistance, at least for anyone who is beginning his studies; for me, however, it is excellent, since I only have to review the ideas and especially do the exercises. I also got them to send me Pushkin's[3] "The Peasant Girl" in the Polledro edition: text, literary and grammatical translation, and notes. I memorized the text; I think Pushkin's prose is very good and therefore I'm not afraid that I might be stuffing my memory with stylistic blunders. I consider this memorizing method excellent from every point of view.

I've received, forwarded from Ustica, a letter from my sister Teresina with a photograph of her son, Franco, who was born a few months after Delio. They don't seem to resemble each other at all, whereas Delio looks very much like Edmea. Franco's hair is not curly and must be dark chestnut; besides, Delio is certainly more beautiful: Franco's basic features are already too marked, something that leads one to expect them to develop in a harsh and exaggerated manner; instead, Delio's features are very childish, while the seriousness of his general expression and a certain melancholy that is not childish at all is cause for concern. Did you send his photograph to my mother, as you had promised? You would be doing a great good: the poor woman has suffered much because of my arrest and I believe she suffers all the more since in our villages it is difficult to understand that a man can go to prison without being a thief, crook, or murderer; she has lived in a condition of permanent fear since the outbreak of the war (three of my brothers were at the front) and she had and still has a sentence all her own: "they will butcher my sons," which in Sardinian is terrifyingly more expressive than in Italian: "*faghere a pezza.*" *Pezza* is the meat put up for sale, whereas for a human being the term *carre* is commonly used. I really don't know how to comfort her and make her understand that I'm fairly well and not exposed to any of the perils that she imagines: this is very difficult, because she always suspects that people hide the truth from her because she has a very limited notion of present-day life; just remember that she has never traveled, she's never even been to Cagliari and I suspect that she's convinced that the many descriptions we've given her are just fairy tales.

Dearest Tania, I really can't manage to write to you today; they've again given me a nib that scratches the paper and forces me to perform digital acrobatics. I look forward to your letters. I embrace you.

Antonio

I've noticed that it is less than a month to Easter. Now you should know that Easter is one of the three days in the year on which the prisoners can eat sweets. I definitely want to eat sweets sent me by you. Will you have time enough to send them to me? I hope so. Let me know how many letters of mine you have received until now. I know that the first, which I wrote to you on February 12, cannot have arrived.

1. In several letters, Tania confused Saint Anthony of Padua, whose day is June 13, with Saint Anthony of the Pig, celebrated on Gramsci's birthday, January 22.

2. Tania replied to Gramsci's complaints and criticisms with characteristic good humor tinged with a touch of self-deprecation. Part of her letter of April 12, 1927 reads as follows:

> I assure you that when I read one of your letters, or a letter from one of my friends, I perceive it perfectly not only in its expression but I perfectly hear the tone of the voice, in fact I read it the first time, immediately, with the intonation that it actually presents, and therefore it is out of the question that I was unable to sense your life in Ustica. On your part, you should after all recognize that my writings have not only a psychological and pedagogical aim but are at times the expression of a legitimate joke, like the one about the saints, etc. Please do not think that I took it in bad part, not at all, I only must once more protest that neither father nor you know me at all. In any case the fault (if there is a fault) is entirely mine, I've always concerned myself with those who were dear to me, but I never gave anyone the opportunity to know my intimate life, I've been friend, sister, companion, but vice versa no one has ever been any such thing for me. You write (I don't know why, for my part I've not given you any reason to do so), that if you had thought that you were less dear to me you would no longer have written. Bravo, I'm sorry for you, for all of you, for almost everyone who is endowed with this sort of psychology. You always need to be loved, taken care of etc. etc. Whereas in my relations with those whom I love I do not in the least care about their feelings toward me . . . Why did you stop caring about the friends whom you have neglected because they no longer were as fond of you as before (you say) and with what justification? Might they not perhaps have had more need of love than the ability to give love to others? At any rate, I assure you that since you are one of those people who really have a need for love, I could not possibly let you go without it, precisely because I always feel the necessity, the need, to give what is needed.

3. Alexander Pushkin (1799–1837), Russia's most celebrated poet, several of whose stories Gramsci translated in prison. The story "The Peasant Girl" appeared with the title "The Squire's Daughter" in Alexander Pushkin, *Complete Prose Fiction*, trans. and ed. by Paul Debreczeny (Stanford: Stanford University Press, 1983).

March 26, 1927

Dearest Teresina,

The letter that you sent to Ustica and that contains Franco's photograph was handed to me only a few days ago. And so I have finally been able to see your little boy and I send you my heartfelt congratulations; you will also send me Mimi's photograph won't you? That will make me really happy. I was struck by the fact that Franco, at least going by the photograph, resembles our family very little: he must resemble Paolo and his campidano and perhaps even Maurredina[1] stock: and Mimi, whom does she look like? I want you to write me at length about your children if you have the time, or at least get Carlo or Grazietta to write to me. Franco looks very vivacious and intelligent: I'm sure that he already speaks fluently. In what language does he speak? I hope that you will let him speak Sardinian and will not make any trouble for him on that score. It was a mistake, in my opinion, not to allow Edmea to speak freely in Sardinian as a little girl. This harmed her intellectual development and put her imagination in a straitjacket. You mustn't make this mistake with your children. For one thing Sardinian is not a dialect, but a language in itself,[2] even though it does not have a great literature, and it is a good thing for children to learn several languages, if it is possible. Besides, the Italian that you will teach them will be a poor, mutilated language made up of only the few sentences and words of your conversations with him, purely childish; he will not have any contact with a general environment and will end up learning two jargons and no language: an Italian jargon for official conversation with you and a Sardinian jargon learned piecemeal to speak with the other children and the people he meets in the street or piazza. I beg you, from my heart, not to make this mistake and to allow your children to absorb all the Sardianian spirit they wish and to develop spontaneously in the natural environment in which they were born: this will not be an impediment for their future, just the opposite.

Recently Delio and Giuliano have been ill: they had Spanish fever; I'm now told that they've recovered and are well. Take Delio, for example, he began by speaking his mother's tongue, as was natural and necessary, but he also quickly learned Italian and besides he used to sing little French songs without becoming confused or mixing up the words of the different languages. I wanted to teach him to sing also: *"Lassa sa figu, puzone"*[3] but his aunt in particular strenuously objected. I had a lot of fun with Delio last August: we spent a week together at the Trafoi, in Alto Adige, in a small German peasant house. At that time Delio had just turned two years old, but he was already highly developed intellectually. He used to sing a song with great vigor: "Down with the monks, down with the priests," then in Italian he sang: "*Il sole mio sta in fronte a te*" and a little French song, something to do with a mill. He had become passionately interested in searching for strawberries in the woods and he always tried to run after the animals. His love for animals was used in two ways: in music, since he did his best to produce the musical scale on the piano in accordance with animal voices, from the bear's baritone to the chicks' treble, and also in drawing. Every day when I went to see him in Rome we had to repeat the entire series: first we had to put the wall clock on the table and have him set it in all possible ways; then we had to write a letter to his maternal grandmother with drawings of the animals that had caught his imagination during the day; then we would go to the piano and make his animallike music, then we would play in various ways.

Dear Teresina, in your letter you remarked that my first letter sent from Rome was terribly disconsolate. I don't think I ever was as disconsolate as you say. Indeed, I wrote that letter at a bad moment, relatively speaking; the day before I'd been informed of the decision to send me into police internment for five years and I'd been told that within a few days I would leave for Jubaland[4] in Somalia. Certainly during that night I must have given much thought to my capacity for physical endurance, which I had not as yet been able to test and that I did not think was worth much; it is possible that this state of mind was reflected in the letter. In any case you must believe that, though I may as you say have been somewhat disconsolate, the feeling quickly passed and has not returned. I look upon everything with great coldness and tranquillity, and even though I do not harbor puerile illusions, I'm firmly convinced that I'm not destined to rot in prison. You and all the others must try to cheer up mother (from whom I've received a letter that I don't know how to answer) and to assure her that my honor and my rectitude are not at all in question: I'm in prison for political reasons, not for reasons of honor. I really believe that the contrary is taking place: if I did not value my honor, my rectitude, my dignity, if, that is, I had been able to undergo a so-called crisis of conscience and change my opinion, I would not have been arrested and would not have gone to Ustica in the first place. You must convince mother of this; this is very important to me. Write to me and get everyone else to write: I've no longer seen even a sign of Grazietta's signature; how is she? I embrace Paolo with affection: many kisses to you and your children.

Antonio

1. The plain between Oristano and Cagliari.
2. Gramsci's conception of Sardinian as a distinct and autonomous Romance language is shared by many contemporary linguists. For a comparison of the position Gramsci takes in this passage with other things he had to say on language learning and on the whole "language question" in Italy, see the relevant sections in *Selections from Cultural Writings*, ed. Forgacs and Smith as well as in *A Gramsci Reader*, ed. Forgacs and *Selections from the Prison Notebooks*, ed. and trans. Hoare and Geoffrey Smith.
3. "Hey bird, leave the fig tree alone."
4. An area of 36,000 square miles, acquired from Kenya by Italian Somaliland in 1924.

April 4, 1927

My dear, dear Tania,

Last week I received your two postcards (of March 19 and 22) and the letter of the twenty-sixth. I'm very sorry if I've distressed you; I also think that you did not really understand my state of mind, because I did not express myself properly, and I'm grieved that there might arise misunderstandings between us. I absolutely assure you that I never had even a fleeting doubt that you might forget me or be less fond of me; certainly if I had thought such a thing even remotely, I would no longer have written to you at all; this has always been my character and because of it in the past I have broken off many old friendships. Only face to face would I be able to explain to you the reason for the nervousness that seized me when I hadn't had news from you for two months; I won't even attempt to do it in a letter, so as not to run into further painful misunderstandings. It's all over now and I don't even want to think of it again.

A few days ago I moved to another cell and another tier (the prison is divided into sections) as you can see also from the heading of the letter; first I was in section one, cell thirteen; now I am in section two, cell twenty-two. Let us say my penitentiary situation seems to me improved. But my life goes by as before. I'll describe it to you in some detail, so that day by day you will be able to imagine what it is I am doing. My cell is as large as a student's small room: I would say that roughly it measures three by four and a half meters and three and a half meters in height. The window looks out on the courtyard where we exercise: of course it is not a regular window; it is a so-called wolf's maw with bars on the inside; only a slice of sky is visible and it is impossible to look into the courtyard or to the side. The position of the cell is worse than that of the previous one whose exposure was south–south–west (the sun became visible around ten o'clock and at two it occupied the center of the cell with a band at least sixty centimeters wide); in the present cell, which I think has a south–west–west exposure, the sun shows up around two and remains in the cell until late, but with a band twenty-five centimeters wide. During this warmer season it will perhaps be better this way. Besides: my present cell is located over the prison's mechanical workshop and I hear the rumble of the machines; but I'll get used to it. The cell is at once very simple and very complex. I have a wall cot with two mattresses (one filled with wool); the sheets are changed approximately every fifteen days. I have a small table and a sort of cupboard–night stand, a mirror, a basin and pitcher made of enameled iron. I own many aluminum objects bought at the Rinascente department store that has set up an outlet in the prison. I have a few books of my own; each week I receive eight books to read from the prison library (double subscription). Just so that you can get an idea I'll give you this week's list, which is however exceptional because of the relative high quality of the books I happened to get: (1) Pietro Colletta, *Storia del Reame di Napoli* [History of the Kingdom of Naples] (excellent); (2) V. Alfieri, *Autobiografia* [Autobiography]; (3) Molière, *Commedie scelte* [*Selected Comedies*], translated by Signor Moretti (ridiculous translation); (4) Carducci, two vols. of the complete works (very mediocre, among Carducci's worst); (5) Artur Lévy, *Napoleone intimo* [The intimate Napoleon] (a curious apology of Napoleon as a "moral man"); (6) Gina Lombroso, *Nell'America meridionale* [In South America] (very mediocre); (7) Harnack, *L'essenza del Cristianesimo* [The essence of Christianity]; Virgilio Brocchi, *Il destino in pugno* [My fate in my fist] a novel (this is enough to give a dog rabies); Salvator Gotta, *La donna mia* [My woman] (luckily she's all his, because she's extremely boring). In the morning I get up at half past six, at seven they sound reveille: coffee, wash up, cleaning of the cell; I drink half a liter of milk and eat a roll with it; approximately at eight we go for exercise, which lasts two hours. I stroll, study German grammar, read Pushkin's "The Peasant Girl" and memorize about twenty lines of the text. I buy *Il Sole*, the industrial-commercial newspaper and read some economic news (I've read all the annual reports of the various Stock Companies); on Tuesday I buy the *Corriere dei Piccoli* (a children's weekly), which amuses me; on Wednesday I buy the *Domenica del Corriere* (a popular illustrated weekly); on Friday I buy *Guerin Meschino*, a so-called humorous weekly. After exercise, coffee; I receive three dailies, *Il Corriere*, *Popolo d'Italia*, and *Secolo* (now *Secolo* comes out in the afternoon and I will no longer buy it because it has become worthless) and I read them; lunch arrives at different hours, between twelve and three; I heat the first dish (soup or pasta), I eat a tiny piece of meat, (if it isn't beef, because I'm still not able to eat beef), a roll, a small piece of cheese, fruit that I don't like, and a quarter liter of wine. I read a book, walk up and down, reflect on many things. At four to four-thirty I receive two more newspapers, *La Stampa* and *Il Giornale d'Italia*. At seven o'clock I eat dinner (dinner arrives at six), soup, two raw eggs, a quarter liter of wine; I can't manage to eat the cheese. At half past seven, taps; I get into bed and read books up to eleven or twelve. Starting two days ago, around nine I drink a small cup of chamomile (the sequel will appear in the next issue, because I want to write to you about something else).

I don't need any new linens, etc. I have enough and I wouldn't know where to put other things. The shoes I have are very good; I also have your slippers. For the time being the suit is fine, as a prison suit. I have the overcoat that served me well during the cold months and has now already become useless. I have your spoons and teaspoons, which served me well (also without handles), I have six or seven cakes of soap, brushes, toothbrushes, comb, etc., etc. I really don't need anything essential. Your coming here, being able to see you, would be a great thing for me, as you can well imagine! But first, it is necessary to know whether I'll remain here, and second, we must find out whether they'll give you the permit for the visit. You must remember that juridically we're not related, because my marriage has not been recorded in Italy; juridically I'm single and you cannot prove that you are my sister-in-law. I tell you this because it would be horrendous for me if you were to come and then would be unable to see me. But you must know that it is not impossible to obtain the visit; I know that some of my friends have visits from their companions, who are not juridically their wives, so why should it be impossible for sisters-in-law. You ought to talk to an attorney; in Milan you ought to go to Attorney Arys¹ (Via Unione 1) who, as Bordiga has written to me from Ustica, has taken over my case. Dear Tania, I would be so happy to see you; but you mustn't write me any more about this unless you have already made sure that you will be able to obtain the visit; otherwise I would suffer too much from the disappointment. I embrace you.

Antonio

Listen, my dear, let us arrange the following for the correspondence: I will write you a letter every Monday (in this section we write on Mondays); you will write me a letter every week, plus two postcards, even picture postcards and will send me Giulia's letters. You know, the thought of my letters being censored deprives me of all spontaneity, as happened during the early times in Ustica.² I hope to become "shameless" as before, but I still can't manage it. Write Giulia that I think a lot about her and the children, but I really can't write; I would write like a file clerk and that horrifies me.

1. The correct spelling is Ariis. Giovanni Ariis was one of Gramsci's three defense lawyers (the other two were Adelmo Niccolai and Giuseppe Sardo) at the trial of Italian Communist leaders held in Rome before the Special Tribunal for the Defense of the State from May 28 to June 4, 1928.
2. See letter to Tania, December 27, 1926, n. 4.

April 11, 1927

Dearest Tania,

I received your postcards of March 31 and April 3. I thank you for the news you sent me. I look forward to your visit here in Milan, but, I must confess, I won't count on it too much. I've decided that it is not very pleasant for me to continue the description of my present life, which I undertook in my last letter. It is best that each time I'll write whatever comes into my head, without a preestablished plan. Writing has become a physical torment too because they give me horrible nibs that scrape the paper and demand an obsessive attention to the mechanical aspect of writing. I thought I might be able to obtain the permanent use of a pen and I had planned to write the studies that

I mentioned; but I did not receive the necessary permit and don't like to insist.[1] So I write only during the two and a half or three hours when we take care of our weekly correspondence (two letters); of course I can't take notes, in fact I can't study in an orderly fashion and profitably. I read desultorily. Yet the time goes by, more quickly than I would have thought.

Five months have passed since the day of my arrest (November 8) and two months since the day of my arrival in Milan. I can hardly believe that so much time has passed. It must however be taken into account that during these five months I've seen all manner of things and I've received the strangest and most exceptional impressions in my life.[2] Rome: November 8 until November 25: absolute and rigorous isolation. November 25: Naples, in the company of my four fellow deputies until the twenty-ninth (three not four, because one of them[3] was separated from us in Caserta and sent to the Tremiti). Embarkation for Palermo and arrival at Palermo on the thirtieth. Eight days in Palermo: three failed crossings to Ustica because of stormy seas. First contact with the Sicilians arrested as Mafia members: a new world that I had known only intellectually; I verify and check my opinions on the subject, which I recognize to be rather correct. On December 7 arrival at Ustica. I get to know the world of the detainees: fantastic and incredible facts. I get to know the colony of Bedouins from Cyrenaica,[4] political deportees: an Oriental picture, very interesting. Life on Ustica. On January 20 I leave again. Four days in Palermo. Boat trip to Naples with common criminals. Naples: I become acquainted with a series of types who are of the greatest interest to me, since when it comes to the south I was physically acquainted only with Sardinia. In Naples, among other things, I witness a scene of initiation into the Camorra:[5] I meet a lifer (a certain Arturo) who makes an indelible impression on me. After four days I leave Naples; stop over at Cajanello, in the carabinieri barracks; I get to know my chain companions, who will travel with me as far as Bologna. Two days at Isernia with these types. Two days at Sulmona. One night at Castellammare A.,[6] in the carabinieri barracks. Then two days with approximately sixty detainees. A number of entertainments are organized for the occasion in my honor; the Romans improvise a wonderful group recital, Pascarella and popular sketches of the Roman underworld. Men from Apulia, Calabria, and Sicily present a knife-fencing clinic in accordance with the rules of the four states of the southern underworld (the Sicilian State, the Calabrian State, the Apulian State, and the Neapolitan State): Sicilians against Apulians, Apulians against Calabrians, because the hatred between these two states is powerful and the clinic even becomes serious and bloody. The Apulians are the masters of all of them: unsurpassed knife wielders with a technique full of secrets and very lethal, developed in line with all the others and in order to outdo them. An old Apulian, age sixty-five, much revered, but without "state" recognition, defeats all the champions of the other states; then, as the grand finale,[7] he fences with another Apulian, a young man, with the most beautiful body and surprisingly agile, a high dignitary whom they all obey and for half an hour they demonstrate all the normal techniques of all the fencing schools. A truly grandiose and unforgettable spectacle in every way, because of the performers and the spectators: a whole subterranean world was revealed to me, extremely complicated, with its own life of emotions, of points of view, of points of honor, and formidable, iron hierarchies. The weapons were simple: spoons rubbed against the wall, so that the chalk marked off the blows on the clothes. Then Bologna, two days with more spectacles; then Milan. Certainly these five months have been exciting and rich in impressions, enough for one or two years of rumination. This will also explain how I pass the time when I am not reading; I think back over all these things, analyze them in the finest detail, become intoxicated with this Byzantine labor. Besides, everything that happens around me and that I'm able to perceive becomes extraordinarily interesting. Of course I assiduously control myself, because I do not want to fall into the sort of mono-manias that characterize the psychology of prisoners; I'm helped in this especially by a certain ironic spirit full of humor that always accompanies me. And what are you doing and what are you thinking? Who buys adventure novels for you now that I'm not there? I'm convinced that you have reread the wondrous stories of Corcoran and his charming Lisotta.[8] Are you attending this year's lessons at the Rome General Hospital? And Professor Caronia, is he the one who discovered the German measles bacillus? I've read all about his lamentable troubles; I didn't understand from the newspapers whether Professor

Cirincione has also been suspended.[9] All of this is, at least in part, linked to the problem of the Sicilian Mafia. It is incredible how the Sicilians, from the lowest stratum to the highest peaks, have such solidarity with each other and how even scientists of undeniable stature skirt the edges of the Penal Code due to this feeling of solidarity. I've become convinced that the Sicilians are truly a people apart; there is more resemblance between a Calabrian and a Piedmontese than between a Calabrian and a Sicilian. The accusations that southerners in general bring against the Sicilians are dreadful: they even accuse them of cannibalism. I would never have believed that there existed such feelings among the people. I think that one would have to read many books on the histories of the last centuries, especially on the period when Sicily and the South were separated during the reigns of Joseph Bonaparte and Joachim Murat[10] in Naples, to track down the origin of such feelings.

I'm absolutely delighted with the little bonnet; where did you manage to find it? I think it is the bonnet from Orgossolo, red and blue, which I had no longer been able to find. I won't be able to send the papier-mâché ball, so you won't be able to send me the varnish: I believe that it is absolutely impossible, especially for the varnish, which can be considered a poison, according to regulations, and would require a whole series of very complicated checks. There, you see; another very interesting subject for analysis: prison regulations and the psychology that develops among the prison personnel, partly based on those same regulations and partly on contact with the prisoners. I always believed that two masterpieces (I say this very seriously) summarized the thousand-year-old experience of mankind in the field of mass organization: the corporal's manual and the Catholic catechism. I've become convinced that it is necessary to add, though in a field that is much more restricted and of an exceptional nature, prison regulations, which contain true treasures of psychological introspection. I'm waiting for Giulia's letters: I think that after having read them I will be able to write to her directly. Don't think that this is childishness. An important piece of news: for a few days now I've been eating a lot; but I still can't manage to eat vegetables; I've made the most strenuous efforts but I find them terribly revolting. And yet, I'm unable to forget that perhaps you'll come and that perhaps (alas!) we'll be able to see each other if only for a few minutes. I embrace you.

Antonio

1. In March 1927 Gramsci made a first unsuccessful request for the right to use pen, ink and paper in his cell.

2. This wonderfully detailed account of his first five months of internment and imprisonment was deemed unacceptable by prison authorities and confiscated. See letter to Tania, May 2, 1927.

3. Enrico Ferrari

4. Cyrenaica, especially the capital and main seaport of Bengasi, had been administered by the Italian government since the conquest of Libya in 1912. The Bedouins referred to in this letter probably belonged to the opposition groups that fought against the Italian occupation of their land.

5. The Camorra, frequently compared with the Mafia because of its rituals and organized criminal elements, is a secret society that originated under the Neapolitan Bourbons in the first half of the nineteenth century. The links between this society and the Camorra today are tenuous. The gangsterism and corruption in contemporary Naples have very little to do with the original society.

6. Castellammare Adriatico.

7. Gramsci uses the French word *clou*, which means "nail," but one of its figurative meanings is the high point or feature attraction of a play or of a spectacle that captures the audience's attention.

8. The reference is to a book for children by Alfred Assolant (1827–1886), *Les merveilleuses aventures du capitaine Corcoran* [The marvelous adventures of Captain Corcoran]. Lisotta is a tiger, an inseparable companion of Captain Corcoran.

9. In Rome, because of her scientific studies at the university, Tania had friends and professional contacts in medical circles, which explains Gramsci's questions and remarks to her about Professors Caronia and Cirincione. The former was professor of pediatrics, the latter professor of opthamology, at the University of Rome. Caronia was briefly suspended (he was absolved of charges against him) from teaching because of several accidents that had occurred in the pediatric clinic under his supervision. He was rector of the University of Rome from 1944 to 1947.

10. During the Napoleonic era, southern Italy was governed first by Joseph Bonaparte, from 1806 to 1808, and then by Joachim Murat, from 1808–1815. Murat promoted some social reforms in accordance with principles inspired by the French Revolution. Sicily, on the other hand, continued to be governed by the reactionary Bourbon monarchy and remained largely cut off from the new European reformism. This accentuated the already existing alienation of the Sicilians, which led to the popular uprisings of 1820 and 1837 for insular autonomy and in protest against domination by Naples.

April 18, 1927

Dear Tania,

I've received your note of April 4 together with Giulia's two letters; I have not yet received the other letters you promised. I spent Easter waiting for your greetings, but I didn't receive anything (remember? you wrote that you were sending various additional things to the prison in Rome, because each one of them was like a greeting from you). But I assure you that this did not upset me; I was almost certain that you would not be able to send me the sweets precisely for Easter day. When I wrote to you it was too late due to the postal backlog that occurs on such occasions and I believe that even if something arrives after the day set by the regulations, it will not be forwarded. Too bad. Another regulation day is Statute Day[1] (the first Sunday in June): I reveal this to you after a long pro and con debate with myself. The debate came to this conclusion: it will be a most beautiful epigram if I should celebrate Statute Day! Therefore I count on your sweets for that occasion; you have all the necessary time to think about it, select, prepare, etc., etc. Don't worry too much about the choice. I like all kinds, provided they are not too sweet. Yesterday (Easter) I bought two hundred grams of Easter dates and a biscuit dove; but I wasn't able to eat the dates because they hurt my gums too much. So I decided to report to the doctor and have him prescribe a palliative; I also thought that I should get some injections in view of the imminent heat. What do you think of it? The beginning of the good weather has already begun to make me unwell. I absolutely cannot eat meat; the very smell of it revolts and nauseates me. And so I sleep less than before; no more than three and a half hours. It's not a nervous insomnia because I'm not agitated and I don't dream: it is insomnia pure and simple. So that you may understand and be able to give me some advice let me describe it to you. I get into bed at half past seven and by half past eight I ought to be asleep. But if I fall asleep at half past eight I wake up at midnight when the inspection comes and then I can't fall asleep again. Therefore I make an effort to stay awake until the nine o'clock inspection, and go to sleep after that; so I fall asleep around ten, do not hear the midnight inspection, but when the inspection at three arrives I've already been awake for at least an hour. So as you see I have no difficulty in falling asleep and I think that this is important; but I can only sleep very little and this always leaves me a bit tired and depleted. By sleeping like this from ten to half past one I feel more rested than if I sleep from half past eight until midnight. I think that the injections might be helpful, by stimulating my appetite; if I ate more, I would perhaps sleep more.

Now that the good weather is starting I will bathe more often: there are only showers, there's no tub, and when I take a shower even though it is hot I feel a terrific, abnormal cold afterward (my blood temperature must still be five degrees below normal and that explains everything). I embrace you affectionately.

Antonio

At this very moment I have received your card of the ninth with the view of Trafoi.[2] Good girl!

1. The 1848 constitution of Piedmont-Sardinia, which became the fundamental law of the Piedmontese state from 1848 to 1861 and, with minor modifications, of the unified Italian kingdom until the last years of the Fascist dictatorship. The liberal provisions of this constitution, if observed, ought to have protected Gramsci against imprisonment; hence his ironic allusion to epigrams and festivities.

2. A resort town near Bolzano, in the Dolomites, where Gramsci had spent a brief vacation with his wife and son Delio in August 1926.

April 18, 1927

My dearest Julca,

I resume writing to you after such a long time. Only a few days ago I received two of your letters: one of February 14 and the other of March 1, and I've been thinking about you a great deal; I actually made an inventory of all my memories and do you know what image struck me most? One of the first, from a long time ago. Do you remember when you left the silver forest,[1] after your month of vacation? I accompanied you to the edge of the main road and stood there for a long time watching you walk away. We had just met, but I had already teased you several times and even made you cry; I made fun of you about the assembly of the owls and I'd felt the electricity of the cats when you played Beethoven. And so I always see you as you walk away with small steps, your violin in one hand and your picturesque traveling bag in the other.

What is my state of mind right now? I will write to you at greater length in the future (I will ask permission to write a double letter) and try to describe for you the positive aspects of my life during these months (the negative aspects are forgotten by now); a most interesting life, as you can imagine, because of the men I met and the scenes I witnessed. My state of mind is in general marked by great tranquillity. How can I sum it up? Remember Nansen's journey to the Pole? and do you remember how it went? Since I'm not really convinced that you do, let me recall it for you. Having studied the marine and atmospheric currents of the Arctic Ocean and having observed that on the shores of Greenland there were trees and detritus that must have been of Asiatic origin, Nansen thought he could reach the Pole or at least come close to it by letting his boat be carried along by the ice. So he let himself be imprisoned by the ice and for three and a half years his ship moved with excruciating slowness in accord with the ice. My state of mind can be compared to that of Nansen's sailors during this fantastic voyage, which has always struck me because of its truly epic inspiration. Have I conveyed the idea? (as my Sicilian friends at Ustica would say). I could not convey it in a briefer and more concise fashion. So don't worry about this aspect of my existence. Instead, if you want me to always remember you with tenderness (I'm joking, you know!), write to me at length and describe for me your life and the children's. Everything interests me, even the slightest details. And send me photographs every now and then. That way I'll be able to follow the children's growth with my eyes too. And write to me also about yourself, a lot. Do you see Signor Bianco sometimes?[2] And do you see that curious Africanist type[3] who once promised me a dish of fried rhinoceros kidneys? Who knows if he still remembers me; if you see him ask him about those fried kidneys and tell me what he answers. I'll enjoy that very much. As you know, that's all I do: think about the past and relive all the funniest scenes and episodes; it helps me pass the time, sometimes I really laugh wholeheartedly, without even realizing it. My dear, Tania announces other letters of yours; how I await them! Greet all of your family for me. I love you very much.

Antonio

Tania is really a very fine girl. That's why I have tormented her quite a bit.

1. The sanatarium outside of Moscow, called "The Silver Forest," where Gramsci was undergoing treatment in 1922 and where he met Giulia, who had gone there to visit her sister Eugenia.
2. Vincenzo Bianco (1898–1980), a Turinese worker whom Gramsci had befriended in the early 1920s. He emigrated to Moscow in 1923, became a friend of the Schucht family, and corresponded with Gramsci prior to his imprisonment. He fought in the International

Brigades in Spain, and later played an active part in the politics and the eventual dissolution of the Communist International (CI) in 1943.

　3. Evidently someone whom Gramsci had met in Moscow during his stay there in 1922–1923.

April 25, 1927

Dearest Mother,

I just received your letter today. Thank you. I'm very happy about the good news you've given me, especially about Carlo. I knew nothing about his working and living conditions. I believe that Carlo is a fine boy, despite his wrongheadedness in the past, and I believe that when it comes to business he is more reliable than were, and perhaps still are, both Nannaro and Mario, who had a tendency to see fabulous profits and build castles in the air at the drop of a hat. Alas! everyone in our family (with the exception of myself) believes he has a special talent for business and I wouldn't like all of them to have an experience like the famous one with the "chicken coop"; do you remember it? and Carlo, does he remember it? One ought to remind him of it to the eternal shame of all Gramscis who want to go into business. I will always remember it also because those chickens, which never laid an egg, pecked and wrecked three or four of my Carolina Invernizio[1] novels (thank goodness!).

My life goes by always the same. I read, eat, sleep, and think. I can't do anything else. But you mustn't think all the things that you do think, and especially you mustn't delude yourself. Not because I am not superconvinced that I will see you again and have you meet my children (you will receive Delio's photograph, as I have mentioned; but hadn't Carlo given you one in 1925? when Carlo came to Rome? and Chicchinu Mameli had given you a silver coin that I had sent Mea so that she would make it into a teaspoon? and a special wooden snuffbox for you? I always forgot to ask you about these things), but because I'm also supercertain that I will be sentenced and who knows for how many years. You must understand that neither my rectitude[2] nor my conscience nor my innocence nor guilt figure in this at all. This is something that is called politics, precisely because all these fine things don't figure in it at all. You know what is done to little children who pee in their beds, don't you? They are threatened that they will be burned with hemp flaming at the end of a pitchfork.

Well: just imagine that in Italy there is a very big child who continually threatens to pee in the bed of this grand genetrix of oats and heroes; and I and a few others are the flaming hemp (or rag) that is waved about to threaten the impertinent one and prevent him from soiling the snow-white sheets. Since this is how things are, one must be neither alarmed nor harbor illusions; one must just wait with great patience and endurance. Come, come, you are still strong and young and we shall see each other again. Meanwhile write to me and get all the others to write to me: send me lots of news about Ghilarza, Abbasanta, Boroneddu, Tadasuni, Oristano. Is Aunt Antioga Putzulu still alive? And who's the mayor? Felle Toriggia, I think. And what is Nessi doing? And the uncles and aunts from Oristano, are they still alive? Does Uncle Serafino know that I've given the name Delio to my boy? And what about the small hospital, did they finish it? And did they continue with the work on the low income houses at Careddu? See all the things I want to know. And is there talk, as I believe, of uniting Ghilarza and Abbasanta? and without the people of Abbasanta rising up in arms? And the Tirso basin, is it finally being used for something? Write to me, write to me and send me photographs, especially of the children. Kisses to all and many, many of them to you.

Nino

And why doesn't Grazietta write me even as much as a line?

1. Carolina Invernizio (1851–1916), author of popular serial novels on sentimental and sometimes macabre subjects such as *Il bacio della morte* [The kiss of death] (1889) and *L'orfanella di Collegno* [The little orphan girl of Collegno] (1893).

2. Gramsci's use of the word *rectitude* was determined by a letter he had recently received from his mother. On March 10, 1927, Peppina began a letter to her son in the following manner: "My dearest Nino, I received your dear letter and you can imagine my state of mind, although you reassure me about your morale. I am so confused that I don't feel strong, but I want to assure you that I too, with the help of God, will bear what he ordained for me, adding another cross to my Calvary. Knowing your honesty quite well, I want to hope that everything will turn out to be a soap bubble, and in this way make evident your innocence and rectitude." (*Le donne*, p. 117.)

April 25, 1927

Dearest Tania,

I received your letter of the twelfth and I have coldly, cynically, decided to make you angry. Do you know that you are entirely too presumptuous? I want to demonstrate this to you objectively and it already amuses me to imagine your anger (but don't get too angry; I would regret that). It is certain that the letter you sent me while on Ustica was completely mistaken; but you cannot be held responsible for this. It is impossible to imagine life on Ustica, the environment of Ustica, because it is absolutely exceptional, it is outside any normal experience of human cohabitation. Could you imagine anything like this; listen. I arrived at Ustica on December 7, after an interruption of eight days in the steamer's arrival and after four failed crossings. I was the fifth political internee to get there. I was immediately advised to stock up on cigarettes because supplies were down to almost nothing; I went to the tobacconist and asked for ten packs of Macedonia (sixteen lire), putting a fifty lire note on the counter. The vendor (a young woman, with an absolutely normal appearance) was astonished by my request, made me repeat it, picked ten packs, opened them, began to count the cigarettes one by one, lost track of her count, began again, picked up a sheet of paper, performed some long additions with her pencil, broke off, picked up the fifty lire, looked at it from all sides; finally she asked me who I was. Having found out that I was a political internee she handed me the cigarettes and returned the fifty lire, saying that I could pay her after changing the note. The same thing happened elsewhere and here is the explanation: on Ustica there exists only the economy of the *soldo*,[1] all commerce is in *soldi*; one never spends more than fifty *centesimi* [cents].

The prototype[2] of the Ustica economy is the convict who receives four lire a day, already owes two of them to the moneylender or the wine seller and feeds himself with the remaining two, buying three hundred grams of pasta and seasoning it with one *soldo* worth of ground pepper. Cigarettes are sold one at a time; one Macedonia costs sixteen *centesimi*, that is, three *soldi* and one *centesimo*; the convict who buys one Macedonia cigarette a day, leaves one *soldo* in deposit and he uses up one cent of it each day for five days. In order to calculate the price of one hundred Macedonia cigarettes it was therefore necessary to carry out one hundred times the calculation involving the sixteen *centesimi* (three *soldi* plus one *centesimo*) and no one can deny that this is a fairly difficult and complicated calculation. And she was the tobacconist, that is to say, one of the major merchants on the island. Well: the predominant psychology throughout the island is the psychology that has as its foundation the economy of the *soldo*, the economy that knows only the addition or subtraction of single units, an economy that lacks the multiplication table. And listen to this (I tell you only about things that happened to me personally; and I tell you things that I don't think are subject to censorship): I was called to the office by the employee in charge of reviewing incoming mail; I was handed a letter, addressed to me and was asked to explain its contents. A friend was writing to me from Milan, offering me a radio and asking me for technical information in order to buy one with the Ustica-Rome range. To tell the truth, I did not understand the question they were asking me at the office and I told them what was involved; they thought that I wanted to speak with Rome and I was denied the permit to have the radio sent to me. Later on the Podestà[3] called me on his own initiative and told me that the town authority would buy the radio on its own account and therefore I should not insist, the mayor was in favor of my receiving the permit, because he had been to Palermo and had seen that it is impossible to communicate with a simple radio. Could you have imagined all of this? No. Therefore my remark did not contain even the slightest malice toward you. No one can be expected to imagine new things; but one can expect people (let me put it this way) to exercise their fantasy so as to round out the full living reality on the basis of what they know. This is how I want to get at you and make you angry. You, like all women in general, have plenty of imagination and little fantasy, and what's more in you (as in women in general) imagination operates only in one direction, in the direction that I would say characterizes (I can see you jump) . . . that of societies for animal protection, vegetarians, nurses: women are lyrical (just to raise the tone) but they are not dramatic. They imagine the life of others (of their children too) only from the point of view of animal suffering, but they don't know how to recreate with their fantasy all of another person's life, as a whole, in all its aspects (mind you, I am observing, not judging, nor dare I draw consequences for the future; I describe what exists today[4]). This is what I want to get at. You know that I'm here, in prison, enclosed in a confined space, where I "must" lack for many things; just think of the bath, the insects, the linens, etc. If I wrote to you that I lack a particular toothpaste, for example, you would certainly be capable of running all over Rome, neglecting lunch and dinner, and even getting a fever; I'm sure of it. But instead you write to me announcing a letter from Giulia, then you write to me again announcing another; then I receive a letter from you (and your letters are very dear to me) but I don't receive Giulia's letters and I still haven't received them. Well, you cannot picture my existence here in prison. You can't imagine how having received the announcement I wait every day and am disappointed every day, and this affects in turn all the minutes of all the hours of all the days: how I sit reading and at every moment I jump up from my reading and begin to pace up and down and think and think again and rack my brain and say over and over: Oh, that Tania, that Tania! But you mustn't get too angry, you know, and you mustn't be too hurt either (a little bit, however, yes; so that you will send me the letters right away without announcing them beforehand and always make me think that they've gone astray). Do you see what a roundabout way I've taken to tell you something so simple? and how many stories I've dusted off? I'm wicked, really wicked. But why is it you don't understand that often I mean to joke and then you answer me so seriously? Do you know how much I laughed when you answered me in all seriousness about the photographs that I took with me into the cell? And the same goes for your confusing the two Saint Anthonys; I was joking then too. And there's another thing you didn't understand.[5] You, none other than you (and how could you forget?) had written to me that (when I didn't receive any letters from you) I shouldn't think that you were less fond of me or had forgotten me. And I replied that if I had thought this, I would not have written to you again, as I have sometimes done in the past, certainly not because I "always need to be loved, cared for, etc. etc." (or some such . . . animal protection psychology!) but because I hate everything that is conventional and smacks of bureaucracy. I am not an afflicted person who must be consoled; I shall never become one. Even before having been thrown in prison, I knew all about isolation and knew how to find it even in the midst of multitudes. But it's not this, this isn't what you thought. The exact opposite is true. A letter from you fills several of my days. If you could see me when I receive a letter, you certainly would write me one a day (though this in its turn would be bad). But enough of all this. In any case this week I won't be able to write to Giulia.

You know, your parcel has arrived and I've seen the wonderful things you sent me: but only the chocolate has been given to me. It is not to be excluded that the remainder will also be handed to me: it requires an application that is already under way. The chocolate is very good: I eat it in tiny bits because of my teeth (here is something of interest to you: they've given me the chocolate but not the colored paper of the wrapper because I could actually have used it for coloring: the ball however is a nice natural papier-mâché color that is very good now that it is completely dry). My mother's address is: Peppina Gramsci, Ghilarza (Cagliari); I'll write to her today telling her that she will receive the photograph. You will receive (or so they assure me) a parcel of Pantelleria grapes for Delio and Giuliano; you'll see what wonderful grapes they are; forget about Greek raisins! I herewith give you permission to eat some so that you can find out for yourself. Giulia will be very happy and Delio will want to eat them all immediately. I assure you that these grapes astonished me with their fragrance, their flavor, and the fleshiness of their tart pulp. Dear Tania, don't get too angry with me; I care for you very, very much and I would really be desperate if I were to cause you too stinging a pain. I embrace you.

Antonio

1. The *soldo* was a copper coin, worth five one hundredths of a lira.
2. The typical consumer.
3. Under Fascism, the figure of the *podestà*, who was appointed by the king after being proposed by the government, replaced that of the *sindaco*, or mayor, who was elected by the people.
4. This is one of several places in the letters where Gramsci expresses a conventionally condescending attitude toward women. For a brief discussion of this question as it manifests itself in his correspondence with Tania, see my article "Three Essays on Antonio Gramsci's *Letters from Prison*," *Italian Quarterly* 25 (Summer-Fall 1984): 27–29. The most complete analysis of Gramsci's sexism, somewhat marred by a doctrinaire "psychoanalytic" orientation, is Adele Cambria's *Amore come rivoluzione*. See also Renate Holub, *Antonio Gramsci: Beyond Marxism and Postmodernism*, ch. 7.
5. See letter to Tania, March 26, 1927, nn. 1 and 2.

May 2, 1927

Dearest Tania,

I've received your postcard of April 15 together with a letter from Giulia, mailed by you on the twentieth; I've also received your postcard of April 26, in which you mention a letter of yours that I did not receive. Was it perhaps inside the envelope that contained Giulia's letter? Or was it some other envelope that besides your letter contained something from Giulia? Or was it just a postcard? You must believe that I care a great deal about correspondence: it is the only link that connects me with the world and it is what every now and then breaks my segregation and my isolation. I would like you always to number (1) your postcards; (2) your letters; (3) Giulia's letters with independent progressive numbers, so that I'll be immediately able to see if there's been an interruption and of what sort and degree it is.[1] As for my letters, you can easily keep count of them week by week; there can be a change only if they move me to another section and if in the new section the day for correspondence is different from the present one or if I should become so sick I'm unable to write (in which case I believe a telegram would be authorized). I'm sorry that you didn't receive my letter of April 11 because this means that a whole area of memories and impressions has to be ruled out; I don't even remember precisely what that letter contained. Ah well. You know, I've received your sweets (Tuesday the twenty-sixth) and I thank you once again; they were very fresh and excellent also from the point of view of my poor teeth. I too would like to send you a present, but I don't know how to go about it. With infinite patience I have fashioned a small wooden letter opener. The wood is certainly not of the best quality (anything but), its fibers aren't too strong and compact, but I think that this little object turned out quite nicely; besides, I scraped away for fifteen days to give it the desired shape, and I stored in it several hundred lire of work wages, to say the least. In any case, you know that I have here at your disposal a small paper knife. This reminds me of the story of the small handles for the bone spoon and fork, which are still without any handles; I always use the fork, even without the handle: not so the spoon, which frightens me with its bulk and intimidates me. In its place I use the two wooden spoons of modest proportions, one for the soup and the other for stewed fruit (which however I'm not able to get them to send me regularly); so I never use the two bone teaspoons, but only the two wooden ones, which have become very black because of the coffee. In this regard I would also like to mention the daily tragedy of washing and drying my cutlery, but I prefer to skip it. And there it is—a letter in perfect penitentiary style. The next time or times I will write you much more genteel things:

the song of tiny birds at sunset and dawn, the rapid budding of beans and gladiola in the courtyard where I exercise every morning, the changes of luminosity in my cell according to the sun's position on the horizon, etc. etc. I still haven't found a spider to train; there aren't any mice and the remaining zoology is not very attractive. For the rest, nothing interesting or new. I embrace you.

Antonio

I think that in my letter of the seventh I was asking you whether you're attending the courses at the General Hospital this year and whether you still read adventure stories: did you get the continuation of Kipling's sea novel I was supposed to buy for you when I was arrested?

1. Evidently Tania found it impossible to fulfill Gramsci's request, since her letters and those of Giulia written after this date are not numbered.

May 2, 1927

Dearest Giulia,

I believe it is healthier for my correspondence not to keep the promise I had made of describing at least the positive side of my adventure. I regret this very much, believe me, because I'm always obsessed by the thought of being reduced to conventional epistolography and, what is worse than conventionality, to a conventionally prison epistolography. I would have had so many little stories to tell you! Did Tania pass on the story of the pig's arrest? Perhaps not, because Tania didn't believe it; she thought that it was a pure invention of mine to keep her in good cheer and make her smile. Besides, you too will not believe many of these stories (green spectacles, etc.), which are however beautiful precisely because they are true (really true): you didn't even want to believe the story of the airplanes that catch birds with bird lime and Loria's theory[1] on the subject, although there was the magazine with Loria's article as supporting proof. How can I get you to know my way of living and thinking? A great part of my existence I can leave to your imagination; for example that I think a lot about you and about all of you. My physical life can be imagined just as easily. I read a lot: during these three months I've read eighty-two books from the prison library, the most bizarre and extravagant (the possibility of choice is very small); I have a certain number of books of my own that are a little more homogeneous and that I read with more attention and method. Furthermore, I read five newspapers a day and a couple of magazines. Also: I study German and Russian and I'm memorizing from its original text a short story by Pushkin, "The Peasant Girl." But, actually, I've realized that exactly contrary to what I've always thought, studying is difficult in prison, for many reasons, technical and psychological.

Last week I received your letter of March 15. I look forward to your letters very anxiously and I'm very happy when I receive them. I wish you could find the time to describe your life and Delio's life, especially. But I imagine how busy you must always be. There are so many things I would like to know.

You know, when I received your letter in which you speak of the famous Atlas, I had only a few days earlier returned *Guerin Meschino* to the library, a very popular Italian knightly romance, much read by peasants etc., especially southerners; I would have liked to transcribe a few geographic passages contained in the novel, some of the most amusing (Sicily, for example, is set among the Polar regions) in order to reassure you that there existed somebody whose geography was worse than yours; and we won't talk about history, for in that case it would become necessary to quote the respectfully above-mentioned Prof. Loria, who during one of his conversations made it quite clear he believed that in the time of Julius Caesar Venice existed and that in Venice people spoke as they do now: ("the soft dialect of the Lagoon," according to his imaginiferous effrontery). My dear, I try to write to you as long a letter as possible about things that I believe will not result in the letter being stopped: therefore I must bother you with all this silly stuff. A very, very strong embrace.

Antonio

1. Achille Loria (1857–1943), Italian economist. See Joseph Buttigieg's introduction to the *Prison Notebooks* for a discussion of what Loria and "Lorianism" signified to Gramsci.

May 23, 1927

Dearest Mother,

It's been some time now since I received your letters and news from home. I've written to Teresina, but she hasn't answered me. And so for all this time you haven't written me anything about Grazietta and her health.

I'm reasonably well; my life goes by always the same. I read, eat, sleep, and so it goes every day. I'm always waiting for correspondence, but I receive very little of it. Why don't you at least get Carlo to write to me? Is it possible that his business affairs absorb him so much as to prevent him from writing to me now and then? Moreover, I would like to have Mario's precise address; I have had no contact with him since 1921, but now I've heard that he's taken an interest in me and so I would like to write to him to thank him. Write me everything that concerns him, so that from my letters it will not appear that I have not taken any interest in him during all these years: how many children does he have and what are their names? etc. etc. Embrace everyone at home and delicately tweak Carlo's and Teresina's ears. For you an affectionate embrace.

Nino

May 23, 1927

Dearest Tania,

Last week I received a letter and a postcard from you together with Giulia's letter.

Let me reassure you with regard to my health: I'm reasonably well, I really mean it. In fact during this last week I've been eating with a diligence that surprises even me: I've been able to get them to give me by and large only the food I like and as I like it, and I believe that I've even put on weight. Furthermore, for a while now I've devoted a bit of time both in the morning and afternoon to exercise; indoor exercise, which probably isn't very scientific, but that nevertheless does me a great deal of good, or so it seems to me. This is what I do: I try to make a number of movements that stimulate my limbs and

all of my muscles in an orderly manner and every week I try to increase the number of movements by a few units; that this is useful is
demonstrated, in my opinion, by the fact that during the first days I
ached all over and could make certain movements only a very few
times, whereas now I've already been able to triple the number of the
movements without suffering any discomfort. I believe that this in-
novation has also helped me psychologically, diverting me especially
from too much insipid reading done only to kill time. And you
mustn't think that I study too much either. I believe that real study is
impossible for me, for many reasons, not only psychological but also
technical; it is very difficult for me to become completely absorbed in
a train of thought or subject and delve into it alone, as one does when
one studies seriously, so as to grasp all possible relationships and connect them harmoniously. Something along those lines is perhaps beginning to happen with the study of languages, which I try to carry
out systematically, that is, not neglecting any grammatical aspect, as
I've never done before, because I used to be satisfied with knowing
enough to speak and especially to read. That's why until now I
haven't written you to send me any dictionaries: Kohler's German
dictionary that you had sent me on Ustica was lost by my friends
there; I'll send you a request for another dictionary, based on the Langenscheidt system, after I've studied all of the grammar; then I'll also
ask you to send me Goethe's *Gespräche* [*Conversations with Eckermann*],
to use it for syntactic and stylistic analyses and not only for reading;
right now I'm reading the fairy tales of the brothers Grimm, which
are very elementary.[1] I have definitely decided to make the study of
languages my main occupation;[2] after German and Russian, I want to
systematically take up again English, Spanish and Portuguese, which
I had studied rather superficially in recent years; and also Rumanian,
which I had studied at the university only in its Romance aspect and
that I think I can now study completely, that is, also in the Slavic part
of its lexicon (which in fact is more than 50 percent of the Rumanian
vocabulary). As you see, all of this proves that I'm also completely at
ease psychologically; in fact I'm no longer affected by nervousness
and by fits of blind rage as during the first days; I've adjusted and
time passes for me quickly enough; I reckon it in weeks and not in
days and Monday is the point of reference, because that's when I write
and shave, two eminently topical operations.

Let me give you a catalogue of my permanent library, that is, of the books that belong to me, which I peruse continually and try to study. Now let's see. *Il corso di scienza delle finanze* [The course in financial science] published by Einaudi, here is a solid tome to be digested systematically. Concerning finance I also have: *Gli ordinamenti finanziari italiani* [Italian financial regulations], a collection of lectures presented at the University of Rome by experts in government administration; an excellent book of great interest. A *Storia dell'inflazione* [History of inflation] written by Lewinsohn, very interesting, though of a journalistic character. A book on the *Stabilizzazione monetaria nel Belgio* [Monetary stabilization in Belgium] written by Frank, the minister. I have no books on economics: on Ustica I had Marshall's excellent book, but my friends kept it for themselves. I do however have Mortara's *Prospettive economiche* [Economic perspectives] for the year 1927; the *Inchiesta agraria* [Agricultural survey] by Stefano Jacini; Ford's book *Oggi e domani* [Today and tomorrow] that I find very amusing because Ford, though he is a great industrialist, seems to me quite comical as a theoretician; Prato's book on the economic structure of Piedmont and Turin and a bulletin of the *Annali di economia* [Economic annals] with a diligent study of the economic structure of the Vercelli area (where Italian rice is grown) and a series of lectures on the English economic situation (that includes a lecture by Loria). I have very little history and the same goes for literature: a book by Gioacchino Volpe[3] on the last fifty years of Italian history, which is, however, topical and has a rather polemical slant; and both *History of Italian Literature* and *Critical Essays* by De Sanctis.[4] The books I had in Ustica I had to leave with my friends there, who are also rather badly off in this respect.

I wanted to write all this to you because I believe it is the best way for you and Giulia to get some vague idea of my life and the ordinary train of my thoughts. On the other hand you mustn't think that I am totally alone and isolated; every day, in one way or another, something happens. In the morning there is our walk; whenever I happen to take up a good position in the small yard, I observe the faces of those who come or go to occupy the other small courtyards. Then there is the sale of the newspapers that all the prisoners are allowed to buy. After my return to the cell, they bring me the political newspapers that I am allowed to read; then there is the shopping, and then they bring in the things you ordered the day before, then they bring lunch, etc. etc. In short I continually see new faces, each of which conceals a personality to be fathomed. On the other hand, I could by giving up my reading of the political papers stay in the company of other prisoners for four or five hours every day. I thought about it for a while, but then I decided to remain alone and keep up my newspaper reading; some casual company would amuse me for a few days, perhaps for a few weeks, but after that, in all probability, it would not be able to make up for my reading of the newspapers. What do you think? Or do you perhaps think that company in and of itself is a more valuable psychological factor? Tania, you as a doctor should give me some truly expert advice, because it is quite possible that I might be unable to judge with the objectivity that would perhaps be really necessary.

And so there you have the general structure of my life and my thoughts. I'm not going to talk about my thoughts insofar as they are directed to all of you and the children: you'll have to imagine this aspect on your own, and I believe that you feel it.

Dear Tania, in your postcard you still talk about your coming to Milan and the possibility that we might see each other during a visit. Will it really be true this time? Do you realize that it's more than six months since I've seen a member of the family? This time I really expect to see you. I embrace you.

Antonio

1. Gramsci translated large sections of the *Gespräche* in Turi prison, which can be found in Notebook 26. He also translated some of the stories in the Grimms' *Fünfzig Kinder und Hausmärchen* (usually translated as *Household Tales* or *Household Stories*).

2. As far as can be determined, Gramsci had a thorough reading knowledge of French, German and Russian, but his spoken command of these languages was rather limited. He was considerably less proficient in English.

3. Gioacchino Volpe, *L'Italia in cammino: L'ultimo cinquantennio* [Italy on its way: The last fifty years], (Milan: Treves, 1927).

4. Francesco De Sanctis (1818–1873), one of Italy's greatest literary historians and the author, among many other works, of *History of Italian Literature* (1870–71), which exerted a strong influence on Gramsci's conception of the relationship between a nation's political history and social development on the one hand, and the character of its literary production on the other.

June 6, 1927

Dearest Mother,

I've received your letter of March 23. Thank you for writing at such length and for sending me such interesting news. You should always write to me like this and always send a lot of news about local life even if to you it doesn't seem to have much significance. For instance: you tell me that in Ghilarza they will attach another eight municipalities to the town; but which ones are they? And besides: what does this consolidation mean and what will its consequences be? Will there be only one mayor, and a single municipal administration, but the schools, for instance, how will they be organized? Will they leave the elementary schools in each of the present communes, or will the children of Norbello or Domusnovas have to come to Ghilarza every day even for the first grade? Will they institute a single communal tax? Will the taxes paid by the people from Ghilarza who own land in all these communes be spent in the separate hamlets or will they be spent to beautify Ghilarza?

This is the principal question, it seems to me, because in the past Ghilarza's town budget was very poor since its inhabitants owned property within the territory of the neighboring communes and paid the larger part of their local taxes to them. This is what I want you to write about instead of forever thinking about my critical, sad, etc. etc. situation. I would like to reassure you on this point. Let's understand each other. Of course: I don't believe that my situation is very brilliant. But you know that everything has its value, depending on the way in which we see it and feel it. Now, I am much more tranquil and I see everything with great calm and confidence, not because of the immediate events that concern me but because of my more distant future; I am convinced, as I have already written to Teresina, that I won't have to rot in prison forever; I believe that in one way or another, I won't stay here any longer than three years, even if they were to sentence me, let us say, to twenty years. You can see that I write to you with the utmost sincerity, without trying to give you any false hopes. I think that only in this way will you too be strong and patient. What's more, you absolutely mustn't worry about the state of my moral strength and physical health. When it comes to moral strength you do know me somewhat. Remember the time (but perhaps we never told you then) when we boys made a bet on who would have greater endurance after banging our fingers with a rock until a drop of blood appeared at the fingertips. Perhaps now I would no longer be able to stand up under such barbaric tests, but I have certainly become much more capable of enduring the hammer blows on the head that events have inflicted on me and will continue to inflict. Just think, it's about ten years now that I've been in an atmosphere of struggle and that I have become sufficiently tempered; I could have been killed a dozen times and instead I am still alive: this in itself is a point of incalculable gain. On the other hand I've also been happy for a period of time; I have two very beautiful children who are certainly being raised and growing up as I would like and who will become two energetic, strong men. So I am tranquil and quiet and I definitely am not in need of either compassion or comforting. And physically too I am very, very much stronger than I myself thought. I am sure that I'll be able to bear up in the future too and I am therefore absolutely sure that I will embrace you again and see you happy.

From time to time I have a yearning for Giulia and our boys and I know that they're fine. I'm certain that the children are being raised with even too many comforts and too much care: their mother, their grandparents, and their aunts would deprive themselves of bread so that they should not miss their cookies and their pretty little clothes. I've never been able to find out anything precise about Nannaro: I only knew that he was living in Paris, that he was working, but nothing else. Nannaro is quite mad and strange and I believe that it is indeed he himself who decided not to let me know anything, perhaps because he thought I was very angry with him for having collected my salary for five or six months without letting me know anything, while I was ill in the sanatorium. At least that's what I think; and that's why I think he's crazy. I knew what state he was in, how he had been wounded because of me[1] and I wouldn't even have thought of reproaching him or asking him for a penny.

Dear mother, keep strong and calm and don't be too fierce with the Abbasanta people. I embrace you affectionately.

Nino

1. In 1922, Gennaro was working in the administrative offices of the newspaper *L'Ordine Nuovo*, founded by Gramsci in Turin. On December 18 of that year, he was beaten and seriously hurt by a gang of Fascists. This occurred while Gramsci was living in Moscow.

June 27, 1927

Dearest Mother,

I have received your letter of the 2d with Mea's photograph. What's more, I had received your previous letter and I've also answered it. My situation is always the same; my health is fairly good and I get by. During these last weeks I had a great disappointment; my sister-in-law Tatiana came from Rome to Milan to visit me, but she has fallen ill and since the fourteenth has been in hospital, without having yet been able to come and see me. I hope that she's well now (at least that's what she writes) and that in a few days she will visit me.

I don't like Mea's photograph. Do you know what I was thinking? That you have put the silver coin that I sent to have a tea spoon made for her into the piggy bank or in her postal savings account. It seems to me that in the face of this little girl I see the potential lineaments of a church-going bigot[1] who lends money at 40 percent interest. I have the feeling that all of you together, you, Grazietta and Teresina have ruined Edmea. I will never forget that the first time Mea came for a walk with me, when I asked her whether she wanted chocolate, she asked me to give her the money so that she could put it into her postal account. Do you think that this is the proper way to bring up children? I ask myself whether a girl brought up like this would be repelled at the thought of becoming a prostitute, if you have taught her that money is a value in itself and not for the services it can procure? I really want Mea to have a little spoon and not a coin, you must write to me if you have taken care of it.

I would like you to send me, you know what? the sermon of *Fra Antiogu a su populu de Masuddas*[2] [Brother Antioch's sermon to his people of Masuddas] that you can buy at Oristano because recently Patrizio Carta[3] has reprinted it in his famous print shop. Since I have a lot of time to kill, I want to compose a poem in the same style in which I will include all the illustrious personages that I have known as a child; tiu[4] Remundu Gana with Ganosu and Ganolla, maestru Andriolu and tiu Millanu, tiu Micheli Bobboi, tiu Iscorza "alluttu," Pippetto, Corroncu, Santu Jacu "zilighertari,"[5] etc. etc. I will have great fun and then I will recite the poem to the children, in a few years. I think that now the world has become more refined and the scenes that we have seen as children will not be seen again. Do you remember that beggar from Mogoro who had promised to come and get us with two white horses and two black horses so we could go and discover the treasure protected by the Musca Maghedda[6] and how we waited for him month after month? Now children no longer believe these stories and so it is a good idea to tell them in song; if we were to meet with Mario again we could have another poetic competition! I remember Uncle Iscorza "alluttu," as Aunt Grazia[7] demurely used to put it: is he still alive? do you remember how he made us laugh with that horse of his that had a tail only on Sunday? You see how many things I remember? I bet I managed to make you laugh. An affectionate greeting to everyone. I embrace you tenderly.

Nino

1. Gramsci uses the word *beghina* here. The word derives from the name of a medieval order of Belgian nuns who followed the teachings of Lambert Le Begue from Liège. It has a strongly pejorative connotation, meaning a bigoted and greedy woman.

2. As evidenced in this and the preceding letter, Gramsci had a keen interest in Sardinian language, customs, folklore, and politics. The "style" of the sermon he refers to here was one of severe moral denunciation.

3. Patrizio Carta was a friend and distant relative of the Gramsci family. His printing shop in Oristano went bankrupt, which is why Gramsci ironically calls it "famous."

4. *Maistru* (maestro, master) and *tiu* (zio, uncle) are Sardinian terms of respect used when speaking to elderly or esteemed men.

5. *Alluttu* (alert or vivacious) and *zilighertari* (lizard) probably contained a double entendre alluding to the phallus.

6. In Sardinian folklore, the *musca maghedda* is a huge, diabolical fly. The word *maghedda* derives from the verb *magheddare*, "to whip or otherwise mistreat cattle."

7. Grazia Delogu, at whose home Gramsci's mother lived for a while with her children after the imprisonment of Francesco Gramsci.

July 4, 1927

Dear Berti,

I've received your letter of June 20.[1] I thank you for writing. I don't know whether Ventura has received my many letters, because it's been quite a while since I have received any correspondence from Ustica.

At this moment I'm going through a certain period of moral lassitude, because of events concerning my family. I'm very nervous and irascible; I'm unable to concentrate or focus on any subject, even if interesting, such as the one you deal with in your letter. On the other hand, I've lost all contact with your milieu and I cannot imagine what sort of changes have taken place among the run of internees. In my opinion one of the most important activities that the teaching faculty ought to perform is that of recording, developing, and coordinating the pedagogical and didactic experiences and observations; only from this uninterrupted work can be born the kind of school and the kind of teacher that the environment requires. What a wonderful book could be based on these experiences and how useful it could be. Since this is my opinion I find it difficult to give you advice or even dish out, as you put it, a series of "inspired" ideas. I believe that inspiration should be dropped into a "ditch" and instead one should apply the method taught by the most particularized experiences and the most dispassionate or objective self-criticism. Dear Berti, don't think that I'm trying to discourage you or add to the uneasiness you already have, as you tell me: Since you don't think like this, I will tell you that I am convinced that you, after having youthfully exaggerated your self-assurance, are now exaggerating by underestimating yourself. Do you mind my telling you this? Your adolescence has lasted a bit (let us even say a big bit) longer than it commonly lasts in men. But I believe that the energetic massages to which you've been subjected have been beneficial, have hardened your bones.

I resume. I think, by and large, that the school should be divided into three grades (fundamental ones, because each grade could be divided into courses): the third grade would have to be that of the teachers, or the equivalent, and function like a club rather than a school in the ordinary sense. That is, each member would have to offer his contribution as lecturer or reporter on specific scientific, historical, or philosophical but especially didactic or pedagogical subjects. For the philosophy course I believe, still by and large, that the historical presentation ought to be summary while on the other hand the course should emphasize a concrete philosophical system, the Hegelian, dissecting and criticizing it in all of its aspects. I would also set up a course in logic, I would even say including the *barbara, baralipton*,[2] etc., and a course in dialectics. But we'll be able to discuss all this at greater length if you write to me again; I do not feel like writing and thinking about all that.

Who is Parri,[3] whom you mention? I knew (he was at the university three years before me) a Francesco Parri, who became a professor of modern history and I believe a specialist in the history of the Risorgimento. The Parri in question followed, if I remember rightly, a particular school of history, those who approached history from an economic point of view and descend directly from Adam Smith and Ricardo, continuing the scientific tradition of the economic study of history (Einaudi, Prato, Porri, etc.) and could present a very interesting analysis of the origins of the unified Italian State. Since you know Rosselli[4] (I don't know him), I ask you to tell him that I would be grateful if he could get me the printed pages N. 8 (from page 113 to page 128) of his brother's book on the Italian cooperative movement during the Risorgimento, my copy lacks this set of pages and it repeats note twenty-one due to a mistake in book binding; I don't know how to get it otherwise (the book costs twenty-six lire!) and just that chapter is extremely interesting.

Dear Berti, give my regards to our friends and believe me cordially yours,

Antonio

I received at this very moment Marcucci's letter of June 29. I'm really glad that Marcucci has decided to write me. Let him tell you about it. Marcucci has taken seriously one of my jokes that you told him. Assure Marcucci for me and tell him that in my cell I have a sparrow who plays on his shoes, embroidering them prettily with an equivocal splatter, to my enormous amusement; I will not clean them until I'm sure that they are embellished to the right artistic point. (Artistic in relation to your course on the history of art, about which in fact Marcucci writes).

A supplementary book for the history course that I recommend is the recent one by Corrado Barbagallo, *L'oro e il fuoco* [Gold and fire], Corbaccio Publishers, Milan, Buenos Aires. 69, L. 14.

1. This letter, in which Berti gives an interesting account of the "school" set up by the political prisoners on the island of Ustica, has been published in Antonio Gramsci, *Lettere dal carcere*, ed. Caprioglio and Fubini, pp. 102–03. See Introduction, n. 11, for names of internees at Ustica with whom Gramsci exchanged letters. Pietro Ventura was one of them.

2. *Barbara* and *baralipton* are terms used as student mnemonic devices for the study of logic. *Barbara* designates the type of syllogism in which both the two premises and the conclusion are universal affirmative statements. *Baralipton* designates the type of syllogism in which the first two premises are universals, but the conclusion is restrictive to particular instances.

3. In his letter of June 20, 1927, to Gramsci, Berti had jokingly said that if he had not

agreed to teach the history course for the internees at Ustica, the job would have fallen to Professor Parri or to Professor Rosselli; to protect them from such a burden, Berti said, he had accepted the task instead. This explains why Gramsci refers to a Francesco Parri and to Carlo Rosselli in this letter. The Parri who was with Berti at Ustica is Ferruccio Parri (1890–1981). In May 1927 Parri and Carlo Rosselli had both been exiled to Ustica as a consequence of their part in assisting the Socialist leader Filippo Turati to escape from Italy to Switzerland. Parri was to become one of the major figures of the Action party during the second World War and the first prime minister of postwar Italy in 1945.

4. Carlo Rosselli (1899–1937), one of the titans of Italian anti-Fascism. After participating in the anti-Fascist movement in Florence, he escaped to France and founded the Justice and Liberty movement in Paris in 1929. In 1936, he led an Italian detachment of volunteers in Spain. Ten months later, on June 9, 1937, in Bagnoles-de-l'Orne, a resort town in Normandy, he and his brother Nello were assassinated by French right-wing terrorists. The study of the Italian cooperative movement to which Gramsci refers is Nello Rosselli's *Mazzini e Bakunin: Dodici anni di movimento operaio in Italia, 1860–1872* [Mazzini and Bakunin: Twelve years of the workers movement in Italy, 1860–1872] (Turin: Bocca, 1927).

July 11, 1927

Dearest Carlo,

I've received your postcard of July 2. Perhaps by now mother has gotten my letters. At any rate I have not received an answer to my last two letters and so I imagine that they are still on their way. But do you know what I thought? That you've written that you didn't receive any more news from me only as a pretext for your postcard, since it is quite some time since you have written to me. Why don't you write to me sometimes? Could you possibly be so deeply immersed and absorbed in your business? Or is it that Giulia and Lia[1] deafen you all day long with their chatter and gossip? I can imagine what a delightful amusement it must be to have them for neighbors. Did they already find a way to set up some new and original enterprise, like that of the little crowns or of the saint's pictures and the picture postcards? What a shame that the famous Juanna Culamontigu died, now that the company has been established; do you remember? But does tia Tana still exist?

I always feel the same, that is, fairly well. I study, read, and time passes quite rapidly for me, more than I would have thought. I try not to think about anything else beyond my penitentiary occupations, in order to keep my peace of mind. I don't know whether I'll always succeed, but until now I have. From this point of view you may reassure mother. Besides, if I were ill, or needed something I would write to you or Teresina.

Embrace everyone. Affectionately,

Nino

1. Giulia and Lia Delogu, sisters of Serafino Delogu, with whom Gramsci lived during his student days in Oristano. The Delogus were cousins of Gramsci's mother.

July 18, 1927

Dearest Tania,

I've received your letter of the eleventh. I did not write to you directly sooner, because I didn't know your precise address.[1] But I thought that Ester[2] always showed you my letters that were written especially for you. Dear Tania, you can certainly imagine how sorry I have been and still am over this turmoil of illness in which you have been caught up because of me. I don't understand anything about it, but when I hear certain words buzzing like huge flies I believe that some extremely complicated things are involved. The fact that you've already been able to leave the hospital has comforted me greatly. Do you know what it is that especially caused my anxiety? Not knowing anything concrete and thinking that while you were sick here in Milan, I might from one day to the next be transferred to Rome without having seen you. I have to turn in the pen and must stop. I embrace you tenderly with the hope of seeing you soon.

Antonio

1. Gramsci did not know Tania's exact address because for most of July and early August 1927 she was undergoing treatment in a Milan hospital. Tania suffered from a number of chronic physical ailments, including gastro-intestinal disturbances, phlebitis, headaches, thyroid deficiency, and respiratory problems. But as she herself said in several of her letters, she was one of those people who are never entirely sick or entirely well and who constantly suffer from one symptom or another. She ate irregularly and inadequately. There were times when she weighed about 110 pounds, 20 pounds less than her ideal weight. Her close friend, Nilde Perilli, recalls that Tania "was the enthusiastic friend of doctors and nurses, she was always happy when she could find a reason to enter and spend a few days in the hospital, in a private room." (Quercioli, ed., *Gramsci vivo*, p. 159.)

2. Ester Zamboni (1890–1963), a teacher from Bologna and member of the PCI. She had been entrusted with the task of giving Gramsci instructions for his escape to Switzerland in early November 1926, in accordance with a plan that had been worked out several months earlier. Before emigrating to France, Belgium, and then finally to the Soviet

Union, she befriended Tania and helped her during the latter's hospital stay in Milan in the summer of 1927. (Cambria, *Amore*, p. 203, n. 47). Gramsci's letters to Ester Zamboni have not yet been found.

July 25, 1927

Dearest Tania,

This week I have received only a letter from Ester. Yesterday, Sunday, I was absolutely convinced that you would come at the visiting hour. But you mustn't believe, dearest, that I've ever been irritated because you haven't yet been able to come and see me, and that I have, in any way whatever, thought that the delay was caused by a lack of diligence on your part. I had the impression of reading something of this sort in Ester's letter. No. I've been anxious because I was not receiving news from you regularly and because your news was vague and uncertain. I understood why you wrote to me the way you did because on other occasions I've seen how little importance you attach to your health, but I don't understand why at least Ester didn't realize that she should have written to me and put things more concretely. Even now I understand very little. Ester had written to me that you had already undergone the appendicitis operation; but from your last letter it would appear that the operation has yet to take place. You must then connect this uncertainty with the fact that at the end of May and almost all of June I thought I would have to leave for Rome from one day to the next. You can imagine my state of mind in such a situation. At moments I was truly enraged. Those "fairly well's" that you wrote me stung like thorns. You know, in my town, they tell this story: A very long time ago the government through its prefects sent to all the municipalities a circular letter in which it asked how far the cemetery was from the inhabited area. The first time the mayor answered: "A shotgun blast away." The form was sent back with a request for greater precision and the mayor specified: "The distance traveled by a stone flung by the hand of a champion"; the form was sent back once again and the mayor was once again even more precise: "A flight of larks from a second brood." Wouldn't you say that you and Ester have shown and still show the same aversion as that mayor for the decimal metric system of information?

Dearest Tania, despite everything, I feel very guilty and I am sorry at having lost control of myself in such a way. Please do not neglect anything in order to regain your health and do everything the people at the hospital consider necessary. I can wait with great patience. I feel great fondness for you.

Antonio

August 1, 1927

Dearest Mother,

I've received your letter of July 12 and the photograph of Teresina's two children. Did you receive another letter of mine in which I wrote to you about Nannaro? If you did not receive it, you mustn't think that I sent you precise news about him, for I too have never been able to obtain any; I only tried to explain to you the probable reasons for Nannaro's silence, at least as regards me.

The group picture of the two children seems to have turned out very well, even if the photograph itself did not. One can see that they are two beautiful children. In the other photograph of Franco that you had sent me, the boy looked like a little old man; he was very thin and without vitality. It's been some time since I've received news from Giulia; for about three months now I have heard nothing about her or the children. My sister-in-law is still sick in hospital; I think that just during these days she's been operated on because I haven't had news from her for twenty days. I'm getting accustomed to not thinking of anything and letting things go as they will. I embrace you all.

Nino

So that you won't let them cheat you, just in case, I warn you that the silver coin is not only worth five lire but today is worth twenty lire. When I sent it, it was worth about thirty lire and it was perfectly possible to make it into a small children's spoon.

August 8, 1927

Dearest Tania,

I've received your letter of July 28 and the letter from Giulia. I had not received any letters after July 11 and I was in great distress, so much so that I did something that you will consider foolish: I don't want to tell it to you, but I will do so when you come to visit me. I'm sorry to hear that you are so dispirited. I'm all the more sorry because I am convinced that I've contributed to your depression. Dear Tania, I'm always terribly afraid that you are worse than you say and that you might be having serious problems. Because of me. And this is a state of mind that nothing can destroy. It is deeply rooted in me. You know that in the past I've always lived the life of a bear in its den precisely because of this state of mind; because I did not want anyone to be mixed up in my misfortunes. I've tried to make even my family forget me, by writing home as little as possible. Enough! I would like to do something at least to make you smile. I will tell you the tale of my little sparrows.[1] Now you should know that I have a little sparrow and that I had another one that died, poisoned I think by some insect (a cockroach or millipede). The first sparrow had a much more winning manner than the present one. He was very proud and extremely vivacious. This one is very demure, with a servile nature and devoid of initiative. The first immediately became the lord of the cell. I think that he had an eminently Goethean spirit, according to what I have read in a biography of Goethe, *Über allen Gipfeln*[2] [Above all peaks]. The sparrow conquered all the peaks that existed in the cell and then he sat down for a few minutes to savor this sublime peace. To climb onto the cork stopper of a small bottle containing tamarind was his perpetual aspiration; and so he once fell into a container full of coffee grounds and almost drowned. What I liked about this sparrow is that he did not want to be touched. He would rebel fiercely, spreading his wings and pecking at my hands quite energetically. He had become domesticated, but without permitting too much familiarity. The strange thing is that his relative familiarity was not gradual but sudden. He would move about the cell but always at the opposite end from me. In order to attract him I would offer him a fly in a match box; he would not take it unless I was far away. Once instead of one fly there were five or six in the box; before eating he danced around frenetically for a few seconds; this dance was always repeated when there were many flies. One morning, upon returning from my walk, the sparrow came quite close to me; he never again left me, in the sense that from then on he always kept close to me, watching me attentively and coming every now and then to peck at my shoes so that I would give him something. But he never let me hold him in my hand without rebelling and immediately trying to escape. He died slowly, that is, he had a sudden seizure, in the evening, while he was squatting down under the table, he screamed like a child, but he died only the next day: his right side was paralyzed and he dragged himself about painfully to eat and drink. Then all of a sudden he died. The present sparrow, on the other hand, is nauseatingly domestic; he insists on being hand fed even though he eats perfectly well on his own; he alights on my shoe and settles in the cuff of my trousers: if his wings weren't clipped, he would fly on to my knee; you can see that he wants to do so because he stretches, shivers, then hops onto the shoe. I think that he too will die, because he is in the habit of eating burnt match tips, on top of the fact that always eating soaked bread must cause fatal ailments among these little birds. For the time being he is fairly healthy but he isn't lively; he doesn't run about, he always stays close to me and he already has inadvertently received a few kicks from me. And so there you have the story of my little sparrows.

You will write to Giulia on my behalf too, won't you? I thought of writing to her directly; what do you think. It would be the same, but how can I write every week to you and Giulia separately? That would take up all of my correspondence; besides, I do want to write to you every week. Dear Tania, I am so very fond of you, and I embrace you.

Antonio

1. This is one of several examples in the letters of Gramsci's ability to turn his prison experiences into fables with moral and political significance.

2. "Over all the Peaks," the first line of Goethe's lyric poem "Wanderer's Nightsong" and also the title of a fictionalized biography of Goethe by Paul Heyser, *Über allen Gipfeln* (Berlin: W. Heitz, 1895).

August 8, 1927

My dear Berti,

I've received your letter of July 15. Let me assure you that the condition of my health is no worse than it has been in recent years; in fact I believe that it has somewhat improved. On the other hand, I'm not doing any work, because reading pure and simple cannot be called work. I read a lot, but in a disorderly fashion. I receive a few books from the outside and I read the books from the prison library, just like that, at random, week by week. I possess a fairly fortunate ability to find interesting things even in the lowest intellectual production, such as serial novels, for example. If it were possible I would accumulate hundreds and thousands of index cards on various subjects of common popular psychology.[1] For example: how was the myth of the "Russian steamroller" of 1914 born; in these novels you can find hundreds of clues in this regard, and this means that there existed a whole system of beliefs and fears rooted in the great popular masses and that in 1914 the governments imposed what might be called their campaigns of nationalistic agitation. In the same manner you can find hundreds of clues concerning French popular hatred for England, which is linked to the peasant tradition of the Hundred Years War, the burning at the stake of Joan of Arc, and later on Napoleon's wars and exile. Isn't it extremely interesting that the French peasants during the Restoration believed that Napoleon was a descendant of the Maiden? As you see I also scrabble on the manure heaps! In any case every now and then I do run into an interesting book. I am now reading *L'Eglise et la bourgeoisie* [The church and the bourgeoisie] volume one (300 pages in octavo) in *Origines de l'esprit bourgeois en France* [Origins of the bourgeois spirit in France] by a certain Groethuysen.[2] The author, whom I do not know but who must be a follower of Paulhan's[3] sociological school, has had the patience to carry out a molecular analysis of the collections of sermons and devotional books published before 1789, so as to reconstruct the points of view, beliefs, and attitudes of the new ruling class that was then being formed. On the other hand I had a great intellectual disappointment with the highly touted book by Henri Massis, *Défense de l'Occident* [Defense of the West]; I think that either Filippo Crispolti or Egilberto Martire would have written a sparer book if the subject had occurred to them.[4] What makes me laugh is the fact that this eminent Massis, who is dreadfully afraid that Tagore's[5] and Gandhi's Asiatic ideology might destroy French Catholic rationalism, does not realize that Paris has already become a semicolony of Senegalese intellectualism and that in France the number of half-breeds is increasing by leaps and bounds. One might, just for a laugh, maintain that, if Germany is the extreme outcrop of ideological Asianism, France is the beginning of darkest Africa and the jazz band is the first molecule of a new Euro-African civilization!

I thank you for having tried to get me the pages that are missing from my copy of Rosselli's book.[6] Have you read the book? I don't know Rosselli, but I would like to tell him that I don't understand why in a history book there should be as much acrimony as he puts in his. This in general. In particular: the main thrust of his book seems to me dramatic to the point of histrionics (of course, the reviewer in the *Giornale d'Italia* has seized on this motif and twisted it about with the greatest possible vulgarity). Rosselli also does not even mention the fact that the famous 1864 meeting in London for Polish independence had already been requested for several years by the Neapolitan Societies and was convoked precisely because of an explicit letter from a Neapolitan Society. This fact seems to me of capital importance. In Rosselli there is (for him) a strange intellectual distortion. The moderates of the Risorgimento who, after the Milan events of February 1853 and a few days after the hanging of Tito Speri, had sent an address of homage to Franz Joseph, at a certain point, especially after 1860 but even more after the Paris events of 1871, co-opted Mazzini and turned him into a bulwark, even against Garibaldi (see for example Tullio Martello in his *History*).[7] This tendency has survived to this day and is represented by Luzio.[8] But why also by Rosselli? I thought that the younger generation of historians had freed themselves from such diatribes and the acrimony that accompanies them and that it had replaced acts of God with historical criticism. In any event Rosselli's book really "fills a gap." I received a postcard from Amadeo. My affectionate greeting to everyone, also to Rosselli and Silvestri.[9] I embrace you.

Antonio

---

1. This is a project that was realized, in some measure, in the many pages of the *Prison Notebooks* dedicated to analysis of popular culture. The "myth" of the Russian steamroller

involved the fear, in the early years of the first World War, that the vast population of Russia would one day inevitably overrun Europe.

2. Bernhard Groethuysen (1880–1946), prolific German author of philosophical works, among which are *Philosophische Anthropologie* [Philosophical anthropology] (1928), *Die Dialektik der Demokratie* [The dialectic of democracy] (1932), and *Montaignes Weltanschauung* [Montaigne's worldview] (1929).

3. Frédéric Paulhan (1856–1931), French psychologist and educational theorist; among his works are *Fonction de la mémoire* [The function of memory] (1904), *Logique de la contradiction* [The logic of contradiction] (1911), and *Puissance de l'abstraction* [The power of abstraction] (1928).

4. Filippo Crispolti (1857–1942) and Egilberto Martire (1887–1952) were journalists and exponents of the Italian Catholic movement who became supporters of Fascism.

5. Rabindranath Tagore (1861–1941), Indian poet and philosopher.

6. The reference is to Nello Rosselli's *Mazzini e Bakunin: Dodici anni di movimento operaio in Italia, 1860–1872* (1927). See letter to Berti, July 7, 1927, n. 4.

7. Tullo Martello (1841–1918), *Storia dell'Internazionale dalla sua origine al congresso dell'Aja* [History of the International from its origin to the congress of the Hague], first published in 1873 and reprinted in 1921 (Florence: Società Anonima editrice Francesco Perrella).

8. Alessandro Luzio, author of various books and compiler of documents on the events of the Risorgimento, published from 1913 to the late 1930s.

9. Carlo Silvestri, Italian journalist. He was one of the political internees on the island of Ustica with whom Gramsci exchanged letters in 1927 and 1928. Police records list him and Nello Rosselli as "Masonic liberals."

August 22, 1927

Dearest Mother,

I haven't received any letters from you for about a month. How are you? I'm writing to tell you not to worry if you receive (or have already received) a notice from the State Railways in which there is talk about three railroad tickets that, as a deputy, I issued to three fellows, and that have been contested, I don't remember well whether at the end of 1925 or the beginning of 1926. At least I believe it is about this matter, because two days ago they asked me for my family's address that was requested by the State Railways in connection with an "administrative matter." At first I replied that being of age I myself was my family, but since the request was very concise, they asked me for the address of my parents. Let me explain what happened. As a deputy, every year I was entitled to eight first-class tickets and four second-class tickets for members of my family or anyone who traveled with me as a companion for reasons of health. Sometimes I used these tickets to have someone accompany me because throughout those last years I was always very weak and sometimes suffered from fainting spells and dizziness. One time when I went from Rome to Milan the person who accompanied me had to return immediately; what to do? I questioned the clerk in charge of special tickets and asked for clarification; he told me that I could issue the tickets specifying: "returning after having acted as companion." I did this and did so another two times later on. In May of '26, when I was supposed to obtain the tickets for the new legislative year, they were refused and I was informed that in order to receive them I would have to pay several thousand lire, the price of three tickets plus a fine. I think I don't have to pay anything: (1) because there was no fraud on my part; at the window I presented tickets that were accepted despite the fact that clearly written on them was: "returning after having acted as a companion"; this means that the regulations are not clear and that the clerks do not know how to interpret them; (2) because I suffered harm by not having the use of tickets during the year 1926. I've explained all this to you so that you may see that I did nothing objectionable. At any rate I'm the only person responsible and I don't know what they think they can demand from my parents. So if you receive a notice of this kind I want you to answer that you have nothing to do with it, that it is twenty years now that I have been independent and have my own family. I await news from you. I embrace you affectionately.

Nino

August 22, 1927

Dearest Tania,

It is almost a month since I have received any news from you; your last letter is dated August 29.[1] I've become more patient, true; yet this state of affairs is very painful for me. Last month, before receiving your letter of the twenty-ninth and not knowing what to think, I wrote to Signorina Nilde. She answered very politely and assured me that Professor Bastianelli[2] does not think an operation is necessary for your illness and that he has written this to a doctor at the hospital. Professor Bastianelli believes that you need calm, fresh air, and good nourishment. All this is very good, but it doesn't exactly calm me because I believe that you have neither calm nor fresh air and that probably you are eating very little. Write to me as often as possible; at least some of your letters will get to me and give me a bit more patience. And do write to Giulia, to reassure her. Her last letter was rather melancholy (have you read it?) I embrace you.

Antonio

1. Gramsci's error. This should read July 29.
2. Raffaele Bastianelli (1863–1961), eminent Italian surgeon. He was named Senator in 1929.

August 29, 1927

Dearest Mother,

I received your letter of the seventeenth and I am answering you right away, even though I wrote to you last week.

Mario came here on Thursday and we spoke for about a quarter of an hour. He is very well. He told me something about his business affairs, which also seemed to be going quite well. It seems to me that he has a slight tendency to put on weight, like father. Before coming to see me, Mario had paid a visit to my sister-in-law at the hospital, so he told me about her and reassured me somewhat. He promised he would write to you immediately that he found me in very good health. I think what you wrote to me about him is rather exaggerated. No one, in this instance, can be more dispassionate and objective than I because Mario is fighting in the opposite camp.[1] When I paid him a visit, a couple of years ago, at his home, I believe that I was able to form a precise opinion about the entire milieu in which he figures as a sort of hero. But these are things that are best not written and besides Mario is my brother and I love him despite everything. I hope that now he is taking better care of his affairs and that he will settle down. If he comes to see me again, as he told me, I will try to find a way to say something to him, especially about his wife, who certainly is not a woman like you, and who would become limp as a rag if she had to struggle with the slightest bit of serious difficulty. Something more serious than having to give up the seaside, or a summer vacation, or a new dress.

I'm sorry that Grazietta is still unwell; why doesn't she write to me sometimes? I embrace you all affectionately; to you many, many kisses.

Nino

And what about Father Poddighe's sermon, when are you going to send it?

1. See the note on Mario in list of correspondents and family members.

August 29, 1927

Dearest Tania,

Thursday I received a visit from my brother Mario who has reassured me about your health. I was so overwrought due to the lack of news from you that after the visit and the nervous charge caused by it, I felt ill: I didn't sleep all night and I must have had a bit of a temperature. Nevertheless I cannot explain the lack of letters from you. Mario told me that he invited you to spend a few days in Varese, at his home. Why don't you accept? It is no longer hot, but the countryside must still be very pleasant and the lake region in Lombardy is worth seeing. My brother is a good boy and I am sure that you will feel *à ton aise* in his home. I don't know his wife very well; I saw her only once, quite a few years ago, when she was about to give birth and I don't believe that this is the most opportune moment to make a lady's acquaintance. You would still be able to take a few nice walks; Varese itself has a lake and some very beautiful hills. Meanwhile, how about you? how do you spend your time? Do you have books? I could send you some books, but I don't know how to go about it. I read a novel by an English writer, Margaret Kennedy, which seems very worthwhile to me. Its title, *The Constant Nymph*, is rather silly, but the book is really interesting: I don't know why, but it reminds me of Dostoyevsky's *Idiot*. Don't think that it has the same intensity; however, it certainly is remarkable, both because it is written by a woman and because of the psychological atmosphere in which it is conceived and also for the world it describes; what's more, it's well translated. You will certainly read it, because I'll have to send you the books I have here, either when I leave from Milan, or from Rome, when I'm assigned to a permanent penitentiary after the trial. When you've read this novel I would like you to send it on to Giulia. When the time comes, I'll write and tell her why this book should interest her. You know, the novel deals with a sort of phalanstery of musicians, who live, develop ways of thinking and judging centered on this fundamental fact: musical creation and sensitivity. Giulia once told me that as a young girl she thought about transforming the world with music. In the novel it is the world that smashes the characters: in any case, the book is interesting and well translated. Do you realize how badly Conrad's novels are translated? Not only do they lack a style and expression in Italian equivalent to the English original, but the Italian language itself is massacred.

I look forward to receiving direct news from you. The cold weather is approaching: I imagine that you arrived in Milan with a small bag, thinking that you would stay only a few days and that you are inconvenienced in many small ways. When I am able to tell you in person everything that I've thought during this month, I'll certainly make you laugh: I really believe that too much imagination is a great misfortune. I embrace you affectionately.

Antonio

———————————

September 5, 1927

My dear Berti,

I received your postcard dated August 11. I had already received a number of your letters, which I answered, either directly, or when I wrote to Lauriti.[1] During these last weeks however I have not received mail from anywhere, except for: (1) a postcard from the Tussi couple, which I answered with my kindest regards; (2) a postcard from Renzo Menotti[2] about whom you have written to me and who I thought was from Turin; now I remember him and return his greetings. Would you take care of this distribution of greetings?

Here autumn has already begun, with its accompaniment of very melancholy atmospheric conditions. I have already felt it in my old bones. I foresee a very hard winter; but never before as in these days did I feel that I had physically grown older more than my actual age would warrant and that I have a very meager store of reserves. The crisis of exhaustion that I had in the years '22–'23 really wore me out;

I tried to overcome it slowly, leading a middling, limited, passively vegetative existence, but today I again feel the same leaden mantle descend upon me that then seemed to crush me. Perhaps this is all a consequence of the Milanese humidity and also of the isolation in which I have found myself for the last seven months; especially since more than once during these last weeks I have thought of giving up reading political newspapers and spending time with people. I have hesitated to do so until now because of the fear that the remedy might be worse than the disease. Any possible company is divided into two strata: common people or professional criminals, with whom conversation can be interesting for two or three weeks, until one exhausts that certain amount of the picturesque and the typical that is inherent in their condition; and intellectuals, or almost, accused of bankruptcy, fraud, etc., in whom there probably isn't even a minimum of the picturesque and typical that there is in the former. I've had some of them as neighbors in nearby cells and I was struck by the fact that they become demoralized in childish and primitive ways; they weep, exactly like children, with great loud sobs, invoking Mama; even if she, poor woman, probably died quite some time ago. They always ask for something, in order to be able to see the guard, exchange a few words, and so feel connected with life, proving that they still have rights. When I think of all this, the idea of giving up the newspapers and having such deadheads for company is less cheering to me. Another nightmare has again begun to obsess me since the change in the weather: the nightmare of transfers in the cold and all the rest of it. My dear Berti, I'm sorry to afflict you with all these sad tales; I give vent to them with you because I do not want to write these things to my family. Write to me and press our other friends so that they too will write me, about any subject whatever; in this way I'll feel less isolated and I will be distracted from the obligatory course of my thoughts. I embrace you fraternally, together with our other friends.

Antonio

1. Mario Lauriti, a Communist from Rome who was one of the anti-Fascists held in police internment on the island of Ustica in 1926 and 1927. Lauriti recalls the impact that Gramsci had on him and on other prisoners in "L'università di Ustica," *Rinascita Sarda* (November 1, 1970): 10.

2. The Tussi couple and Renzo Menotti were with Gramsci on the island of Ustica. Some of the internees were allowed to live with their spouses.

Dear Grazietta,[1]

I hope that these lines find you still at Oristano. You say that you've written other things on other occasions. You have my word that when I answered you it was the first time that I had received direct news from you. I assure you that I'm less indifferent and less lazy than it may appear to some. Oh god, I'm not a demon of expansiveness and often I have to make an effort to write an affectionate word, but neither you nor anyone else at home should be surprised by this fact. Give many kisses to Uncle Serafino's little daughter and give my regards to all the uncles and the cohorts of aunts and tell them to write to me sometimes and I'll answer: to write to everyone is impossible, to choose among the many is discourteous; therefore if it matters to anyone at all that I am alive and wearing clothes,[2] I am waiting to know who this someone is. But I won't count on it. Endless kisses to everyone.

Nino

1. It has not been possible to date this letter. Its placement here is in conformity with the 1965 and 1988 Italian editions.
2. The expression "wearing clothes" seems a rather odd and puzzling choice of words, but the puzzle was solved by Massimo Lollini, who drew my attention to Dante's *Inferno*, canto 33, verse 141. Frate Alberigo, one of the sinners in the next-to-lowest rung of Hell, reserved for the souls of those who murdered their guests for money, explains to Dante that in this circle of Hell one encounters the souls of people whose bodies may still be living in the world. The reason, he says, is that the instant after an act of treachery of this kind is committed, the soul of the perpetrator is cast into hell, leaving its body to walk the earth until its allotted lifespan is finished. Not knowing this, Dante, upon hearing that the soul of Branca d'Oria is in this rung of hell, says to Alberigo, "I believe that thou deceivest me: for Branca d'Oria did not die; he eats and drinks and sleeps and wears clothes." The singularity of the expression makes it virtually certain that this was a conscious borrowing by Gramsci of a verse from Dante, similar to other borrowings that appear in his writings before and after his imprisonment.

September 12, 1927

Dearest Tania,

I've received your two letters; every day I receive the fruit you are sending me. I was very happy to see you and to have been able to exchange a few words with you.[1] It was really a great consolation to see you, after four months of anxieties and grim thoughts. Why did you find me changed? I'm not aware of it. It is true that with this kind of life changes follow one another so slowly that the "patient" may not notice them. You don't seem to have changed a great deal; perhaps you were too overwhelmed by the fear of seeing me, am I right? I on the contrary think that I have "developed" in the direction of coldness and outward indifference, I've lost many of my "southern" qualities. I don't believe that I'm sensitive, just the opposite; instead I have perhaps acquired a bit of nervous and morbid sensitivity but I've lost the outward habit of sensitivity. It's true that you reminded me of Giulia; you resemble each other very much, despite a number of conspicuous traits of personality that are unique and unmistakable. In any case, do you remember how one afternoon in Rome I spoke to you, thinking you were Giulia?

I don't know when you will be able to have a second visit. I would like to tell you face to face, more convincingly than I did last time, that you mustn't worry too much about me. Do you know that ten months have already gone by since my arrest? Time passes very quickly that's true, but it is still a long time. I think that I've already imposed too many sacrifices on my brothers and on you as well. On my brother Mario I can no longer count.[2] I understood this a month ago after a letter from my mother. Mother wrote me that she had received a letter from Mario's wife with many complaints, etc. I wrote to Mario to come and visit me; he seemed to be very embarrassed. After the visit he wrote home, to my brother Carlo, in a most alarming manner, from what I can imagine. Carlo writes to me as though I had one foot in my grave; he talks about coming to Milan himself and he has even thought of bringing mother, a woman about seventy years old, who has never left her village and has never taken a train trip longer than forty kilometers. Absolute madness, which made me sad and also somewhat annoyed with Mario, who could have been franker with me instead of terrorizing our old mother. Enough. Because of all this I have decided to put an end to this state of affairs, limiting myself, if necessary, to the prison diet pure and simple. But there are some obligations and these worry me a lot. Forgive the outburst, dear Tania, and don't be grieved. You see that I'm writing to you as I would to a sister and during all this time you've been more than a sister for me. So I've also tormented you a bit, at times. But isn't it true that we torment precisely those who are most dear to us. I want you to do everything to recover and stay healthy. In that way you'll be able to write to me, keeping me informed about Giulia and the children, and be able to comfort me with your affection.

I've received the 300 lire you sent me in June; I must have also written to you about it. They still haven't given me the German dictionary; but why did you send it? I could have done without it for the time being, waiting to have my own. In a general way you mustn't send me anything that I don't ask for and that I have not agreed to have shipped. Believe me, this is the most rational way, aside from the fact that, as you say, I never ask for anything. That's not true; when I need something I do ask; but I try to do this rationally, in order not to create bad habits for myself that later on are more painful to give up. To live untroubled in jail one must get accustomed to the bare necessities; you well understand that every small comfort in this environment becomes a kind of vice that it is then difficult to eradicate due to the absence of distractions. If one wishes to remain strong and keep intact one's power of resistance one must subject oneself to a regime and follow it with an iron will. For example: why did I suffer so much because of your silence? Because I was accustomed to a certain regularity in your correspondence: so every irregularity took on a sinister significance. But I want you to create for me this habit of regular correspondence, do you hear? Don't think that I'm authorizing you not to write to me because of this theory of nonhabits! Dearest, I wait for your new visit, even despite the fact that we can't even clasp hands. By the way, do you know that for a long time I had thought of giving you some flowers grown in my cell (this is the height of prison romanticism!)? But the plants have withered by now and so I've not been able to keep any of the five or six small blossoms that had opened, rather stunted, if the truth be told. I embrace you affectionately.

Antonio

1. On September 5, 1927, Tania visited Gramsci at the Milan prison. This appears to have been the first time she had seen him after his arrest in November of the previous year.

2. In his letter to Tania written on the same day, Gramsci explains that, after a visit to the Milan prison in August, Mario had written a letter home that gave the impression that he, Gramsci, was at death's door. But no doubt there were political reasons for Gramsci's

loss of confidence in his brother: in 1927 Mario was secretary of the local section of the National Fascist party in the town of Varese.

September 12, 1927

Dearest Carlo,

Your letter of August 30 and your certified letter of September 2 have reached here together. I thank you with all my heart. I don't know what Mario wrote to you; I have the impression that he has alarmed you too much, while I had thought that his visit would have helped reassure mother. I was wrong. Your letter of August 30 is indeed overwrought. From now on I intend to write to you often to try and convince you that your state of mind is not worthy of a man (and by now you are no longer so very young). It is the state of mind of a person in the grip of panic, a person who sees dangers and threats on all sides and so loses the power to function seriously and to overcome real difficulties, after having identified them properly and set them aside from the imaginary ones created by fantasy alone. And first of all I want to tell you and everyone else at home that you know me very little and therefore have a completely mistaken opinion about my power of endurance. It seems that it is almost twenty-two years since I left the family and during the last fourteen years I've come home only twice in '20 and in '24. Now, in all this time I never lived like a rich man; just the opposite; I've often gone through very difficult times and I've also gone hungry in the most literal sense of the word. At a certain point this is something that must be said, because (. . .)[1] one can be reassured. You have probably envied me sometimes, because I was able to study. But you certainly do not know how I was able to study. I only want to remind you of what happened to me during the years between 1910 and 1912. In 1910, since Nannaro had a job in Cagliari, I went to live with him. I received my first monthly allowance, then I no longer received anything: I was totally dependent on Nannaro who did not earn more than one hundred lire a month. We moved to another pensione. I had a small room that had lost its plaster because of the dampness and had only a tiny window that looked out onto a sort of well, more a latrine than a courtyard. I immediately realized that we couldn't go on like this, because of the ill humor of Nannaro, who always found fault with me. I began by no longer drinking a bit of coffee in the morning, then I put off lunch later and later and so I saved dinner. Thus for about eight months I ate only once a day and I made it to the end of the third year of *liceo*, in a seriously undernourished condition. Only at the end of the school year did I find out about the existence of the Carlo Alberto school scholarship, but in order to compete for it one had to take an examination in all the subjects taught during the three years of *liceo*; so I had to make an enormous effort during the three months of vacation. Only Uncle Serafino² noticed my deplorable weakness and invited me to live with him at Oristano as Delio's tutor. I remained there one and a half months and I almost went crazy. I couldn't study for the competition, since Delio absorbed me completely and my anxiety, together with my weakness, shattered me. I slipped out on the sly. I had only one month of time left to study. I departed for Turin almost in a somnambulistic state. I had fifty-five lire in my pocket. I had spent forty-five of the hundred lire received from home for the trip in third class.³ The Exposition⁴ was on and I had to pay three lire a day just for the room. I was reimbursed with about eighty lire for the trip in second class, but this was nothing to make merry over because the exams lasted around fifteen days and for the room alone I had to spend about fifty lire. I don't know how I managed to sit for those exams, because I fainted two or three times. I did it but then my troubles began. When I got home it took them two months to send me the documents to register at the university, and since registration was suspended, the seventy lire of the scholarship was also suspended. I was saved by a school janitor who found me a pensione that cost seventy lire a month, where I was given credit; I was so depressed that I thought of being sent home by the police. So I would receive the seventy lire and spend seventy lire for a very shabby pensione. And I spent the winter without an overcoat, wearing a light mid-season suit good for Cagliari. Along about March 1912 I was in such a miserable state that I stopped speaking for several months; and when I did speak I misused the words. On top of this I lived right on the banks of the Dora River, and the freezing fog was destroying me.

Why have I written you all this? Because I want to convince you that at other times I have been in dreadful situations but without despairing. This past life has tempered my character. I have become convinced that even when everything is or seems lost, one must quietly go back to work, starting again from the beginning. I've become convinced that one must only count on oneself and on one's own strength; expect nothing from anyone and so avoid creating disappointments. That one must set out to do only what one knows one can do and go one's own way. My moral position is very good; some people think of me as a devil, others think of me as almost a saint. I don't want to be either a martyr or a hero. I believe that I am simply an average man who has his own deep convictions and will not trade them away for anything in the world. I could tell you some amusing anecdotes. During my first months here in Milan, one of the guards naively asked me if it was true that if I had been a turncoat I would have become a minister. I smiled and told him that minister was a bit too much, but I might have become undersecretary of the Postal Service or Public Works, since those were the posts in the government that were given to the Sardinian deputies. He shrugged his shoulders and asked me why I hadn't gone over to the other side, touching his brow with his finger. He had taken my answer seriously and thought that I was completely crazy.

So then cheer up and don't let the small town Sardinian environment engulf you: one must always stand above the environment in which one lives, without therefore despising it or believing that one is superior to it. We must understand and reason, not whine like foolish women! Do you understand? Is it possible that I, who am in prison, with rather grim prospects, must encourage a young man who can move about freely, who can exercise his intelligence in his daily work and make himself useful? I embrace you affectionately together with everyone at home.

Nino

Send me as soon as you can what you promised me because I really need it. I hope that in the future I will not have to enlist your help.

1. The manuscript contains several illegible words at this point.

2. Serafino Delogu, a cousin of Gramsci's mother, was the proprietor of a pharmacy in Oristano. Delio was Serafino's son.

3. Third-class fare for the poor on public transportation was in effect in Italy until shortly after the end of World War II.

4. Three large fairs were held in 1911 in Turin, Florence and Rome to celebrate the fiftieth anniversary of the founding of the kingdom of Italy.

September 19, 1927

Dearest Tania,

Are you happier after our Wednesday visit? It was very picturesque, wasn't it? I saw that you too were laughing because of all that
deafening racket; are you sure you didn't cry afterward? I was very
happy because it seemed to me that you were feeling a little better.

Thank you for what you send me every day. I try to eat absolutely
everything that you send me: but at times it is quite impossible. How
could I eat so many nuts, for example? Instead I really ate with great
zest the prosciutto and the fresh cheese, which I liked very much and
the grapes and the figs, etc. But don't send me any bread: here we
must buy it by the half kilo each time and so I always have a surplus;
it is fresh and good just like the bread you can buy on the outside.
Besides, since yesterday I have begun receiving lunch from the trattoria (at least I received it yesterday; right now as I write I have not
yet received today's, but it is still too early). It has been a few days
now since I gave up reading the political daily newspapers and spend
time with company instead. That is, from approximately one till five
another prisoner comes to my cell. He is waiting for trial and hails
from a small town near Monza, charged with theft and with wreck-
ing a house of ill repute: an excess of zeal in the search for cocaine on
the part of the vice squad. Having this company has been an enormous diversion during these days; he is a rather alert and witty young
man, this prisoner, and I hit it off easily with anyone. For the time
being at least, the subjects for conversation are not yet exhausted.

Did you read Kennedy's novel? Another rather interesting novel is
the one by Henri Beraud; if you have read it, don't you think that it
reproduces the dry and nervous style of the old French chroniclers
rather well? Also worthy of being read is a book of memoirs by
André Gide,[1] I don't know whether you are aware of the rest of his
poetic or novelistic works. R. Bacchelli's novel—*Il Diavolo al Ponte
Lungo* [The devil at Ponte Lungo]—has had a great success, from
what I have read in the press. You know, Bacchelli belongs to a school
that was much discussed after the war, the school of the so-called
Rondisti (because the name of their magazine was *La Ronda*[2]); they
"discovered" that Leopardi is the greatest Italian writer and that Leo-

pardi's prose offers the best model for modern literature. They published a very beautiful anthology of Leopardi's prose, but it seems to me that their entire effort was exhausted with this anthology; from his novel it is not quite clear in which way Bacchelli is an innovator of modern Italian literature and marks a stage. There certainly does not appear in it the harmony of parts and the complete fusion between expressive form and conception that are typical of Leopardi.

Let's hope that you will now be able to recover your health quickly. I look forward to another visit so as to see you even happier and stronger. I embrace you.

Antonio

1. *Souvenirs d'enfance et de jeunesse* [Memories of childhood and youth] (1927).
2. *La Ronda*, a literary review published in Rome from 1919 to 1922, championed Italy's classical cultural and literary heritage and regarded Giacomo Leopardi (1798–1837) as an exemplary prose stylist and lyric poet.

September 26, 1927

Dearest Tania,

I had thought of writing this letter to Giulia. But I am absolutely unable to; I couldn't even begin it. I'm still under the impression of her last letter that I received on May 31, but it certainly is an anachronistic impression. It seems to me that during these months Giulia's life must have undergone many changes, because Giuliano is probably beginning to speak and walk and she must have experienced once more, but with new variations, the sensations awakened by the first steps taken by Delio, who today must already be a wise spectator of his little brother's great exploits; thus all emotional relations are complicated by essential novelties of enormous import. As you can imagine. So my letter would be inopportune and certainly jarring: this worries me and robs me of initiative. Do you really think that Giulia will be very saddened by not receiving my letters directly? (Mind you, I do not want to put her sensitivity in doubt!) I think about it, but I still can't do it. I really must have in hand some of her more recent letters. But we could do this: forward this letter to her, for example. When she reads it she will understand my state of mind perfectly well and will forgive me. Perhaps she won't even think that there is a need for a true and proper forgiveness. I now ought to write a great paean to her goodness, but someone might think that I do it on purpose *ad captandam benevolentiam!*[1]

Dear Tania, I hope that I will find you somewhat better than last time; you seemed a trifle feverish. I expect you on Wednesday. I embrace you.

1. Latin for "to get on someone's good side."

Antonio

October 3, 1927

Dearest Mother,

I received your insured letter of September 26; many thanks to Carlo. I've also received Father Poddighe's sermon, but it isn't very amusing; it definitely does not have the fresh and rustic humor of the sermon to the "populu de Masuddas" [people of Masuddas]. By an effort of memory, despite having heard it only a few times, I've been able to remember entire passages and that's why I asked you for it. And *ita ca no meis bogauchi si noi boghint is ogus—e un arrogu e figau*[1] etc. etc; I like this very much. I think I wrote you a number of letters that you didn't receive: otherwise I cannot explain the lack of news. I've not been ill and I don't feel unwell. In recent times I have given up reading the daily newspapers in order to spend a few hours in the company of other prisoners. This company, as you can imagine, is the sort prison can offer, because I'm not permitted to go with other political prisoners: so these are people charged with common crimes. Yet this offers me some diversion and time passes more quickly.

My sister-in-law has left the hospital and comes to see me now and then. She is still convalescing and makes great sacrifices for me. She comes to the prison every day and sends me some delicious morsel to eat: fruit, chocolate, fresh dairy products. Poor woman, I'm unable to convince her not to tire herself out so much and to give more thought to her health. I'm even a bit humiliated by so much abnegation, which sometimes one doesn't even find in one's own sisters.

I meant to tell you something. I no longer remember which of my books are still in Ghilarza. I remember that in 1913 in Turin I had bought a batch of books about Sardinia from the library of a certain

Marquis Di Boyl, whose heirs had discarded all the books with a Sardinian subject. I think I remember that I had taken some of them to Ghilarza during my vacation. If they are still there, I would like to have General Lamarmora's book about his travels in Sardinia (it is written in French) and Baron Manno's histories.[2] I'm quite sure that these two are in Ghilarza. I used to have a large bound volume (very large, weighing at least ten kilos) containing a collection of all of the papers of Arborea, but I don't remember whether I'd brought it with me.[3] But a small volume that should be there is by Engineer Marchesi, *Con Quintino Sella in Sardegna* [In Sardinia with Quintino Sella]. If you find any of these books around the house have them sent to me. Tell Carlo that if he happens to buy a copy of the magazine *Il Nuraghe*, he should send it to me after reading it. Whenever you can, send me some of those Sardinian songs that the descendants of Pirisi Pirione from Bolotana sing in the streets, and if during some feastday they have poetry contests write and tell what themes are sung. Do they still hold the feasts of Saint Constantine at Sedilo and of Saint Palmerio, and how do they turn out? Is the feast of Saint Isidor still a big event? Do they carry the banner of the four moors in procession and do they still have the captains dressed up like ancient militiamen? You know that these things have always interested me very much, so write to me about them and don't think they are foolish things without head or tail.[4]

I've had no news about the children for some time, but I hope they are well. I embrace you affectionately together with everyone at home.

Nino

1. "What slanders you've come up with—May they gouge out your eyes and liver!"
2. Alberto Lamarmora (1789–1863), *Voyage en Sardaigne de 1819 à 1825* [Journey in Sardinia from 1819 to 1825] (Paris, 1826); Giuseppe Manno (1786–1868), *Storia della Sardegna dai più antichi tempi alla morte di Carlo Emanuele III* [History of Sardinia from ancient times to the death of Carlo Emanuele III], 4 vols. (1825–27); and *Storia moderna della Sardegna dall'anno 1773 al 1799* [Modern history of Sardinia from 1773 to 1799] (1842).
3. Documents on the history and literature of Sardinia from ancient times to the Middle Ages were discovered in 1845 by a Cagliari monk, who published them as papers from the archives of the Judges of Arborea, the name Arborea referring to one of four zones into which Sardinia was divided in the Middle Ages.
4. Gramsci wrote "without head or tail" in Sardinian: *senza cabu né coa*.

October 3, 1927

Dearest Tania,

I've received your two postcards of September 21 and 23. You mustn't always think about what I want and might like to have. I assure you that if I lack for something necessary or useful I ask you for it without much ado. But just to keep you happy, with regard to books, I'll tell you that I would like to get the recent publication by Daudet and Maurras, *L'Action Française et le Vatican* [French action and the Vatican], which can be bought in Milan too.[1] Besides that, I would like to get the *Manualetto di linguistica* [Manual of linguistics] by Giulio Bertoni and Matteo Giulio Bartoli, printed in Modena in 1925 or 1926. I had ordered a small book by Finck from the Sperling and Kupfer bookstore (Via Larga 23); since I didn't remember the title, instead of the book I wanted they've sent me one that might be rather interesting for a person who wants to study Chinese, Lap, Turkish, Georgian, Samoan, and the dialect of the Negroes of Zambia, but is not yet of interest to me, since I have not as yet decided to undertake such arduous labors. The exact title of the book I want is: F. N. Finck,[2] *Die Sprachstamme des Erdkreises* [The language families of the world] published by Teubner in Leipzig, in the collection "Aus Natur und Geisteswelt" [Of nature and the spiritual world]. This is a classification of all the languages in the world, but the subject of the book is only the classification and not the separate study of the languages. Instead, the book that I received is definitely devoted to the basic grammatical elements of the languages I mentioned above (as well as Arabic and modern Greek), together with a collection of short essays. I would like to tell you a Zambian Negro story about some young girls who were playing in the forest with snakes, which is entitled *Za bakazana n in-zoca* (literally: concerning some organisms—persons—girls with snake-organisms), but it would be too complicated; in any case, you can admire the Negroes' concision as compared with European prolixity; actually I'm not quite sure whether some of the sounds shouldn't be reproduced by a clack of the tongue and not by a vocal articulation. I want to hold on to this book: I will send it to Giulia with the recommendation to study Lap, Samoan, and Negro; I really want her to get angry. It will be a complement to her geography studies, which have cost me so much agitation and propaganda effort. What do you say about that? Don't go to too much trouble for these books. You can go to the Sperling Bookstore in my name and ask them to send the books to me. If possible I would like to have the special number of *Europe Nouvelle* devoted to the Vatican and France, which appeared some time around last February or March. You could also send me a few issues of *Die literarische Welt* (The Literary world), which perhaps is on sale, as it is in Rome, at the Modernissima Bookshop. I embrace you.

Antonio

1. The Action Française movement, founded in 1899 by Charles Maurras (1868–1952) and other intellectuals of the Ligue de la Patrie Française, provided the French extreme Right with a doctrine combining "organic" nationalism, monarchism, and rejection of democracy and socialism. Léon Daudet (1867–1942) was the first editor of the movement's newspaper, *Action Française*.

2. Franz Nikolaus Finck (1867–1910), author of books on the languages of the Celts, Armenians, Gypsies, and Bantus. In prison Gramsci translated the book by Finck that he mentions into Italian.

October 10, 1927

Dearest Tania,

After Thursday's visit, I spent a long time thinking and I have decided to write what I didn't have the courage to say to you in person. I believe that you should not stay in Milan any longer on my account. The sacrifice you are making is too disproportionate. You will not be able to recover your health in this damp climate. Of course seeing you is a great comfort to me, but how can you believe that I don't continually think about your sickly appearance and that I'm not filled with remorse at being the cause and object of your sacrifice? I believe I've guessed the main reason for your desire to remain: you think you might be able to leave with the same train on which I will be transferred and that, during the trip, you might in some way be able to comfort me. Did I guess right? Well: this aim of yours hasn't the slightest chance of being realized. The orders for the transfer will certainly be very severe and the escort will under no circumstances allow "Christians" to take an interest in the prisoners (I open a parenthesis to explain to you that convicts and detainees divide the public into two categories: "Christians" and convicts and detainees). Your plan would be futile and perhaps harmful, because it might lead to distrust and an increase in severity and strictness. You would only manage to travel under the worst conditions and arrive in Rome ill for at least another four months. Dearest Tania, I think that one should be practical and realistic even when doing good. Not that you are wasting your goodness, but you are wasting your energies and your strength; and I can no longer consent to this. I've really thought about this matter at length and I would have liked to tell you in person; but my courage really failed me on seeing you and at the thought that perhaps I would sadden you even more. My dear, I embrace you tenderly.

Antonio

October 17, 1927

Dearest Tania,

The day before yesterday I received your letter of September 27. I'm happy to hear that you like Milan and that it offers you some opportunities for diversion. Did you visit the museums and the arcades? because I think that from the point of view of urban structure one's curiosity will be exhausted rather quickly. The fundamental difference between Rome and Milan seems to me to consist precisely in this: that as an urban "panorama" Rome is inexhaustible, while Milan is inexhaustible *chez soi*, that is, in the intimate life of the people of Milan, who are linked to tradition more than one might think. So Milan is little known by your average foreigner, while it has greatly attracted men such as Stendhal,[1] who were able to gain entry to its families and its salons and got to know it intimately. Its most substantial social nucleus is the aristocracy, which has been able to preserve a homogeneity and compactness that is unique in Italy, while the other groups, including the workers, are more or less gypsy encampments with neither stability nor structure, composed of layers from all the Italian regional groups. This is the strength and the national weakness of Milan, a gigantic emporium of industry and commerce, effectively dominated by an elite of old aristocratic families that have the strength of a tradition of local government (you should know that

Milan even has a special Catholic cult, the Ambrosian cult,[2] of which the old Milanese are most jealous and that is tied to this situation). Forgive the digression. But you know that I am a big chatterbox and get carried away whenever a subject interests me.

About the books. Of course, you mustn't drag such heavy luggage around. I also believe that it would be better to send the books to my address at the Roman prison,[3] so that the customs check and the police investigation can take place at the prison.

Here in storage I have a fibreboard suitcase and a traveling sack, both of which are quite capacious; they'll be sufficient. For my personal use I won't need more than a pillow case in which I will pack linens and other indispensable objects. I'll put in a request that these things be handed to you at the door. In the suitcase there should be: a thermos bottle that I don't need because I don't use it, some tins of Nestlé's milk, some cakes of soap as well as my watch and my fountain pen that might be damaged if they are not used. So you can keep them for me and use them, although the watch is anything but elegant and modern (by the way: Giulia has often tried to get the chain, which is actually worse than the watch and that I haven't given her precisely because it seemed to me such an odd whim).

Write me more about your impressions of Milan. I embrace you affectionately and look forward to seeing you.

Antonio

1. Henri Beyle (1783–1842), known as Stendhal, was born in Grenoble but took Milan as his adopted city and made it one of the settings of his novel *The Charterhouse of Parma*.
2. A reference to the special attachment the Milanese feel to Saint Ambrose (340?–397), bishop of Milan and one of the greatest fathers of the Church.
3. Gramsci mistakenly thought that he was about to be transferred back to the Regina Coeli prison in Rome.

October 24, 1927

Dearest Mother,

I haven't received anything from you after the insured letter, but I am writing to you all the same for various reasons: (1) because I have the impression that for a few months now my correspondence has become very irregular in its arrivals and departures; one more letter sent is one more probability that one of them will arrive. (2) because it is probable that I will soon be moved from Milan to Rome for the trial and for some weeks I may not be able to write.[1] You mustn't become too anxious because of all these problems; just think that I am absolutely at peace and that I am sure that the whole matter will end well, not immediately, but at least in a couple of years. And I have learned to wait without losing my patience. My affectionate greetings to all. I embrace you.

Nino

1. Gramsci did not leave the Milan prison for Rome until May 11, 1928.

October 31, 1927

My dear Berti,

It's been about a month now that I haven't received any letters from you. Nor have I have received a letter from Lauriti that you had mentioned and Amadeo's[1] announcement contained in a postcard—"we shall write"—has not been followed by any writing. I believe that you have written to me and that the letters are still on their way; it is probable that my letters too have run aground near some Cape of Good Hope. I write you all this also because the anniversary of my arrest is approaching, I have calculated that this year is the most epistoliferous of my entire life; it is possible that I didn't write as many letters in all of my (preceding!) existence as I've written this year.[2] Let this be said especially for you, who again and again have insinuated calamitous rumors with regard to my congenital antiepistolography!

It seems that we shall remain in Milan all through this year. Affectionate regards to all our friends.

Antonio

1. Amadeo Bordiga.
2. There are 188 letters in Gramsci's private correspondence and seven political letters, several quite long and cosigned by other Italian Communists, in Antonio Santucci's critical edition of Gramsci's *Lettere, 1908–1926* (Turin: Einaudi, 1992).

October 31, 1927

Dearest Tania,

I have at this very moment received your letter of the twenty-first together with the two letters from Giulia. Didn't you really know anything about her illness? Often during your visits I had the impression that there was something you were holding back, and a few weeks ago I had really decided to ask you; but in prison a person acquires a very complicated psychology, unfortunately! and at the last moment I didn't want to. You promised to always tell me the truth; and I don't even want to begin doubting your promise. Rest assured; I will not take it in bad part and I will not wrack my brain senselessly. But I want to be informed, always. You too should write to Giulia to send me photographs of herself and the children. Those taken after her illness. I've delayed writing this letter to wait for the mail distribution. It is too late and I don't want to write to Giulia too hastily. I embrace you tenderly.

Antonio

November 7, 1927

Dearest Mother,

I've received Carlo's insured letter of October 28 and your letter of the twenty-fifth. Please thank Carlo very warmly for the money he has sent me; tell him that now I'm taken care of for some time and that if I need anything I will certainly write to him. I really don't want him to sacrifice too much for me; who knows when I'll be able to pay him back!

I don't have the news about the trial that you say you have read in the newspapers, because for several months now I no longer read the dailies. I too thought that I would have to leave for Rome and that in fact is what I wrote you in my last letter; but a few days ago I was informed that the trial would take place only at the end of January or the beginning of February. So I will remain in Milan for a few more months, which does not displease me at all, for it is not pleasant to travel at this time of year (to travel as a prisoner of course!). You mustn't have any anxieties, and you must only think that I am calm. Ah! what are we going to do about these mothers! If the world had always been in their hands, men would still be living in caves, clad only in the skins of billy goats! And you mustn't worry about my health either. I've been informed that abroad they have published some nonsense in this regard, and I wouldn't like some "compassionate" soul to make sure that you hear it (it is true, unfortunately, that bad news always reaches to the ends of the earth), you must believe only what I write you since I am better informed than everyone else and I have no reason to hide the truth from you. My sister-in-law is still here in Milan and she continues to spoil me like a child, sending me every day something that gives me the impression that I am free to eat everything I might desire. I am unable to convince her to return to Rome, among other reasons because Milan's climate at this time of year is not the best. I have finally received news about the children, who are well and getting big; Giulia, however, has been ill for a few months. I'm very sad about the death of Aunt Maria Domenica,[1] she was good, at bottom, notwithstanding her coarseness, and she was certainly the only likable relative we had (after Uncle Serafino). I remember very well the ways and words of all these people, when we were children, and I remember that I went to Aunt Maria Domenica's house most willingly; you understand certain things even though I don't put them into words. Dear mother, an affectionate embrace for everyone and many kisses to you.

Nino

1. Maria Domenica Corrias, a cousin of Gramsci's mother.

November 7, 1927

Dearest Tania,

Wednesday, during your visit, I was really a fool. I've thought it over for several days. It seems to me I acted with almost brutal coldness. I did not thank you for the fifty lire deposited by you and I did not even inform you that they had been entered in my account. I'm ashamed of myself, truly.

Saturday I received the two towels, the dust cloth, and the other items that I've not yet been able to identify exactly: one that could be a handkerchief I'm using as a napkin; in any case I don't think this will be too much of a drop in status for it. I will put aside the other colored pieces, presumably handkerchiefs, until you instruct me as to their intended purpose. I believe in any event that you have formed too lofty an idea what the dishrag-towels should be made of and that you would have done well to follow my realistic suggestion that hemp is the most appropriate textile material. The linen of the dust cloth is too noble a fiber to fall so low; in my village they use linen only for the trousseaus of young brides. Dear Tania, I embrace you affectionately.

Antonio

November 7, 1927

Dearest Julca,

I've received your two letters, written around the middle of September. So I have forgotten the long period of time that went by without news from you. But it is really dreadful to remain without news for so long. I'm no longer able to orient myself, for instance; I feel rather confused, and I will also have to make a certain effort to stop soft pedaling the flow of my thoughts and feelings. You mustn't let these words upset you. Of course I feel somewhat numb and want to inform you of my precise state of mind. You must help me to unwind myself little by little. You must write to me at length and whenever possible, about your life and that of the children, about whom I know nothing, save for the general news concerning their health. I embrace you tenderly.

Antonio

November 14, 1927

Dearest Tania,

I already have several books with me in my cell. The *Quintino Sella in Sardegna* [Quintino Sella in Sardinia] and the Mondadori catalogue. Finck's book and the book by Maurras have arrived, but they have not yet been handed to me. It is strange that I had asked my mother for the book on Quintino Sella; I believe it is one of the first books I ever read, because it was among the books in the house, and yet it has not evoked anything for me. I would also like to have the following publications:

1. Benedetto Croce, *Teoria e storia della storiografia* [Theory and history of historiography] (Laterza, Bari).

2. Machiavelli, *Le più belle pagine* [The best pages] edited by G. Prezzolini (Treves).

3. Mario Sobrero, *Pietro e Paolo* [Peter and Paul] (Treves).

4. De Agostini Atlas-Calendar for 1927.

5. Catalogue of the Vallecchi Publishing house in Florence, which you can request from the Sperling bookstore. Find out whether in the "Complete Works" series of the Barbera publishing house in Florence the complete Machiavelli has appeared and how much it costs; but I'm afraid it is a bit too expensive, at least a hundred lire. In that case *The Best Pages* in the Treves edition will be sufficient. When the Machiavelli centenary occurred, I read all the articles published by the five dailies that I used to read at the time; later on I received the special issue of *Marzocco*[1] on Machiavelli.[2] I was struck by the fact that none of the writers on the centenary made a connection between Machiavelli's books and the development of the States in all of Europe during the same historical period. Deflected by the purely moralistic problem of so-called Machiavellianism they did not see that Machiavelli was the theoretician of the national States ruled by absolute monarchies, i.e., that he in Italy theorized about what in England was energetically accomplished by Elizabeth, in Spain by Ferdinand the Catholic, in France by Louis XI, and in Russia by Ivan the Terrible, even though he was not and could not be acquainted with some of these national experiences, which in reality represented the historical problem of the epoch that Machiavelli had the genius to intuit and present systematically. I embrace you, dear Tania, after this digression that will probably have a very limited interest for you.

Antonio

1. *Il Marzocco* was a cultural review published in Florence.

2. See letter to Tania, March 19, 1927, n. 1. For an example of Machiavelli's influence on Gramsci's political thought, see especially section 2, "The Modern Prince," in Hoare and Smith, eds., *Selections from the Prison Notebooks*, pp. 123–205.

—————————

November 14, 1927

Dear Giulia,

I want to send you at least a greeting every time I'm allowed to write. A year has passed since the day of my arrest and almost a year since the day I wrote you my first letter from prison. I've changed very much during this time: I believe I've grown stronger and more stable. The state of mind that dominated me when I wrote you that first letter (I won't even try to describe it to you, because it would horrify you) now makes me laugh. I believe that during this year Delio must have had the possibility of receiving impressions that will accompany him throughout his whole life; this cheers me up. I embrace you tenderly.

Antonio

—————————

November 21, 1927

Dearest Mother,

It has been a few weeks now since I received any news from you or Carlo. I think that I have already informed you that I will remain in Milan for some time yet. I still haven't received the books you promised. My health is quite good. During these last days I've been feeling really well, since I'm living in a cell together with a friend,[1] the company reduces the feeling of boredom and this results in a better appetite. I hope to get letters from you in the coming days and then I will be able to write at greater length. Greet everyone affectionately for me. I embrace you.

Nino

1. The friend was Enrico Tulli (1898–1942), a left-wing Catholic journalist who joined the PCI in the mid–1920s and worked briefly for the Communist daily *L'Unità*. He was arrested in 1927 and was Gramsci's cell mate for several months at San Vittore prison in Milan. He was sentenced to thirteen years in prison, part of which he served in Turi, where he again was a fellow prisoner with Gramsci. According to the testimony of Umberto Clementi (Quercioli, ed., *Gramsci vivo*, p. 199), Tulli was among the group of Communist prisoners at Turi whose ideological disagreements with Gramsci led to hostility and to Gramsci's isolation. Tulli was amnestied in 1937 and soon thereafter escaped clandestinely to France. His wife, nicknamed "Pina," is mentioned several times in Gramsci's prison letters.

1. Gramsci's mother, Giuseppina, holding her granddaughter Mimma in a photo taken in the early 1920s.

2. Gramsci's father, Francesco.

3. Gramsci's sister Teresina as a young woman, in a traditional Sardinian dress.

4. The Schucht family in a photo taken in Rome around 1912–1913, not long before the family's return to Russia after an exile of twenty years. In front, Giulia at the age of sixteen or seventeen. In the center row, from left to right, Apollon Schucht, Eugenia, Lula, and Tania. Top row: Nadine, Anna, and, with his head partly covered, Vittorio.

5. Gramsci's younger son, Giuliano (center at top) as a little boy with his school-mates in Moscow.

6. Two identity cards issued to Gramsci by the Comintern at the beginning of the Fourth World Congress of the Communist International held in Petrograd and Moscow in November and December of 1922. The card on the left is headed "Russian Socialist Federated Soviet Republics." In the center are the words *Administration of the Affairs of the Council of People's Commissars,* and at bottom "Moscow, September 13, 1922, the Kremlin." On the right is pass number 704 "issued to Comrade Gramsci—Member of the Presidium of the E.C.C.I. [Executive Committee of the Communist International] for the period up to January 1, 1923."

7. Giulia Schucht in the late 1920s.

8. Tania Schucht in a photo showing her resemblance to Giulia. In late 1924, before his first actual meeting with Tania in February 1925, Gramsci had seen her in a trolley car and had momentarily mistaken her for his wife.

9. A portrait of Tania Schucht taken in the mid 1920s, at around the time of her first meeting with Gramsci in Rome.

10 and 11. Two portraits of Piero Sraffa. The photo on the left shows Sraffa in the mid-to late 1920s, at about the age of twenty-eight. The photo on the right was taken about thirty-five years later. With Tania Schucht, he became a mainstay of Gramsci's material and intellectual support system in prison.

Scrittura (autografa)

Impronte simultanee delle quattro dita lunghe della mano destra

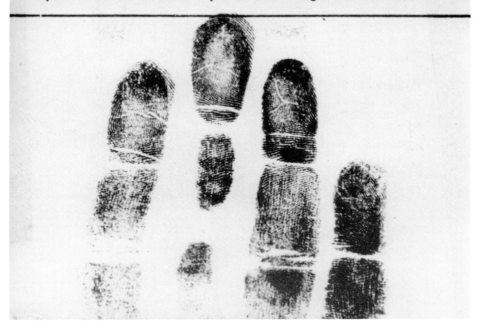

12. Gramsci's signature and fingerprints after his arrest in Rome on November 8, 1926.

10 maggio 1928

Carissima mamma,

sto per partire per Roma. Ora
mai è certo. Questa lettera mi è stata
data appunto per annunziarti il
trasloco. Perciò scrivimi a Roma d'ora
innanzi e finché io non ti abbia avver
tito di un altro trasloco.

Ieri ho ricevuto un'assicurata di
Carlo del 5 maggio. Mi scrive che mi
manderà la tua fotografia: sarò molto
contento. A quest'ora ti deve essere giunta
la fotografia di Delio che ti ho spedito
una decina di giorni fa, raccomandata.

Carissima mamma non ti vorrei ripe
tere ciò che ti ho spesso scritto per rassi
curarti sulle mie condizioni fisiche e

14. The first page of a letter from Gramsci to Tania written from Turi prison on July 10, 1933.

Facing page: 13. The first page of a letter from Gramsci to his mother written from San Vittore prison in Milan on May 10, 1928, the day before his departure for Rome. Three weeks later he was sentenced to twenty years, four months, and five days imprisonment by the Special Tribunal for the Defense of the State.

15. The prison at Turi di Bari, where Gramsci was held from July 19, 1928, to November 19, 1933.

Facing page: 16. Under the heading "First Notebook," dated February 8, 1929, Gramsci listed sixteen topics he intended to study in the following years. The first twelve are 1) theory of history and of historiography; 2) development of the Italian bourgeoisie up to 1870; 3) formation of Italian intellectual groups: development, attitudes; 4) the popular literature of "serial novels" and the reasons for its continued success; 5) Cavalcante Cavalcanti: his position in the structure and art of the *Divine Comedy;* 6) origins and development of Catholic Action in Italy and in Europe; 7) the concept of folklore; 8) experiences of prison life; 9) the "southern question" and the question of the islands; 10) observations on the Italian population: its composition, the function of emigration; 11) Americanism and Fordism; 12) the language question in Italy: Manzoni and G. I. Ascoli. Items 13 to 16 are "common sense"; types of periodicals; neo-grammarians and neo-linguists; and Father Bresciani's progeny.

Primo quaderno (8 febbraio 1929)

Note e appunti.

Argomenti principali: —

1) Teoria della storia e della storiografia.

2) Sviluppo della borghesia italiana fino al 1870.

3) Formazione dei gruppi intellettuali italiani: – svolgimento, atteggiamenti.

4) La letteratura popolare dei «romanzi d'appendice» e le ragioni della sua persistente fortuna.

5) Cavalcante Cavalcanti: la sua posizione nell'economia e struttura nell'arte della Divina Commedia.

6) Origini e svolgimento dell'Azione Cattolica in Italia e in Europa.

7) Il concetto di folklore.

8) Esperienze della vita in carcere.

9) La «quistione meridionale» e la quistione delle isole.

10) Osservazioni sulla popolazione italiana: sua composizione, funzione dell'emigrazione.

11) Americanismo e fordismo.

12) La quistione della lingua in Italia: Manzoni e G. I. Ascoli.

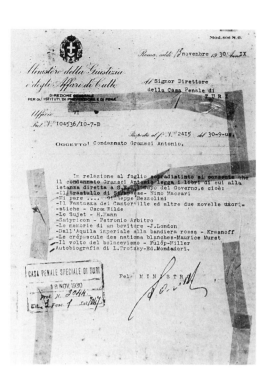

Mod. 606 M.G.

Roma, addì 13 novembre 19 30 Anno IX

Ministero della Giustizia
e degli Affari di Culto
DIREZIONE GENERALE
PER GLI ISTITUTI DI PREVENZIONE E DI PENA

Ufficio

Div. N. 104536/10-7-D

Al Signor Direttore
della Casa Penale di
T U R I

Risposta al f. N. 2415 del 30-9-us.

OGGETTO: Condannato Gramsci Antonio.

In relazione al foglio sopradistinto si consente che il condannato Gramsci Antonio legga i libri di cui alla istanza diretta a S.E. il Capo del Governo, e cioè:
- Il trastullo di Shakespeare- Nino Maccari
- Mi pare ..... Giuseppe Bezzolini
- Il Fantasma dei Canterville ed altre due novelle umoristiche - Oscar Wilde
- Le Sujet - H.Mann
- Satyricon - Petronio Arbitro
- Le memorie di un bevitore -J.London
- Dall'Aquila imperiale alla bandiera rossa - Krasnoff
- Le crépuscule des nations blanches-Maurice Muret
- Il volto del bolcevismo - Fülöp-Miller
- Autobiografia di L.Trotzky-Ed.Mondadori.

Pel MINISTRO

CASA PENALE SPECIALE DI TURI
18 NOV. 1930
Prot. N. 3044
Cat. 2 Fasc. 1 Col. 1047

ROMAIN ROLLAND
ANTONIO GRAMSCI
CEUX QUI MEURENT DANS
LES PRISONS DE MUSSOLINI

19. The building in Formia that housed the Cusumano clinic, where Gramsci was a patient but still held under police guard from December 17, 1933, to August 24, 1935.

Facing page:
Top: 17. A directive from the Ministry of Justice, dated November 13, 1930, to the warden of Turi prison granting Gramsci permission to read the books mentioned below, including Fülöp-Miller's book on Bolshevism and Trotsky's autobiography. At the lower left are the protocol number 3044 and Gramsci's prison identification number at Turi, 7047.
Bottom: 18. The cover of a pamphlet published in 1933 or 1934 written by the French novelist Romain Rolland. Under Gramsci's name are the words *Those who are dying in Mussolini's prisons.* The pamphlet was translated and distributed in many countries.

Above: 20. Tania Schucht standing beside Gramsci's grave in the English cemetery in Rome, in 1937 or 1938, shortly before her return to the Soviet Union. The plot in which Gramsci was buried had been purchased by the Schuchts years earlier.

Right: 21. Gramsci's grave in Rome, in a photo taken in the mid- to late 1940s. The words at bottom, in Latin, read "The ashes of Antonio Gramsci." These words inspired the title and the tormented political and spiritual ambivalence of Pier Paolo Pasolini's poem "Le ceneri di Gramsci."

22. A portrait of Gramsci's elder son, Delio, together with his aunt Eugenia (left) and mother Giulia. The photo was taken in the early 1960s.

Top: 23. Bronze busts of Garibaldi and Gramsci belonging to the estate of Giulia Schucht. The idea of the PCI as the heir to the political and military legacy of Giuseppe Garibaldi was central to the party's propaganda from the time of the Spanish Civil War.

Bottom: 24. A PCI meeting shortly after World War II. The banner is a close-to-exact quotation from Gramsci's statement at the proceedings of the Special Tribunal in May and June 1928 at which he and other Communist party leaders were sentenced to long terms in prison. It reads: "The day will come when you Fascists will bring Italy to ruin and then it will be up to us Communists to rebuild the country."

November 21, 1927

Dearest Tania,

I've received the following books: Francesco Crispi,[1] *I Mille* [The Thousand]; Broccardo,[2] Gentile,[3] etc.: *Goffredo Mameli e i suoi tempi* [Goffredo Mameli and his times]; C. Maurras: *L'Action française et le Vatican*[4] [French action and the Vatican].

During our last visit I forgot to thank you for the handkerchief and to compliment you as you deserve. I think that the tiny geese turned out marvelously. I don't remember whether I ever told you the story of the handkerchiefs embroidered by Genia. I had great fun teasing her, insisting that the swallows and other embroidered ornaments were all lizards. And actually both the ornaments and the initials on those handkerchiefs had a decided tendency to assume saurian features: Genia used to get really angry at seeing the value of her domestic efforts go unappreciated. I must admit, in all sincerity, that your creations are much more successful and I compliment you again.

I would like to write you at length about this question of the new suit. As far as I'm concerned it is a totally idle question. We should keep in mind that the trial will take place relatively soon and that after a person is sentenced and sent to a penitentiary, the prison administration issues the convict's regulation clothes. It is true that in this regard the regulation adopts a somewhat vague formulation: it says more or less this: "The prisoner's hair will be shaved and he will wear a loose-fitting jacket *if required*." It would seem that there can be exceptions. But I have no specific objection against the jacket and I will not initiate any procedures in order to become an "exception." So why should I have a new suit made? Since for the trial some people might say that my present jacket is a "demagogic" exhibition,[5] I will wear the suit that I have in storage and is in fairly decent condition. Of course I do not want to quarrel with you on this subject and neither do I want to displease you; I set out from absolutely utilitarian presuppositions, which can be corrected or modified only by my concern with not displeasing you. I embrace you tenderly.

Antonio

1. Francesco Crispi (1819–1901), a leader of the Italian Risorgimento who, after a youthful commitment to republican radicalism, became an exponent of Italian nationalism,

imperialism, and authoritarianism. He was prime minister for all but two years from 1887 to 1897.

2. The correct spelling is Broccardi.

3. Giovanni Gentile (1875–1944) was a longtime intellectual partner of Benedetto Croce, until the two men broke over their differing responses to Italian Fascism. His *Manifesto of the Fascist Intellectuals* of April 21, 1925, was followed on May 1 by Croce's *Manifesto of Anti-Fascist Intellectuals*. Despite some misgivings, Gentile remained loyal to Fascism until his death by assassination on April 15, 1944, in Florence. His assassins were members of the Patriotic Action Groups, urban guerrillas organized by the PCI.

4. Charles Maurras (1868–1952), founder of the French Catholic-Monarchist movement L'Action Française. See letter to Berti, January 30, 1928, for Gramsci's observations on the French Catholic movement.

5. Gramsci meant that if he were to wear a threadbare jacket at the trial, Fascist journalists would seize on this fact to accuse him of trying "demagogically" to win public sympathy.

November 21, 1927

Dearest Giulia,

In the yard, where I take my regular exercise with the other prisoners, an exhibition of the photographs of the prisoners' respective children has been held. Delio was greatly admired. Since a few days ago, I am no longer isolated but live in a common cell with another political detainee who has a pretty, charming, three-year-old little girl whose name is Maria Luisa. In keeping with a Sardinian custom, we have decided that Delio will marry Maria Luisa as soon as they will both have reached the marriageable age; what do you think of it? Of course we await the consent of both mothers, in order to give the contract a more binding value, though doing so represents a serious deviation from the customs and principles of my hometown.[1] I imagine that you are smiling and that makes me happy; it is only with great difficulty that I can imagine you smiling. Dearest, I embrace you tenderly.

Antonio

1. A joking reference to the fact that in patriarchal societies such as Italy (where traditional paternal authority was reinforced by the mores of Fascism), all decisions concerning the marriage of children are subject to final approval by the male heads of family.

November 28, 1927

Dearest Tania,

I've received your letter of 11/17; it seems to me that during our visit I already told you everything that might have reference to what you write to me. My fever lasted only a few days; it was certainly due to a slight pharyngitis that has also disappeared. The overall condition of my health has improved enormously. For the first time in a long while, I go through entire days without the slightest headache and in the morning I get out of bed truly rested, sometimes even with a tremendous desire to have a fist fight with someone, which I hope will not have any deleterious consequences for the physical integrity of my cell mate! In short, the change has done me a lot of good; the new food, prepared with Christian kindness by Tulli's wife, has had the virtue of stimulating my appetite, which had been almost assassinated by the persistent dishwater taste that characterized the food from the trattoria, as, moreover, it characterizes trattoria food in the entire universe. I sleep more and I think that I am well on the way to becoming a perfect Philistine, and this worries me very much, since I read very little and when I do it is with a conspicuous propensity for the novels of Ponson du Terrail.[1] I'm waiting for the letter in which you promised to report in minute detail the wondrous progress of Delio's physical development. I embrace you affectionately.

Antonio

1. Pierre-Alexis Ponson de Terrail (1829–1871), author of immensely popular *feuilleton*-type novels, among which are *Les exploits de Rocambole* (1859), *Les chevaliers du clair de lune* (1862), and *Le forgeron de la Cour-Dieu* (1869).

November 28, 1927

Dearest Giulia,

Last Saturday Tania personally gave me the news she had received, especially about Delio. I'm waiting for your letters and your photographs. It really seems to me that everything must have changed, in such a way that I cannot without a visual impression picture the reality of the current phase. I embrace you.

Antonio

December 5, 1927

Dearest Tania,

I have just at this moment received your letter of November 28, with the news you had hinted at during our penultimate visit. I do not feel like writing; I'm completely exhausted because of a long hair-cutting and shaving session. However I want to reassure you again and seriously with regard to my cell regime; the business of the coffees and cigarettes is definitely only a joke. In reality I am most temperate and I myself must continually overcome my retiring nature in order to admire myself; I only drink three coffees a day and I do not smoke more than fifteen cigarettes. This doesn't seem too much, or even much to me. I could cut the coffees down to two and the cigarettes to ten without difficulty and where the cigarettes are concerned I will do so. Believe me that it was only a joke. I embrace you tenderly.

Antonio

December 12, 1927

Dearest Mother,

I received your letter of November 30, after almost a month without news. You will do well to write to me or have someone write to me at least once every fifteen days; even just a postcard will be enough. With the life that I am forced to lead, the absence of news sometimes becomes a true torment. I no longer know what to write to you to comfort you and set your mind at peace. As for my peace of mind you must never have any doubts. I'm neither a child nor a simpleton, don't you agree? My life has always been ruled and directed by my convictions, which certainly were never passing whims nor momentary improvisations. Therefore prison, too, was a possibility to be faced, if not as a light diversion, certainly as a de facto necessity that did not frighten me as a hypothesis and does not depress me as a real state of affairs.[1] Besides, today I feel more confident about the state of my health, which at the start worried me somewhat. This experience has proven to me that I am also much stronger physically than I myself thought; everything contributes to making me look upon the near future coldly and with serenity. I wish that you too could become convinced of this.

I've received fairly good news from the children and from Giulia. Delio is developing very nicely. He is only three years and four months old and is already a meter tall and the little suit for a five-year-old child bought in Rome is already too small for him; his intellectual development keeps pace with this very promising physical development.

If you want to send a package to Tatiana I think you will do well to address it to the lady with whom she is lodging: Signora Isabella Galli—Via Montebello, 7, Milan—in case there should be a sudden departure for Rome, which is becoming more likely every day. At best, given the short time and the large number of packages that travel due to the coming holidays, your package could get here for New Year's or the Epiphany; so you should not send anything that is very perishable.

My warmest wishes for the Christmas holidays; I hope that you spend them without sadness, with the thought that we will surely be able to celebrate many more Christmases together, eating many roasted kid heads. I embrace you tenderly together with all the others at home.

Nino

1. For an analysis of some of Gramsci's attitudes and feelings as a political prisoner, see Frank Rosengarten, "Three Essays on Antonio Gramsci's *Letters from Prison*," *Italian Quarterly*, nos. 97–98 (Summer-Fall, 1984): 9–19. The best general account in English of his prison years is in Spriano, *Antonio Gramsci and the Party*.

December 12, 1927

Dearest Tania,

I've received the following books: (1) The De Agostini Atlas-Calendar for 1927; (2) Mario Sobrero, *Pietro e Paolo*[1] [Peter and Paul], (3) Benedetto Croce, *Stora della storiografia italiana nel secolo XIX* [History of Italian historiography in the nineteenth century]. I still haven't received Pascarella's[2] Sonnets, and the books of short stories by

Chekhov and Maupassant that you had mentioned during that other visit.

The book by Croce is not the one I had specified, which is entitled: *Teoria e storia della storiografia* [Theory and history of historiography]; this is a single volume and costs twenty lire, whereas the one I've received is in two volumes and costs forty lire. It is true that the two volumes complement each other in a certain sense and perhaps it would be a good idea to read them together, but from the "prison" point of view the one I've received is not the best. The other one contains a synthesis of the entire Crocean philosophical system, together with a true and proper revision of that system, and can give rise to lengthy meditations, (this is its specific "prison" utility). If you can procure it, I'd be thankful. You must inform the bookstore that I haven't received a book ordered quite a long time ago: Giulio Bertoni and Matteo Giulio Bartoli's *Manualetto di linguistica* [Small manual of linguistics], printed in Modena in 1925 by a publisher whose name I don't recall. If it is difficult to obtain, you can forget about it, because at this point I have abandoned my plan to write (by force majeure, given the impossibility of getting the necessary writing materials) a dissertation on the theme and with the title: "This Round Table Is Square," which I think would have become a model for present and future intellectual prison endeavors. The question, unfortunately, will remain unsolved for some time yet and this for me is a cause for real regret. But I assure you that the question does exist and already has been discussed and dealt with in several hundred academic dissertations and polemical pamphlets. And it is not a small question, if you consider that it means: "What is grammar?" and that every year, in all the countries of the world, millions upon millions of textbooks on the subject are devoured by specimens of the human race, without those unfortunates having a precise awareness of the object they are devouring. I will not develop my argument here, even schematically, because I would not have enough space; without taking into account the preoccupation that, given the relative public nature of my correspondence, these arguments might reach some student on the lookout for subjects for doctoral theses in philology and I might be defrauded of the just fame that I propose to acquire by means of my lucubrations. So if the book is hard to find, there is no need to insist.

I am advising you in case it was sent to me and has been lost and could be tracked down.

Dear Tania, you must not be upset if sometimes, during your visit, you see me nervous, disquieted and restless. I believe that this is due to the fact that in a cell one becomes used to muffled sounds and the racket of the crowd, with the dominant note of women's metallic shrieks, fills one with an unpleasant nervous disquietude. You mustn't think that I have a fever or that I am worried for other reasons. I embrace you tenderly; I would like to kiss your hands.

Antonio

1. Gramsci appears as a character, with the name Raimondo Rocchi, in Sobrero's novel *Pietro e Paolo* (1924), which is set in Turin during the years 1919–20.
2. See letter to Tania, March 12, 1927, n. 4, on Pascarella.

December 19, 1927

Dearest Tania,

I had the impression, especially during the last visit, that a certain misunderstanding has arisen between us with regard to my letters. It seemed to me that, when you allude to this you feel ill at ease, because you believe that I am prey to bad thoughts or worries that I don't want to confess. I would like to radically destroy this misunderstanding by reassuring you. One thing is true: I hesitate to speak or write about my most intimate matters because of a reticence that I absolutely cannot overcome in the presence of third parties. Therefore, sometimes, when you hint at something, in an involuntary and instinctive way I change the subject with a certain abruptness to which I hope you will not attach the slightest negative significance. Dear Tania, I'm sorry that here too I may have caused you moments of dejection and sadness. At least this is what I thought I understood, when in my cell I reflected on your attitudes and facial expressions.

How will you spend the Christmas holidays? I'm glad that you will have company and will be able to have some diversion. Will you have a Christmas tree? I trimmed my last Christmas tree in 1922 to amuse Genia, who could not leave her bed yet, or at least could not yet walk without holding on to the walls and furniture. I don't remember exactly whether she had gotten out of bed; I do remember that the small tree stood on the table next to her bed and was thickly covered with small wax matches that were all lit simultaneously as soon as Giulia, who had given a concert for the patients, returned to the room, where I had also stayed to keep Genia company.

Dear Tania, I would like to comfort you, because I'm still under the impression of your sorrowful, dispirited state of mind; I embrace you tenderly.

Antonio

December 19, 1927

Dearest Mother,

I received your insured letter of December 12; a few days before that I received Boullier's book on Sardinia[1] that I didn't even remember I had. Thank you for the money you sent. I have expressly bought a wedge of Christmas panettone, which I intend to eat as though you yourself had sent it to me directly. Of course I would prefer a nice dish of *kulurzones*[2] like those made by tiu[3] Franziscu Frore, with a pair of roasted kid's heads; don't you agree? But perhaps Franziscu Frore died, taking the culinary secret with him to his grave. I hope that all of you will have a good time during the holidays, without melancholy and without regrets; I wish this for you with all my heart. I too am sure that I will enjoy them well enough; for my health is good and I will eat my panettone with a glass of white wine drunk to your health. I embrace you tenderly, together with everyone at home.

Nino

1. Auguste Boullier, *I canti popolari della Sardegna* [Popular songs of Sardinia], trans. Raffaele Garzia (Bologna, 1916). The original French edition was published in 1864.
2. See letter to mother, February 26, 1927, n. 3.
3. In this instance, as in some other letters written to his mother, Gramsci used the Sardinian word for uncle, *tiu*.

December 26, 1927

Dearest Tania,

And so holy Christmas has also passed, and I can imagine how fatiguing it must have been for you. In truth, I've thought of its special nature only from this point of view, the only one that could interest me. The sole remarkable fact here was a general excitation of vital spirits throughout the prison environment; one could notice this phenomenon developing for an entire week. Everyone looked forward to something exceptional and the expectation gave rise to a whole series of small typical manifestations, which as a whole imparted this impression of an outburst of vitality. For many the exceptional thing was a portion of spaghetti and a quarter liter of wine, which the administration issues three times a year instead of the usual soup: but what an important event this is nevertheless. Don't think for a moment that I'm amused by it or laugh at it. I perhaps might have done so before having experienced prison. But I've seen too many moving scenes of prisoners who were eating their bowl of spaghetti with religious scrupulousness, sopping up with a small piece of bread even the faintest trace of grease that might still cling to the earthenware bowl! One of the prisoners wept because in a carabinieri barracks where we were in transit only a double ration of bread was distributed instead of the regulation soup; he had been in jail for two years and the hot soup was for him his blood, his life. It is quite understandable why the reference to daily bread has been included in the Our Father.

I thought about your kindness and your abnegation, dear Tania. But the day passed rather like all the others. Perhaps we chatted less and read more. I read a small book by Brunetière on Balzac,[1] a sort of punitive drill for disobedient children. But I don't want to bore you with this subject. Instead I want to tell you an episode of my childhood that occurred around Christmas, which will amuse you and show you a characteristic feature of life in my part of the world. I was fourteen years old and I was in the third grade of gymnasium at Santu Lussurgiu, a small town about eighteen kilometers from mine and where I believe there still exists a town high school that to tell the truth is quite run down. In order to have twenty-four extra hours at home, another boy and I started off on foot on the afternoon of December 23 instead of waiting until the next morning for the stagecoach. We walked and walked and walked and we were about half way there, in a completely deserted and solitary spot; to our left, approximately one hundred yards from the road, there stretched a row of poplars surrounded by thickets of mastic bushes. We heard a first rifle shot over our heads; the bullet whistled by at a height of about ten meters. We thought this was a random shot and continued on unconcerned. A second and then a third closer shot immediately warned us that we were being fired at and so we threw ourselves into a ditch, and stayed there, hugging the ground for quite a while. When we tried to get up, another shot and so it went for approximately two hours with about a dozen shots pursuing us, as we crawled along, each time that we tried to get back on the road. It was certainly a group of pranksters who wanted to amuse themselves by frightening us—but what a sense of humor eh? We arrived home when it was pitch dark, quite tired and muddy, and we didn't tell the story to anyone, so as not to frighten the family, but we weren't too frightened ourselves for during the following carnival holiday we repeated the journey on foot without incident. And so I've almost completely filled my four pages! I embrace you tenderly.

Antonio

But the story is really true; it isn't one of those tall tales people reel off about bandits!

1. Ferdinand Brunetière (1849–1906), French literary critic who was for many years editor of the *Revue des Deux Mondes*. Gramsci refers to his *Honoré de Balzac, 1799–1850* (Paris: Calmann-Lévy, 1905).

December 26, 1927

My dear Berti,

I've received your letter of November 25 with a certain delay. I knew that the group of internees had been sent to jail in Palermo, but I did not know the precise charge; I thought that what was involved was a disciplinary hearing before the local magistrate, moved to Palermo only because of the limited capacity of the jail on the island. Well! dear Berti we must have patience![1]

My acquaintance with lawyers is more or less the same as yours. I think that you'll have time to think about it, if the pretrial investigation is thorough and they pack you off to Rome. I, personally, have not yet given thought to this serious problem, which rather makes me laugh. I would quite possibly even dispense with counsel, if I were not amused in advance at imagining his speech, that is to say, his harangue, and if I did not follow the general principle of not neglecting any legal possibilities. My amusement would be greatest if I could choose some dormant Freemason democratic lawyer, who would be embarrassed and get red in the face;[2] but, unfortunately, it will be necessary for us to ration our amusements (for instance can you imagine the position today of one of those lawyers who in 1924–1925 maintained and wrote that we were in agreement with the government, or something of that sort?).

Dear Berti, keep up your good spirits; worry only about your physical health, so that you will be able to steadfastly endure any hardship. A fraternal embrace.

Antonio

Give my cordial greetings to Maria and many compliments for her offspring. Tulli is with me in the cell and sends his affectionate greetings.

1. In October 1927, Berti, with other political internees on the island of Ustica, had been arrested on the charge of using the "school" (that Gramsci and Bordiga had created a year or so earlier) for anti-Fascist activities. See letters to Sraffa, December 21, 1926 and January 2, 1927; to Tania, January 3, 1927; and to Julca, January 15, 1927.

2. Gramsci is poking fun at lawyers who would have been embarrassed if their previous or still "dormant" ties to Freemasonry, which was outlawed by Fascism, were to surface.

1928

January 2, 1928

Dearest Mother,

How did you spend this series of holidays? I hope very well; without worries and without having to complain about your health. I spent them very simply, as you can well imagine; but as long as we have our health! . . .

For Christmas I would have liked to send you a telegram with my best wishes, so that it would arrive piping hot for the occasion; but I didn't get permission. Prisoners, it would seem, do not have the right to send their family good wishes that arrive precisely on the day established by the traditional calendar as the family holiday. I really regret this for you, dearest mother, since you would have been less sad on that day if you had received my greetings. Ah well!

At any rate another year has passed, more quickly than I would have imagined, and not completely useless for me. I've learned a lot of things that otherwise I would never have known, I've seen a series of spectacles that otherwise I would never have had the chance to see. In short, I'm not completely displeased with 1927. And for a prisoner this is a great deal, don't you think? It means that I'm an exceptional prisoner and that I hope to remain such throughout the time I will have to spend in this category. I embrace you affectionately, together with everyone at home.

Nino

January 2, 1928

Dearest Tania,

And so the new year has also begun. One ought to make plans for a new life, as is the custom; but despite all my thinking about it I have not yet been able to put together such a program. This has always been a great difficulty in my life, since the early years when I began to reason. In elementary school every year around this time as the theme for an essay we were given the question: "What will you do in life." A difficult question that I solved the first time, at the age of eight, by fixing my choice on the profession of carter. I had decided that a carter united all traits of the useful and pleasant: he cracked his whip and drove his horses, but at the same time he performed a labor that ennobles man and earns him his daily bread. I remained faithful to this orientation the following year also, but for reasons that I would call extrinsic. If I had been honest, I would have said that my keenest aspiration was to become bailiff at the magistrate's office. Why? Because that year there had arrived in my town as the magistrate's bailiff an old gentleman who possessed a most appealing little black dog that was always dressed up: a red bow on his tail, a tiny saddlecloth on his back, an enameled necklace and a horse's trappings on his head. I was definitely unable to separate the little dog's image from that of his owner and the latter's profession. And yet, with much regret I gave up beguiling myself with this prospect that was so seductive to me. I was a formidable logician and had a moral integrity that would have put to shame the greatest heroes of duty. Yes, I considered myself unworthy of becoming a magistrate's bailiff and therefore of possessing such a marvelous little dog: I did not know by heart the eighty-four articles of the Statute of the kingdom![1] Just that. I had finished my second grade in elementary school (initial revelation of the carter's civic virtues!) and I had thought of taking the exemption exams in November that would have allowed me to skip third grade and go into fourth: I was convinced I could do this, but when I presented myself to the superintendent to submit my duly compiled application, I was faced by the point-blank question: "But do you know the eighty-four articles of the Statute?" I hadn't even given a thought to these articles: I had confined myself to studying the notions of "a citizen's rights and duties" contained in my textbook. And for me that was a terrible omen, which impressed me even more since on the previous twentieth of September I had participated for the first time in the commemorative procession, carrying a small Venetian lantern, and had shouted together with everyone else: "Long live the lion of Caprera!" "Long live the martyr of Staglieno!" (I don't remember whether we were shouting the "martyr" or the "prophet" of Staglieno, perhaps both of them for the sake of variety!), certain as I was that I would pass the exam and attain all the juridical rights for the electorate, becoming an active and perfect citizen.[2] But I did not know the eighty-four articles of the Statute. What sort of a citizen was I? And how could I ambitiously aspire to become a magistrate's bailiff and to possess a dog with a bow and a saddlecloth? The magistrate's bailiff is a small wheel of the state (I thought it was a big wheel); he is the repository and custodian of the law even against any possible tyrants that might want to trample it underfoot. And I did not know the eighty-four articles! and so I restricted my horizons and I once again exalted the civic virtues of the carter who at any rate can also have a dog, though without bows and saddlecloth. There you see how programs preestablished in too rigid and schematic a way crash into and shatter against harsh reality, when one has a vigilant sense of one's duty!

Dear Tania, would you say that I've walked this dog too long from tree to tree and without profit? Laugh and forgive me. I embrace you.

Antonio

1. See letter to Tania, April 18, 1927, n. 1.

2. Giuseppe Garibaldi (1807–1820) was called "the lion of Caprera" because he was interned by Cavour on the island of Caprera, off the Sardinian coast, after the victorious Sicilian expedition of 1860. "The Martyr of Staglieno" is Giuseppe Mazzini (1805–1872), who was buried in Staglieno cemetery in Genoa.

January 9, 1928

Dearest Mother,

Your package arrived on Saturday. My sister-in-law has already sent me ———[1] the sugar candies and fresa.[2] I thank you very much and I also pass on regards and thanks from Tatiana.

As for myself nothing new yet. I believe I will soon have to leave for Rome, but I do not yet know anything certain. My health is pretty good. Regards and kisses to everyone. I embrace you.

Tenderly Nino.

1. Illegible word.
2. Fresa is a type of fine-grained Sardinian bread of Arab origin.

January 9, 1928

Dearest Tania,

Let me repeat in writing the titles of the three books I mentioned to you during our last visit:

Roberto Michels,[1] *Francia contemporanea* [Contemporary France] published by Corbaccio, Milan.

Roberto Michels, *Corso di sociologia politica* [Course in political sociology], Milan, Istituto Editoriale Scientifico.

Henry Sée, *Matérialisme historique et interprétation économique de l'histoire* [Historical materialism and the economic interpretation of history], Paris, M. Giard.

These three books are favorably reviewed in the last *Riforma Sociale*. The *Corso di sociologia politica* by Michels interests me particularly because I am sure it is the reprint of the first series of lectures held at Rome University under the auspices of the department of political science recently established and inaugurated precisely by Michels: I have already read his other course on the science of administration which however was not very interesting; it dealt with "technical" presentations made by high functionaries of the state, each for his own department. Dear Tatiana, the weather is really grim, my nib demands an exceptional effort of attention so as not to splatter ink everywhere, and I am unable to make this effort right now. I embrace you affectionately.

Antonio

Yesterday I received the finished suit. Tulli assures me that it fits perfectly. The cost of the tailoring was moderate. I've also received the four Maupassant volumes and the two by Chekhov. I thank you.

1. Roberto Michels (1876–1936), German-born Italian sociologist influenced by the sociological and political theories of Vilfredo Pareto and Gaetano Mosca. His writings deal with mass parties in the modern age, bureaucracy, and problems of democracy. His pessimism concerning democracy led him eventually to accept the need for Fascism. Gramsci may be referring here to the Italian translation of Michels's *Zur Soziologie des Parteiwesens in der modernen Demokratie* [On the sociology of the party system in modern democracy] (1911).

January 23, 1928

Dearest Mother,

It's been almost two months since I have received news from you. What has happened? I hope it is only a matter of postal inefficiency, yet I cannot help but feel a certain anxiety. Why don't you at least get Carlo, Teresina, and Grazietta to send some picture postcards.

My life continues always the same. I embrace you affectionately.

Nino

At this very moment I have received your letter of January 2. Your insured letter, which arrived here on the seventeenth of December, had been mailed seven or eight days before. I already wrote to you about the package. Tatiana has written to you. Kisses.

January 30, 1928

Dearest Tania,

I hope that you have already recovered, as you read this. I think that I have been partly responsible for your ailment. I should have insisted more energetically on making you leave and not have allowed you to spend the winter season in Milan. These mists and this humidity are bad for a temperament like yours. I'm really filled with remorse. And besides you, who every week preach to me that I should take care of myself, eat, etc. etc., probably take no care whatsoever of yourself and probably waste your energies on a great heap of useless or at least unnecessary actions. But enough of that. I don't want to continue writing reproaches. I already have the impression that my letter of a fortnight ago immediately contributed to your feeling unwell. Instead I would like to cheer you up or at least make you smile.

But it isn't easy for me at this moment. Knowing that you are indisposed forces my train of thoughts into a not very happy groove and in any case I do not want to be the "journalist" with you. I hope to see you on a visit even before you've received this letter. I embrace you tenderly.

Antonio

January 30, 1928

My dear Berti,

Your letter of the thirteenth came a week ago, when I had, however, used up my two regulation letters. No news here. The usual squalor and the usual monotony. Even reading becomes more and more a matter of indifference. Of course I still read a lot but without interest, mechanically. Despite having company, I read a book a day and even more. Disparate books, as you can imagine (I've even reread *The Last of the Mohicans* by Fenimore Cooper) since that's what is distributed by the prison's rental library. During these last weeks I've read a few books sent by my family, but none of overwhelming interest. I will list them for you just to pass the time.

1. *Le Vatican et l'action française* [The Vatican and French action]. This is the so-called yellow book of the Action Française; a collection of articles, speeches, and circulars, the greater part of which I already knew because they appeared in the "Act. Franç." of 1926. In the book the political substance of the conflict is disguised by seven times seven veils. There is only the "canonical" discussion of the so-called mixed material and the "just (according to the canons) freedom" of the faithful. You know what is involved: in France there exists a Catholic mass organization, along the lines of our homegrown Catholic Action, presided over by General de Castelnau.[1] Up until the French political crisis of 1926, the nationalists were in fact the only political party that was organically tied to this organization and exploited its assets (four to five million yearly subscriptions, for example). That is, all Catholic forces were exposed to the backlashes of the adventures of Maurras and Daudet, who in 1926 had already prepared a provisional government to hoist into power in case of a collapse. The Vat., which however foresaw a new wave of anticlerical laws of the Combes[2] type,

decided to carry through a demonstrative break with "Act. Franç" and to set about organizing a democratic Catholic mass party that would have the role of a parliamentary center, in keeping with the politics of Briand-Poincaré. In Act. Franç., for obvious reasons, only semiobsequious and moderate articles were published: the violent and personal attacks were left to *Charivari*, a weekly publication that has no equivalent in our country and did not officially belong to the Party; but this part of the polemic is not reported in the book. I've seen that the orthodox have published an answer to the "yellow book" compiled by Jacques Maritain,[3] a professor at the Catholic University in Paris and the acknowledged leader of the orthodox intellectuals: this means that the Vatican has marked up a remarkable success, because in 1926 this Maritain had written a book defending Maurras and before that had signed a declaration to the same effect: today, therefore, these intellectuals have split and the isolation of the monarchists must have increased.

A book by Alessandro Zévaès, *Storia della Terza Repubblica: La Francia dal settembre 1870 al 1926* [History of the Third Republic: France from September 1870 to 1926], very superficial, but amusing. Anecdotes, ample quotations, etc. It helps to recall the most important events of French parliamentary and journalistic life.

R. Michels, *La Francia contemporanea* [Contemporary France]. This is a publishing fraud. What we have here is a totally disconnected collection of articles about certain quite special aspects of French life. Since he was born in the Rhine district of Prussia, the zone of confluence between Romanism and Germanism, Michels believes that he is destined to cement the friendship between Germans and neo-Latins, whereas he himself embodies the worst characteristics of both cultures: the haughtiness of the Teutonic philistine and the miserable fatuity of the southern attitude. And besides, this man who flaunts his repudiation of the German race like a cockade and boasts that he has given the name Mario to one of his sons to commemorate the defeat of the Cimbri and the Teutons, leaves me with the impression of a most refined hypocrisy aimed at furthering an academic career.

A collection of essays for the Goffredo Mameli centennial (Gentile, etc.)—The second edition of *I Mille* [The Thousand] by Francesco Crispi—the most interesting of them all. And there you have it— because I won't tell you about some other less notable books of a romantic character. Write to me whenever you can; but I should imagine that your possibilities are even less than mine. Cordially

Antonio

Tulli sends his regards. I must correct a mistake contained in one of my letters from Ustica. I mentioned a book on the historical method, attributing it to a certain Bernstein, whereas the person is Bernheim[4]: my memory really does not serve me well, because I used this book for two years as a text in school: obviously I've aged more than I supposed. The correct name suddenly floated up without any attendant reason. I wanted to tell you this for the sake of accuracy. Affectionate greetings.

1. General Noël-Marie-Joseph-Edouard de Currières de Castelnau (1851–1944) commanded the second French Army in World War I.

2. Emile Combes (1835–1921), radical French prime minister from 1902 to 1905, who promoted a series of laws that led to the separation of State and Church in France and to a break in diplomatic relations between France and the Holy See.

3. Jacques Maritain, *Primauté du spirituel* [The primacy of the spiritual] (Paris: Plon, 1927).

4. Ernst Bernheim, *Lehrbuch der historischen Methode* [A textbook of the historical method], the two parts of which were translated into Italian in 1897 and 1908, respectively.

February 6, 1928

Dearest Mother,

Last week I received two of your letters: one of January 25 and the insured one of February 1 with the 200 lire. For once your correspondence has arrived within a decent interval.

I assure you that my health is fairly good; if last time I only wrote some short notes, it was simply because I wasn't receiving news from you. The last fifteen days I've been getting bioplastine injections and this will at least help to bolster my strength. For the rest, I spent the first half of the winter without too many shocks. It has been rather cold, and so I got chilblains, which I never had before: obviously I'm getting old and my blood has cooled off somewhat. Your two letters made me a bit angry. I hope you will not have any masses said for the favorable outcome of my trial! You mustn't worry about these things. I'm very calm and will be so even more if I can be certain that you are calm and serene. And why shouldn't you be? The fate that awaits me, as you say, is after all not so frightful: it is simply a matter of time and patience.

Give my warmest thanks to Carlo for the insured letter. Embrace everyone affectionately and to you many, many embraces.

Nino

Tatiana has fallen ill and is once again in hospital;[1] Milan's terrible climate and the drudgery of bringing me food every day are certainly responsible for her illness. So it seems to me that I, despite being in prison, am better off than all of you. Now Tatiana feels better, she has overcome the critical phase of a bronchial pneumonia. The most recent news about the children is rather good.

1. See letter to Tania, July 18, 1927, n. 2.

February 6, 1928

Dearest Tania,

I've received news about your health and also about your impatient desire to get out of the hospital. Your impatience seems utterly unreasonable. I truly regret not having the possibility of using means more persuasive than words to force you to take care of yourself in a rational manner; what makes me fly into an absolute rage is the fact that you of all people have always preached to me with such tenacity that I must take care of myself, take care of myself, take care of myself. Does that seem right to you? In this instance I feel Kantian to the tips of my hairs: "Do not ask others to do what you yourself would not be willing to do." For our situations are identical. Besides, you are undoubtedly more convinced than I of the morality of Kant's categorical maxims and you should furthermore remember the professional principle: "*Medice, cura te ipsum.*"[1] In short, you mustn't force me to present you with ultimatums. Because I'm perfectly capable not only of stopping my injections but also of no longer showing up for a visit with you if I become convinced of your lack of wisdom, and of ordering Signora Pina to box your ears.

Dear Tania, I really hope that you won't do anything contrary to the doctor's advice. Knowing that you are unwell adds to the many anxieties that besiege me; when I heard that you were ill for four or five days I was so furious with myself that I would no longer talk even to Tulli. If you want me to remain calm, you must prove to me that you are well, really well, because I cannot bear to think that I'm the cause of your illness. This is something you must absolutely promise me. It is possible that I may have to leave even before we can see each other again: but that after all is not a serious matter because we will meet again in Rome. I want you to travel under the best possible conditions. I want you to make a reservation on the express train and take a sleeping berth. In second class a berth used to cost sixty lire and I don't think the price has gone up: the reservation must be made a few days in advance. Will you do this? Do you promise? I wish I could give you a caress: I embrace you tenderly.

1. "Physician, heal thyself."

February 13, 1928

Dearest Tania,

Yesterday I heard that you are better and that perhaps you will soon be able to leave the hospital. I am very happy about the good news, but I must insist that you take the time to take care of yourself. You mustn't fool yourself into thinking that the good season and fine weather have arrived: actually I think that in Milan this is the worst time of the year because of the sudden changes in temperature. Last year it snowed through all of March. How do you pass the time? Do you have books to read? I continue to give myself injections: today it will be the 20th; you see how good I am!

I've been told that there is a letter from you, but I have not yet received it. The first time you come for a visit I want you to be completely recovered; I want to see you healthy, otherwise I'll become terribly angry and I'll ask for permission to reach over the grill to box your ears. I embrace you tenderly.

Antonio

February 20, 1928

Dearest Tania,

I've received your letter of the ninth; I am answering you at your home address, as a good omen that in a few days you will be able to leave the hospital and resume your normal life (always on the condition that you are really cured and have regained your strength).

The series of injections is going ahead full tilt: indeed, this morning I had authentic and irrefutable proof of my incipient march toward obesity, the testimony of the barber. He assured me that his razor glides more smoothly because in recent times my cheeks have plumped out a bit. This should settle the problem of my health once and for all.

I've begun sending out some books: up until now I've sent out about forty volumes. From the bookstore I've received the book by Sée you had ordered. As soon as you are able to resume a normal life, I will let you know about some other publications to be sent to me. Actually I had decided, for a while, not to ask for anything more, but I hadn't thought that we were at the beginning of a new year and that Professor Giorgio Mortara's *Prospettive economiche per il 1928* [Economic prospects for 1928] and the *Almanacco letterario Mondadori* [The Mondadori literary almanac] were about to be published. Despite everything, I cannot stifle the need to follow, though very approximately, what happens in the vast and terrible world. Dearest Tania, I hope to see you soon. This time they ought to grant you a visual visit too, so that I will be able to embrace you. If they wish to protect themselves against my terrible schemes they could give orders to subject me to a special body search before and after the visit. I embrace you.

Antonio

February 20, 1928

Dearest Teresina,

Your letter of January 30 arrived with the photograph of your children. I thank you and I would be very happy to receive more letters from you.

The worst hardship of my present life is boredom. These days that are always the same, these hours and these minutes that follow one another with the monotony of dripping water, have ended by corroding my nerves. At least the first three months after my arrest were full of movement: bounced from one end of the peninsula to the other, though at the cost of much physical suffering, I did not have the time to be bored. There were always new sights to observe, new exceptional types to be catalogued: I actually thought I was living in a fantastic fairy tale. But now it is more than a year that I have been stuck in Milan, in enforced idleness. I can read, but I cannot study, because I have not been allowed to have pen and paper at my disposal, even with all the surveillance demanded by the boss,[1] since I'm considered to be a terrible individual, capable of setting fire to the four corners of the country or something along those lines. Correspondence is my greatest diversion, but very few people write to me. Besides it's a month now that my sister-in-law has been ill and I no longer have my weekly visit with her.

I'm very worried about mother's state of mind, however I don't know what to do to reassure and comfort her. I would like to infuse her with the conviction that I am very calm, as I really am, but I can see that I'm not succeeding. There is a whole area of emotion and ways of thinking that forms a kind of abyss between us. For her my incarceration is a dreadful misfortune, somewhat mysterious in its concatenation of causes and effects; for me it is an episode in the political struggle that was being fought and will continue to be fought not only in Italy but throughout the world, and for who knows how much longer. I have been caught in it, just as during the war one could become a prisoner, knowing that this could happen and that even worse could happen. But I'm afraid that you think the same as mother and that for you these explanations are like a riddle expressed in an unknown language.

I've examined the photograph at length, comparing it to those you had sent me before (I had to interrupt this letter to let them shave me; I no longer remember what I meant to write to you and I don't feel like thinking about it again. Let's leave it for next time). Affectionate greetings to all. An embrace.

Nino

1. Gramsci uses the word *capo*, referring to Benito Mussolini. In prison, hoping to obtain as many privileges as the system legally allowed, Gramsci scrupulously complied with the rules, regulations, and terminology of the Fascist government, provided that such compliance did not involve making unacceptable political or moral compromises with the regime.

_____

February 27, 1928

Dearest Tania,

Due to a most fortuitous conjunction of favorable stars, your letter of the twentieth was delivered to me on the twenty-fourth, together with Giulia's letter. I have much admired your diagnostic talents but I did not fall into the subtle snares of your literary cunning. Don't you think it would be preferable to apply one's talents to other subjects rather than on one's own person? (Not that I want evil to befall my neighbor, that is, of course, if one can speak of a neighbor in this instance. Have you read and studied Tolstoy's ideas carefully? I would like you to confirm for me the precise meaning that Tolstoy gives to the evangelical concept of "neighbor." It seems to me that he holds to the literal, etymological meaning of the word: "one who is closest to you, the people in your family and, at the most, the people of your village"). In short, you did not succeed in putting up a smokescreen by displaying before me your abilities as a physician so as to make me think less about your condition as a patient. What's more, when it comes to phlebitis, I've been able to acquire specialized knowledge, for during the last two weeks of my stay in Ustica, I was compelled to listen to the long disquisitions of an elderly attorney from Perugia who suffered from it and had made sure to receive four or five publications on the subject. I know that it is a rather serious and very painful illness; will you really have the necessary patience to cure yourself properly and unhurriedly? I hope so. I can contribute to your being patient, by writing you longer letters than usual. This is a small effort that will not cost me much, provided you are satisfied with my chatter. And besides, I'm feeling much more cheerful than before.

Giulia's letter has certainly put my mind more at ease. I will write to her separately at some length, if I'm able to, because I do not want to reproach her and I still don't see how I will be able to write her a long letter without reproaching her. Do you think it is right, in fact, that she doesn't write to me when she feels ill or in distress? I think that it is precisely under such circumstances that she ought to write to me more often and at greater length. But I don't want to turn this letter into a communication from the complaints department.

To help you pass the time, I'll tell you about a small "penitentiary" disputation that has unfolded in fits and starts. A certain fellow who I believe is an Evangelist or a Methodist or a Presbyterian (I was reminded of him in connection with the above-mentioned "neighbor") was very indignant because those poor Chinese, who sell small objects certainly manufactured on the assembly line in Germany, but that give our compatriots the impression of annexing at least a small piece of Cathay folklore, were still allowed to circulate freely in our cities. According to our Evangelist, the danger to the homogeneity of beliefs and the ways of thinking of Western culture was great; what we have here, in his opinion, is a grafting of Asiatic idolatry onto the trunk of European Christianity. These small images of the Buddha would in the end exert a particular fascination that might act as a reagent on European psychology and lead to ideological neoformations totally different from the traditional one. That an individual such as the above-mentioned Evangelist should entertain such preoccupations was certainly very interesting, even though the preoccupations had a very remote origin. But it was not difficult to trap him in a briar patch of ideas with no way out, by pointing out to him that:

1. The influence of Buddhism on Western civilization has much deeper roots than it might seem, because throughout the Middle Ages, from the Arab invasion until approximately 1200, Buddha's life circulated in Europe like the life of a Christian martyr, sanctified by the Church, which only after several centuries realized its error and deconsecrated the pseudosaint. The influence that such an event may have had in those days when religious ideology was very lively and constituted the masses' only way of thinking is incalculable.

2. Buddhism is not an idolatry. From this point of view, if there is danger, it is instead represented by the music and dance imported into Europe by the Negroes. This music has actually conquered an entire stratum of the cultivated European population, indeed it has created a real fanaticism. Now it is quite impossible to imagine that continuous repetition of the physical movements that Negroes perform in dancing around their fetishes, that continually having dinned into one's ears the syncopated rhythms of jazz bands, should not have ideological consequences: (a) this is an enormously widespread phenomenon involving millions upon millions of people, especially among the young; (b) these are very forceful and violent sensations that thus leave behind deep and enduring traces; (c) these are musical phenom-

ena, that is, manifestations that express themselves in the most universal language in existence today, in the language that most rapidly communicates total images and impressions of a civilization not only alien to ours but certainly less complex than the Asiatic, primitive and elementary, that is, on the basis of the music and dance, easily generalizable and assimilable to the entire psychic world. In short, the poor Evangelist became convinced that, just when he was afraid of turning into an Asian, he in fact, without realizing it, had become a Negro and that this process was already terribly advanced, at least to the point of his being a half-breed. I don't know what the final results were: but I believe that he is no longer able to give up having coffee with jazz on the side, and that from now on he will look at himself more attentively in the mirror in order to catch a glimpse of the colored pigments in his blood. Dear Tania, I wish you a full and rapid recovery: I embrace you.

Antonio

February 27, 1928

Dearest Giulia,

I've received your letter of December 26, 1927, with the postscript of January 24 and the attached notes. I was really very happy to get your letters. But for some time now I had already become calmer. I have changed a great deal in all this time. There were days when I thought that I had become apathetic and inert. Today I believe that I've been mistaken in this self-analysis. And so I no longer even believe that I was disoriented. It was a crisis of resistance to this new way of life that was implacably imposing itself through the pressure of the prison environment, with its rules, its routine, its deprivations, its needs, and an enormous mass of very small things that follow each other mechanically for days, for months, for years, always the same, always with the same rhythm, like grains of sand in a gigantic hourglass. My entire physical and psychic organism was resisting tenaciously, with all of its molecules, to being absorbed by this external environment, but every now and then I had to recognize that some of this pressure had succeeded in overcoming my resistance and in modifying a certain area of myself, and at that a swift, total upheaval would take place in order to suddenly repel the invader. Today a whole cycle of changes has already unfolded because I've reached the quiet resolve not to oppose what is necessary and ineluctable with the earlier means and modes that were ineffective and inept but to dominate and control the process under way with a certain ironic spirit. Besides, I've become convinced that I will never turn into a perfect Philistine. At any given moment I will be able to throw off with a shrug the half donkey and half sheep hide that this environment grows over one's natural skin. Perhaps this is something I will never obtain again: to give my natural, physical skin its smoky color. Valia will no longer be able to call me his smoky companion. I'm afraid that Delio, despite your contribution, by now is probably much smokier than I! (Are you protesting?) This winter I lived almost three months without seeing the sun, except in some distant reflection. My cell receives a light that is midway between that of a cellar and an aquarium.

However you mustn't think that my life goes by as monotonous and the same as it might seem at first sight. When one has become accustomed to aquarium life and has adapted one's sensory system to seize the muffled and crepuscular impressions that flow through it (always assuming a somewhat ironic standpoint), an entire world begins to teem around you, with a particular vivacity of its own, with its peculiar laws, with its essential course. What happens is the same as when one casts a glance at an old tree trunk half ruined by time and inclement weather and then little by little one focuses one's attention ever more fixedly. At first one sees only some damp, mushrooming fungus, with a big snail here and there, which drips slime and slithers by slowly. Then, a little at a time, one sees an ensemble of colonies of tiny insects that move about and work, repeating the same efforts and going over the same path again and again. If one preserves one's aloof posture, if one does not turn into a big slug or a small ant, everything in the end becomes interesting and helps to pass the time.

Every detail that I am able to gather about your life and the life of the children offers me the chance to try to elaborate a larger picture. But these elements are too scanty and my experience has been too meager. What's more, the children must be changing too quickly at this age for me to be able to follow them in all their movements and conjure up a picture of them. Of course I am sure that about all this I am very disoriented. But I suppose this is inevitable. I embrace you tenderly.

Antonio

March 5, 1928

Dearest Mother,

I'm terribly sorry that you didn't receive the letters that I wrote you in January and February and as a result thought I was indisposed, as you say in your letter of February 27, which arrived very quickly. Certainly during this period I wrote you at least six letters, which have all probably arrived by now. I write to you at a minimum every fifteen days, sometimes I have even written to you every week. I received the insured letter of January 6 and on the ninth following I told you about it. A few weeks ago I got a letter from Teresina with a photograph of the children; I answered immediately.

These mixups pain me very much because of their effects on your spirit. But you must not always imagine the worst possibilities and torment yourself continually. You should know that if I were ill, if I did not feel well in any manner or degree, I would inform you immediately, because I think that it would be even worse not to inform you, and the sudden news of my illness would be even more alarming for you. And so you are wrong to think that I'm always gloomy and at the mercy of who knows what despair. But no, not at all. Of course I'm not always dancing with joy and laughing continually, but neither am I always gloomy and desperate, like a raven perched on a cypress at the cemetery. I'm really calm and serene, as behooves one who has an untroubled conscience and looks upon life without illusion. I'm truly sorry that you are obsessed by the thought that I am in despair; if this were someone else instead of you I would be offended and consider myself mortally insulted. After all, I'm not a child, isn't that so? who has gotten into trouble inconsiderately and frivolously. You see, I was about to get excited and even started to yell at you! But, really, how can I convince you that you too must remain calm and serene? Must I berate you a bit to obtain this?

I'm sorry that Aunt Nina Corrias died.[1] Poor woman. I believe that she was very good, despite her innocent pose of mainland superiority. And besides, she certainly contributed to rejuvenating the environment in Ghilarza to some extent, without fear of offending prejudices, institutions, and persons. Do you remember the first women's club she sponsored? And the time when she had her brother the census taker buried without religious rites? Remember the scandals, the mutterings? I remember absolutely everything and even though many of her "progressive" initiatives made me laugh a bit, I believe that at bottom these were serious matters and she devoted a fervor to them that was in any event praiseworthy. Did she confess and take communion before dying? And Uncle Francesco, is he still alive? (I seem to remember that Giovanna died, but I'm not sure of it). Such news from our town interests me very much. You mustn't believe that these are negligible matters and that they bore me, or that all this is just gossip. I'm always as curious as a ferret and I appreciate even the smallest thing. Besides, what do you expect, that every week in Ghilarza they should invent gunpowder? I was also interested in Corroncu and Brisi Illichidiu and tia Juanna Culamontigu. They were original types, of their kind, more than many others who were popular and were really very boring and with whom one could do nothing but exchange compliments and salaams.

So then, to conclude: my health is fairly good; I'm not at all gloomy and I send you many, many good wishes for your coming name day. Send me a nice photograph, but it must be just the way you are at home without frills, right? without coquettishness! I hug you very, very tightly.

Nino

1. Nina Corrias was an elementary school teacher who founded a women's cultural circle in Ghilarza to which Gramsci's mother belonged.

March 5, 1928

Dearest Tania,

Your letter of February 28 also reached me with marvelous promptness; on March 3 no less, after only four days. I hope that this will continue and that such solicitude extends to all our correspondence. But poor mother is desperate, because for two months now she hasn't received any letters from me. On February 27 she still hadn't received my letter of January 9, which I absolutely remember having written, and so she thinks that I am seriously ill and physically unable to write.

I offer you congratulations on your reacquired strength that has allowed you to get up and walk. But you are on principle too optimistic and believe too much in a sort of cosmic justice! You would do better to be patient and wait until you have completely recovered, beyond any danger of relapse and complications. You really must be reasonable! Otherwise I will take Draconian measures and box your ears, without being worried or moved by your accusations of barbarous treatment!

I've read your letter with great interest, because of your observations and your new experiences. I think that there is no need to recommend indulgence to you and not only practical indulgence but also what I would call spiritual indulgence. I've always been convinced that there exists an unknown Italy, which one doesn't see, very different from the apparent and visible one. I mean to say—since this is a phenomenon that applies to all countries—that with us the difference between what one sees and what one doesn't see is deeper than in other so-called civilized nations. With us the piazza, with its shouts, its verbal enthusiasm, its arrogance, overshadows the *chez soi* more than elsewhere, relatively speaking. And so a whole series of prejudices and gratuitous assertions have come into existence concerning the solidity of family structure as well as the amount of ingenuity that providence has supposedly deigned to grant our people, etc. etc. In a very recent book by Michels, it is reported that the average Calabrian peasant, though illiterate, is more intelligent than the average German university professor; and so a lot of people feel they are relieved of the obligation of wiping out illiteracy in Calabria. I believe that family customs in the cities, given the recent formation of urban centers in Italy, cannot be judged while ignoring the overall situation of the entire country, which is still very deficient and from this point of view can be summed up in this characteristic trait: an extreme egotism in the generations between the ages of twenty and fifty, which above all damages children and the elderly. Naturally this is not a stigma of permanent civic inferiority: it would be absurd and foolish to think so. It is a fact that can be ascertained and explained historically and that will undoubtedly be overcome with a rise in the standard of living. The explanation, in my opinion, is to be found in the demographic structure of the country that before the war carried a load of eighty-three inactive persons for every hundred workers, while in France, with enormously greater wealth, the load was only fifty-two for every hundred. Too many old people and too many children compared to the in-between generations that are numerically depleted by emigration. Here you have the basis for this egotism of the generations, which at times assumes aspects of frightful cruelty. Seven or eight months ago the newspapers reported this ferocious episode: a father had massacred his entire family (his wife and three children) because, upon returning from work in the fields, he had found that his meager dinner had been devoured by his famished brood. In the same manner, and more or less on the same date, there was a trial in Milan of a husband and wife who had caused the death of their four-year-old son by keeping him tied with a wire to a table leg for months. It became clear at the trial that the man doubted his wife's fidelity and that she, rather than lose her husband by protecting her child from abuse, had agreed to his murder. They were sentenced to eight years in prison. This is the kind of crime that in the past was listed in the annual statistics of criminality under a specific heading; Senator Garofalo[1] considered the average of fifty sentences per year for such crimes as only an indication of criminal tendencies, since most often the guilty parents are able to escape all punishment due to the general custom of paying little attention to the hygiene and health of children, not to mention the widespread religious fatalism that regards the elevation of new little angels to the divine court as a special benevolence of heaven. This, unfortunately, is the most common ideology and it is not surprising that, though in attenuated and milder forms, it is still reflected even in the most advanced and modern cities. As you see, indulgence is not out of place, at least for those who do not believe in the absoluteness of principles even in such relationships, but only in their progressive development together with the development of life in general. Many, many good wishes. I embrace you.

Antonio

1. Senator Raffaele Garofalo (1851–1934), first president of the Court of Cassation and one of the founders of the positivist school of criminal law in Italy.

March 12, 1928

Dearest Mother,

In my last letter (of March 5) I made a mistake that you however were able to correct by yourself: I received the insured letter on February 4 and wrote to tell you so on February 6; so it was not January as I wrote but February. I've recently received news about the children and Giulia. Delio has been well, but the little one has been seriously ill, in danger for several months and so they were not sending me any news. The illness has delayed his development in teething and speaking, but for some time now, after his recovery, he has been doing well and making up for lost time. They've written me a world of details that I won't repeat to you because at bottom they are the usual details about the lives of small children, which mothers however consider extraordinary and marvelous and characteristic only of their particular children.

It seems certain, this time, that my departure for Rome and the trial are imminent. Perhaps it is even probable that we will leave very soon; I will try to inform you of my departure by telegram so that you will immediately be able to write to me at the new address of the judiciary house of detention in Rome. I repeat, once again, that you mustn't be alarmed whatever the hodgepodge of news the newspapers will be pleased to print. The same charges, with reference to the same articles of the Penal Code, were brought against me in 1923, when I was abroad. We were already acquitted in the first instance even though there was a document bearing signatures recognized by the defendants as authentic.[1] Now I will certainly be sentenced to many years despite the fact that the charge against me is based on a simple police report and on generic unprovable impressions; but the comparison between '23 and '28 should provide an idea of the "gravity" per se of the present trial and characterize it. That is why I am so calm. Do you think that these attendant circumstances are not what should count, but rather the real fact of the sentence and imprisonment inflicted on me? But you must also take into account the moral position, don't you agree? Indeed only this creates strength and dignity. Prison is a very ugly thing; but for me dishonor due to moral weakness and cowardice would be even worse. So you mustn't be alarmed and grieve too much, and you must never think that I'm downcast and desperate. You must have patience and in any case you mustn't believe the bunkum they might publish about me.

I hope that you have by now received all my previous letters. I send you once again my most fervid and affectionate good wishes for your name day and I embrace you tenderly.

Nino

1. Gramsci refers here to the trial held in Rome from October 18–26, 1923, of himself, Amadeo Bordiga, Ruggero Grieco, Bruno Fortichiari, Umberto Terracini and other Communist leaders on the charge of "incitement to class hatred" and anti-Fascist activity. All of the accused were acquited by reason of insufficient evidence. Gramsci was tried in absentia, since he was in Vienna at the time.

March 12, 1928

Dearest Tania,

I received your letter dated February 21 only a few days ago. I thank you for the news you convey regarding the children's health. Giulia mentioned it only in passing. I want you to keep Giuliano's lock of curly hair and I don't want you to send it to me by applying for a special permit. I can't explain exactly why, but this sort of bureaucratic procedure arouses in me a sense of invincible revulsion. I will be content with your descriptions, I assure you, without experiencing, owing to this solution, the displeasure I would feel if I knew that you on the contrary had requested a permit and given explanations, etc., etc.: I really feel such a revulsion against such things and I would really like to impress this on you.

I'm a bit worried because news of my imminent departure is again circulating, and I would be very upset if by reaching you this news should make you decide to leave the hospital before you are completely cured and possibly even leave Milan when you are still too weak. If this were to take place I would be tremendously sad and I would hold it against you for a long time. All you must think about now is to get better and regain your strength. In any case, if my departure is really imminent, we will see each other again in Rome. I will do everything just so. I've sent out some more books (another twenty-two items) and I shall quickly send off the rest. I will carry with me only the indispensable linens. I will send off the suitcase too, with a pair of shoes, the new suit, and a light overcoat. I think that the suitcase, with the linens that I will send ahead and a few books for the first days in Rome, can be shipped express; the rest of the books can go by slow freight; you will send them back to me only after you receive my instructions, because I will need only some of them for study and reference. The books you can put in a suitcase are Luigi Einaudi, *Corso di scienza della finanza* [Course in the science of finance] and the German vocabulary (I will take the grammars with me). I am also sending out to you the back issues of *Marzocco*, from which I would like to clip some articles of a historical and bibliographic nature.

In order that you not be forced in Rome to go to more trouble for our visit, you would perhaps do well to ask the pretrial judge for advice; perhaps he will be courteous enough to give you a letter of introduction to the person in charge in Rome.

Dearest Tania, you definitely must follow my advice with regard to your release from hospital. To reward you(!) for your obedience, I will explain to you in excruciating detail how it was that as a child my hair was the lightest blond and then turned the color of chestnuts (do you remember how I used to make Giulia angry with this story and with the story of my little sister's eyes that were first blue and then each became half blue and half black, then one completely black and the other blue again, etc., etc.) I embrace you affectionately.

Antonio

March 19, 1928

Dearest Tania,

On Thursday for a few moments I thought that you had already left the hospital. While Tulli was pacing up and down like a lion, waiting to be called for his visit, the door opened and instead of him I was called to go to the office. But it was only to sign the receipt for an insured letter my mother sent. I was really convinced that I was going to have a visit with you and I was very disappointed. But we must be patient. There will be another time. This time the trial is really moving toward its conclusion. This morning I was notified of the decision remanding me to trial and this should mean my imminent departure. I was also asked to appoint my personal attorney and I appointed Attorney Ariis. In truth I attach very little importance to this business of the lawyer; I would only like, before the trial, to obtain some legal information so as to write a defense memorandum that I want to be permanently attached to the dossier.[1] This for the form that I must give the note, not for its substance, which I have already thought out in all of its details.

Tomorrow I'll give myself the fiftieth injection, and that's it. I believe that I'm entitled to some rest. Later on you will advise me as to whether or not the treatment should be resumed after an interval or not. It is a week now since I've had precise news from you: it would appear that generally it is pretty good. I've sent out some more books (another twelve items). For some weeks now I haven't received *Marzocco* and since February 1, I no longer receive *Critica Fascista*[2]: the bookstore should be notified. As soon as I leave it will also be necessary to notify them of the change of address. In *Marzocco* I read that Hoepli in Milan has published a book by Arnaldo Bonaventura entitled: *Storia del violino, dei violinisti, e della musica per violino* [History of the violin, of violinists, and of music for the violin]; perhaps Anna would be happy to have it: she might be able to use it in her teaching and perhaps even translate it; what do you think?

Dear Tania, I'm glad that I haven't left yet, because of the possibility that I might see you once more in Milan; but once again I urge you to take good care of yourself, not to leave the hospital too early, and afterwards to make the trip from Milan to Rome in the most comfortable conditions possible. I embrace you tenderly.

Antonio

1. The memorandum written by Gramsci to the President of the Special Tribunal on April 3, 1928, was published by Domenico Zucaro in two books: *Vita del carcere di Antonio Gramsci* [The prison life of Antonio Gramsci] (Milan/Rome: Edizioni Avanti, 1954), pp. 108–120, and *Il processone: Gramsci e i dirigenti comunisti dinanzi al tribunale speciale* [The big trial: Gramsci and the Communist leaders before the special tribunal] (Rome: Editori Riuniti, 1961), pp. 135–146.

2. The periodical *Critica Fascista* was founded in 1923 by Giuseppe Bottai (1895–1959), minister of national education from 1936 to 1943. The review attracted "left-wing" Fascists who believed that Fascist corporativism "offered an alternative to capitalism and communism" (*Historical Dictionary*).

March 26, 1928

Dearest Mother,

Your insured letter of March 12 arrived within three days (on the fourteenth). I could have informed you of this immediately last Monday, but I had already been assigned the weekly letters that I am granted and I did not think I would be doing you a grievous wrong. I thank you and I thank Carlo very affectionately.

As you see, I haven't left for Rome yet, but certainly this will be the time I do; at any rate it will be a matter of days and no longer of months as was the case in the past. I've already received the information that I'm being remanded to trial, issued by the Pretrial Commission of the Special Tribunal.[1] From it I haven't learned anything new. No concrete charge, supported by documentary and testimonial proofs, is being brought against me.[2] There are four police functionaries who declare that I am responsible for all the bad things that happened in Italy in 1926, even the bad harvest. Among other things I see they've actually mentioned my trip to Ghilarza in 1924 as part of the charge.[3] Now look at that! And you were always complaining that I didn't visit! Luckily, I didn't travel much. Naturally all of this shouldn't give you any illusions and lead you to think that I might be acquitted. You will have to get used to the thought that I will be sentenced and that I will of necessity have to spend a certain number of years in jail, which I hope will be brief, but that this is inevitable. By now I am thoroughly accustomed to it and I would like everything to go more quickly and I wish I were already in a penitentiary with my head shaved and wearing prisoner's striped overalls. This for example would once and for all put an end to my sister-in-law's torment, who, in order to remain close to me and be able to make my life easier, has spent almost six months in hospital during the last year and must again be hospitalized because of her extremely weak condition.[4]

A few days ago I received the most recent news about Giulia and the children, rather good news. Believe me, and you shouldn't have any doubts about it, I am absolutely untroubled. Indeed, with each passing day, I become stronger and less susceptible to emotional agitation. I've never been excessively emotional, as you well know, and perhaps this apparent insensitivity has often caused you pain; today I must have lost even the small quota of emotionalism I once had. As with flint, only the sharp impact of steel can draw sparks from me. But you, along with very few other people, certainly have this steel-like power: I give you a warm embrace.

Nino

1. The Special Tribunal for the Defense of the State was instituted on November 5, 1926 by the Council of Ministers presided over by Mussolini, during the course of the same meeting at which decisions were made to suppress anti-Fascist parties and newspapers, to arrest parliamentary deputies who had opposed the Fascist regime, and to establish the death penalty for "crimes against the state."

2. See introduction for the charges against Gramsci. As Gramsci himself pointed out on several occasions, the generic nature of the charges revealed the essentially political nature and purposes of the trial. The dossier on Gramsci declared that he was "one of the chief exponents and one of the most active and influential members of the Communist party, especially in his capacity as deputy. And the fact that he is on the Central Committee makes him, as well as all the other members of this body, directly and primarily responsible for all the illegal and criminal activities of the Communist organization as sponsored by the organs and general policy of the Party itself." See Zucaro, *Il processone*, p. 220.

3. In October 1924, four months after the assassination of the Socialist deputy Giacomo Matteotti, Gramsci spent several days in Ghilarza visiting his family. He took advantage of the trip to hold a meeting on October 26 of several local sections of the PCI near Cagliari, and also to meet with leaders of the anti-Fascist Sardinian Action party.

4. Tania was suffering from the effects of bronchopneumonia.

March 26, 1928

Dearest Tania,

A few days ago I received a letter from you that presents a number of peculiarities. It is dated February 5 by you, but it seems to me that it must be more recent; perhaps you wrote 5. II instead of 5. III. Furthermore it isn't signed, it has no conclusion, at least from an epistolary point of view. They are two small sheets, the second numbered second, written partly in pen and partly in pencil, on which you summarize for me three letters from your father, your mother and Genia. The second sheet continues with two lines written at the beginning of its first page side, which ends the sentence left dangling on the fourth side, but are not a conclusion. I write you all these details to assist your memory; in fact, rereading it, I realize that your letter could indeed be dated February 5, because the chronological facts that are mentioned before and after might also refer to this date.

In any event, if your letter is more recent, it does not contain news about you; if it was written on February 5 it means that all during these twenty-five days of March you did not write to me or at least I didn't receive anything from you.

The news you've sent me has aroused a world of very lively but also very painful impressions, because I am in a position to recreate the whole material environment and all the physical difficulties that exist in the life of our loved ones; and with two children these difficulties can only be multiplied geometrically. Perhaps you have already realized this: it is precisely this sort of preoccupation that has always harassed me most intensely and has made me feel all the powerlessness of my situation. To this is added my preoccupation about your health, and about your whole immediate life that I would like to know fully and that you try by every means to make me believe is without excessive problems. Dear Tania, you really must be very reasonable and not make the slightest effort, relying simply on your will. I will not be able to be at peace until I know with certainty that you have followed to the letter all the doctor's instructions and advice: I wish you could leave Milan and live for a few months in a healthy climate that would help you regain your strength. You mustn't worry about me, for I am absolutely well and need nothing: I only need to know that you are taking care of yourself and have completely recovered. Otherwise how could you undertake long and uncomfortable journeys? I really believe that you must make up your mind to go and visit your mother.[1] Perhaps in the past I was never able to express the intensity of her desire to see you again. Sometimes I think that your mother, notwithstanding her great kindness, must hold it against me that she hasn't seen you in such a long time: already in 1922 she hoped that I would be able to persuade you. I embrace you tenderly.

Antonio

1. Although Domenico Zucaro says that Tania went now and then to Moscow to bring news of Gramsci to her family (Zucaro, p. 71), as far as can be determined, she did not leave Italy during the entire period of Gramsci's imprisonment. She returned to the Soviet Union in the latter part of 1938.

April 2, 1928

Dearest Tania,

Why don't you write me a bit more often? I don't believe that your treatments in the hospital take up your entire day. Do you read? Did you get some of the books I sent back? I don't know if any of them might interest you, but you could at least leaf through some of the magazines, such as *Nuova Antologia*. For my part during these weeks I've been able to obtain from the library a series of *Revue des Deux Mondes* of 1846–1868 and 1873, in which I found a number of very interesting articles on history and science. For example, the repercussions of the debates provoked by Claude Bernard's and Charles Robin's studies in physiology and on the question of so-called final causes; I didn't even know Robin's name and I don't know what position he held in the world of science and methodology.[1] Some of his observations were of extreme interest to me and therefore I would like to know, even in a general way, what consideration is given to his works and research. I think that you can tell me something about it.

From the bookstore I have received several volumes that I list here for your information: (1) Pasquale Jannacone, *La bilancia del dare e dell'avere internazionale con particolare riguardo all'Italia* [The balance of international debit and credit with particular regard to Italy]; (2) Benedetto Croce, *Storia d'Italia dal 1871 al 1915* [The history of Italy from 1871 to 1915]; (3) Giovanni Carano-Donvito, *L'economia meridionale prima e dopo il Risorgimento* [The southern economy before and after the Risorgimento]; (4) Antonio Graziadei, *Capitale e salari* [Capital and wages]; (5) Marcel Proust, *Chroniques* [Chronicles]. I will also be getting Mortara, *Prospettive economiche* [Economic perspectives] and the *Almanacco letterario Mondadori per il 1928* [The Mondadori literary almanac for 1928] about which I had written to you; so don't bother about it any longer.

On Thursday I received news about your health that was better than the previous news. But, to tell the truth, I can't make head or tail of it. It seems that you are hiding your true condition from Signora Tulli; so these deductions may or may not be well founded. In short, I "demand" most energetically that you write to me more often and that you tell me about yourself in greater detail.

My own health, however, is good. Tulli even says that I'm growing wattles. Marvels will never cease! There is still no word about my departure; I'm not too unhappy about this because I would rather leave with better weather than we have now and I hope that spring will finally agree to stage its grand opening. With many good wishes for the holidays, I embrace you tenderly.

Antonio

1. Gramsci is referring to an essay by Paul Janet, "Le problème des causes finales et la physiologie contemporaine," in *Revue des Deux Mondes*, February 15, 1873, pp. 861–88, in which two long paragraphs are devoted to *Leçons sur les propriétés des tissus vivants*, by the physiologist Claude Bernard (1813–78) and to *De l'appropriation des parties organiques à des arts déterminés*, by Charles Robin (1821–85).

April 9, 1928

Dearest Tania,

Yesterday I received your letter of the fifth with completely Easterly swiftness. I've also received Giuliano's lock of hair and I'm very happy about the news that you are passing on. To tell the truth, I'm unable to come to any conclusions about it. As for the rapidity or the opposite with which children learn to speak[1] I have no way of judging save for an anecdote about Giordano Bruno, who so it is said, did not speak until he was three, despite the fact that he understood everything: one morning, upon awakening, he saw that from a crack in the wall of the humble little house in which he lived a large serpent was coming toward his pallet; he immediately cried out for his father, whom he had never called before by name, was saved from danger and from that day on he began to talk too much, as is known even by the Jewish peddlers on Campo dei Fiori.[2]

I am unhappy to hear, as you write, that you feel disheartened and that you therefore consider yourself excused from writing more often. This is a manifest injustice, because I could declare myself to be even more disheartened than you and not write to you at all; something that will certainly happen if you should again provoke me with such disheartenings. You should write to me at least twice a week: how is it that you have become so lazy? What are you doing all day long? And how did you spend Easter?

A few days ago I received *Prospettive economiche* [Economic perspectives] and the *Almanaco letterario* [Literary almanac]. I've been giving this almanac to Giulia every year since 1925. I wouldn't do so this year. It has deteriorated a great deal. It contains so-called witticisms, which before were the preserve of silly semipornographic publications, put together for young recruits who had come to the city for the first time. True, even making such an observation has some value. Saturday I received a new parcel of books that however have not yet been given to me; I believe these are a certain number of history and philosophy reviews, since I was able to take only a peek when I was signing the postal receipt. In any case, I've again laid in a certain stock of reading material for the period that I will have to stay here in Milan.

I've been thinking that Delio will be four on August 10 and that now he is already old enough to receive a serious present. Signora Pina has promised to let me have the Meccano catalogue: I hope that the various sets are presented not only according to price (from 27 to 200 lire!) but also with reference to their degree of difficulty and the child's age. The principle of the Meccano is certainly excellent for modern children; I'll select the set that seems most appropriate and then I'll write to you about it. From now until August there is plenty of time. I do not know what Delio's chief interests are, assuming that he has already given clear signs of having any. When I was a boy I had a pronounced preference for the exact sciences and mathematics. I lost it during my high school studies, because I didn't have any teachers worth a straw. And so, after my first year in *liceo*, I stopped studying math and chose Greek instead (there was an option at the time); but during my third year in *liceo* I suddenly gave proof that I had preserved a remarkable "ability." In those days in the third year of *liceo*, in order to study physics one had to know the elements of mathematics that the pupils who had opted for Greek were not obliged to know. The physics professor, who was a most distinguished gentleman, got great amusement out of embarrassing us. During the last interrogation of the third trimester, he presented me with questions in physics linked to mathematics, saying that my answers would determine my average for the year and thus whether I would or would not have to take exams for my diploma: he was very amused at seeing me stand in front of the blackboard where he let me stand as long as I pleased. Well, I stood in front of that blackboard for half an hour, I covered myself with chalk from head to toe, I tried, tried again, wrote, erased, but finally I "invented" a demonstration that was considered excellent by the professor, even though it did not exist in any treatise. This professor knew my older brother in Cagliari and he tormented me with his cackling all through the school year: he called me the Hellenistic physicist.

Dearest Tania, banish all depressions and write me often. I embrace you.

Antonio

I forgot to tell you how yesterday I tried to embarrass Signora Pina. Since on Saturday Tulli was called for a visit, he asked me whether I had any special wishes for my Easter meal. I've always had wishes that I've never been able to satisfy: I would like to eat rhinoceros kidneys and the leg of a pangolin; for a second choice I would be satisfied with a roasted young goat's head. Tulli refused to perform the errand with regard to the rhinoceros and pangolin, rightly concerned not to burden his wife with overlong searches in the butcher shops; he insisted on asking only for the young goat's head. But yesterday, naturally, the head did not arrive; it was announced only for tomorrow, Tuesday. I don't believe in tomorrow either because lambs and young goats reach town without heads, but I want to know the results of this whole affair. I hope that Signora Pina will not be too angry with me; do me the favor of putting in a good word with her on my behalf.

1. Gramsci had learned recently that Giuliano was a late talker.

2. The allusion to Bruno's having "talked too much" is to the fact that his voluminous philosophical treatises questioning some of the dogmas of the Catholic church led to his imprisonment and trial by the Inquisition, and to his being burned at the stake on February 17, 1600, on Campo dei Fiori. A statue of Bruno on Campo dei Fiori (located in the heart of one of the busiest and oldest quarters in Rome, which explains the reference to the Jewish street vendors) is a reminder of this event.

———————————

April 9, 1928

Dearest Mother,

It's been about three weeks since I last heard from you. I hope you didn't think that I already left Milan for Rome and so have begun to write to me at my future address. As you can see, I haven't left yet and it appears that I will have to remain in Milan for at least all of April. At any rate, before changing my address, you must wait for a confirmation from me: I think I will be allowed to send you a telegram.

There is nothing new in my life. My sister-in-law is still in hospital, sick: her pneumonia has brought about a complication, phlebitis, which for some time yet will compel her to remain in bed; for her recovery she will have to go to a sanatorium outside Milan. So for more than two months I haven't had any visits and I don't see anyone. I have stopped writing to Mario and I definitely won't write to him again. I've heard that he's very afraid of being compromised and I don't want to cause him even the slightest trouble.[1]

Just yesterday I received word about the children, who are well; they even sent me a big lock of Giuliano's hair, which is a very lovely ash blond.

I hope that all of you spent the holidays very well and quietly. I myself have been quite cheerful: I had a guest, besides the friend with whom I share the cell: we ate the Easter *colomba*,[2] which they sell in Milan, and we drank white wine. I also want you to know that every Sunday morning I listen to the Mass and yesterday we actually had a high mass with a special organ or rather harmonium accompaniment; not that you can really hear the Mass, because the altar is far from the cell, but still it is something similar; however, you can't smell the incense.

By the way: you keep forgetting to send me the sermon "a su populu de Masuddas" that you had promised me. And besides I wanted to ask you for a piece of information that interests me very much: did you teach Franco the song about the old sergeant with the rataplàn, rataplàn?

Affectionate greetings to all. I embrace you tenderly.

Nino

1. See note on Mario Gramsci in the list of correspondents and family members.
2. A cake shaped like a dove.

April 16, 1928

Dearest Tania,

I haven't received any letters from you during this past week and neither have I received more precise news about you from Signora Pina. I hope that everything is well with regard to your health. I've been sent several magazines from the bookstore that have absorbed me completely, awakening in me a very lively interest in the development of the various cultural activities that I thought I had lost. I would never have believed that publishing activity was so intense, especially in historical studies of all kinds. The plans for translations of historical works, especially from the German, and of novels from the English, are at times spectacular. All this seems to me of great cultural import: the fact that the attention of the average public has switched from French to Anglo-Saxon fiction and that not only a restricted circle of university people and academicians but also the greater public that obviously constitutes the customers of the large publishing houses wish to be kept abreast of German intellectual activities.

I've also received two books: a novel, *Le pétrole* [Oil] by Upton Sinclair and *La vie de Disraeli* [The life of Disraeli] by André Maurois. I've read the latter, which has given me a very interesting "specimen"[1] of the new success obtained by "fictional" biographies in France. The Life of Disraeli has already had 170 printings.[2]

This pen drives me into a fury. I really don't know what contortions I should perform to prevent the ink from splattering on all sides. And in any event today I find it very fatiguing to write. The course of my thoughts does not coincide perfectly with the things I must write to you, just to amuse you a bit. I embrace you with many, many good wishes.

Antonio

1. In English in original.
2. Gramsci probably meant seventeen editions, not one hundred and seventy. In any event, he may have been misled by the fact that the biography had appeared originally in serial form, in the *Revue de Paris*, in five successive issues. The first and second editions in book form were published by Gallimard in 1928 and 1929.

April 23, 1928

Dearest Mother,

I've received your insured letter of April 12. As you can see, I am still in Milan and perhaps will remain here for a few more weeks: it appears that the trial has been set for the twelfth of June.

My news, always the same. My health is fairly good. My state of mind is tranquil and without shocks of any kind. I'm thinking of sending you my copy of the photograph taken of Delio in June 1926: I'll find out today if I can mail it and in what manner so that it won't be damaged. You will then write me your impressions: I especially want to know whether he resembles us when we were children. You will see how beautiful your grandchild is; you will be very happy about it. There is one thing that I want: do not erase the prison stamp on the back. The photograph should remain as it is, bearing the mark of its having gone through prison where I have been shut away for so long a time. Not only am I not ashamed of being in prison but on the contrary I feel extremely honored by it; certainly this will also be the boy's feeling when he is able to understand these things.

I'm waiting for the more lengthy letter that you have announced. I embrace you affectionately.

Nino

April 30, 1928

Dearest Mother,

I'm sending you Delio's photograph. My trial has been set for May 28: this time my departure must be imminent. In any case I will make sure to send you a telegram. My health is fairly good. The closeness of the trial makes me feel better because at least I'll leave this monotony behind. Don't worry and don't get frightened whatever sentence they may give me: I believe that it will be fourteen to seventeen years, but it might even be worse, precisely because there is no evidence against me: after all, what deeds might I not have committed without leaving any evidence behind? Take heart. I embrace you.

Nino

April 30, 1928

Dearest Tania,

I've received your letter of April 25 together with Giulia's letter. I thank you for the news you have passed on to me. I was really very happy to get it; I was extremely worried.

I don't know whether you have been informed of the fact that my trial has been set for May 28, which means that my departure is drawing near. I've already seen Ariis, the lawyer. These approaching events rather excite me; but in a pleasant way. I feel more vibrantly alive; there will be a certain struggle, I imagine. Be it only for a few days, I will find myself in an environment different from that of prison.

I wish to protest against your deductions concerning . . . young goat heads. I'm very well informed about this particular commerce. In Turin, in 1919, I made a broad survey because the city's administration was boycotting Sardinian lambs and goats to the advantage of Piedmontese rabbits: in Turin there were approximately 4,000 Sardinian shepherds and peasants on a special mission[1] and I wanted to enlighten them on the subject. Southern lambs and young goats arrive here without heads, but there is a small percentage of local trade that also supplies the heads. That it is difficult to find them is proven by the fact that the head, promised for Sunday, could be obtained only on Wednesday. Besides, I wasn't quite sure whether it was that of a lamb or young goat, despite the fact that it was very good (for me; Tulli was horrified by it). It must have been a strange young goat, without brains and without one eye, with a skull that greatly resembled that of a German shepherd (but, I beg you, don't say this to Signora Pina!) crushed by a street car! Ah, these butchers!

I'm very sorry that Giulia went without news for so long. Will we see each other before my departure? I don't think so. I don't want you to do anything imprudent. You must take good care of yourself. Only in this way will I be at peace. You must realize that from now on I will be able to write very infrequently.[2] I embrace you.

Antonio

1. The reference is to the 4000 soldiers of the Sardinian Sassari Brigade sent to Turin in the early part of 1919 to put down angry protests by workers caused by high prices, food

scarcities, and layoffs. Gramsci carried on some effective propaganda among the soldiers, many of whom were peasants and shepherds.

2. On May 11, Gramsci was transferred to the Regina Coeli prison in Rome, where he arrived on May 12 and remained until July 8. During this period he was allowed to write to family members only once every fifteen days, as Gramsci says in letter to Tania, July 20, 1928. It was during his two-month stay at Regina Coeli in 1928 that Gramsci, together with his comrades and fellow prisoners Umberto Terracini and Mauro Scoccimarro, began to develop a "democratic and parliamentary" strategy for the Italian Communist party that diverged radically from the one then advocated by the Communist International. In a clandestine letter written in the summer of 1930 on the turn to revolutionary intransigence taken by the Party in 1930, Terracini refers back to his talks with Gramsci at Regina Coeli: "And since I have referred to the common ideas of the guests of Regina Coeli in 1928," Terracini wrote, "I want to horrify you by saying that not only was the democratic perspective, that is, the return of the bourgeoisie to the democratic method of government taken for granted, but that we also talked about the tactics that the Party would have to adopt in the period between the end of the Fascist 'ministry' and the formation of a parliamentary government; not only that, but also about our electoral tactics for the first democratic assembly . . . " Umberto Terracini, *Sulla svolta: Carteggio clandestino del carcere 1930, 1931, 1932* [On the turn: The clandestine prison letters of 1930, 1931, 1932] ed. Alessandro Coletti (Milan: La Pietra, 1975), pp. 35–36.

April 30, 1928

Dear Giulia,

I've received your note of April 3. Tania has passed on to me the news concerning the children's life. I am quite happy.

One period of my life as a prisoner is about to end, for on May 28 I will go on trial. I don't know where they will toss me afterward. My health is fairly good. I've heard from the judiciary and prison authorities that many incorrect things have been published about me: that I was dying of starvation,[1] etc. etc. This has upset me very much because I believe that in such matters one mustn't ever invent or exaggerate. It is also true that one lacks the means to verify things and in truth I know no more than what has been reported to me. But you have always been informed by Tania and therefore you have had no reason to be troubled. I do not want to write abroad: perhaps they would permit me, but I don't want to do so as a matter of principle. I have for instance recently received a strange letter signed Ruggero,[2] which requested an answer. Perhaps prison life has made me more distrustful than normal prudence would require; but the fact is that, despite its stamp and its postmark, this letter made me lose my temper. It too said that my health must be bad! or that there are rumors to that effect. I wasn't well during the first months after the journey from Ustica to Milan; then I was able to rest and recover satisfactorily. I study, I read, within the limits of possibility, which isn't much. Systematic intellectual work is impossible due to the lack of technical means.

Dear Giulia, it saddens me to receive such scant news about your life and the life of the children. I'm afraid that in the future it may become even scanter: this is my greatest preoccupation. My dear, I embrace you tenderly.

Antonio

1. Periodic attempts were made throughout Gramsci's imprisonment to enlist the support of governments and political organizations in securing his release. This reference is to an article written by Gramsci's Communist comrade Alfonso Leonetti (who in 1927 was living clandestinely in Genoa) published in *Correspondance Internationale* on September 24, 1927 with the title: "Antonio Gramsci se meurt de faim! Il faut le sauver!." [Antonio Gramsci is dying of hunger! We must save him!] The article was reprinted later in various Italian anti-Fascist émigré newspapers.

2. Ruggero Grieco (1893–1955) joined the Italian Communist party in 1921, and became a member of the Party's executive committee. He broke with Amadeo Bordiga in 1924, and supported the Lyons Theses written in 1926 by Gramsci and Palmiro Togliatti. He was active in the Communist International, and in France as an anti-Fascist organizer during the 1930s.

A letter (published in English translation in Spriano, *Antonio Gramsci and the Party: The Prison Years*, pp. 151–153) that Grieco wrote from Basel, Switzerland on February 10, 1928, and had sent from Moscow to Gramsci (and similar letters he wrote to Mauro Scoccimarro and Umberto Terracini, who were also then facing trial) provoked intense anger and suspicion in Gramsci, since the letter (called "strange" and "infamous" by Gramsci), which highlighted the leadership role played by him in the Italian Communist party, was read by prison authorities and could therefore only aggravate his legal status vis-à-vis the Fascist government. Gramsci's suspicions were further aroused when the judge in charge of gathering evidence against him, Enrico Macis, referring to Grieco's letter, said: "Honorable Gramsci, you have some friends who certainly want you to stay in prison for quite a while." No doubt Macis's purpose was to sew discord among the Italian Communists, and in this he succeeded, at least as far as Gramsci was concerned. But, as amply documented by Michele Pistillo in his book *Gramsci come Moro?* [Gramsci like Moro?], there is no reason to suspect Grieco (or Togliatti) of malicious intent, since there was nothing in the letter that was not already known by Fascist authorities. A note of November 10, 1924, from the Ministry of the Interior to prefects throughout the country described Gramsci as "new secretary of the Executive Committee of the Communist party" (Spriano, *Antonio Gramsci and the Party: The Prison Years*, p. 23), so his leadership role was no secret to Fascist authorities. Moreover, a decision had already been made by Mussolini prior to receipt of Grieco's letter not to make any concessions to Gramsci and the other Communists facing trial. Yet Gramsci was firmly convinced, as was Tania, that the letter destroyed whatever chance he had to be freed in 1928, through negotiations then underway between the Vatican and the Soviet government concerning the possibility of an exchange of prisoners: Gramsci was to be freed in return for the liberation of several Catholic priests imprisoned in the Soviet Union. One of several indications that Gramsci was bitterly resentful over this incident is

APRIL 1928 / 203

to be found in a letter from Tania to Piero Sraffa of February 11, 1933. She referred therein to a talk she had had recently with Gramsci. "A part of our talk," she wrote, "was used by him to explain to me past facts relative to his situation in '28 before the trial. Nino says that what was aimed at was an avoidance of the trial itself and that moreover in the meeting between Litvinov and Grandi the question of his liberation was to be dealt with, when the "infamous letter" arrived." (Natoli, *Antigone*, p. 252)

There is reason to believe that Gramsci was mistaken about talks between Litvinov and Grandi. In an interview with Renzo De Felice held in 1977, Grandi "completely dismissed the suggestion that Litvinov had spoken of [the Gramsci question], even in an informal manner." (Spriano, *Antonio Gramsci and the Party*, p. 87) What did occur in 1927 was an attempt by Vatican and Soviet authorities to negotiate a prisoner exchange, but on October 20, 1927, four months before Gramsci received Grieco's letter, the Jesuit Pietro Tacchi Ventura "reported to the Vatican Secretary of State Cardinal Gasparri Mussolini's refusal to intervene in favor of Gramsci and Terracini before the trial and sentence of the [Special] Tribunal." (Sraffa, *Lettere a Tania*, p. xxvi).

May 7, 1928

Dearest Tania,

I've received your two letters, dated April 17 and 20, which reached me after the letter of the twenty-fifth, which I answered last Monday. I'm happy with the good news you give me about your health; but I don't think that we will be able to see each other before my departure. Besides, I don't want you to take the risk of leaving the hospital before your condition has improved and you are absolutely certain about your leg. I think that you should keep very quiet and wait for them to assign me to a prison after the trial. They might even send me back to northern Italy from Rome, and so you could come from Milan without too much traveling inconvenience.

I did not address my letters to the hospital before, because I had been told that any day you might be transferred to the Central Hospital: owing to my uncertainty about your address, I decided to go on writing you at home.

My remarks concerning a letter from you dated February 2 were not in the least intended to "make you blush" over the manner in which it was written, or its literary form. I attach very little importance to such things. I had the impression that a sheet might be missing from the envelope, lost perhaps during review by the censor. But you don't say a word about this. I minutely described the letter to you so as to help you remember it, because it was dated February 2 and my answer would have reached you a good two months after that date. As for the news that you were passing on to me, you were right: you must write everything to me, even the bad side of things.

Please be advised that I have sent out my winter coat: I would like to have the stains removed. I also sent out a heavy sweater. I believe that you would do well to deliver to attorney Ariis all the books that I've sent out from prison; he'll keep them at my disposal and ship them to me wherever I'll finally be sent after the trial. I believe that this is the best solution from every point of view: you must worry only about your health and you mustn't make problems for me, do you understand? You must no longer tire yourself out as you have done in the past, you must no longer be so prodigal with your strength, which is not very great. I'll always write to you assiduously; and you must write to me, but nothing more. Concern about your health, for a whole year now, has often tormented me too much and made me feel the bitterness of my loss of freedom. Dear Tania, I ask you with all my heart to make sure that you take very great care of yourself. I embrace you tenderly.

Antonio

May 7, 1928

Dear Borioni,

I received your postcard of April 30. I did not know where they had bounced you. You cannot possibly know a detail that will interest you. In November 1926, when I was arrested and taken to the Regina Coeli prison, I would spend hour after hour listening to your and Ottavio's[1] voices as you were talking with a third prisoner, who was clearly from the South. I wouldn't be able to tell you where my cell was located (I believe it was on the second tier of the third section); but it is a fact that your voices reached me with a distinct and clear sound; I still remember the subject of your conversation. To tell you the truth, your voices caused me a certain anger; I was unable to understand (or I understood all too well!) the reason for my absolute isolation, although I was held only at the disposal of the police, while you were allowed to be together and while away the time chatting. For seventeen days I had nothing I could read. I only managed to obtain a volume containing the speeches of the Subalpine Parliament for 1848–1849 and, irony of fate, precisely the one that contained the debates on parliamentary immunity[2] in regard to the newly granted and promulgated statute. I spent the time making papier-mâché balls from old *Sports Gazettes*: I've become remarkably specialized in this craft.

I no longer receive any news from Ustica: before the October 1927 arrest some people would write to me and I would answer within the permissible limits. So, since you've resumed the tradition, I take advantage of it to ask you for a favor. I would like you to try and track down what has become of some of my things that had remained in the care of Pietro Ventura. They are mostly books and correspondence. I really would like to have the correspondence returned to me. As for the books, I make a distinction.[3]

Give my greetings to friends who still remember me. Cordially yours,

Gramsci

If possible I would like to have the collection of the following magazines that arrived for me in Ustica in 1927: *La Critica* [edited] by B. Croce and the *Leonardo*. I have found the list of my Ustica books. I list the ones I would like to receive, if they can be recovered. (Besides the already ———[4] Windelband—*The History of Modern Philosophy*, three volumes).

1. Ottavio Gianotti, one of the group of Communists sent to police internment at Ustica in late 1926 or early 1927.
2. The *Statuto* stipulates in Article 45 that "Except for the case of flagrante delicto, no Deputy shall be placed under arrest while the Chamber is in session nor may he be brought before a court in a criminal proceeding without the prior consent of the Chamber."
3. At this point, the letter is torn, showing only that the missing page dealt with book titles. The letter then skips to a salutation and postscript, as given here.
4. Illegible word. Gramsci refers here to Wilhelm Windelband, *Die Geschichte der neuren Philosophie* (Leipzig: Breitkopf, 1922).

———

May 10, 1928

Dearest Mother,

I'm about to leave for Rome.[1] Now it's certain. In fact I've been allowed this letter to inform you of my transfer. So write to me at Rome from now on and until I inform you of a further transfer.

I have received an insured letter from Carlo dated May 5. He writes that he will send me your photograph: it will make me very happy. By now you must have received Delio's photograph that I sent you about ten days ago, registered.

Dearest mother, I don't want to repeat what I have always written to reassure you about my physical and moral states. In order to be completely tranquil, I would like you not to be too frightened or too perturbed by whatever sentence they are about to give me. I would like you to understand completely, also emotionally, that I'm a political detainee and will be a political prisoner, that I have nothing now or in the future to be ashamed of in this situation. That, at bottom, I myself have in a certain sense asked for this detention and this sentence, because I've always refused to change my opinion, for which I would be willing to give my life and not just remain in prison. That therefore I can only be calm and content with myself. Dear mother, I would really like to embrace you and hold you tight to make you feel how much I love you and how I would like to console you for this sorrow that I've caused you: but I could not have acted otherwise. Life is like that, very hard, and sometimes sons must be the cause of great sorrow for their mothers if they wish to preserve their honor and their dignity as men. I embrace you tenderly.

Nino

I will write to you from Rome immediately. Tell Carlo not to lose his good spirits and that I thank him infinitely. Kisses to all.

    1. Gramsci left for Rome the next day, May 11.

May 15, 1928

Dearest Mother,

I arrived in Rome two days ago. I already sent you a telegram. I'm not writing you or telling you anything about the journey from Milan to Rome and about the condition of my health. I want to write you only about a certain series of events because this is the sole way of bringing them to the attention of the person charged with censoring my letters.

Some months ago, in the Milan jail, there was a sort of investigation into the condition of my health, following orders from above. I was almost reproached for not having complained: the pretrial judge on the one hand and the prison warden on the other were almost trying to hold me responsible for certain somewhat alarmist reports published abroad with regard to my health: it almost seemed that I wanted to be ill on purpose so that people could say that I was ill.

Here in Rome almost the contrary occurs: I really don't know what I should do in order to obtain something that my stomach will tolerate. It is impossible to get an interview with the warden. One can only make a single request a week and each week one can only ask for a single thing; before the first request is granted the time is already passed and so they say that it is useless to make requests. Nevertheless I will do everything I can to obtain what I need not to fall ill: at least they won't be able to start further investigations to ascertain whether I was trying to be sick on purpose. Only today will I be able to make a request for the proper food, so as to eat at my expense and also be able to eat only those foods that I can digest: I will do this and wait for the results. I would at least like to go to trial in a condition that will allow me to endure the fatigue of the transports to and fro.

Dearest mother, you mustn't in any event let these events upset you. My willpower is strong enough to withstand these annoyances. I embrace you tenderly.

Antonio

May 22, 1928

Dearest Mother,

I'm waiting for the trial, which will take place in a few days. I still haven't received news from anyone. My sister-in-law had left the hospital three days before my departure from Milan. I had two visits with her. She was still sick: she was extremely weak. She told me that she was leaving for Rome immediately, but I have not heard from her.

Dearest mother, I'm in excellent condition, strong and in a good mood. I beg you not to despair and to always be of good cheer and confident, despite everything. I embrace you tenderly.

Antonio

I have not received the photographs promised by Carlo. Did he send them to Milan? It will be well to keep me informed of what might have been forwarded to Milan, so that I can know what to do.

May 29, 1928

Dearest Mother,

I'm writing you a few lines, hastily. I'm a bit tired because I was at the hearing of the Tribunal and then at a meeting with my attorney.

I have received your insured letter, with the enclosure of one hundred lire and two photographs. The two photographs were handed to me today; the letter not yet. The other day I received a letter from Teresina sent to Milan and forwarded from Milan to Rome; it too contained two photographs. My heartfelt thanks. I'm glad that Delio's photograph arrived without damage and that you were happy to receive it.

I don't feel like writing anymore. My head aches and I don't want to write you empty words. Besides, I wouldn't be able to write you anything about the trial, because it is not permitted. Keep in good spirits and always trust what I write to you. I embrace you tenderly.

Antonio

June 1, 1928

Dearest Mother,

I've already seen Carlo[1] three or four times. I'm very glad that he has come to Rome, because in this way you will be able to hear from him the news that concerns me directly and you will be reassured. Your letter, contained in the insured envelope, has not yet reached me. No news here yet. I think that the sentence will be handed down on Monday. I'm completely sure of myself, that is, I've already adjusted to the worst hypothesis, that is, the maximum sentence allowed by the old code: I believe that Carlo will confirm this impression and he'll be able to convince you that I'm not in the least downcast or despairing. I embrace you tenderly.

Antonio

1. See the note on Carlo Gramsci in the list of correspondents and family members.

June 19, 1928

Dearest Carlo,

I've received your letter of June 15 (postmarked in Ghilarza). I haven't written before today owing to the peremptory reason that I cannot write when it pleases me, but only on the prescribed days. We must become accustomed to this requirement. I will be able to write very little from now on, and I will have to distribute the few letters equally between you and Tatiana.

I haven't had any further visits after your departure; I'm not certain that I'll have any more before I leave for my new destination. It is probable though: the military prosecutor Isgrò[1] who came to the prison once spoke to me in such a way as to make me think that I'll be able to have some visits with Tatiana.

I've received no communications with regard to the penitentiary. I've made an application for a special medical examination and I've spoken about it with the military attorney, who made a note of it. That's all I know. You must realize that I am the least informed about what's going on and especially about what concerns me. I'm sorry that among you there is an "almost morbid sensitivity," as you tell me. I am made of stone and I hope to harden even more. You have witnessed a part of this process; I thought that I had been able to convey less tragic impressions than those that can arise from the simple reading of the press. I embrace you affectionately, together with everyone at home.

Antonio

1. Michele Isgrò, the public prosecutor at Gramsci's trial before the Special Tribunal.

June 27, 1928

Dearest Tania,

Nothing new in sight, up to this moment. I don't know when I will leave. But it is not to be excluded that my departure will take place in a few days; I could be transferred even today.[1] I received a letter from my mother several days ago. She writes that she has not had any letters from me since May 22, that is, since the time I was still in Milan.[2] From Rome I've written home at least three times, my last letter also went to my brother Carlo. I want you to write a letter to my mother, explaining to her that now I can write very little, only once every fifteen days, and that I must distribute my two monthly letters between her and you. However, I can receive an unlimited number of letters: my mother on the contrary believes that there is a limit to the letters one receives. Inform her about the matter of my suspended departure for Portolongone[3] after a special examination by the doctor, and about the probabilities of a better destination. Reassure her in general and write to her that I don't need to be comforted to be tranquil, but that I am very tranquil and very serene all on my own. This is a point on which I've never succeeded in obtaining any sort of success with my mother, who has before her a terrifying and gothic picture of my position as a convict: she thinks that I [am] always brooding, a prey to despair, etc. etc. You can write to her that you've seen me recently and that I'm not in the least desperate, downcast, etc., and that I'm clearly inclined to laugh and joke. Perhaps she'll believe you, whereas she thinks that I write like this just to comfort her.

Dearest Tania, I'm sorry that I'm giving you this epistolary task too. On the other hand, I had decided to write this letter to you and I don't want to depart from the established system. I hope to see you again before I leave. I embrace you tenderly.

Antonio

1. Gramsci left Rome for the prison in Turi di Bari on July 8, 1928.
2. In reality Gramsci had been in Rome since May 12.
3. A prison in Florence.

July 3, 1928

Dearest Mother,

I've received your letter of June 23. As you see, I am still in Rome, waiting to be assigned. I should already have left ten days ago, but the journey was suspended at the orders of the doctor who performed the special examination that I had requested. I don't know whether you have finally received the letters I sent you from Rome: there must have been at least three. In any case you will have to be very patient with regard to our correspondence: I will be able to write to you only once a month. You, though, can write as often as you want. The limitation is inflicted on the convict, not on the family.

I thought that Carlo had persuaded you that I'm absolutely calm and that I don't need any encouragement. But I see that you continue to be worried about my state of mind. So you mustn't expect great things from Tatiana, who would be able to visit me only once every two weeks and so does not have better information on the general condition of my health than I myself can describe to you or to Carlo in my letters. I'm sure that you understand that in cases like this it is especially necessary to be patient: any initiative dictated by impatience is doomed to fail and therefore it is best not to even think of undertaking it. From this point of view I'm in good shape: I've acquired the psychology of the perfect convict. I let the days go by one after the other; I don't get excited about anything, I don't pose any problems for myself that I realize are insoluble, etc. etc. To the extent that this depends on my will, I worry only about preserving my physical health and reading a few books so as not to fall into complete stultification.

Write to me often and get Carlo and Teresina to write to me. I embrace you tenderly.

Antonio

Caserta, July 10, 1928

Dearest Tania,

I made the trip from Rome to Caserta under much better conditions than I thought I would. I've been treated very well and I've been able to breathe easily. In Caserta I got a doctor to examine me and he reassured me about the pains in my midsection. It is not, apparently, an inflammation of the liver but only a herpes that has produced an irritation that is temporary and of no consequence even though very painful. My entire waist is irritated and covered with swellings; I found out about this external irritation only during the trip! I've begun to rub in salve; I hope it will help. The pain continues and gives me no rest, but the doctor told me that in a couple of days it will all be over. I don't know what this herpes is. I never, never had skin infections of any kind, but in recent times I've seen that they're very common among prisoners and that they easily go away with application of salves. At any rate, better herpes than a disease of the liver: don't you think so?

I will be leaving tomorrow morning, but I don't know when I will arrive at Turi. If you could send a few books down there, even right away, you would be doing me a favor. If you have collected my luggage from the prison you could immediately send me the books and the magazines contained in the suitcase and traveling bag. I would particularly like to have the grammars. For German I have only the two small books that you yourself had sent me: the German grammar that I had in Milan has been lost; but among my books in Rome there is the Otto Sauer-Ferrari Method and the Langenscheidt Dictionary. Could you write directly to Ariis, asking him to send me the books I had left with him in Milan? His address is: 1 Via Unione. As you can see, I continue to make you work and tire you out. Your last letter caused me a certain displeasure. I think that you did not interpret very correctly the contents of the letter that you received after such a long delay. I no longer remember it, but I rule out your interpretation as impossible. Dear Tania, how can you think that at any moment in this time full of painful vicissitudes, I could have failed to recognize your great kindness and ceased being so deeply fond of you? And besides, I'm continually filled with remorse at having given you so many worries and having asked you to do so much work for me. I will write to you at length on this subject, when I'm rested and better able to think clearly. I only want you to understand that since I've been in prison, I've made an effort of the will to control my emotions and affections and keep them in check as much as possible: this is a form of self-preservation. And so it may have happened and indeed it must certainly have happened that often in my letters I have seemed arid, dry, a bit selfish, etc. etc. But in any event I categorically exclude that one might draw from them the conclusion that you have drawn. I will write to you at length as soon as I reach my destination and I will write to Giulia. I am waiting with great impatience for the promised photographs. Dearest Tania, I embrace you tenderly.

Antonio

July 20, 1928

Dearest Tania,

Yesterday morning I arrived at my destination. I found your letter of the fourteenth and a letter from Carlo containing 250 lire. I beg you to write to my mother for me and tell her all the things that might interest her. From now on I will write only one letter every fifteen days and this will bring me face to face with real moral dilemmas. I will try to be orderly and make the very best use of the paper available to me.

1. The trip from Rome to Turi was horrible. Obviously the pain that I had felt in Rome and that I thought was liver trouble was only the beginning of an inflammation that became manifest later on. I was incredibly sick. At Benevento I spent two infernal days and nights; I writhed like a worm, I could neither sit nor lie down. The doctor told me that it was St. Anthony's fire and that he could do nothing about it.[1] During the trip from Benevento to Foggia the ailment abated and the blisters that covered the right side of my waist dried up. I remained in Foggia five days and during the last three days I was already healed, I was able to sleep for a few hours and I was able to lie down without having stabbing pains. I still have a few dried out blisters and some tenderness around the kidneys, but I don't think it is anything serious. I can't explain the Roman incubation that lasted about eight days and appeared with extremely violent internal pains on the right front side of my waist.

2. I cannot write you anything about my future life yet. I'm going through my first days of quarantine before being definitively assigned to a section. I don't think however that you can send me anything but books and linen: we are not allowed to receive foodstuffs. So never send anything before I ask for it.

3. Have the books from Milan (Libreria Sperling) shipped directly: there is no point in your spending money to forward things for which postage has already been paid.

4. The memorandum[2] was no longer there: I *had* to take it with me.

The cherries have been very useful, even though I didn't even get a taste of them: they've made my trip[3] easier.

214 / JULY 1928

I've just at this very moment received your letter of the nineteenth, along with Giulia's letter. I would like to write Giulia at length, but I am unable to mail the sort of letter I would like. It is difficult to write. I'll see about it next time, after having rested and after having put my ideas in some better order. So you write to her and send her the usual news.

Dearest, write to Carlo to make sure that he too doesn't get some weird ideas, such as making mother come all the way to Turi. It would be a crime to force an old woman who has never left her village to take such a long and uncomfortable journey. And what's more, I think that seeing me in convict's clothes etc. etc. would make too devastating an impression on her. I embrace you tenderly.

Antonio

1. Henderson identifies this disease as erysipelas, but the more likely diagnosis is the one given by the prison doctor at Caserta and by Tania in a note at the bottom of this letter, which was herpes zoster.
2. The memorandum referred to in letter to Tania, March 19, 1928, n. 1., that Gramsci sent on April 3, 1928.
3. Gramsci may have given the cherries to his police guards, in return for some favors.

July 30, 1928

Dearest Tania,

I've received two of your letters dated July 25. Thank you. Now you will have to be patient, because I'll be able to write to you only a month from now; my next letter, fifteen days from now, will go to Carlo and to mother, who would not be satisfied to receive my news only through you. One would like to be able to satisfy all of one's needs, but I'm only entitled to two letters a month! We must be patient. I will try to write to you in an orderly manner about all the essential subjects one by one, now that I have gotten my bearings and am better informed.

1. It is necessary that you be able to prove my right to write to you and your right to be involved in my affairs.[1] Last week, after having written to you, I was subjected to a sort of interrogation. In my opinion, it will be enough for you to have at your disposal, so that if required you'll be able to send it to this warden's office, a doc-

ument proving that the Special Tribunal in Milan and in Rome as well as the Warden's office in the Rome prison gave you permanent visiting rights. Perhaps a piece of paper from the Visitor's Office in Rome is sufficient; in case of necessity, however, you can also turn to the Military Attorney General Isgrò. Let's hope this is sufficient and that it won't be necessary to spend money for more complicated certificates.

2. The herpes is almost healed. It is a bit irritating, but it no longer gives me sharp pains. It would have healed even sooner if during the trip I had had the possibility of regularly applying a salve prescribed by the doctor at Caserta. This has resulted, I believe, in an inadequate healing of the blisters due to the continuous rubbing against my underwear, and in a slower recovery.

3. As you see from the warning at the top of the sheet,[2] I cannot receive any foodstuffs. I can however receive linens. But the problem of its rational utilization presents itself, because here in my cell I can keep very little of it (the weekly change) and this does not allow for the plan you outlined in your letter. Nevertheless I believe that I need a few more shirts. You will do well to send me the woolen undershirts. Remember that I left some linens in Milan with Tulli; they should be held for me at Ariis's office. You will also have to send me a suitcase and perhaps also the traveling bag to keep stuff in the storeroom.

4. I've received two packages of books sent on by you. I have yet to receive anything directly from the Sperling bookshop. When I was in Rome I kept forgetting to tell you that you must send my address to: "Virginio Borioni,[3] political internee, Ustica" to whom I entrusted the books I left in Ustica at the moment of my arrest. I also left some correspondence and my Gillette razor in Ustica. Write, urging him to make sure that everything is sent here to Turi.

5. Some time will have to pass before I can write to you about my situation in this penitentiary. I'm receiving the infirmary's dairy diet; we exercise twice a day, quite sufficient. I still haven't gotten used to the promiscuous life in the dormitory (there's a group of six of us); and I'm plagued a great deal by insomnia. After a longer trial period, I'll see whether it will be necessary to initiate some special procedures at the Ministry and with the Special Tribunal to be given a cell by myself, which would make it easier to obtain writing materials and so be able to study in a coherent manner.[4] Perhaps I will do so, based

on the precedent that in Milan, when there was the inquiry into the condition of my health I was reproached by the warden for not having complained sooner and not having asked sooner for what I needed.

6. Send me some soap and toothpaste. Could you send me the Sedobrol that you were supposed to send me in Rome? Thank you for the gifts that you sent to Delio and Giuliano in my name: I wouldn't know what to suggest for Giulia; you choose and it will suit me. I embrace you, my dear.

Antonio

(Write often—as much as you can)
When I write to Carlo, I'll ask him to write to you about anything that I might have forgotten or whatever news I have by then.

1. Gramsci's marriage with Giulia was never legally recognized in Italy, so that, in a strict legal sense, none of his wife's relatives could be considered "family members," a requirement for visits and correspondence rights.

2. The words "packages with food in them are not accepted" were stamped on the top of most of Gramsci's letters

3. Virginio Borioni, one of about thirty Communist internees at Ustica, to whom Gramsci wrote the letter of May 7, 1928, published in this book for the first time.

4. Gramsci obtained permission to write in his cell at the end of January 1929: See letters to Tania, September 24, 1928, and January 14, 1929; and to mother, January 28, 1929. The first entry in the notebooks is dated February 8, 1929.

August 13, 1928

Dearest Carlo,

I reached Turi on July 19. I had to write my first two letters to Tatiana to tell her what she should send me out of the luggage I left in the prison in Rome. Tatiana writes that she has sent a letter to mother to give her my news and pass on to her those parts of my letters that might interest her. You must always remember and remind mother that I can only write one letter every fifteen days; therefore I can write you once a month in order to write once a month also to Tatiana. We have to be patient. It means that Tatiana will send on to you those parts of my letters to her that might interest you, and you or mother will send on to Tatiana what might interest her in my letters to you.

1. I've received your insured letter of July 12 with the 250 lire; thank you. I've received mother's letter of August 3: I was sorry to hear about her illness after so much time. I send mother my best wishes for a swift and certain recovery. You must always keep me informed about everything; Teresina has not written to me. I've received news from Giulia and the children. They returned from the country a few days ago; Giulia, who was feeling run down, is fine now. The children are well and are growing. I will receive their photographs and I will write to ask that a copy be sent to mother too. Meanwhile mother still hasn't sent me her impressions of Delio's photograph that I sent to her from Milan and I am very anxious to receive effusive compliments.

2. As soon as you have a bit of time at your disposal, you must take care of a matter that is of great importance to me. You must apply to the proper ministry, on behalf of my family (mother's and yours) and request that instructions be given that I be moved to a cell of my own,[1] here in this jail (its precise name is "Special Penitentiary of Turi"). At present I am in a dormitory with four other men, they too sentenced for political crimes, but they have bronchial and pulmonary diseases. I do not have these diseases and continued proximity, despite all precautions (which in any case are very difficult in prison life) and especially with the approach of winter, which intensifies pulmonary ailments, could have serious consequences. I think that it shouldn't be difficult to obtain this, in view of the fact that the Special Tribunal has sentenced me to time in prison but has not specified that it should be aggravated by tuberculosis. Through Tatiana you'll be able to inform attorney Niccolai;[2] with all such requests the intervention of someone who can go to the offices concerned is worth more than a hundred letters. It should be added that I'm suffering from a serious nervous depression and insomnia, so you can imagine what my nights are like. In the application you must also say that because of my past work as an intellectual I suffer very much from the difficulties of studying and reading that one encounters living in a dormitory full of sick people and you must also ask that when I'll be on my own I will be allowed to have paper and ink so that I may devote myself to work of a literary character and the study of languages. Remember that I've been assigned to Turi not because of pulmonary diseases, but due to chronic uremia that has ruined my teeth

and my stomach and has been the cause of nervous ailments resulting in migraines and chronic neurasthenia.

3. Write to Tatiana that I can have neither suits nor coats: only linens. Either you directly or through Tatiana should send me: a comb—two or three pillow cases—a few packs of Esportazione cigarettes—and to perfume the tobacco get them to send me three or four "American fava beans" (they are sold in large pharmacies in Rome).

4. I don't know what books you should send me, for the time being get them to send me the catalogue of the publisher "Il Nuraghe" and the De Agostini Atlas-Calendar. Write to Tatiana immediately to inform Attorney Niccolai about the application to the Ministry of Justice and to give her my best wishes. Reassure mother about my health. Inform Tatiana that I have not yet received anything directly from the bookshop, but only three parcels forwarded from Rome; have they been informed of my new address? or has the communication gone astray?

Write to me as much as you can and get others to write to me. Embrace mother and everyone at home. Affectionately

Antonio

1. He was moved to an individual cell several weeks after this letter, as seen in letter to Tania, August 27, 1928.
2. Adelmo Niccolai, one of the three defense attorneys at the trial of May 28–June 4, 1928.

———————

August 27, 1928

Dearest Tania,

This month I've received six letters from you. Thank you. As for myself, for a while yet I'll be able to write to you only once a month, that is, I'll be able to write only one letter every fifteen days (the other to mother or to Carlo). And (at least this for now) my letters can only be of an immediate nature, aimed at organizing my life in some way or other. I herewith begin the list of my problems.

1. For goodness' sake, don't start any procedures for any transfer whatsoever to any other prison. Don't even think of it. If I had anything to say about it, I would never travel again. My last trip was

horrendous and I still haven't completely recovered from the brutalized condition into which it plunged me. I spent almost twenty nights
without sleeping!

2. I've been put in a cell by myself. From this point of view I'm
better off than before. However, I want you to continue with the application so that I will be granted paper and pen by the Ministry.
When I'm be able to work in a coherent manner on some literary
research or to do some translations, time will pass easily: I have a
marvelous capacity to adjust. What has made imprisonment difficult
for me until now (apart from all the other deprivations that go with
my situation) has been intellectual idleness.

3. On the problem of books I should write several paragraphs.
Has Sperling bookstore in Milan gotten my new address? Up until
now I haven't received anything directly. So I'm not getting the magazines in their proper order and I cannot check the mailings. What
does Attorney Ariis propose to do with the books I stored with him
in Milan? Did he write you anything? Ask my brother to send him a
reminder, because I think it is necessary. For the Russian books that
you want to send me I would need a dictionary: I should have one,
Makarov's Russian-French. The one you had sent me to Ustica was
French-Russian and I don't know where it ended up (the books I had
in Ustica were, after a letter of mine, handed for safekeeping to Virginio Borioni, who was not among the arrested in Palermo. I don't
know whether you have written to him to give him my address; he
had promised to send me the books to the penitentiary to which I
would be assigned). From among my Roman books I would like to
have the books dealing with history and those concerning Catholic
Action and Catholicism in general. Do not send me *Emporium* or anything similar. I do not want to receive anything else besides what I
myself have ordered from Sperling bookstore. One thing that you
might let me have is the *Secolo Illustrato* of Milan for the photographs
of current events: you can get me a subscription from July 1 (with
back issues) for the second semester of 1928.

4. As you have written to me, Carlo has passed on the list of
things I want. Add: (a) a gutta-percha purse for tobacco; (b) Dr.
Favre's headache pills; (c) some Bayer aspirin.

Uff! I'm fed up with all these things that I must write to you. I
think of all the walking that I'm forcing you to do: and you haven't

kept me up to date on your phlebitis! Let's talk about something else. For example, about the present you want to give Giulia. You know that I've never taken seriously your idea of giving Giulia a present on my behalf. For Delio and for Giuliano it's all right: they may really believe that I'm the one who is giving them the present and they may link my name with the objects that they receive. But Giulia is not a child and it seems to me that this business of the presents is a kind of hoax. At most I could make her a present of my fountain pen, but it would be of no use to her! Don't you agree? On the other hand I feel enormously at fault toward her because I haven't written to her directly for such a long time. I'm sure that she doesn't think that she is less dear to me because of it, but I don't know what to do about it: when I write I feel that I am scribbling some sort of bureaucratic screed and I don't want to write to her when dominated by such a state of mind. You see how sentimental I am! How lucky I am to have you, who are so good and won't be offended if I don't hesitate to send you bureaucratic screeds. This is a fine muddle! Dearest Tania, I want you to write to Giulia for me. And anyway, are you still sending her my letters? They are not only written for you: nor am I always able to think about you as detached from Giulia. Otherwise how could I go on giving you so much trouble? Which would be trouble, in fact, if there were not something of Giulia in you and I did not think of you as inseparable from Giulia. So you see, this is a kind of epistolary Pirandelloism.[1] My dear, I embrace you tenderly.

Antonio

Do you know that hearing you call me Nino has a very strange effect on me: this is what they called me back home a long time ago and this is how my mother and Carlo address me. It also makes me laugh a bit because in my life this evokes a very old and anachronistic scene.

---

1. A reference to the theme of multiple identity and the variety of roles people play at different moments and in different circumstances of their lives, in the plays of Luigi Pirandello (1867–1936), to whom Gramsci devoted a series of articles as theater critic for the Turinese edition of the Socialist newspaper *Avanti!*.

September 6, 1928

Dearest Tania,

I've received your letters of August 31 and of September 1 and 3 after I had already written to you (I wrote to you on August 22 and I sent it registered mail; on September 3 you had not received this letter; keep me informed so that I may put in a claim in case it was lost). I've requested permission to write this extraordinary letter to you to try and stop the flood of initiatives that you have suddenly unleashed.[1] What on earth can you be thinking of? The moment I arrived at Turi I wrote to you "not to send me anything that I hadn't asked for." During an interview the prison warden told me that he had underlined this sentence to give greater emphasis to it. You answered me that it was all right, that you would stick to this rule; why did you change your mind? And the same must be said for the business about Soriano.[2] First you mention the matter, promising me that you wouldn't do anything without my prior consent, then you write to me that you've spoken about it at the Ministry. Why do you act like this? Today my anger has passed, because I've received the four packages and, if nothing else, I've been forced to laugh about your loving naïveté, but I assure you that during the last few days I've been very upset. This has actually made me ill. The impossibility of writing to you right away and being in time to avoid some catastrophic initiative (such as compelling me to travel in my present state) filled me with real fury, I assure you. I have the sensation of being doubly imprisoned, because you too were beginning not to recognize any will on my part, arranging my life at your whim and refusing to hear my opinion, after all I'm in prison, I know what it is, I bear its painful marks on my skin. How can you have any illusions about extraordinary transfers, despite all the promises, when you have seen what has happened to me until now? And besides I don't want to change in any way, even if they were to transfer me in a sleeping car, because in principle I am against any change that isn't necessary and not undertaken for good reason, very good reason. Already in Milan we had a rather lively exchange of opinions on this subject: you had promised me not to start this all over again. Alas! And the same goes for the things that you are sending me and that you still intend to send me. I had to laugh today, but I must tell you there's reason to be sad at seeing what you think I can have. This means that you haven't the faintest idea what prison is like, that is, that you are unable to form an accurate conception of my real situation. You think I'm living in a boarding house or something of the sort. That's it; do you understand? No suit, no coat, etc. etc. Nothing made of metal: not even a tin of Vaseline. You definitely mustn't send me anything that I haven't asked for beforehand and you mustn't take any initiative before receiving my explicit approval. With no exception whatsoever. Otherwise you'll make my imprisonment more difficult rather than easier. Instead, do as I tell you. (1) I'm still not receiving the magazines from the bookstore with any regularity. (2) Instead of sending me a German grammar for Italians, you sent me an Italian grammar for Germans (and that's a fact). (3) My books in Ustica have been held by Virginio Borioni (a political prisoner). (4) I don't know whether you have written to Ariis about the books I left in Milan. Enough. Now don't you too get angry because of what I've written to you: I know very well that you acted as you did for the sake of what you thought was my own good. In any case you mustn't have any doubts: if I need anything I'll write to you. For example: you could send me a few packs of Giubek or Macedonia Esportazione cigarettes. Send me about a dozen of those so-called American fava beans that are used to add scent to tobacco (they are sold in pharmacies). Also send me a few translations from Russian (Slavia Publ.) and Lo Gatto's Literature.[3] I embrace you tenderly, but don't make me angry again. I want you to believe that I have a rational will and what I do I do after having thought it over for some time, a long time.

Antonio

1. As indicated in the introduction, this was a persistent problem in the relationship between Gramsci and Tania. She understood his need to have his will respected in all matters affecting him, but there were times when she felt that she had to intervene with the authorities whether Gramsci approved of her actions beforehand or not. She did so in several attempts to ease the conditions of his imprisonment and in appeals for his transfer from Turi based on his deteriorating health. She also acted independently on a number of occasions in mediating the troubled relationship between Gramsci and his wife.

2. Tania had sought to have Gramsci transferred to a prison in Soriano, near Viterbo. This prison, like the one in Turi, was reserved for prisoners with serious or chronic illnesses.

3. Ettore Lo Gatto, *Letteratura sovietica* (Rome: Istituto per l'Europa Orientale, 1928).

September 11, 1928

Dearest Carlo,

I've received your insured letter of August 27. Thank you. Perhaps Tatiana has already informed you that my situation has much improved due to the fact that for a few weeks now I've been in a cell by myself. The question of having pen and paper at my disposal has not moved one step forward; I don't know what the result is of the applications made by you and Tatiana. In any case you should know that everything depends on the Ministry, as the inspector who recently visited the Turi prison assured me, so that from here I can do little and obtain nothing. You must continue to try to obtain this permission, which is not excluded by regulations and that is given to a good number of people in other prisons. I don't believe that they intend to apply measures of particular severity against me.

I received the package. I don't understand the complications that you've imagined for the Esportazione cigarettes, for which you tell me you have written to the free port in Genoa. Who knows what you thought I was asking for: some extraordinary specialty. You must always remember that I never ask for anything extraordinary or unusual.

There is one recommendation I must make to you, which I have already made to Tatiana rather emphatically. That is, not to initiate any procedure concerning me and not to send me anything if I haven't been informed of it beforehand. Tatiana gave me two dreadful weeks by letting me know that she had said to some clerk at the Ministry that it would be a good thing to transfer me from Turi to Soriano. I don't know whether you too were in agreement with this business. At any rate you are now advised that all these initiatives displease me enormously and that I will not accept changes if I have anything to say about it. I don't want to travel again. The last trip reduced me to a rag. You cannot imagine how much I suffered. The blood and skin irritation that afflicted me during all the changes demanded by the journey was such that I had an attack of so-called St. Anthony's fire, accompanied by atrocious pain. Now I'm getting back to normal, but I'm still half brutalized. You can imagine what an effect it had on me to know that I might be threatened by a new haphazard journey. I've written to Tatiana perhaps even too harshly. But she was still harboring illusions about some extraordinary journey. Illusions, because in the last analysis everything is decided upon by the carabinieri and police headquarters. By order of the Special Tribunal I had to make an extraordinary journey from Ustica to Milan; I was in transit twenty days and I slept in ten different jails. The journey from Milan to Rome was unusual because of its duration, but due to the lack of carabinieri I spent sixteen hours in irons in the prison car; this was instead of third class as per the Tribunal's orders, and they made us travel in the prison car, at night, something that is prohibited by the regulations. For the journey from Rome to Turi I had a medical certificate: at the moment of departure the certificate disappeared and I traveled for twelve days, tormented by "St. Anthony's fire." To sum up, I don't want to travel or change. You are duly advised. Write Tatiana that in her letter of September 1 she refers to news about the children that I'm supposed to have received and that in fact I have not received at all, perhaps a letter has been lost. Tell her also that among the Roman books there should be one entitled: Gino Piastru, *La truffa garibaldina in Francia* [The Garibaldi fraud in France], which I would like to have in order to reconstruct a friendly conversation I had with the pretrial judge in Milan.

Send me a bit more detailed news about mother's health, since she hasn't written to me. Teresina still hasn't written. Among my books in Ghilarza there is one: *Goethe: Über allen Gipfeln* [Goethe: Above all peaks] (in German, bound) that I would like to have. Greet and kiss everyone at home. Embrace mother and give her my best wishes. I embrace all of you.

Antonio

September 24, 1928

Dearest Tania,

I've received your letters of September 15 and 17. I was somewhat anxious, because I hadn't received any word from you since September 3 and I couldn't find a reason for it: you had previously mentioned your rather shaky health and I was afraid that you weren't even able to write to me.

I see that my last, somewhat . . . tragic letter did not perturb you too much. Nevertheless, you must take it into serious account. Apparently you are not disposed to do so; why such obstinacy? For example, you announce that you were going to send me some money. There's no point in your sending it. What Carlo sent me is more than sufficient. One can spend very little: at any rate, I wouldn't know what to buy because the things on sale here are very limited. I never did describe for you my existence, which is not very brilliant and can hardly inspire colorful vignettes. With regard to the material aspect of things, I have already become adjusted. The daily fare: 300 grams of bread, 700 grams of milk, about 200 grams of pasta dressed with butter, and two raw eggs. This is supposed to be infirmary fare that I receive since I cannot eat meat or soups with tomato. I myself buy every day an additional fifty grams of sugar and fifty grams of butter and for some time now one kilo of grapes. Apparently we're allowed to buy one kilo of grapes every day throughout the season: I eat the grapes and very little bread, about 120 grams a day, some of it with milk and some with butter in the evening. I have trouble digesting even this food, although it is so very light. The main problem is sleeping. I sleep too little and I constantly suffer from general fatigue. The Sedobrol helped me, but that soon ran out. All my ailments are due to uric acid, according to the diagnosis of the doctor in Rome, who examined me before my departure. Do you think it might be possible to take a general treatment for uremia? I think that when the cold weather starts I will resume the injections of Bioplastina, which in the past have done me some good.

You haven't told me anything about the application at the Ministry so that I can obtain permission to write in my cell. Carlo hasn't told me anything about it either. What concrete steps have been taken? I thought that if initiated from the outside, by the family, the procedure would be more expeditious. Now, not knowing anything from you, I hesitate to initiate the application myself, in order to avoid overlappings that irk the bureaucratic mentality.

In the same way you haven't written me anything about the periodicals I'm supposed to receive from the Sperling bookstore. I left

Rome two and a half months ago: the change of address should have been requested immediately. Why wasn't this done? Where are the magazines being sent after your departure from Rome? And why aren't they arriving at Turi? I beg you to clear up this matter that concerns me more than anything else, and to make arrangements for me to receive regularly the publications to which I am subscribing. A tremendous confusion has occurred in the meantime: skipped issues, etc. etc. And to think that in Milan the service functioned perfectly and I was able to have the magazines as soon as they came out despite the double control by the Special Tribunal and the prison. I really beg you to look into this and to clear up this matter before any other. This is essential for me. Tell me about your health. Don't worry too much about mine, which will continue to be more or less the same as in the past. The really important thing is that I no longer have to travel and thus won't have further occasions for becoming exhausted. Write to me often or at least with regularity. Every piece of news leads me to imagine all sorts of extraordinary events, illnesses, etc. And I can write to you only once a month. I haven't yet received the packages from Rome. In my opinion, you were wrong not to send them off personally. Let's hope for the best. I haven't received any letters from Carlo either, and for quite some time. Enough. I await your letters. I embrace you.

Antonio

October 8, 1928

Dearest Carlo,

I received your letters of September twenty-third (insured) and of the twenty-fourth, mother's letter of the twenty-fifth, and your postcard of October second. Thanks for the 200 lire and the news that you and mother send me about life in the town. (By the way: I've received the small atlas, the "Nuraghe" catalogue and the cigarettes). You must always send me news about Ghilarza: it is very interesting and significant. It seems to me that one may draw a conclusion from all this. Whereas before, in Sardinia, there existed delinquency of a prevalently occasional or passionate character, undoubtedly linked to backward customs and to old ways of seeing things that, though they were barbaric, nevertheless preserved some traits of generosity and grandeur, now instead there is the development of a technically organized professional criminality that follows preestablished plans, and preestablished by groups of instigators who sometimes are wealthy, who have a certain social position, and who are driven to crime by a moral perversion that has nothing in common with that of classic Sardinian banditry. This is one of the most characteristic and significant signs of the times. And just as significant is the increase of suicides.

You shouldn't have ordered the Goethe book from the Sperling bookstore. I don't believe it can be found simply by giving the title, because it is one of the many Goethe anthologies published in Germany, whose title is taken from the first verse of a very short poem. I really believe it is on the shelf at home, because I remember having seen it in 1924. Anyway, please, never order books for me from Sperling, because an incredible confusion is being created. Instead in Cagliari you might buy me issues of the review *Mediterranea*; I often see it mentioned in other publications in connection with articles on Sardinian history, which at times are very interesting, but I don't know where it is published: I think in Cagliari. In any case it should be easy to find in Cagliari. In your postcard you write that you aren't receiving any letters from Tatiana. Tatiana writes that she has written you and mother and that she hasn't received any replies. There must have been some mixup. I don't know, therefore, whether you know that Tatiana has moved to Milan, where she lives at Via Plinio 34. Just today I received a registered letter from her containing photographs of the children and a letter from Giulia who sends me good news. The children look charming and are well.

I'm glad that you, mother, and Grazietta all feel better. I would like to point out to mother that it seems to me that she takes too much pleasure in writing me that Edmea reproaches her mother because she has married. Couldn't this be somewhat influenced by what she hears said around her? For you the situation is difficult and embarrassing, I understand that, especially now that the girl has grown up. But don't you think that it is a bad thing to set, or contribute to setting, a little girl against her mother? And do you think that when Edmea grows up and will really be able to understand and judge, she might not hold against you the fact of having instilled such morbid feelings in her or of not having prevented them from taking root? It seems to me that her mother was absolutely right to get married. As far as I know she is a good woman who has always worked and has always been treated very badly by Nannaro, not because he refused to marry her, of course, but because of many other wretched acts.[1] Do you believe that one day Edmea might not discover a lot of things and feel that today she had falsified her feelings? I write these things because I myself suffered as a child because of incorrect judgments and some of these sufferings have left a scar on my consciousness.[2]

Tell me about the procedure you have initiated or still must initiate to obtain permission for me to write. You mustn't just write to Attorney Niccolai; you must take care of the procedure in person at the Ministry, on behalf of the family. I thought that you'd be able to do so more quickly than I. If I'd only known, I'd have initiated the procedure directly, through prison channels. Well, patience. Write to me as often as you can. My health is always the same. An affectionate embrace to all.

Antonio

1. See the note on "Nannaro" in the list of correspondents and family members.
2. Gramsci is probably referring to the fact that the truth about his father's imprisonment had been kept from him. See the note on Gramsci's father in the list of correspondents and family members.

October 20, 1928

Dearest Tania,

Am I being punished for that rather wicked letter of mine? For an entire month you've written me only twice: on the fifth and the sixth of October. I was very glad, truly happy, about the photographs of the children, and of Giulia and also yours. But why and how have you become so mean? How could you write and think that receiving a photograph of yours would not please me and that I might send it back to you? The world is truly vast and terrible and especially for someone who is in prison ever more incomprehensible. You write to me once a month and you also write to me in such a mean way! It is true that for two years now I've caused you endless bother and annoyance and then I have even dared to reproach you, but you seem to

me, despite everything, to be at least a bit naive, if you do not understand that my situation makes such needs imperative for me. What I
regret most is that during these two years I have lost almost all of my
sensitivity and that the conviction that I am not understood, within
the limitations in which I am obliged to write, plunges me ever more
deeply into a state of passive and beatific indifference from which I
cannot wrest myself free. So, for example, despite the fact that this
was increasingly becoming a tormenting almost obsessive thought of
mine, I had stopped writing to ask for photographs of the children.
Not receiving them made me suffer cruelly, but I was no longer able
to write on the subject and I was abandoning myself to the drift of
my feelings, without even making an attempt to wrench myself free
from them. I would like to explain to you and Giulia the general state
of mind in which I find myself after two years in jail, but perhaps it
is still too soon. It seems to me, for the time being, that I can only
focus on this point: that I feel rather like a survivor in every sense of
the word. To make myself better understood, I would have to have
recourse to a rather complex comparison: they say that the sea beyond thirty meters of depth is always immobile, well I have sunk to a
depth of at least twenty meters, that is, I am immersed in the layer
that moves only when storms of a certain size, well above normal, are
unleashed. But I feel that I am sinking deeper and deeper and I can
lucidly see the moment in which, by imperceptible degrees, I will
reach the level of absolute immobility, where even the most formidable storms no longer make themselves felt and from where it also
will no longer be possible to see the motions of the upper layers, even
a mere breaker of foamy spume. And, what is worse, it seems to me
that I have already fallen into a trancelike state, which much be typical
of old convicts, who no longer reason by making realistic connections but by intuitions of a magical or spiritualistic character. When
the photographs arrived I went downstairs to sign the log of the registered letters absolutely certain that it would be the photographs. No
prior element could have prompted this thought in me, indeed, your
having written that you would send me some money might have
simply prompted the idea that it had arrived. And there is more. Before I received the things that you sent from Rome (the suitcase and
the package of books), I clearly thought that you would send me a
specific small wooden box. There was nothing particular about it, I

didn't even remember it any longer, or at least nothing could induce me to think of it. And a small box really was there. This episode struck me and even today it strikes me even more than the one with the photographs.

Enough. Perhaps in another letter I will try to explain myself better. For the rest, I don't want you to believe (nor should Giulia believe) that I've become a complete fool. Perhaps sleeping too little has dazed me a bit and induces these states of mind.

So I've received the things that you've sent from Rome and I thank you. Now I also receive directly from the bookstore the subscription magazines. I don't know why I'm not receiving *Critica Fascista* to which I had subscribed in Milan and that I received all through February: in June the bookstore wrote to me in Rome that they would take care of the matter, but I have yet to see any results of this taking care of.

If you don't mind, write to Carlo, telling him that I've received his letter and that he should have them make for me at home some very robust socks, because the prison shoes have ruined my footwear.

For the rest I don't need anything. Dear Tania, don't be mean, write to me often and write to Giulia to tell her of all my joy at having seen her photograph and that of the children. I embrace you tenderly.

Antonio

November 3, 1928

Dearest Tania,

I've received your two letters and the two letters from Giulia. Next time I'll write an entire letter for Giulia. I've written for Carlo to send you the information you request with regard to the petition. I don't know what you will do and in what form. At any rate warn the "personality" who is supposed to support my request (mine because it concerns me, but submitted by my family and not by me) to say that I am ready to have the table I need built at my expense, so that it will not cost the prison administration anything.

Don't worry about the money. I have a lot, approximately 1,000 lire in my pass book; so I'm well stocked for some time against all emergencies.

You may send me the quadrilingual book that you mentioned; it will be very useful for me.

I'm sorry to hear about the great effort your work requires. I do not want to add to it by asking you to write me at length and often. It is enough for me if you write regularly, even only simple picture postcards. Being left without news for a long time makes me nervous and preoccupied.

From Rome I received a small case of books, not just a package: I expressed myself incorrectly. I have not yet been able to obtain them because I have a number of others that I am reading and I cannot keep more than a certain number in my cell. I don't know what the new books are that you say have been sent from Milan: perhaps the books from Slavia? I received them. By the way: as soon as they appear send me volumes 5 and 6 of *War and Peace*.[1] And what about the books I left with attorney Ariis? Up until now I haven't heard anything about them. I'd like to know, not because I need them right away—in fact it would be a good idea to delay their shipment—but so that I know what to think about them. Dearest Tania, I embrace you affectionately.

Antonio

1. Vols. 5 and 6 in a six-volume edition of *War and Peace*, published in 1928 by Slavia.

November 5, 1928

Dearest Mother,

I've received your insured letter of October 24, the cigarettes, the Goethe book. I'm very glad to hear you're better. My health remains the same. The cure that Carlo suggests can also be followed directly in prison by asking that the necessary medicines be bought at my expense; I believe that it is best to do this, after having asked the doctor's opinion. In this way we'll save some mailing costs. Tatiana writes me that she wants to know from Carlo the precise date on which the application for me to be allowed to write was submitted as well as the name of the person to whom the application was delivered. Write to her immediately because she said that she will be able to obtain very authoritative support for it. I am writing half of a sheet of this letter for Tatiana; you will send it to her in Milan (Via Plinio 34) together with the information she is requesting. I already sent you the news about the children last time, which is good. You yourself should write to Tatiana so she'll send you the most recent photographs: I think that if she is leaving she can send you the ones that she herself received. The other news they sent me basically concerns various events in the children's lives. That they love each other, etc. Tell Carlo that if he sends me more cigarettes he should add a bit of nasalina,[1] putting it in a wooden container (a snuff box, for example), because metal objects are forbidden in jail. I've caught some very bad colds. It is very windy here and I want to sleep with my window slightly open; it is easy to catch a cold since I get up sometimes and often at night it is very cold. Write to me more often to reassure me about your health, and the health of everybody else at home. Thank Carlo for what he is doing for me. Hugs for everyone and most tenderly for you.

Antonio

1. Nasal medicine.

November 19, 1928

Dearest Giulia,

I've been very unkind to you. In truth, my justifications are not well founded. After my departure from Milan, I was very very tired. All the conditions of my life deteriorated. I suffered much more from my incarceration. Now I feel somewhat better. The very fact that a certain stabilization has intervened, that life flows according to certain rules, has in a certain sense also normalized the course of my thoughts. I was very happy to receive your photograph and that of the children. When too large a span of time comes between visual impressions, the interval is filled with bad thoughts; especially as regards Giuliano I did not know what to think, I had no image that could sustain my memory. Now I'm really happy. In general, for these last few months, I have felt more isolated and completely cut off from the life of the world. I read a lot, books and magazines; a lot in relation to the intellectual life that one can lead in a prison. But I have lost much of the pleasure in reading. Books and magazines only offer general ideas, sketches (more or less successful) of general currents in the world's life, but they cannot give the immediate, direct, vivid impression of the lives of Peter, Paul, and John, of single, real individuals, and unless one understands them one cannot understand what is being universalized and generalized. Many years ago, in 1919 and 1920, I knew a very naive and very pleasant young worker. Every Saturday evening, after work, he would come to my office to be one of the first to read the review I was editing. He often said: "I wasn't able to sleep, oppressed by this thought: what will Japan do?" Japan of all places obsessed him, because the Italian newspapers write about Japan only when the Mikado dies and an earthquake kills at least 10,000 people. Japan escaped his grasp; therefore he was unable to form a systematic picture of the world's forces and so it seemed to him that he understood nothing at all. In those days I laughed about such a state of mind and I made fun of my friend. Today I understand it. I too have my Japan: it is the life of Peter, Paul, and also of Giulia, Delio, and Giuliano. I completely lack the molecular sensation: how could I, even summarily, perceive the life of the complex whole? Even my own life feels shrunken and paralyzed: how could it be otherwise, when I lack the sense of your life and that of the children? Moreover: I'm always afraid of being overwhelmed by the prison routine. This is a monstrous machine that crushes and levels according to certain set phases. When I see men who have been in jail for five, eight, ten years act and speak, and I observe the psychic deformations inflicted on them, I truly shudder and wonder about the outlook for my own future. I believe that the others too have thought (not all of them but at least some) that they would not allow themselves to be overwhelmed and instead, without even being aware of it, the process is so molecular and slow, today they find themselves changed and do not know it, cannot judge it because they are changed so completely. But, for example, I realize that I am no longer able to laugh at myself, as in the past, and this is serious. Dear Giulia, are you interested in all this chatter? And does it give you an idea about my life? However, you know that I do take an interest in what happens in the world too. Recently I've read quite a number of books on Catholic activities. This is a new "Japan." Through what stages will French radicalism pass in order to split and give rise to a French Catholic party? This problem "won't let me sleep," as happened with that young friend of mine. And there are others too, naturally. Did you like the letter opener? Do you know that it cost me almost one month of work and half my finger tips worn down? My dear, write me more extensively about yourself and the children. You should send me your photographs at least every six months, so that I'll be able to follow their development and see your smile more often.[1] I embrace you tenderly, my dearest.

Antonio

P.S. For Tania. How unkind you are Tania. How long it's been that I haven't received any news from you? You don't have to write long letters, even a picture postcard will do. Do you know that I too am increasingly engulfed by an inertia that keeps me from writing? And I must struggle to overcome it. But will I always overcome it? There are people here who haven't written for months and years. I too will come to the same end, certainly, unless I find active correspondents. Dear Tania, I embrace you hoping that you are not ill.

Antonio

1. For many people, looking at photographs can be disturbing because they stop a moment in time, thereby heightening the sense of difference between past and present. For a prisoner, on the other hand, who is out of touch with loved ones for many years, photographs become a precious record of precisely that passage of time, and of the differences that time has wrought.

December 3, 1928

Dearest Carlo,

During the past month I've received very little news from all of you: a letter from mother dated November 8 and one from you dated the eleventh, then nothing (of course I've received the socks, the cigarettes, and later on the nose and eye drops). Why do you leave me without any information for such a long time, especially during a period when mother is ill? I understand that one need not write long letters: there may be neither the desire nor the material that could be considered interesting; but it would be enough to write a postcard now and then with a few lines of essential news!

Please write to Tatiana to tell her these little things that she has been anxiously asking me: I've deposited 930 lire in my account which however at the end of the month will be reduced to approximately 700 lire, because besides ordinary expenses I will have to pay for a chest that I had made and don't know how much it will cost, but I imagine it will be more than 50 lire. Last month I spent exactly 120 lire. When I arrived at Turi I had 650 lire. In Rome nothing was deposited for me. And there you have my basic budget. As regards my estimate for the future: I think it will be a good idea to have in my account a permanent fund of at least 700 lire for any extraordinary event, for instance, an illness, owing to which I might have to go to hospital, take a transfer journey, etc. Once things have been arranged in this way, Tatiana can be reassured and need not worry about my finances. I tell you, I wouldn't like her to send me any money because I know what sacrifices she makes and how in the end she pays with her health. So you too must try to convince her and reassure her. Tell her that should I need anything, I will certainly ask her, but that for the time being I don't need anything at all.

So she mustn't worry about initiating any applications to increase the amount of money I am allowed to spend daily. It's not worth the effort, because there isn't anything to buy here. Turi is a small agricultural center and it certainly doesn't shine because of its opulent market; furthermore, I believe that the overwhelming majority of the prisoners cannot buy anything, since they have no money and as a result the available items for sale are very limited. This is a matter of fact. As a matter of principle: one must never ask for more than one thing, if one doesn't want to be considered a professional nuisance and not be taken seriously for anything. Right now we are working on the application for writing. This one application is quite enough.

Tatiana has disappointed me; I thought she had a more sober imagination and that she was a more practical person. Instead I see that she spins wild tales, such as the one that, due to reasons of health, it might be possible to change my imprisonment into internment: possible in the ordinary way, obviously, that is, by virtue of written laws and regulations. But this would be possible only through a personal act of mercy,[1] which would be granted only following an application that is motivated by a change of opinion, acquiescence, etc. etc. Tatiana doesn't think of all of this: she has a pure naïveté that sometimes frightens me because I haven't the slightest intention of getting on my knees before anyone or of changing my behavior in the slightest. I am stoic enough to look with the greatest calm on all the consequences of the aforementioned premises. I've known for a long time what could happen to me. Reality has confirmed me in my resolution and has not at all shaken me. In view of all this, Tatiana must realize that she shouldn't even talk about such fanciful notions, because just talking about them might lead people to think that these are approaches that I might have suggested. The very idea of it irritates me. Do me a favor and write these things to Tatiana because if I write them I'm afraid of losing my temper and hurting her feelings. What's more, write to her that I've left my winter slippers and my over-stockings in Milan: I could really use them because it is starting to get cold.

I would also like you to send me the "Casali serum," as you once wrote you would. With the approaching cold I feel weaker. You should also send me some Ovaltine so that the treatment to rebuild my strength will be more complete. As for the amount, send enough for a complete treatment. You ought to send me some felt soles to slip inside my shoes to prevent my socks from getting worn out and also to keep warmer. You can send me everything when you send me the cigarettes.

Dearest Carlo, write more often; why don't you write about the cooperative dairies where you work? I would be very interested.

Embrace mother most affectionately. Kisses to all.

Cordially. Antonio

(For your information, just in case it got lost, I didn't receive any money from you in November).

1. "Grace" or an act of mercy granted by the head of state requires a plea for mercy on a prisoner's part and an implicit admission of guilt. In any event, Gramsci was convinced that, given the circumstances of his arrest and imprisonment, such a concession by Mussolini in his regard would inevitably be interpreted as a sign of moral and political compromise. The letters Gramsci sent to Mussolini during his imprisonment were intended to obtain the best possible conditions for himself by making full use of existing Italian legislation regarding the rights of political prisoners.

December 17, 1928

Dearest Tania,

This month you've been very good: you've written me four letters! I thank you with all my heart. Now I'll try to answer all the questions that you have raised, in an orderly manner.

(1) I think you're absolutely right to join your family. Especially your mother, who will be comforted and made happy by it. But I also think that you would be wrong to go during the winter. In my opinion, you ought to go in May. For various reasons, all of them valid. Your health. I think that it would be unpleasant for you and for everyone if immediately upon your arrival you were to fall ill and be forced to lie in a hospital. Besides, in winter, life is all curled up in itself and if one doesn't have a large apartment, the addition of another person becomes irksome and diminishes the joy of seeing you. This is simply a suggestion. (2) Today I'm not answering many of the questions in your letter of November 25 because I delegated Carlo to write you about them fifteen days ago: I hope he did so. (3) About the books that the attorney is still holding. You can have them sent to me and free him of the bother. I've prevailed on them to make me a very capacious chest and so I can keep my books nicely packed and all together in the prison storeroom. I would like to know whether my books in Milan are all there, or which ones have been lost. I write this because to my great surprise and some disappointment in the Rome jail I came across a prisoner who had my German grammar: Signora Pina had thought it might be a good idea to make him a present of it. I still need almost all of the books I had in Milan, because I wasn't able to read some of them and there are others I would like to reread and study. And so I would like to know whether there are still books of mine in Rome or whether those that didn't fit into the footlocker have been lost. Furthermore, from the Rome jail I sent out the first volume of Salandra's *Memorie* [Memoirs], which I haven't found in the footlocker. Can you inform me about all of this?; meanwhile get the attorney to send me the books that were delivered to him by the prison in Milan. (4) Here is a list of the books that you can have sent to me: (α) Hegel, *Introduzione alla storia della filosofia*, [Introduction to the history of philosophy] edited by F. Momigliano

(Laterza, Bari); (β) Guido de Ruggero, *Sommario di storia della filosofia* [Summary of the history of philosophy] (Laterza, Bari); (τ) A. Gerbi, *La politica del Settecento* [The politics of the eighteenth century] (Laterza, Bari); (δ) A.C. Jemolo, *Il Giansenismo in Italia* [Jansenism in Italy] (Laterza, Bari); (Σ) Ben. Croce, *La poesia di Dante* [Dante's poetry] (Laterza, Bari); (θ) Ben. Croce, *Poesia e non poesia* [Poetry and nonpoetry] (Laterza, Bari). And in addition: *L'Almanacco letterario per il 1928* [The literary almanac for 1928] (Unitas Milan); *Il calendario-atlante De Agostini per 1929* (The De Agostini atlas-calendar for 1929) and a book by Vincenzo Morello on the tenth canto of Dante's *Inferno* published by Mondadori, whose exact title I do not know.[1] (5) Advise the bookstore that I have not received number thirty-eight (September 11) of the Rassegna Settimanale della Stampa Estera [*Weekly Review of the Foreign Press*] and the September number of Benedetto Croce's *Critica*. Maybe they were sent to Rome and have gone astray. I would really like to have them.

Dearest Tania, so now I've gotten rid of practical matters. I would really like to write to you about many other things, to chat with you, as you say. But I'm not yet psychologically ripe, I don't feel like it at all during the half hours every second Monday when I'm summoned to write. You provoke me, very amiably, but I will not be carried away even by, how shall I put it? paternal vanity. Perhaps, when I feel better and have fewer headaches, I'll again find the impelling desire that I had in Milan. But in those days things were very different: I would write two letters every week and I wrote them in my cell, with four and a half hours at my disposal. In Rome and here things have changed, also technically, because we write in a common room, at school desks, and we must work as quickly as possible. I write very swiftly and I tend to write only about very concrete matters.

Write me at greater length about your health. You know that five months ago, when I saw you in Rome, you looked like a skeleton. Because of this too your father is right when he lectures you wisely about your trip. You must recover properly before deciding to undertake such an exhausting effort. Next time I'll write for Giulia. I'll write mother tomorrow, because we are granted an extra letter for Christmas.

Dearest, I embrace you tenderly, with many good wishes.

Antonio

I've just remembered that I had decided to ask you to have them send me an English grammar. I would like the one by Pietro Bardi, Laterza, Bari, which I already used for study for a while at the university where I had also taken a course in English language and literature. For the time being don't send me a dictionary, I'll ask you for it in due time, when I've reviewed the grammar and gotten my bearings. I didn't quite understand what you wrote me about Fabrizio.[2] You should remember that I don't know anything. For example, I haven't even found out what happened to Tulli,[3] my cellmate in Milan.

1. Gramsci's request for Croce's *La poesia di Dante* and especially for the book by Vincenzo Morello, *Dante, Farinata, Cavalcanti* (Milan: Mondadori, 1927), gives the first hint of his intention to study canto 10 of Dante's *Inferno*, to which he devoted some pages of the notebooks published in English translation in *Selections*, pp. 147–163. See letters to Tania, August 26, 1929, September 20, 1931, February 22, 1932, and April 3, 1933, for subsequent remarks and pages of critical analysis concerning canto 10.

2. Fabrizio Maffi. See letter to Tania, December 19, 1926, n. 1.

3. Enrico Tulli

December 31, 1928

Dearest Carlo,

I've received a lot of things: the medicines, 200 lire, etc. My heartfelt thanks. The doctor[1] said that the Casali serum will certainly do me good. It apparently is the most suitable cure. Tatiana came here for Christmas; she stayed long enough for us to have several visits. I was really sorry that I didn't feel too well precisely during the Christmas holidays. I had an attack of uremia, with intense pains in the kidneys, intestines, and bladder, but it is already beginning to disappear. So I am afraid that Tatiana must have received a wrong impression of my general health. Actually, this illness is painful only when it becomes acute; this happens infrequently, provided one is careful to exclude all irritating and spicy foods from one's diet. From now on I will be even more careful than before and I hope to avoid any further mishaps. Aside from this unpleasantness, Tatiana's visit was a delight for me, as you can well imagine.

I've received mother's letter of the twenty-fourth with Edmea's note and drawing. I'm glad that mother is feeling better and on her way to recovery. Give Edmea many kisses from me, together with a few soft pinches in the plumper parts, and thank her for her very kind and very well expressed thoughts. It does however seem to me that even though she composes quite well and knows how to put her emotions into spontaneous and lively sentences, she does make quite a few spelling blunders that are too many even for a pupil who is only in the third grade. She must be very inattentive and always in a great rush; I also think that when she speaks she sometimes resembles a whirligig and mouths half of her words, swallowing the *r*'s with particular relish. You must make her do her homework with diligence and much discipline. In Sardinian village schools it will happen that a girl or boy who is accustomed to speaking Italian at home (even though little and badly) by that simple fact is superior to his classmates, who know only Sardinian and thus learn to read and write, to speak, to compose sentences in a completely new language. The former seem to be more intelligent and quick, whereas sometimes this is not so, and therefore both at home and at school people neglect training them to do methodical and disciplined work, thinking that with their "intelligence" they will overcome all difficulties, etc. Now spelling is precisely the stumbling block of this sort of intelligence. Unless Mea studies diligently and this deficiency is corrected, what is one to think? One will think that she is one of those many little girls with ribbons in their hair, nicely ironed little dresses, etc., who in fact have dirty bloomers. Tell this to her with a certain tact, so as not to hurt her feelings too much. As for her little drawing, I don't like it at all: it has neither spontaneity nor taste. And yet it would be fine if she could learn how to draw.

Dear Carlo, you mustn't worry too much about the money you are sending me. I don't want you to make silly, useless expenditures. You know that I'm very precise and practical when it comes to such matters, at this moment my deposit book shows 950 lire in my account, free of any unpaid debts (I've already paid for the chest). This means that I can't possibly have any urgent needs and that you mustn't worry if for a few months you find it difficult to send me even a cent. Don't you agree? Many good wishes for everyone for the New Year. I kiss you affectionately.

Antonio

1. Probably the prison doctor, named Cisternino.

1929

January 14, 1929

Dearest Tania,

I've received a postcard from you since your arrival in Milan and a package of books that you ordered from the bookstore in accordance with my letter before Christmas. Thank you so much for having come all the way to Turi: I was very glad to see you, as you can imagine. I was only afraid that such a long trip might be too tiring for you and perhaps make you ill. In Milan I spent some awful days when you fell ill after your trip from Rome to visit me.

My health has improved somewhat. The intense pains in the kidneys and intestines have not come back. I'm continuing with the Casali serum cure and as the doctor recommended I also take Wassermann's Valero-Fosfer: when I've taken all three bottles of the Casali I'll get Bioplastina injections and take the Glicerofosfati that you left with me. I've also received the hot water bottle, but I'll use it only if the sharp pains should return. Actually in Turi the winter is rather mild (these days there is a springlike sun) and I hope that I won't have any relapses. I've systematically excluded from my diet everything that might irritate the stomach: instead of the 200 grams of wine that I used to get, they now give me 300 grams of milk: so I have one liter of milk a day that I drink in the morning and the afternoon. In the same way I eat pasta only with ricotta and not with the pecorino cheese that is too sharp (but soon I will be able to obtain nonfermented cheese). Quite soon I will also be able to have writing materials in my cell and thus my greatest aspiration as a prisoner will be

241

satisfied. The books I have already received and that are mentioned in my December letter are: *L'Almanacco letterario Unitas* [The Unitas literary almanac] and Antonello Gerbi's *La politica del 700* [The politics of the eighteenth century]. So don't include them any longer in the list. Instead add a small book: Adriano Tilgher's *Storia e antistoria* [History and antihistory] (Biblioteca Editrice, Rieti). Have you received any more news from Giulia? I'm writing her a few lines, as I wait for an answer to my last letter. I have no word from home. Mother is sick. Could you send her Delio's and Giuliano's photograph? You would make her happy. You'll be able to get others, I believe. Dear Tania, I embrace you tenderly.

Antonio

January 14, 1929

Dearest Giulia,

I'm still waiting for your answer to my last letter. When we will have resumed a regular conversation (even though at long intervals), I will write you many things about my life, my impressions, etc. etc. Meanwhile you must let me know how Delio is interpreting the Meccano erector set. This interests me very much, because I've never been able to decide whether, since it deprives the child of his inventive spirit, Meccano is the modern toy that one ought to recommend the most. What do you think about it and what does your father think? In general I think that modern culture (of the American type) of which Meccano is the expression, makes people somewhat dry, mechanical, bureaucratic, and creates an abstract imagination (in a sense different from what was understood as "abstract" during the last century). There has been a type of abstraction determined by a metaphysical intoxication and an abstraction determined by a mathematical intoxication. How interesting it must be to observe the reactions to these pedagogical principles in the brain of a small child, who after all is ours and to whom we are bound by much deeper emotions than a simple "scientific interest." Dearest, write me at length. A very strong embrace.

Antonio

January 28, 1929

Dearest Mother,

I've received your letter and Grazietta's; I've also received a pack of cigarettes. Thank Grazietta very much for the news she sent me about Teresina's children and about Edmea: I'm sure that Delio and Giuliano would also be very fond of her if they could get to know her. Children immediately become attached to anyone who is fond of them and takes seriously their small interests and even their whims. And what are their whims if not their will and their feelings trying to affirm themselves and develop in conflict with the will and feelings of the grown-ups? And if the latter do not understand this and often have recourse to spankings and authoritarian intimidations, they only succeed in making these children into hypocrites and to embittering them for no good reason.

Dear mother, I believe that you should really follow the doctor's advice: you must leave Ghilarza for a while; only in this way will you recover. I myself meant to give you this advice. Why don't you go to Macomer with Carlo? Perhaps to Boroneddu with Antioga Putzulu, if she is still alive.

Did Tatiana write to you about her trip to Turi? Did she send you the photographs of the children? Please send her the page I wrote for her.[1]

Tell Carlo that I will be very grateful if he can procure the following publication for me: Raffaele Ciasca, *Momenti della colonizzazione in Sardegna nel secolo XVIII* [Moments of the colonization of Sardinia in the eighteenth century]. It is not on sale. It was published in the *Annals* of the Department of Literature of the Royal University in Cagliari where Ciasca teaches modern history, and it is printed in abstracts. Carlo can obtain it through his friends; some of them probably know the author personally. He can also procure it through the editorial offices of *Mediterranea* if he knows someone there. Also tell Carlo that I've obtained permission to write in my cell and that I thank him for everything that he did. Kiss everyone affectionately. To you many good wishes and all my tenderness.

Antonio

Do thank Teresina for the postcards.

1. Gramsci is referring to his letter to Tania dated January 29, 1929, which he attached to this letter to his mother.

January 29, 1929

Dearest Tania,

I've received your letter of the thirteenth and after that Giulia's letter. Did you see the story Giulia tells Delio, giving him a license to be mischievous? And besides, if it is true that I stretched out on the snow and began to smoke,[1] it isn't true that some peasants (who knows how many!) walked by and looked at me in astonishment. No one at all passed by and Giulia was the only one who laughed. Indeed, peasants are never astonished by anything and certainly not by a man who smokes after dusk while lying on the snow in the open countryside, while a young lady (this expression would make Giulia very angry) now serious, now laughing, stands there watching him. Dear Tania, I have a number of suggestions for you: (1) do not send me and do not have the bookstore send me any new books. Now that I'll be able to write I'll draw up a study plan and I myself will ask for the books that I need. For now I don't need any. I don't like money to be spent for almost useless or superfluous books, when later on I'll need more substantial books! (2) Tell the bookstore that I have received neither *Rassegna Settimanale della Stampa Estera* [Weekly review of the foreign press] nor the *Marzocco* issue for the first of January. Probably the subscription wasn't renewed in time. Only for the sake of precision I inform you that *Critica Fascista* [Fascist critique] was still being published at least until December 15, 1928. I've seen a table of contents for that date. If the subscription was paid at the beginning of 1928, as the Sperling bookstore wrote to me at the prison in Milan, you will have to ask for the issues from February on: because as a matter of fact I received only the two issues of January 1928. In any event I can do without this magazine. (3) Write Signor Antonio Pescarzoli, editor of *Fiera Letteraria,* Piazza S. Carlo 2, Milan, a note saying more or less this: Antonio Gramsci, a prisoner in the penitentiary of Turi of Bari, kindly asks you to send him the catalogues of the principal Italian and French publishing houses. Gramsci subscribes to *Fiera Letteraria* through the Sperling and Kupfer bookstore.

The postal charges will be reimbursed. Many thanks, etc. If you are in the vicinity of Piazza San Carlo see if you can speak directly to Pescarzoli, who is very nice. I embrace you tenderly.

Antonio

1. This occurred during Gramsci's stay at the "Silver Forest" sanatarium, in 1922.

February 9, 1929

Dearest Tania,

Did you receive the half page I wrote to you fifteen days ago as part of a letter to my mother? I've received your two letters of February 4 and 5 (together with the letter from Giulia). Here there have been four or five days of intense cold with an exceptional snowfall; but it was a parenthesis. The weather is fine again and the sun is once again springlike. The famous hot water bottle has been most useful: it helped me come through the situation brilliantly, without serious disturbances.

Just today I received the five issues of *Marzocco* that hadn't arrived week by week. Perhaps you've already informed the bookstore that since the first of the year a number of magazines had not arrived, as I wrote to you, and so now the service has been resumed: however, I still haven't received *Rassegna Settimanale Della Stampa Estera* [Weekly review of the foreign press]. And in the same manner I haven't received the January 29 issue of *Fiera Letteraria*, which I'm anxious to get. (I did receive the other issues). I repeat to you once more that you must tell them not to send me any more new books. Now that I can write in my cell, I will make lists of the books that I need and every so often I will send them to the bookstore. Now that I can jot down my ideas in a notebook, I want to read according to a plan and delve more deeply into specific subjects and no longer "devour" books. I think that only as an exception, for some books on current topics whose existence I may not be aware of, you may go ahead without any request from me. Besides, the bookstore, which doesn't seem to have a card index for the books that have already been sent to me, has already shipped me duplicates twice. Do you know? I'm already writing in my cell. For the time being I'm only doing translations to limber up: and in the meantime I'm putting my thoughts in order. I keep forgetting to ask you for a piece of information that interests me very much: you'll be able to find out from the attorney. Did the military pretrial judge have any problems because of the declaration made by myself and Terracini[1] before the Special Tribunal?[2] Did he complain about this to the attorney? What he had told me was too important for my defense for me to be obliged to observe discretion: on the other hand, he didn't speak to me in confidence, but in the presence of the clerk of the court and with a great abundance of details so that I considered myself authorized to make use of his statements. However, if he had any trouble because of this I would be sorry, because he showed no animus against me. Dear Tania, write to me more often: did you forget about the existence of postcards? I embrace you.

Antonio

I've also received your letter of the eighth.

1. Umberto Terracini (1895–1983) was a leading Italian Communist activist and thinker, and cofounder, with Gramsci, of the review *L'Ordine Nuovo* in 1919. He was sentenced on June 4, 1928, to twenty-two years, nine months, and five days in prison and was not freed until September 1943. He was elected a deputy to the Constituent Assembly of 1946, and became its president in 1947. In 1948 he was named an honorary Senator of the Republic.

2. In Milan, Gramsci had had a conversation with Enrico Macis, the judge in charge of the investigation prior to the trial, during which Macis had shown Gramsci a communication from the attorney general adding new accusations against him (and the others who were to be tried with him) that had not appeared in the original indictment.

February 9, 1929

Dearest Giulia,

I had thought of writing a separate, really personal letter for Delio. But Tania tells me that he is at Anna's house and in any case your brilliant narrative about the consequences of having told him about my smoking on the snow makes me hesitate. I first want your advice. It seems to me that Delio is very impressionable, as he already was in Rome and Trafoi, and I wouldn't like to make too strong an impact on his sensibility. So I prefer to await your opinion.

My impression of Tatiana is rather good. When I last saw her in

Milan, but especially in Rome, about seven months ago, she was very weak. In December, however, it seemed to me that she had partly recovered and was stronger. I would have preferred if she hadn't made such a long journey for a few half hour visits: but she arrived unexpectedly, and then, of course, I was very happy about it. Now I should launch into great praises of Tatiana and of her great kindness. But I won't do so, because sometimes she exaggerates and ends by acting as though she considered me completely lacking in common sense, absolutely incapable of living without a tutor or a nursemaid. There are times when she has even made me angry, but most often she has made me laugh, though I haven't laughed much for a while now and I don't feel like joking as I used to. I believe that this is the most noticeable change that has taken place in me. In short I've concluded that Tatiana is the best specimen of the entire Schucht family, which the famous Diogott[1] told me was a model family (I never told you this, but I tell you now to get your goat!); she is the only one who truly takes after your mother.

My dear, what you wrote is really true: I too would like to write to you about many things, but I'm unable to take the plunge, to overcome a certain reticence. I believe this is due to the modern education of our minds, which has not yet found its own adequate means of expression. I'm always a bit skeptical and ironic and it seems to me that if I were to express all that I wish I would be unable to go beyond a certain conventionalism and a certain melodramatic tone, which is almost incorporated in the traditional language. The selfsame professional study that I've made of the technical forms of language obsesses me, setting before me again all my utterances in fossilized and ossified forms that arouse my repugnance. Nevertheless I am convinced that the intimate link between us will never be broken. I embrace you with all my strength.

Antonio

1. Vladimir Aleksandrovich Diogott, Russian representative of the Comintern in Italy in 1919, whom Gramsci had met in Turin. By "model family" Degott no doubt meant "Bolshevik" family. However, needless to say, Gramsci was not referring here to Tania's political credentials.

February 24, 1929

Dearest Mother,

I received your letter of the twelfth, after about one month of silence on your part and that of the others at home. I'm glad that your health has improved and I hope that with the coming spring you'll rid yourself completely of your ailments. Bravo! you have written to me at length and I thank you for the news you have sent me, which interests me to the nth degree. You and also the others who sometimes write to me, such as Carlo and Grazietta, must always remember that I'm almost completely immersed in darkness as to what happens and unfolds in the world. When I read my magazines, I must make a great effort of the imagination to try and reconstruct any sort of panorama of the life outside. I must do what naturalists do: from a tooth, from a tiny tail bone found in a prehistoric cave, they try to reconstruct an extinct animal that perhaps was larger than a whale. So I particularly like news culled from the living existence of a town that I know and whose extent and repercussions I can evaluate. For example, Carlo ought to write me something about the present cooperative dairies for which he works. I imagine that their development must proceed amidst great difficulties. Sometimes I ask myself how it is that the old milk monopolists have not yet been able to hand Honorable Pili[1] his head, since it seems to me that he had too many illusions about the efficiency of the forces available for opposition to the financial organization of the hoarders that previously had the monopoly of the pasturelands and dairies. If Carlo could send me a few publications about the commercial and credit efficiency of the Federation of Fascist dairies, he would be doing me a great favor. And if possible also about the competition the Federation is mounting against the old speculative dairies. Similarly, I would like to know what festivals and solemnities took place in Ghilarza to celebrate the recent reconciliation[2] between the Vatican and the state: who spoke, if they did speak, etc.

My health has considerably improved: the tonic treatments that I've followed have helped me greatly. Here the weather, relatively speaking, has been less wicked than elsewhere: it has snowed and rained, but there have always been intervals of springlike sun. In conclusion, despite the crisis of uric acids from which I suffered at the end of last year, I spent a much better winter than in Milan; and we won't mention the winter of 1926–1927 because I spent it on the road traveling in summer clothes in detention cars that had been covered with snow throughout the night; it is since then that my health suffered a serious blow. I've received the cigarettes. I embrace you tenderly.

Antonio

Please do me a favor, send Tatiana the half sheet I have written for her.

1. Paolo Pili, a founding member of the radical Sardinian Action party in 1921, who in 1923 converted to Fascism and became a Fascist deputy. Within the limits allowed by the Fascist regime, he sponsored two cooperative federations in the housing and milk industries.
2. See letter to Carlo, March 22, 1929, n. 3.

February 24, 1929

Dearest Tatiana,

I've received your three postcards (including the one with Delio's scribbles). Then I received the books that I had in prison in Milan and I could observe the fact that your little English trunk has wrought miracles, because undeterred it has survived the slow freight journey, with its usual jolts and tumbling without suffering permanent damage or scars; furthermore I've received the two pairs of mended socks that I left with you in Rome and Salandra's[1] *Memoirs*. Thank the lawyer for the trouble he's taken with my books, although the trunk was packed a bit as if it were filled with potatoes: I still haven't been able to find out exactly what there is in it but it seems to me that a number of books are missing; it doesn't matter! I was very amused by the story about Innocenzo Cappa's[2] lecture. This fellow is a bit like the parsley in every Milanese intellectual sauce; and yet this image is too kind to him, because in a sauce parsley performs a useful and congruous function, whereas Cappa is to the cultural world what a moth is to the art of clothing. At one time he was hired by Lombard democracy to issue complaints; indeed they gave him an even better name: since Cavallotti[3] had been called the bard of democracy, Cappa was called its *bardotto*, which is the mule born from the crossbreeding of a donkey and a horse. An intellectually null and morally equivocal figure.

The weather here seems to have improved; you could say that we are finally smelling the scent of spring. This reminds me that the mosquito season is approaching and that last year they tormented me enormously. So I would like to have a piece of mosquito netting, in order to protect my face and arms as soon as the necessity arises. Not very large, of course, for otherwise it perhaps might not even be permitted; I'm thinking of a surface of one and a half square meters. And while I'm at it I'll express a few more desires: I want to have a few small skeins of wool to mend my socks. I've studied the mends in the two pairs that I've received and I think that they do not exceed my abilities. I also ought to have a needle made of bone, suited for wool. Further I'd like to have a number of American fava beans for the tobacco, because my old ones have already lost their aroma. I keep forgetting to tell you not to send me the Sterno set, because I already have one made of aluminum; I haven't asked them to let me keep it in my cell because I've heard that it has been refused to others; besides, it isn't much use. I've kept it because I'm convinced that in time they'll permit it in all penitentiaries since it's already arrived in many of them and is issued by the administration itself. Dearest, I embrace you affectionately.

Antonio

If you can, also send me the seeds for some pretty flowers.

1. Antonio Salandra (1853–1931), Italian prime minister at the start of World War I, later delegate to the Paris Peace Conference and the League of Nations. After several years of support for Fascism, he called for a return to constitutional government.
2. Innocenzo Cappa (1875–1954), Italian deputy and, in 1929, senator. In a letter to Gramsci, Tania had described a lecture by Cappa on Tolstoy as "a disaster."
3. Felice Cavallotti (1842–1898), playwright, poet, and radical democrat known as "the bard of democracy."

March 11, 1929

Dearest Tatiana,

I really must thank you cordially for writing to me so often: whenever I receive correspondence I experience a joy that is very real, even a bit childish. This very day your 200 lire postal order arrived; a few days ago I got 200 lire from Carlo and so by the end of the month I will still have on deposit 1150 lire, a respectable sum, as you can see. In today's card you write about "letters from Giulia and books" that I should have received. I got Giulia's last letter on March 2, sent by you on February 28: are you referring to that one? I haven't gotten any others. Fifteen days ago I wrote you half a letter, which perhaps was sent you by Carlo with some delay, a letter in which, among other things, I asked you for a number of items: but I forgot to ask you to send me some tins of Ovaltine, since I'm about to finish the one Carlo sent me a couple of months ago. I did get the books sent by the attorney. A number are missing: certainly, as I've been able to check, the following are missing: Benedetto Croce, *Storia della storiografia italiana nel sec. XIX* [History of Italian historiography in the nineteenth century]; Guglielmo Ferrero, *Le due verità: La terza Roma* [The two truths: The third Rome]; Alessandro Zévaès, *Histoire de la IIIème République* [History of the third republic]; Upton Sinclair, *Le pétrole* [Oil]; Enrico Ferri, *Mussolini: Uomo di stato* [Mussolini: Statesman]. A book by somebody with a name like "Bucard"[1] on the English intelligence service with a preface by Stéphane Lauzanne (I don't remember the title). These books must be at Signora Pina's house and I would like to have them, especially the book by Croce: why, just think, I've already bought this book three times and it's always been stolen. This is too much. It cost 40 lire: I've already spent 120 lire and I must spend another 40 (that is, 160 lire) to own a book that is indispensable for me: it seems to me that this is too exaggerated an exaggeration. So I beg you to look for them and keep me informed: I really have the impression that they've been selected and held back on purpose and this exasperates me. It appears to me that it would be foolish to just let it go, and one mustn't be too tactful about certain kinds of rudeness; these people know very well that I'm in prison and that the sacrifices my relatives make for me ought not to be exploited by third parties. Believe me, I'm really exasperated. If necessary you can go ahead and say as much to Signor Tullo, or make it clear to him somehow or other. I saw him in Milan, while Tulli[2] and I were called for a visit with him and he made a disagreeable impression on me, a real hypocrite. After seeing them I felt very sorry that you have to become acquainted with such people. Enough. The nineteenth is my mother's name day: can you send her a telegram with my best wishes? It will be a pleasant surprise for her. Dearest Tania, I'm always writing to you in order to bother you and saddle you with errands that tire you out. Be fond of me in spite of all this.

Antonio

I haven't received *Rassegna Settimanale della Stampa Estera* [Weekly review of the foreign press] since the first of the year. But I'll wait a while longer. I embrace you.

1. Robert Boucard, *Les dessous des archives secrètes (d'un espionnage à l'autre)* [The hidden aspects of the secret archives (from one epionage to another)], preface by Stéphane Lauzanne (Paris: Les Editions de France, 1929).
2. Enrico Tulli.

March 11, 1929

Dearest Giulia,

I've received your letter of February 21 to which the only possible reply would be a caress. But . . . after having caressed you I would like to add something. I already knew what you wrote to me, I already knew it because I imagined it. Do you understand? I knew that your "Japan" existed at the such and such longitude and latitude, etc. What escapes me is how does this "Japan" develop, through what concrete forms of life does its existence unfold? I know too little about your life and the life of the children, and my fantasy, without nourishment, spins in a void. Perhaps this is an obsession caused by prison life, but, in short, I feel it and I do not want to hide it from you. From your photograph it seems to me that you have been unwell; you yourself have mentioned that you must undergo certain cures and that abstaining from certain medicines harms you. But beyond these fleeting and vague things I know nothing, and at times this truly obsesses me.

I've always forgotten to write to you that Maestro Domenico Alaleona,[1] your professor at the Conservatory, died a few months ago. He had a bad death, at the worst moment of his life. I've learned these details from a literary journal. After the suppression of *Il Mondo* [The World], of which Alaleona was an editor, he moved immediately to *Lavoro d'Italia* [Labor in Italy], which was also recently suppressed, and together with other former editors of *Il Mondo* became a big wheel in the Syndicate of Fascist Artists and Writers; before his death there was a small scandal, because somebody published the fact that *Lavoro d'Italia* had paid 150,000 lire for a pulp novel, written collectively by ten of these former editors, the majority of whom were democrats until November 1926 and had become Fascists after the Special Laws. The old Fascists mounted an all-out offensive against these newcomers and the government disbanded the artists' organization, firing Alaleona from the cushy position he had arranged for himself. A short opera of his, in one act, I think, had been something of a fiasco just before this.

My dear, I hope that you will decide to give me more details about your health. How cold was it where you are and how did you take it? I myself feel very well now and I sleep a half hour longer from time to time. Besides that I've become immersed in translations from the German and this work calms my nerves and relaxes me. I read less, but work more. Apparently there are some other letters of yours on their way to me, as Tatiana has indicated: if you'll give me more details, I'll write to you at greater length next time. A very very strong embrace.

Antonio

1. Domenico Alaleona (1881–1928), music critic and composer, held a professorship in the history of music at the Conservatory of Santa Cecilia in Rome.

March 22, 1929[1]

Dear Carlo,

Thank you for your letter about the milk Cooperatives.[2] I think however that I can hold to my opinion about the causes that have led to Pili's misfortunes. Naturally I didn't know before and I don't know now the details concerning the concrete unfolding of events and the specific form they have taken. Whenever there is a profound conflict of material interests, none of the contenders proclaims that he is fighting for a material interest; he will try to find rallying cries that are as disinterested as possible, abstract principles concerning civilization, the people, the future of history, etc. etc. And I imagine that this is what must have happened between Pili and Putzolu, if there has been a public polemic between them. The fact is that although I could not follow these events in any way, by and large I guessed them, based on what Pili represented and on the repercussions that his activity would have, and the enormous power that was opposing him and that certainly could not remain inert at the sight of his progressive ruination. It seems to me that Pili's defeat is the decisive defeat of the Sardinian Action party, which Pili was trying to acclimate to the new, at present dominant political setup: something that I never doubted.

I cannot write anything about my personal opinions regarding the Concordat.[3] In general I expressed my opinion in the speech I gave in the Chamber of Deputies in 1925 when the political action that was to lead to today's event was undertaken.[4] It is a complex matter that involves a general vision of Italian history, from 1848 on. It seems to me, in brief, that two important points are these: (1) it put an end to the moral split that existed within the ruling class: this split had lost much of its harshness after the formation of the popular party; nevertheless it did exist. Perhaps it was only a corpse to be buried: but corpses must be buried so that they will not infect the environment; (2) it allowed the Italian government to enter into competition with other governments, especially the French, to utilize for its own ends the importance of the Church in the world, especially the colonial or semicolonial world. As for the rest one would have to write a book.

I've received the package with the mosquito net, which is fine, and the cigarettes. The Casali serum has done me a lot of good. But I still haven't taken some tonics and injections bought by Tatiana when she came here for Christmas; therefore for the time being there is nothing to be sent. We'll talk about it again next fall.

Tatiana, who arrived at Turi a couple of days ago and will remain until Easter, has told me that she sent a telegram for mother's name day. I've received two letters; I'm very sorry about Edmea's illness. But it's just a childhood disease that must inevitably come sooner or later and I hope there won't be any complications. In a few months I will send you a case of books and old magazines. I've begun to go through them, in order to make notes and comments on the subjects that interest me. Naturally I'm sending them to you with the understanding that nothing will be lost and that you will not lend anything to anyone. During the last ten years I've lost at least 20,000 lire worth of books. In Turin I had sixteen huge cases of books that were burnt in a fire. I bought books all the time, often depriving myself of many other things. I would pick them out at secondhand bookstores and I had managed to build a small personal library that was precious to me, beyond its commercial value, because it called to mind my various researches. Everything went up in smoke, together with huge stacks of notes. Therefore I set much store on preserving the books and magazines that I now have at my disposal. Is that clear? In due time I'll let you know about the modalities of the shipment.

Give my countless good wishes to everyone for the holidays; let's hope that everyone is in good health, at least for now. Tell Mea that I'm translating a series of little German folk tales for her: Red Riding Hood, Tom Thumb, etc. etc. I will copy them in a separate notebook, write a preface, add some footnotes, and then if they allow me, I'll send it to her as a gift from prison. Naturally this will take time, because I'm doing the translations in sections every day, to practice my German. Many affectionate kisses to all, especially to mother.

Antonio

1. The Caprioglio and Fubini 1965 edition of the prison letters, and the Santucci edition of 1988, contain only the first two paragraphs of this letter, which they did not date. The complete letter appeared in *Antonio Gramsci e la questione sarda*, ed. Guido Melis (Cagliari: Edizioni della Torre, 1975), pp. 258–59. A photocopy of this letter at the Gramsci Institute is dated March 22, 1929.

2. See the note on Carlo in the list of correspondents and family members.

3. This is a reference to the Lateran Accords signed on February 11, 1929, which marked a "reconciliation" between the Italian government and the Vatican and a solution of the historic Roman Question. In *A History of Modern Italy* (New York: Columbia University Press, 1968), Salvatore Saladino writes: "The basis of the solution was a compromise in which in return for the Church's recognition of the Kingdom of Italy, the Italian government would recognize the papacy's rights of temporal sovereignty over a territory eventually to be known as the Vatican City and would also agree to a Concordat on religious questions" (pp. 474–75).

4. Gramsci gave his first and only speech in the Chamber of Deputies on May 16, 1925, when he addressed himself to a new law sponsored by Mussolini and Alfredo Rocco concerning the activity of private and "secret" associations and institutions and membership in them of public employees. The law was generally believed to be directed mainly against the Masonic order. Gramsci argued, amidst constant harassment by Fascist deputies, that the Masons had in effect been the best organized segment of the Italian bourgeois class. "In reality," he said, "fascism is fighting against the only efficiently organized force that the bourgeoisie had in Italy, in order to replace it in the occupancy of positions that the state gives to its functionaries. The Fascist revolution is only the substitution of one group of administrative personnel for another." ("L'intervento alla Camera dei Deputati nel 1925," in Ferrata and Gallo, eds., *2000 pagine di Gramsci*, pp. 748–761).

March 25, 1929

Dearest Tania,

I'm sending you a list of books that should be in Rome, unless my memory betrays me regarding some of them. Naturally this does not mean that they should be sent to me immediately. On the contrary. For the time being I have a great deal to read. But they are books that I had bought with the intention of doing specific studies and that therefore fall within a cultural framework and will be of use to me in the future. This is the list of those I remember (in some cases the title is only approximate): (1) *L'Europa politica nel secolo XIX* [European politics in the nineteenth century]. This is a thick volume in octavo, published in Brescia under the sponsorship of their chamber of commerce in 1926. It is a collection of lectures. I would be very glad to get this book right away. (2) Benedetto Croce, *Elementi di politica* [Elements of politics]; (3) B. Croce—*Breviario di estetica* [Breviary of aesthetics]; (4) B. Croce—*Hegel* (I am not sure that this is among them; I may have lent it to someone to read); (5) Gaetano Salvemini[1]—*Mazzini* (there must be some other books by Salvemini); (6) Roberto Michels—*Il partito politico: Le tendenze oligarchiche della democrazia moderna* [The political party: The oligarchical tendencies of modern democracy], 1924 Italian edition published by Utet in Turin. There is also the French prewar edition. (7) Raffaele Ciasca—*Origini del programma dell'unità nazionale* [Origins of the program for national unity]. (Send these books first); (8) a French volume on Italian finances in the years after 1890. I do not recall the title or the author. (9) Jeanroy. I have already received a book by Signorina Jeanroy on the history of the Italian language; but I also had a second volume on the same subject[2]; (10) Maurice Pernot—*L'expérience italienne* [The Italian experience]; (11) Maurice Pernot—*La politique du Vatican* [Vatican politics], Colin, publisher; (12) Werner Sombart—*Il capitalismo moderno* [Modern capitalism], Vallecchi, publisher; (13) Dambrini-Palazzi—*La filosofia di Antonio Labriola*[3] [The philosophy of Antonio Labriola]; (14) there must be the posthumous edition of Labriola's lectures at the University of Rome, perhaps entitled "From One Century to Another"—and a book on *Socrates* edited by B. Croce; (15) Marx—*Storia delle dottrine economiche* [History of eco-

nomic doctrines]—volume 1. *Dall'origine della teoria del valore ad
Adamo Smith* [From the origin of the theory of value to Adam
Smith]—volume 2. *David Ricardo*—volume 3. *Da Ricardo all'economia
volgare* [From Ricardo to vulgar economy] in all eight small volumes—Costes publisher; (16) one entire number of the *Rassegna Italiana* devoted to the first twenty-five years of the reign of Victor Em-
manuel III; (17) Don Ernesto Vercesi—*Storia del movimento cattolico in
Italia* [History of the Catholic movement in Italy], *La Voce*, publisher;
(18) Maurice Muret—French title more or less like this: *La decadenza
delle razze bianche* [Decadence of the white races]; (19) De Rossi—*Il
Partito Popolare della fondazione al 1920* [The popular party from its
foundation to 1920]; (20) *Congresso dell'Unione Nazionale* [Congress
of the National Union]; (21) Jacques Maritain—*Difesa di Carlo Maurras* [Defense of Charles Maurras]; (22) Books on the activity of Am-
bassador Georges Louis; these must be three or four small books; (23)
Paolo Cambon—*La diplomazia* [Diplomacy]; 24) Mathiez—The first
two volumes of the *Rivoluzione francese* [French revolution] in the
Colin Manuals; (25) *Report on the Activity of the Commission of the Eighteen for the Corporative State*—State Publisher for Parliament; (26) Ro-
dolfo Mondolfo—*Il materialismo storico di F. Engels* [The historical materialism of F. Engels], Formiggini, Publisher; (27) Lévy—
Introduzione alla scienza delle finanze [Introduction to financial science]
(in French). These are the books I remember were there. The first
seven I would like to have as soon as possible. The others much later.
I have finally received *La Rassegna Settimanale*. The bookstore sent me
a few more books. As I already wrote to you several times, it is a
good idea that no more books be sent, unless I myself first ask for
them. For many reasons: (1) because I've got enough to read for quite
a while; (2) and more importantly, because only if I myself ask for
them will the books fit into the intellectual plan I want to construct.
I've decided to concern myself chiefly and take notes on these three
subjects: (1) Italian history in the nineteenth century, with special attention to the formation and development of intellectual groups; (2)
the theory of history and historiography; (3) Americanism and Fordism. I have two volumes by Ford published in French: *My Life, Today
and Tomorrow* and a few volumes: *Siegfried* and *Lucien Romier*.[4] If they
have been translated into French I would like to have some of Sinclair
Lewis's novels, especially *Elmer Gantry*. On the theory of history I

would like to have a French book published recently: Bukharin—
Théorie du matérialisme historique [Theory of historical materialism]
Editions Sociales, Rue Valette 3, Paris (Ve) and *Œuvres philosophiques
de Marx* [Marx's philosophical works] published by Alfred Costes—
Paris: volume 1: *Contribution à la critique de la philosophie du droit de
Hegel* [Contribution to the critique of Hegel's philosophy of law]—
volume 2: *Critique de la critique* [Criticism of criticism] against Bruno
Bauer and company. I already have Benedetto Croce's most important books on this subject. I've seen that recently they've published a
book by Enrico Ruta: *Politica e ideologia* [Politics and ideology], but I
didn't see mention of the publisher: perhaps it is Laterza in Bari. I
already have something on the first subject. I remember that in Rome
I should also have a book on the Risorgimento by Piero Gobetti:[5] *La
rivoluzione liberale* [The liberal revolution] and a book by Giuseppe
Prezzolini: *La cultura italiana* [Italian culture]—and that's all.

I've received a postcard from Signora Malvina Sanna,[6] Corso Indipendenza, 23, who asks me for some advice about philosophy
books for her husband. Write to her that I cannot answer her directly,
that I'm fairly well, etc. etc., that I send cordial regards to her husband, etc. And also transcribe for her what follows: "The best manual
for psychology is the one by William James, translated into Italian
and published by Libreria Milanese:[7] it must be quite expensive because before the war it cost twenty-four lire. There is no treatise on
logic, save for the usual school manuals used in the *Liceo*. It seems to
me that Sanna is setting out from criteria that are too scholastic and
that he is under the illusion that he can find more in books of this
kind than they can really give. Psychology, for instance, has moved
completely away from philosophy to become a natural science, like
biology and physiology: indeed, a thorough study of modern psychology requires a great deal of knowledge, especially of physiology.
In the same way formal, abstract logic today no longer has many
adepts, except in the seminaries where Aristotle and St. Thomas are
studied in depth. What's more, dialectics, that is, the form of concrete
historical thought, has not yet been manualized. In my opinion this
is what Sanna should do to improve his philosophical education: (1)
study a good manual of the history of philosophy, for example, the
Sommario di storia della filosofia [Summary of the history of philoso-
phy] by Guido De Ruggero (Bari, Laterza) eighteen lire, and read

some of the classics of philosophy, even in abstracts, like those published by the same publisher, Laterza of Bari, in its Piccola Biblioteca Filosofica [Small philosophical library] in which have appeared small books of selected passages from Aristotle, Bacon, Descartes, Hegel, Kant, etc., with notes. To bring himself up to date on dialectics he should read, even though they are very hard going, some big books by Hegel. However, his *Encyclopedia*, admirably translated by Croce, costs a lot today: about one hundred lire. There is a good book on Hegel also by Croce, provided one remembers that in it Hegel and Hegelian philosophy take one step forward and two back; Croce goes beyond his metaphysics, but he goes backward on the question of the relationship between thought and natural and historical reality. In any case I think this is the route to follow: no new manuals (Fiorentino is enough), and instead a personal reading and criticism of the great modern philosophers." I think this should suffice.

The series of dictionaries is called "Toussaint-Langenscheidt." I used to have the German-Italian and the Italian-German in Rome. I would like to have English-Italian or English-French, not the other way round, for now. The Russian-Italian that Giulia wanted in 1925 was still in preparation in 1925: perhaps it has come out by now. Dearest, I embrace you affectionately.

Antonio

I would like to have the speeches of the Head of the Government for 1927 and 1928, which are published by "Alpes" in Milan, and as soon as it comes out the *Annuario statistico italiano, 1929* [Italian statistical annual report for 1929] published by the Istituto Centrale di Statistica dello Stato [Central state institute for statistics].

1. Gaetano Salvemini (1873–1957), historian and founder of the influential review *L'Unità* in 1911 (not to be confused with the Communist daily *L'Unità*, founded in 1924). He was a leader of the Italian anti-Fascist movement. After a stay in France, he emigrated to the United States, where in 1934 he began teaching at Harvard University.

2. Thérèse Labande-Jeanroy, *La question de la langue en Italie: L'unité linguistique dans les théories et les faits* [The language question in Italy: Linguistic unity in theory and in fact] (Strasbourg-Paris: Istra, 1925) and *La question de la langue en Italie de Baretti à Manzoni* [The language question in Italy from Baretti to Manzoni] (Paris: H. Champion, 1925).

3. Antonio Labriola (1843–1904) was one of Italy's first and most original disciples of Marx, on whom he lectured for many years at the University of Rome. Labriola's *Essays on the Materialist Conception of History* were of considerable importance to Gramsci's development as a Marxist thinker.

4. Gramsci places Siegfried and Lucien Romier in quotation marks as if they were book titles, but these are the names of writers whose books deal with aspects of the theme of Fordism: André Siegfried, *Les Etats-Unis d'aujourd'hui* [The United States Today], and Lucien Romier, *Qui sera le maître, Europe ou Amérique?* [Who will be the master, Europe or America?] (Paris: Hachette, 1927).

5. Piero Gobetti (1901–1926), the leading figure among Turin's liberal intellectuals after World War I, founded several political and cultural reviews, the most influential of which was *La Rivoluzione Liberale*, published from 1922 to 1925. He was severely beaten by a Fascist gang on September 5, 1924. On February 6, 1926, he left Italy for Paris and died there on the 16th of that month.

6. Malvina Sanna was the wife of Antonio Sanna (1879–1973), a native of Sardinia. He was a "third-internationalist" Socialist in the early 1920s. Subsequently, he joined the Communist party and worked in its clandestine organization until his arrest in 1927. After serving seven years in prison, he was amnestied and resumed his underground anti-Fascist activities. He was active in the Resistance during World War II.

7. The Italian translation is *Principii di psicologia*, trans. G. C. Ferrari (Milan: Società Editrice Libraria, 1905).

April 22, 1929

Dearest Tania,

I've received your postcards for April 13 and 19. I will patiently wait for news from home. I believe that you too must have noticed, during the few moments in which we've seen each other, how patient I've become. I was also patient before, but only by virtue of a great effort to control myself: it was a certain diplomatic quality, necessary when coming into contact with imbeciles and boring people, whom unfortunately one cannot do without. Now, on the other hand, it costs me no effort at all, it has become a habit, it is the necessary expression of prison routine and it is also an element of instinctive self-preservation. Sometimes however this "patience" becomes a kind of apathy and indifference that I'm unable to overcome: I believe that you have noticed this too and that it has saddened you a bit. And you know, this isn't anything new either. Your mother had noticed it as early as 1925 and Giulia told me about it. The truth is that already in those years, to tell it by using an image from Kipling, I was like a goat that had lost an eye and turns around in a circle, the radius always being the same. But let's go on to something more cheerful.

The rose has fallen victim to a dreadful sunstroke: all the leaves in the more tender parts are burnt and carbonized; it has a desolate, sad aspect, but it is putting out new buds. It isn't dead, at least not yet.

The solar catastrophe was inevitable, because I was able to cover it only with paper, which the wind kept blowing away; it would have been necessary to have a nice bundle of straw, which is a poor conductor of heat and at the same time protects from direct rays. At any rate the prognosis is favorable, unless there are extraordinary complications. The seeds have been very slow in pushing up small sprouts: an entire series obstinately insists on living a *podpolie*[1] life. Certainly they must have been old and partly worm-eaten. The ones that have come into the light of this world are developing slowly and are unrecognizable. I think that the gardener, when he told you that part of the seeds were very beautiful, probably meant that they were good to eat; in fact some of the small seedlings strangely resemble parsley and baby onions rather than flowers. Every day I am seized by the temptation to pull at them a little in order to help them to grow, but I remain undecided between the two concepts of the world and of education: whether to follow Rousseau and leave things to nature, which is never wrong and is basically good, or to be a voluntarist and force nature, introducing into evolution the expert hand of man and the principle of authority.[2] Until now the uncertainty persists and the two ideologies joust in my head. The six chicory plants immediately felt at home and haven't been afraid of the sun: they are already pushing up the stem that will deliver seeds for future harvests. The dahlias and the bamboo are sleeping underground and have yet to give a sign of life. I believe that the dahlias in particular are truly done for. While we are on the subject, I want to ask you to please send me four more kinds of seeds: (1) carrot seeds, but of the *pastinaca* quality that is a pleasant memory of my early childhood: in Sassari there are some that grow large enough to weigh half a kilo and before the war they used to cost one *soldo*, competing to some extent with licorice; (2) sweet peas; (3) spinach seeds; (4) celery seeds. On one fourth of a square meter I want to plant four or five seeds of each kind and see how they turn out. You can find them at Ingegnoli's, who has shops in Piazza del Duomo and Via Buenos Aires; you can get them to give you the catalogue too, which indicates the months most propitious for planting.

I received another note from Signora Malvina Sanna (Corso Indipendenza 23). Transmit the following lines to her:

"I understand the financial difficulty of obtaining the books I previously suggested. I myself had pointed this out; but my task was that of answering precise questions. Today I will answer a question that, though not addressed to me, was implicit and because I realize that it answers a general need of someone who is imprisoned: how not to waste time in prison and how to study something somehow? It seems to me that first of all one must shed the "scholastic" mental habit, and not set one's mind on following regular and thoroughgoing courses; that is impossible even for someone who finds himself in better conditions. One of the most profitable studies is certainly that of modern languages: it is enough to have a grammar, which can be found on the secondhand book stalls for very little money, and a few books (also secondhand if necessary) of the language chosen for study. It is impossible to learn the pronunciation, true enough, but one will be able to read and this is already a considerable achievement. Furthermore: many prisoners underestimate the prison library. Of course prison libraries in general are a jumble: the books have been gathered at random, from donations by charitable organizations that receive warehouse remainders from publishers, or from books left behind by released prisoners. Devotional books and third-rate novels abound. Nevertheless I believe that a political prisoner must squeeze blood even from a stone. It is all a matter of setting a purpose for one's readings and of knowing how to take notes (if one is permitted to write). I'll give two examples: in Milan I read a certain number of books of all kinds, especially popular novels, until the warden allowed me to go to the library myself and choose among the books that had not yet been distributed for reading or among those that due to a particular political or moral flavor, were not given to everyone to read. Well, I found that even Sue, Montepin, Ponson du Terrail, etc. were sufficient when read from this point of view: why is this sort of literature almost always the most read and the most published? what needs does it satisfy? what aspirations does it answer? what emotions and points of view are represented in these trashy books for them to be so popular? How is Eugene Sue different from Montepin? And does Victor Hugo too belong to this series of writers because of the subjects he deals with? And are *Scampolo* or *L'Aigrette* or *Volata* by Dario Nicodemi perhaps not the direct descendants of this late 1848 romanticism[3]? etc etc. The second example is this: a German historian, Gruithausen,[4] has recently published a big book in which he studies the links between French Catholicism and the bourgeoisie during the two centuries before 1889. He has studied all the devotional literature of these two centuries: collections of sermons, catechisms from the various dioceses, etc. etc. and he has put together a magnificent book. It seems to me that this will suffice to prove that one can squeeze blood even from stones for in this instance there are no stones. Every book, especially if it is a history book, can be useful to read. In any small unimportant book one can find something useful . . . especially if one is in our situation and time cannot be measured with the normal yardstick."

Dear Tatiana, I've probably written too much and I will force you into an exercise in calligraphy. By the way: remember to give instructions so that no more books are sent to me until there is word from me. Perhaps if any books should come out that you think might be useful to me have them put aside to be sent when I ask for them. Dearest, I really hope that the trip did not tire you too much. I embrace you affectionately.

Antonio

1. *Podpolie* means "underground" in Russian. For about a year, prisoners at Turi were allowed to grow flowers on small plots of ground in the prison courtyard.

2. Gramsci's lifelong tendency to allegorize his experiences with plants and animals is nowhere better exemplified than in this letter.

3. This is a good example of the connections between the prison letters and the notebooks: Some of the questions Gramsci was to ask himself in the notebooks on the sociology of literature and on the broader issues of culture and politics are here neatly summarized.

4. Bernhard Groethuysen, *Les origines de l'esprit bourgeois en France* (Paris: Gallimard, 1927).

May 6, 1929

Dearest Tania,

I've received your two letters and the two letters from Giulia: but I have not received the "very long" one announced as imminent on April 30. In fifteen days from now I'll write my entire letter for Giulia and for Delio; so I won't be able to counter the reproaches that, I imagine, you are going to send me. In any case you must never take what I write to you in an absolute sense: of course I'm much changed, but it may be only a temporary phenomenon connected with the unusual life in prison. I think that the events I experienced in the Milan prison and that I reported to the Special Tribunal in answer to Deputy Police Chief De Sanctis have contributed a lot to this. Distrust has changed into a habit of apathy and indifference, which is perhaps an instinctive form of self-defense.

As for the 500 francs that you still have to pay, I think that it would be in your interest to get rid of the obligation altogether by paying off the mortgage with the land itself, that is, by selling it and pocketing the remainder, if there is any[1]. This whole story, when I heard it, made me laugh a bit and has proved to me the total lack of practical sense in all of you: I believe that someone has exploited you, enjoying the land and gathering its fruits. I wouldn't be surprised if, at the very moment in which you paid the last cent of the mortgage, you were to discover that the land no longer belongs to you, by virtue of some article of the Swiss civil code concerning neglect by the owners and the continued possession by third parties, without the owner having in the meantime acted in any way that expresses his ownership. The fact that the children might one day be able to live there seems to me an affectionate notion inspired by past memories. As for Vittorio's[2] projects, don't rely on them, please! I've known some of them, and I had to sweat mightily to prevent him from getting into some really bad scrapes. To conclude, I think that you should write your father the whole truth: the amount that you have spent, reminding him or making it clear to him that at the same time he was spending the same amount, and then how much remains to be paid. Actually you know nothing about what your trustee or friend has done on your account, and I'll bet that among all of you there is not one who any longer even has the documents that prove you have title to the property. As for what I've said about Vittorio, you mustn't think that I don't respect him and am not fond of him: he is indeed original and has a very rich imagination, and his projects suffer a great deal from it; I don't know where he was born, but it would please me to know that he was born in Provence.

I'm anxiously waiting for the Bedouin slippers; I have the feeling that they should be perfect because I've seen them in Ustica during a reception given by the Bedouins confined there. By the way, do you know that one of these Bedouins, a certain Haussiet, used to come and see me almost every day to look at Delio's photograph; he had left behind a child in Bengasi and he was surprised that a photograph could be so expressive, lamenting the fact that his religion forbids the reproduction of the human figure. I told him that Kemal[3] was now permitting people to take their photographs and to that he said that his wife was too stupid to know what a photograph is and that he was going to divorce her. I told him that Kemal forbade polygamy and that saddened him because, despite everything, for him Kemal was like the Pope of Mohammedanism. Dear Tania, I embrace you tenderly and look forward to your long letter.

Antonio

1. In the early 1900s the Schuchts had bought a house and some land outside Geneva, which they still owned in 1929.
2. Viktor Schucht, the youngest of the six Schucht children.
3. Mustafà Kemal (1880–1938), Turkish general and statesman, called Atatürk, father of the country. He was the founder in 1923 of the Turkish Republic, of which he was president until his death. His name is associated with numerous modernizing administrative and cultural reforms.

May 20, 1929

Dear Giulia,

Who told you that I can write more often? Unfortunately it isn't true. I can write only twice a month and only for Easter and Christmas do I dispose of an additional letter. Do you remember what Bianco[1] told you in 1923 when I left? Bianco was right from the standpoint of his experience; I've always had an invincible aversion to letter writing. Since I've been in prison I've written at least twice as many letters as in the previous period: I must have written at least two hundred letters, a true horror! So it isn't correct to say that I'm not calm. Instead I'm more than calm, I'm apathetic and passive. And I'm not surprised at it, nor do I make the slightest effort to come out of this funk. On the other hand, perhaps this is a strength and not a state of decadence. There have been long periods during which I felt very isolated, cut off from any life that was not my own; I suffered terribly; a delay in my correspondence, the lack of appropriate replies to my questions, filled me with an irritability that wore me out. Then time passed and the perspective of the prior period moved further and further away; all that was accidental, transitory, in the realm of emotions and of will gradually vanished and only the essential and permanent reasons of life remained. It is natural that this should happen, don't you think? For a while it is impossible to prevent the past and images of the past from being dominant, but, at bottom, this looking always to the past ends by being uncomfortable and useless. I believe that I've overcome the crisis that takes place in everyone, during the first years in prison and that often leads to a sharp, radical break with the past. To tell the truth, I have felt and seen this crisis more in others than in myself, and it made me smile, which was already a sign of having overcome it. I would never have believed that so many people had such a great fear of death; well, it is precisely to this fear that so many psychological ills in prison can be traced. In Italy it is said that one becomes old when one begins to think about death; this seems to me a very wise observation. In prison this psychological transformation takes place as soon as the prisoner feels that he is caught in a vise and cannot escape it: a rapid and radical change occurs that is all the stronger to the extent that up until then he did not take his life of ideas and convictions very seriously. I've seen some men become brutalized in an incredible manner. And this has been useful to me, just as seeing the helots' depravity was useful to Spartan adolescents.[2] So now I'm absolutely calm and not even a prolonged lack of news makes me anxious, though I know that this could be avoided with a little effort of will . . . also on your part. Besides, Tania makes sure to pass on all the news she receives from you. For example she passed on the news about the children's traits, as accurately described by your father, which engaged my lively interest for several days. And other news, which she accompanies with very graceful comments. I assure you that I don't mean to reproach you! In recent days I've reread all of your letters for the last year and this has again made me feel your tenderness. You know that when I write, I sometimes have the impression of being too dry and severe compared to you who write to me with such naturalness. I truly have the feeling that I am as I was when I made you cry sometimes, especially the first time, do you remember? when I was purposely mean. I would like to know what Tania has written to you about her trip to Turi. For it seems to me that Tania conceives of my life in a way that is too idyllic and Arcadian, so much so that she torments me quite a bit. She cannot be persuaded that I must stay within certain limits and that she mustn't send me anything I didn't request, because I do not have at my disposal a personal storage space. Instead of strictly adhering to my recommendations, she announces the impending arrival of several absolutely senseless things that I will never be able to use.

I'm sending you two photographs: the large one is a picture of my sister Teresina's two children: Franco and Maria, the other is of my mother holding in her arms the same little girl, but a trifle older. My father maintains that the girl resembles Giuliano; I'm not in a position to judge. Certainly the little boy does not resemble anyone in my family: he's the image of his father, who is an authentic Sardinian, whereas we are only half Sardinian: instead, the little girl has more of a family air. What is your opinion?

Just recently I finished reading a history of Russia by Professor Platonov[3] of the former University of Petersburg, a large tome of about 1,000 pages. It seems to me that this is a real publishing fraud. Who was this Professor Platonov? Historiography must have been very poor at that time if this Professor Platonov was one of its standard-bearers, as I see stated by Professor Lo Gatto in his books on Russian culture. Concerning the origins of the cities and Russian commerce at the time of the Normans I've read about twenty pages by the Belgian historian Pirenne,[4] which are worth all of Platonov's cabbage soup. The volume goes only as far as 1905, with two supplementary pages that include the abdication of Grand Duke Michael and that puts the date of Nicholas II's death in a footnote, yet it is entitled *A History from the Origins until 1918*: a double fraud, as you can see. Dear Giulia, write me about Delio's comments on the letter I'm sending him; I embrace you tenderly.

Antonio

1. Vincenzo Bianco. See letter to Julca, April 18, 1927, n. 2.

2. In ancient Sparta the word *helot* was applied to serfs who worked land belonging to the state. Figuratively, the word has been used to describe people who live in a state of degradation and ignorance.

3. Sergei F. Platonov, *Histoire de la Russie des origines à 1918* [History of Russia from the origins to 1918] (Paris: Payot, 1929).

4. Henri Pirenne, *Les villes du moyen âge* [Medieval cities] (Brussels: M. Lamertin, 1927).

May 20, 1929

Dear Delio,

I've heard that you are going to school, that you are a good one meter and eight centimeters tall and that you weigh eighteen kilos. So I think that you are already very grown-up and in a short time you will be writing me letters. While waiting for this, you can even now get your mother to write letters that you have dictated, just as in Rome you got me to write the *pimpò*[1] for Grandma. So you'll be able to tell me whether you like the other children in school and what you are learning and what games you like to play. I know that you're building airplanes and trains and are actively participating in the country's industrialization, but tell me do these airplanes really fly and do these trains run? If I were there, I could at least put my cigarette in the smokestack so that we could see a bit of smoke!

Then you must also write me something about Giuliano. What do you think of him? Does he help you with your work? Is he a builder too, or is he still too small to deserve this qualification? In short I would like to know a heap of things and since you are so grown-up, and, I've been told, also a bit of a chatterbox, I'm sure that with your mother's hand for the time being, you will write me a long long letter with all this information and even more. And I will give you news about a rosebush that I have planted and about a lizard that I want to train. Kiss Giuliano for me and also mother and everyone at home and mother in turn will kiss you for me.

Your Papa[2]

I've realized that perhaps you do not know what a lizard is: It is a kind of crocodile that remains forever tiny.

1. Evidently a word designating some sort of children's picture or word game.
2. The letter is signed "Your Papa," in Cyrillic letters.

June 3, 1929

Dearest Tania,

I have here before me your two letters and five postcards (the most recent is of May 23) that I should answer in order, diligently. But I will not do so. Did you receive the letter mailed from home and the other for Giulia? The first must have arrived after a great delay, according to what my mother writes me.

The change of season, with a considerable heat that one can feel already, has depressed and is stupefying me. I'm oppressed by an enormous fatigue and a certain general weakness, despite the fact that I continue to take the tonics; but I believe that it will not last long. This isn't anything new and therefore it doesn't worry me. It irritates me because it robs me of the pleasure of reading and it blunts my memory and overall sensitivity.

Saturday I received your package, which as an exception was given to me. Thank you. But I thought that in it there would be wool for the socks etc.; instead I was disappointed and worried. Truly. And I must urge you not to get carried away by fantasy and by the abstract conception of what is "useful" and "necessary," but stick to the concreteness of what is allowed in prison, that is, the things I've requested from you. In this regard your two postcards sound like the plot of a novel with resolutions, regrets, lacerating dilemmas, unreasonable ambitions, desires, etc. Would it not be better to be more down-to-earth and resolute? Don't you agree? It is true that your ways amuse me, but this is not a justification (at least not for you). It amuses me because it convinces me that you are the least practical person ever, despite all the boasts that you've often regaled me with. I instead have always been the most practical man in this entire world: I didn't do many things only because I didn't cheerfully give a damn, that is, I did not appear practical because I was too much so, to the point of exaggeration. And no one understood me! A real tragedy.

Now I believe that it is possible to draw up a final, fairly exact floral balance sheet. All the seeds have failed except one; I don't know what it is, but probably it is a flower and not a weed.[1] The chicory is all in bloom and will yield many seeds for future seasons. The cane has already put out a leaf as broad as my hand and is preparing another: it seems to be taking root well. The dahlias are still in incubation and there is no word from them; therefore we may presume that some day or other they may decide to be born, because I do not know when they are in season. The rose is beginning to bud, after it had seemed reduced to desolate twigs. But will it manage to survive the approaching summer heat? It looks too puny and run down to be up to the task. It is true of course that, at bottom, the rose is nothing but a wild thorn bush, and therefore very vital . . . We shall see. I would have liked to send you a chicory flower, but then I thought that at the very best it can only serve as the start of a folk ditty.[2]

From your postcard of May 14 I see that you want to have a new list of the books I'd requested of you when you were here. I think I have received everything. If anything is missing, it doesn't matter: if it is important I'll remember what it is. Don't send me any translations that aren't published by Slavia, even if they are presented as being authoritative—I've received everything published by "Slavia,"[3] save for the first out-of-print volume and the most recent [except] *Anna Karenina* that I have yet to receive. I see that they have reprinted Dostoyevsky's *Il villaggio di Stepancikovo*, [The Manor of Stepancikovo] that you can ask them to send me. I would also like to have these other books: Henri de Man, *Il superamento del Marxismo* [The surpassing of Marxism], Bari, Laterza (just published); Ferdinando d'Amato, *Gentile,* and Francesco Flora, *Croce*—two small books published in Milan by "Edizioni Athena" in the "Thinkers of Today" series, and Adolfo Omodeo's *Storia delle religioni* (History of religions), a small book published by Principato in Messina in a scholastic series. For the books in Rome we'll have to wait a bit longer, because I do not have room: tomorrow however I'm submitting a *domandina* (a little application, this is a prison term) so as to be authorized to send a box of books home.

Dear Tania, let me know something about yourself. How do you feel now? Have you recovered well? I embrace you.

Antonio

1. The sentence "All the seeds . . . weed" was used by Elsa Morante at the end of *History*, as a final expression of hope after the devastating tale of horror she recounts in that novel about a Jewish woman in Rome during World War II. See Elsa Morante, *History*, trans. William Weaver (New York: Avon Books, 1979), p. 687.

2. Gramsci uses the word *stornello*, an Italian folk-lyric poem that typically consists of a short opening line, usually an invocation to a flower, followed by two eleven-syllable lines. (Ernest Hatch Wilkins, *A History of Italian Literature* [Cambridge: Harvard University Press, 1954], p. 322).

3. Slavia was a Turinese publisher that, from 1926 to 1938, published many Italian translations of Russian literature.

Undated[1]

Dearest Giulia,

I greet you together with Delio and Giuliano. And since there are often many delays before my letters reach you I will have to send my good wishes today for Delio's coming fifth birthday. At any rate, I'm giving you the task of conveying these good wishes: many, many of them. Do you remember? Five years have already passed. And now Delio is already grown-up. I wonder what you experience at seeing him grow. I remember him in April 1925, when he had *coqueluche*[2] and seemed to me so unhappy! When I saw him again in 1926 he was another person, absolutely different. Now, going by the legal limits of my sentence, I ought to be able to see him again when he's twenty-three years old and, considering the haste of young people, when he will already have a wife and children. He will be even more different than in April 1925. I'm joking. But I think that he will have children because, if the city wants to defend itself against the invasion from the countryside and not lose its historical hegemony, the new generations will have to change their attitude toward fertility. Especially in your country. If the city grows through immigration and not through its own genetic force, will it be able to fulfill its leadership function or won't it be submerged, along with all its accumulated experiences, by the peasant rabbit hutch? I think that Delio's generation will have to confront this problem and that based on this a new sexual ethic superior to the present one will have to come into being.[3] I embrace you tenderly.

Antonio

1. This undated letter was probably sent together with or shortly after the preceding one to Tania, since Delio had his fifth birthday on August 10, 1929.

2. *Coqueluche* means "whooping cough" in French.

3. See Gramsci's remarks on the sexual question in Hoare and Smith, eds., *Selections from the Prison Notebooks*, pp. 294–298.

June 17, 1929

Dearest Carlo,

I've received your insured letter of the fourth with the 150 lire. I believe that you were probably somewhat annoyed by my previous letter[1] because you haven't answered me yet. I've thought about it and it also seems to me that I exaggerated. This can be laid to the fact that the unproductive prison life, which forces one to become someone else's parasite, also makes one touchy and irritable to the highest degree. I should have realized that it was mother who was writing and therefore many expressions, which could seem harsh, should have been ignored since they certainly were not intentional. So, I beg you, I want only you to write me about such matters, and not ask mother to do it, and I want you to write with the greatest frankness. You know mother too: if she must write to me that you have no money and therefore haven't sent me anything (and I didn't need anything, because besides my 700 lire fund I had another 400 lire) she begins by writing that in all of Sardinia there is great poverty, that taxes have gone up, that the harvest will fail, that the mayor is ordering everyone to redo the facades of the houses and the sidewalks along the streets. In short I thought she was writing a letter that was supposed to be read by the tax collector. The fault is mine, because I should have remembered how mother thinks, but all the same it seemed to me that such a way of writing meant that I had become like a stranger, somebody to whom an income is owed and since one cannot pay it, one begins to beat around the bush remembering that the hen has crushed the chicks, the mare of Zuri's rector has dropped a little foal with horns, which means that the end of the world is near and we ought to think about the salvation of our souls rather than money, etc. In short, I felt stricken by this sense of detachment and estrangement. Now I smile and think about the times when I used to fight every day with mother who was trying to convince me that a bit of barley in coffee is refreshing: "but I don't want to be refreshed, I want to drink some coffee!" It is always the same way of looking at things. I can also imagine how annoyed she must have been because the warden's office refused to accept the package, I was sorry only because it happened on this of all occasions. I did however receive Tatiana's package that had arrived earlier and I was able to eat a bit of chocolate all the same. You may thank Teresina: I've eaten Tatiana's chocolate as if it were hers and I hope that the feelings were the same.

I have prepared a box of books to ship by rail but the Turi-Bari line does not accept freight beyond Bari; therefore I will have to prepare several packages to be sent by mail. Here is a list so they can be checked:

1. Ben. Croce, *Teoria e storia della storiografia* [Theory and history of historiography].

2. G. Mortara, *Prospettive economiche, 1927* [Economic perspectives, 1927].

3. G. Mortara, *Prospettive economiche, 1928* [Economic perspectives, 1928].

4. Rabelais, *Gargantua e Pantagruele*, five volumes.

5. Col. Lawrence, *La révolte dans le désert* [Revolt in the desert].

6. Broccardi, Gentile etc., *G. Mameli e i suoi tempi* [G. Mameli and his times].

7. C. Marchesi, *Il letto di Procuste* [Procruste's bed].

8. Zeromsky, *Tutto e nulla* [All and nothing].

9. S. Aleramo, *Amo, dunque sono* [I love, therefore I am].

10. I. Bunin, *Il villaggio* [The village].

11. Delemain, *Pourquoi les oiseaux chantent* [Why birds sing].

12. Dostoevski, *La voce sotterranea* [Notes from underground].

13. J. Conrad, a novel.

14. Letters of Madame d'Epinay to Abbot Galiani.

15. L. Tolstoi, *Résurrection*, two volumes.

16. R. Kipling, *Les plus belles histoires du monde* [The finest stories in the world].

17. L. Tolstoi, *La tempesta di neve* [The snowstorm].

18. Pirandello, *L'esclusa* [The excluded one].

19. Maupassant, *Novelle* [Short stories], four volumes.

20. Chekhov, *Novelle* [Short stories], two small volumes.

21. Giannini, *Storia della Polonia* [History of Poland].

22. Panait Istrati, *Domnitza de Snagu*.

23. Pedrazzi, *La Sardegna* [Sardinia].

24. G. Piastra, *Figure e figuri della Superba* [Male and female figures of "la superba" (Genoa)].

25. McCarthy, *Villon*.

26. A. Londre, *De Paris à Buenos Ayres* [From Paris to Buenos Aires].

27. Dorgélès, *Partir . . .* [Leaving . . .].

28. Meeserel, *Die Sonne* [The sun].

29. *Almanacco letterario, 1927* [Literary almanac for 1927].

30. *Almanacco letterario, 1929* [Literary almanac for 1929].

31. Panait Istrati, *Mes départs* [My departures].

I want you to keep these first thirty-one items for me without giving them or lending them to anyone. They must not leave the house: I want to be able to count on them at any moment.

32. L. Einaudi, *Corso di scienza delle finanze* [Course in the science of finance]. You can do what you want with this, for I have another copy.

33. Petrocchi, *Dizionario della lingua italiana* [Dictionary of the Italian language].

34. Orlandi, *Il giov.[ane] filologo* [The young philologist].

These last two I give as a gift to Mea, with the hope that she learns her orthography properly.

The packages will reach you, I believe, only next month. I beg you to write me and give me news about the family council and the new administrative setup in Sardinia.[2] An affectionate embrace for everyone at home, especially mother. Cordially.

Antonio

1. The annoying "preceding letter" to which Gramsci refers here has not been found. To grasp the kind of insults of which he was capable when writing to Carlo, see letter of September 25, 1933.

2. The new administrative structure of Sardinia reflected the centralizing impulse of Fascism. Prefects were given wider powers (in effect the prefect of Cagliari was the governor of the island); political activity was coordinated to assure "unity of political aims"; elected mayors were replaced by appointed officials called *podestà*; and tight control was imposed on communal and provincial administrative bodies. Autonomist ideas such as those previously advocated by the Partito Sardo d'Azione were rigorously repressed.

July 1, 1929

Dearest Tania,

I've received the famous Bedouin over-stockings, together with the other things: they are perfect, they seem to have been invented just for my needs. As for the other things in the package I can't say anything about their usefulness, because I can't use them now and I've left everything in storage. During this past month the ailment from which I suffered before has passed, but it has left me with a great listlessness: the other prisoners tell me that this is the most conspicuous symptom of incarceration, which in the most resistant sets in during the third year, causing precisely this psychic enervation. In the third year, the mass of latent stimuli that each of us carries with him from freedom and active life begins to dry up and there remains just a glimmer of will that is exhausted in fantasies of never-to-be-realized grandiose plans. The prisoner lies supine on his cot and passes his time spitting at the ceiling, dreaming unrealizable dreams. This I certainly will not do, because I almost never spit and besides the ceiling is too high!

Apropos: you know the rose has completely revived (I write *apropos* because all during this time observation of the rose has perhaps taken the place of spitting at the ceiling!). From June 3 until June 15, all of a sudden it began to grow buds and then leaves, until it turned completely green again: now it already has little, fifteen centimeter long twigs. It also tried to put out a tiny, tiny bud that at a certain point however has begun to languish and is now turning yellow. In any case the plant has taken and next year it will certainly produce flowers. Nor is it excluded that even this year it will bring to completion a few tiny, very shy roses. This pleases me, because for a year now I've been interested in cosmic phenomena (perhaps, as they say in my hometown, my bed is placed in accordance with the proper direction of terrestrial fluids and when I rest the cells of my organism rotate in unison with the entire universe). I've been waiting with great anxiety for the summer solstice and now that the earth is bowing (actually it straightens up after the bow) to the sun, I am happier (the question is related to the lamp they bring me at night and so there we have identified the terrestrial fluid!); I experience the cycle of the seasons, linked to the solstices and equinoxes, as though they were flesh of my flesh; the rose is alive and will certainly bloom again, because heat prepares the frost and beneath the snow the first violets are already throbbing, etc. etc.; in short, since space no longer exists for me, time seems to me a corporeal thing. Dear Tania, I put an end to these divagations and embrace you.

Antonio

July 1, 1929[1]

Dear Giulia,

You can tell Delio that I was greatly interested in the news he sent me, because it is important and extremely serious. Nevertheless I hope that someone with a bit of glue has repaired the damage done by Giuliano and that therefore the hat has not been turned into wastepaper. Do you remember how in Rome Delio used to believe that I could fix anything that was broken? By now he has certainly forgotten. And what about him, does he have a tendency to fix things? This, in my opinion, would be a sign . . . of constructiveness, of a positive character, more than the Meccano toy. You are wrong if you think that as a child I had . . . literary and philosophical tendencies, as you have written. On the contrary, I was an intrepid pioneer and I wouldn't leave the house unless I had in my pocket some grains of wheat and some matches wrapped in scraps of oilcloth for the eventuality that I might be flung on a desert island and be left to my own devices. I was also a daring builder of boats and carts and I knew seaman's nomenclature inside and out: I had my greatest success when a tinsmith in town asked me for a paper model of a superb schooner with two bridges, because he wanted to reproduce it in tin. Indeed I was obsessed with these things, because at the age of seven I had read *Robinson Crusoe* and *Treasure Island*. Indeed I think that a child's life like that of thirty years ago is impossible today: children today are already eighty years old when they are born, like the Chinese Laotze.[2] The radio and airplane have forever destroyed Crusoeism, which was the way in which so many generations fantasized. The very invention of Meccano shows how quickly the child is intellectualized; his hero can no longer be Robinson Crusoe, but instead is the policeman or the scientific thief, at least in the West. So your judgment can be exactly reversed and only then is it accurate. Don't you agree?

You have told me Giuliano's weight, but not his height. Tatiana informs me that when he weighed eighteen kilos Delio was one meter and eight centimeters tall. Such information interests me very much, because it gives me concrete impressions: but you always send me too few. I hope that when she is with you Tatiana, continuing to be better than you, will send me a great deal of news of all sorts about the children and also about you. Do you know that she is going to bring you a camera? I remembered that I had promised you one in 1926 and I have enlisted Tatiana's help. For your mother, since it is not the chestnut season (in 1925 your mother was very disappointed, because I didn't bring her any chestnuts) I will tell Tatiana to make a collection of cigarettes from various countries and bring them to her in my name; will she like them? I'm sure she will. My dear, I embrace you together with the children.

Antonio

1. The letter is undated. Archivists at the Gramsci Institute attach it to this date.
2. Lao Tse or Tsu (604–531?B.C.), Chinese philosopher considered the founder of Taoism. Lao Tse means the "old master or philosopher." According to legend, the mother of Lao Tse, after a supernatural conception, carried him in her womb sixty-two years (other versions say seventy-two, or eighty-one), so that, when he was finally born, his hair was white as with age.

July 14, 1929

Dearest Tatiana,

I've received a letter from the bookstore with a list of the year's expenses, from the time we started the magazine subscriptions until today, I think, and a notice according to business procedures that within one month from the notice's date, that is, on July 30 (the letter is dated June 30) a draft in my name will be issued. This is a mistake, a disagreeable mistake, but meanwhile I do not know whether I will be able to inform them in time with a special letter, for which I'll ask permission of the warden's office when it is my turn. I don't even know whether you are still in Milan and whether, if that is the case, you are in bed with enterocolitis. In any case do not get out of bed because of this. Turn to somebody and get him to run the errand. Piero would be the best, if he's in Milan, because he's very well known at the Sperling bookstore. In fact it was actually Piero who told me about the store when I was at Ustica and he again recommended it to me in Milan when he was granted a visit by the pretrial judge. Make sure that they are told that mistakes of this kind must not happen again. I've thought of Piero also for these other reasons: I would like you to see him in any case to ask him whether from his uncle,[1] who is first president of the Court of Appeals, it is possible to find out whether the petition for a revision of our trial has been received and what became of it. This is a petition that Terracini on behalf of everyone had forwarded to the Court of Appeals exactly one year ago. The special law provides for the possibility of a petition requesting a revision but does not indicate under which jurisdiction; in the absence of this indication we have addressed it to the Court of Appeals, as it is the supreme judicial jurisdiction. The petition was based on the following facts: (1) that some of the codefendants (Grieco, Molinelli, etc.) considered to be members of the Central Committee, that is, the chief perpetrators like myself, Terracini, Roveda, and Scoccimarro, have been sentenced only to detention, with a maximum of seventeen years for Grieco, who is contumacious; (2) that the defendants Masieri,[2] etc., from Florence have been acquitted of the charge of insurrection and sentenced only to detention, whereas we have been sentenced as instigators of the crime of which Masieri has been acquitted. All of this by the same tribunal at different times. With these data, Piero can have these facts brought to the attention of his uncle and obtain a precise answer. He could also ask him whether or not it is probable that the Special Tribunal will continue in existence. Perhaps Piero himself could obtain the parliamentary records (Senate and Chamber of Deputies) with a stenographic transcript of the debates on the Concordat (I've seen that his uncle made a speech before the Senate) I would like to read them in order to round out my scholarship in this field. If Piero doesn't have time, could you perhaps send a note to Senator Bastianelli?[3] At the Senate's secretariat he can find the records of the Chamber of Deputies.

Do you know that your plans to travel to Calabria, Sardinia, etc. have filled me with the greatest astonishment? You are marvelous, truly marvelous! I believe this is due to the fact that you are terribly afraid of getting on a train and so you console yourself with fabulistic projects. I'm writing to you without any assurance as to your health. I hope to receive news from you soon. I embrace you affectionately.

Antonio

The rosebush has more than forty buds and supports them very well. It will become very beautiful even if it is of a common species.

1. Senator Mario D'Amelio (1871–1943).
2. Gramsci refers to the trial of a group of twenty-three Communists held on January 31, 1928, before the Special Tribunal in Defense of the State.
3. See letter to Tania, August 22, 1927, n. 2.

———————

July 30, 1929

Dearest Tatiana,

Yesterday I received Giulia's letter. I also hope that the photographs haven't been lost and that you will be able to send them to me soon. I should be answering your many questions and instead I would only like to chat with you about this and that; your fierce and passionate outburst against landlords amused me very much. Nevertheless I will try to answer some of the questions. I believe that you should not encourage but rather discourage Vittorio's plan to come to Italy. The position of pharmacist's assistant is very badly paid and besides there's a lot of unemployment in this field; I've known adjunct chemistry professors who went to wrap powders for 600 lire a month. With the new laws concerning pharmacies the situation must have gotten even worse. To any other steady occupation abroad (that is, far from his family and environment, where in an emergency it is always possible to find some help) Vittorio's temperament is unsuited since in my opinion he is too childish and whimsical. In the last few years I've known him as a functionary of the Ministry of Foreign Affairs (translations), as a broker, as a journalist, as a dramatic actor on tour in Samarkand and environs. His instincts are too inclined to wanderlust. His is a temperament that I know because I studied it in my brothers, especially my eldest brother: Italy is the last country one ought to recommend to such types, unless they live on an income, because the excessive population and chronic unemployment in entire sectors of activity (but particularly in middle level technical-intellectual activities) caused by the fact that Italy has a sufficient number of cadres for a country with a highly developed industrial sector, whereas she has had only a mediocre development—leads the state authorities to plant everyone rigidly in his job. The relative popularity that the corporative system[1] enjoys among the middle strata of intellectuals is due precisely to the precariousness of positions and to the situation's lack of elasticity: everyone would like the law to guarantee him against untrammeled competition. Anyone who loses his job can remain unemployed for month after month without any resources. I'll give you an example. An electro-technical company opened a competition for twenty-five engineers, to be hired for a three-year trial period at 300 lire a month; more than 200 applied. Vittorio would find himself in an environment under an atmospheric pressure twenty times greater than normal and he would soon regret his decision. And another reason: we can grade the members of your family in terms of their knowledge of Italian: first place goes to Eugenia who writes very well in a modern Italian style, second place would go to Giulia, who has an almost classical style, forms a sentence to perfection, but commits errors that are noticeable; the third place would go to you, you've recently improved a great deal, but one can tell that Italian is not your language (it is French, in my opinion, not even Russian). Vittorio, though he studied in Italy, has forgotten a great deal. In 1922 he wrote a number of articles for me that couldn't even be corrected; everything needed to be done over from scratch, in terms of orthography, morphology, and syntax. This is an important matter and so I have gone on at length, without hiding any of my thoughts.

Dear Tatiana, I can chat no longer. I did immediately take the small box with me; but I forgot to write to you about it. It is pretty, but it is a snuffbox; let's say a pretty snuffbox. I haven't made up my mind to put salt in it, because I am afraid that if I go into the yard with such a salt shaker, all the others will ask me to let them have a sniff. The rosebush already has more than twenty small roses in bloom, and I like them very much. For the time being I don't need anything; perhaps you could bring me a few cakes of soap and a bit of Ovaltine. You mustn't believe that I'm grumbling or in a bad mood etc. Sometimes I write like this to tease you a bit, but I'm very fond of you. I embrace you.

Antonio

1. The Italian Fascist corporative system combined the ideologies of syndicalism and authoritarian nationalism. It was a system of institutional arrangements by which capital and labor were integrated into obligatory hierarchical organizations called corporations whose activities were recognized and coordinated by the state. (Cannistraro, ed., *Historical Dictionary of Fascist Italy*, p. 138).

July 30, 1929

Dear Julca,

I've received your letter of the seventh. The photographs haven't arrived yet; I hope there will also be one of you. Of course I want to see you too, at least once a year, in order to gain a more vivid impression of you. Otherwise what might I think? That you have changed very much physically, that you've become frail, that you have a lot of white hair, etc. etc. And besides, I must send you my good wishes for your birthday in advance: perhaps my next letter would still reach you in time, but I'm not sure of it. If your photograph reaches me, it means that I'll send you a repetition of my birthday greetings. Of course, I would like to see you in a group with the children, as in last year's photograph, because in a group there is some movement, some drama, it is possible to grasp relationships, which can be extended, imagined in other settings, in episodes of concrete life, when the photographer's lens is not obviously aimed. At any rate I believe I know you enough to imagine other settings, but I cannot sufficiently imagine the children's actions and reactions in their relationships with you, and I mean live actions and reactions as they take place, not general emotions and moods: the photographs say little to me and my childhood memories are of no help, because I think of them as too particular and I imagine that everything is different now, in a new world of emotions and with two generations in between (one might say even more, because between a child raised in a Sardinian village and a child raised in a large modern city, due to this fact alone, there is a difference of at least two generations). You know, sometimes I would like to write to you about yourself, about your strength, which is a hundred times greater than you think, but I've always hesitated because it seems to me I am like a . . . slave trader who palps a beast of burden. There, I wrote it, since I did think it I might as well write it too. I shouldn't think it; but perhaps it is because there still survives in me, in the form of repressed emotions, many past concepts, which have been critically overcome but not completely erased. Certainly I am often obsessed by the thought that to you have fallen the heaviest burdens of our union, heavier objectively, true enough, but this is a distinction and so I cannot think about your strength, which I've admired many times, even without telling you, but tend instead to think about your weaknesses, about your possible moments of weariness, with a great melting tenderness, which could be expressed in a caress but not easily in words. And anyway I'm still very envious, because I cannot enjoy the children's first fresh impressions of life too and help you guide and rear them. I remember many things about Delio's Roman life and also about the principles on which you and Genia dealt with him, and I think about them again and try to develop them and adapt them to new situations. I always arrive at the conclusion that a great impression was made on you by Geneva and the circles saturated with Rousseau and Dr. Fulpius,[1] who must have been typically Swiss, Genevan, and Rousseauian. But I've strayed too far afield (perhaps I'll write to you on this subject some other time, if you are interested) and perhaps I've teased you about Rousseau, which on another occasion (do you remember?) made you so angry. My dear, I embrace you.

Antonio

1. Charles Fulpius, a copy of whose *Cours de morale sociale basé sur l'évolution* [Course on social morality based on evolution] (1905) Gramsci had in prison.

August 26, 1929

Dear Tatiana,

I received the photograph of the children and am very happy, as you can well imagine. I was also very glad because I've been able to see with my own eyes that they have bodies and legs: for three years now I've only seen heads and the doubt was beginning to loom that they had become cherubs without little wings behind their ears. In short, this time I had an impression of a more vibrant life. Of course I do not completely share your enthusiastic judgments. I believe more realistically that their stance is determined by their position in front of the camera; Delio is posed like someone who must go through a boring but necessary chore[1] and who takes himself seriously; Giuliano opens his eyes wide before that mysterious device, not quite convinced that there might not be some rather uncertain surprise in store: an irate cat could jump out or perhaps even a very beautiful peacock.

Why otherwise would they have told him to look in that direction and not move? You're right to say that he has an extraordinary resemblance to your mother, and not only in the eyes but in the entire upper molding of his face and head.

Do you know? I'm writing you halfheartedly because I'm not sure that this letter will reach you before your departure. And besides I'm again a bit out of sorts. It has rained a lot and the temperature has fallen: and this makes me feel unwell. The pains in my kidneys and my headaches return and my stomach rejects food. But this is something normal for me and so I don't worry too much. I do however eat a kilo of grapes a day, when they send them, so I can't possibly die of hunger: I enjoy eating the grapes and they are of excellent quality.

I had already read an article by the publisher Formiggini about bad translations and some of the proposals made to get rid of this epidemic. One writer having actually proposed to hold the publishers legally responsible for the howlers they printed, Formiggini answered by threatening to close shop because even the most scrupulous publisher cannot avoid printing howlers, and, quite humorously, he could already see a police detective accosting him and saying: "Kindly rise and come with me to the police station. It would be necessary that you respond to the accusation of outrage to the Italian language!" (Sicilians talk somewhat like this and many policemen are Sicilians). The problem is complex and will not be resolved. Translators are badly paid and translate worse. In 1921 I approached the Italian representative of the society of French authors to obtain permission to publish a serialized novel.[2] For 1000 lire I obtained both the permit and a translation done by a person who was a lawyer. His office looked quite impressive and the translator-lawyer seemed a man who knew his profession and I sent the manuscript to the typographer so that the 10 installments would be printed and kept in readiness. But on the evening before the beginning of the serial, just to be sure, I decided to check and had them bring me the galleys. After a few lines I jumped out of my chair: I discovered that there was a huge ship perched on top of a mountain. But this wasn't Mt. Ararat and therefore Noah's ark, but rather a Swiss mountain and a large hotel.[3] The entire translation was like this: "morceau de roi" was translated "a small piece of king," "goujat" was "little fish"!, and it became more and more comical as it proceeded.[4] When I protested the office disbursed 300 lire to make a new translation and pay for the printing costs, but what really topped it all was that as soon as the translator-lawyer got his hands on the remaining 700 lire that he was supposed to hand over to his boss, he ran off to Vienna with a girl. Up until now translations of the classics were at least done with care and scrupulously, if not always elegantly. Now the most astonishing things happen in this field too. For a quasi-national collection (the government has granted a 100,000 lire subsidy) of Greek and Latin classics, the translation of Tacitus's *Germania* has been entrusted to . . . Marinetti,[5] who after all obtained a degree in letters from the Sorbonne. In a magazine I've read a list of the vulgarities committed by Marinetti, whose translation has been highly praised by . . . journalists. "Exigere plagas" (to examine the wound) is translated: "to exact the sores" and I would say that's enough: a student in liceo would realize that this is a mindless asininity.

Dear Tatiana, who knows whether this letter will get to you before your departure. In Rome I would like you to take two or three of my books: the collection of lectures on *Europa politica nel secolo XIX* [Political Europe in the nineteenth century], published by the Chamber of Commerce of Brescia, and Michels's book on *Il partito politico e le tendenze oligarchiche della democrazia moderna* [The political party and the oligarchic tendencies of modern democracy], which I have in a prewar French translation and in the new, much expanded and enriched Italian edition of 1924. A long time ago I had asked you to please procure for me a small book by Vincenzo Morello (Rastignac) on canto 10 of Dante's *Inferno*, published by Mondadori a few years ago (1927 or 1928): could you try to remember this now? I've made a little discovery about this canto by Dante that I believe is interesting and that would in part correct B. Croce's thesis on the *Divine Comedy*, which is too absolute.[6] I won't describe the argument here because it would take up too much space. I believe that chronologically Morello's lecture is the last on canto 10 and therefore it can be useful to me to see if someone else has already made my observations; I hardly think so, because in canto 10 everyone is fascinated by the figure of Farinata and they only stop to examine and extol it, and Morello, who is not a scholar but a rhetorician, has undoubtedly kept to the tradition, but I would like to read it anyway. Then I'll write my "Dante comment" and quite possibly I'll send it to you with the author's compliments, indited in very beautiful calligraphy. I say this just for fun, for in order to write a comment of this kind, I would have to review a certain amount of material (for example, the reproductions of the Pompeian paintings) that can be found only in the largest libraries. That is, I would have to collect historical elements that prove how by tradition, from classical art until the Middle Ages, painters refused to depict sorrow in its most elementary and profound forms (maternal sorrow): in the Pompeian wall paintings, Medea, while cutting the throats of the children she had with Jason, is depicted with her face covered by a veil, because the painter considers it superhuman and inhuman to give an expression to her face.[7] I will however write some notes and perhaps sketch the preparatory draft for a future comment. You see what a jumble I've written you? All because I'm not sure that this letter will get to you in time and instead will lie on your desk for several weeks waiting for your return. Except that I would have as usual written the part for Giulia too; I guess that next week I'll write all four pages for her. More: see if you can obtain the *Catalogo generale del materiale scolastico e sussidi didattaci* [General catalogue of scholastic material and teaching aids] published by G. B. Paravia, with branches also in Milan and Rome. More yet: will you remember the American fava beans this time? I believe that you will have to go to a large pharmacy that also has a laboratory in order to find them (all of this on the chance that this letter reaches you!) Dearest, I embrace you affectionately.

Antonio

1. Gramsci uses the French word *corvée*.

2. In the daily newspaper *L'Ordine Nuovo*.

3. The French word *bâtiment* (building) had been translated into the Italian *bastimento* (ship). But *bâtiment* can also mean "ship."

4. *Morceau de roi* means "superb," "excellent," "a choice dish," while *pezzettino di re* means "a little king." *Goujat* means a "cad"or "lout," while *pesciolino* is "a little fish" (the translator may have confused *goujat* with *goujon*, a type of fish).

5. Gramsci refers to the collection edited by Ettore Romagnoli of the Royal Academy of Italy, published by the Istituto Editoriale Italiano. The translation done by Filippo Tommaso Marinetti (1876–1944), futurist poet and supporter of Fascism, had appeared in 1928.

6. As indicated elsewhere, Gramsci was to deal more fully with this canto in a letter to Tania, September 20, 1931, and in the *Prison Notebooks*.

7. What Gramsci says about "veiled suffering" is correct, but in reference to a painting of Agamemnon, not of Medea. The frescoes at Pompei do not show Medea in the act of killing her children. Although Gramsci characterizes a mother's grief at the death of her children as "pain in its most elementary and profound form," the example he gives else-

where in classical painting of a *father*'s pain (in his analysis of canto 10 in the *Prison Note-books*) is the one that is historically accurate. The article "Medea" in the *Enciclopedia dell'arte antica*, pp. 950–57, explains that "in the mural painting of Pompei, Medea is never depicted in the act of killing but rather in the spiritual struggle that precedes the crime."

September 23, 1929

Dearest Mother,

I received your letter of September 18. It seems to me that your writing hand is firmer than on previous occasions and moreover you've written me at greater length, without any sign of weariness showing at the end; this has given me great pleasure because I was afraid that your malarial fevers had returned. Thank you for the news you send me. As I wrote to you at other times, everything about real life interests me, especially if this "everything" can help me to reconstruct and imagine your everyday life that, unchanging and monotonous as it may be, is always more varied and immensely more eventful than mine. Who knows how Giulia and Lia must have aged. Giulia must be more "scarrabudada"[1] than ever; on the other hand I think she's close to sixty, if not more. Lia however must still have "youthful" pretensions and perhaps she still thinks she'll be able to find a husband; but I imagine she already has a rather pronounced mustache. Why not arrange for the friars of Terra Santa to stop at her place when they come for the "search"? You still haven't written me anything about Uncle Achille; is he still in the employ of Uncle Luigi? For me Uncle Achille was the most likable person in the entire family, even more than Uncle Serafino who was actually very pleasant. I would like to know what he is doing now. You know what you ought to do. In your letters you should review for me everyone whom I knew and give me their news, especially those who during these last years have managed to change their situations, for better or worse. I would like to be able to understand whether Ghilarza, with the new administrative situation and the vicinity of the Tirso basin, shows a tendency to become a city; whether there is more commerce, some industries, whether a part of the population has moved from traditional occupations to those of a different type, whether there is any real estate development or on the contrary whether there has been an increase of people living off an income. So that you can understand me, I'll tell you that in my opinion Oristano is not a city and will never become one; it is just a large rural center (relatively large) inhabited by the owners of the land and the fisheries of the nearby territory and in which there exists a certain trade in manufactured goods for the people from the countryside who bring their agricultural products there. A center of merchants and idle owners, of money lenders, that is, it is not yet a city because it does not produce anything important. Does Ghilarza tend to become like Oristano or does the electric energy of the Tirso offer a foundation for an incipient industry? These things interest me and if you'll write me something about them I'll be very glad. You know that boredom is my worst enemy, despite the fact that I read and write all day long; a particular sort of boredom, not that which comes from doing nothing (because I do do something) but comes from not having any contact with the real world. I don't know whether you've read many lives of saints and hermits; these people in fact were tormented by this particular kind of boredom that they called the "noon devil" because precisely around noon, in their solitude, they were seized by a frenzy to change, to return to the world, to see people; they thought it was the devil who tempted them, while it was simply boredom, the terrible boredom that comes from solitude and from always seeing the same things and always performing the same actions.

In a few days I hope to have a visit from Tatiana who must be on her way to Turi. So I'll finally be able to send Carlo the small box and several parcels of books besides the box, together with the dictionary for Mea. I've received the cigarettes and I thank you most cordially. Regards and kisses to all at home, and to you, dearest mother, an affectionate embrace.

Antonio

1. "Scattered and disconnected" in Sardinian.

October 21, 1929

Dearest Mother,

I've received your letter of October 8. Tatiana has not yet come to see me; she stopped in Rome for a while in order to take care of some personal business. I do not know anything about the parcel you mentioned; in any case you've done well not to send it, because it would not have been accepted. Tatiana gets certain things into her head, and I've never stopped reproaching her because of this; but she's incorrigible and sometimes she creates problems for me vis-à-vis the prison administration. Packages of foodstuffs can only be sent on Christmas, Easter, and Statute Day, otherwise they are returned. But since Tatiana has heard that in certain jails they occasionally allow an extra package from time to time she is seized by the inspiration of an experimental initiative. At any rate you are warned and you mustn't follow her suggestions and especially you mustn't think that I have anything to do with them. You know that I have never been gluttonous. When I was in jail in Milan Tatiana's initiatives were unbridled; on some days she would bring me at different hours three, four delicacies that she saw by chance in the shop windows—a quarter pound of goose liver pâté at eleven, a pound of ————[1] at two, mozzarella or whipped cream at five; and the guards at the door, who in the end had gotten to know her, would give in to her pleadings and delivered the small packages to me. This however was a judicial prison[2] and it was possible to do a lot of things: the chief warden would end up by smiling at the assault of all the convicts' women who would beg, insist, and were a continuous nuisance. But Tatiana has not gotten rid of this "vice" and from time to time she succumbs to it again.

I will certainly send the dictionary for Mea. I hope she can wait for it a little longer. As soon as Tatiana arrives I'll get them to send over to her all the books that are be shipped to you and I'll arrange for the dictionary to be mailed by parcel post so that it will arrive quickly. But perhaps it won't be of much use to Mea and somebody will have to explain to her exactly how it works, as regards pronunciation, accents, and ancient and modern words: for the time being it would be better to have an encyclopedic dictionary like the Melzi with illustrations that describe the things, rather than a literary dictionary such as the one I will send that only lists the words used in literary Tuscan.

I found the photograph of the children very interesting, even though it is of very poor quality. Teresina's little daughter particularly resembles Grazietta, she has more of a family air than Mea and Franco. In any case their physiognomies change a lot from one photograph to the next: but they always look very lively and charming. Recently I received a photograph of Delio and Giuliano that isn't very successful; the second copy went astray in transit and I cannot arrange to have it sent to you. Perhaps they will soon send me a new one, taken after they've been on vacation and in the country, and I'll get them to send you a print. They're all well.

And why shouldn't you send the birth certificates to Nannaro?[3] Of course you must send it. I hope that he is wise enough to make good use of it without exposing himself to useless risks. Although legally he has no reason to worry. But in these matters legality counts only up to a certain point. Give him my greeting when you write to him.

But why are they asking you to pay the household tax? This tax was abolished a few years ago by law since it was included in the supplementary tax. It would seem that the mayors, pressured by the demands of the budget, aren't all that scrupulous and get people to pay twice, so that various states ———— ————[4], the same tax. You didn't tell me what Egidio Mass[5] is doing and who Mea's teacher is? Is it perhaps the Tamponi woman? Greetings and kisses to all; and to you an affectionate embrace.

Antonio

1. Illegible word.
2. A "judicial" prison is one in which a person accused of a crime is held while evidence against him is gathered and evaluated by the investigating judge or judges. In Italy judges perform the functions that district attorneys and grand juries perform in the United States.
3. Nannaro was living and working in Paris at this time.
4. Illegible words.
5. The last letters of this name are illegible.

November 4, 1929

Dear Tatiana,

At last, after two months, it is again your turn for a letter. I've reread the postcards you sent me in the meantime, but I haven't been able to reawaken the "frenetic" emotions I experienced when they first arrived. I'm becoming a real fakir; soon I'll be able to swallow swords and stroll barefoot over Gillette razor blades. Perhaps you'll show a perturbed face at this rather melodramatic exordium, and I deeply regret having to reproach you, but I must do so, necessarily, so as not to be compelled at some other time to inflict on you a much more serious displeasure, such as breaking off our correspondence and all other forms of contact. I had warned you many times not to take any initiative either as regards my position in particular or my situation in general without obtaining my prior consent. I don't know why you've always stubbornly refused to take this recommendation seriously or to attach any importance to it. You must have thought it was only some sort of whim or childish tantrum. But in truth, if you had just thought about it for a moment, what conclusions ought you to have drawn? It seems simple to me. Just think along these lines: what do you know that is precise, concrete, about my daily life? Nothing, or almost nothing. How can you possibly know what concrete consequences your initiatives can have for me, even those that you consider most banal and of no importance? You know nothing, nothing at all. The entire concatenation of cause and effect in prison life is fundamentally different from that in ordinary life, because the actions and reactions of emotions and activities are devoid of the fundamental, albeit relative, element of freedom that exists in ordinary life. Is it not right that under such conditions I should be the only one to decide whether a thing should or should not be done, because I alone am in prison and deprived of freedom and the one upon whom the consequences of all initiatives will fall, worsening the conditions of my daily life? Even if one were to admit that this is mere punctilio (and I assure you that this is not the case), well, even if it were childishness, it should be respected because in this situation one's nerves become so overwrought that having some consideration for them is not after all an exaggeration. The fact that has irritated me to the point of frenzy (indeed, precisely, to the point of frenzy) is the application that you have made through Attorney Niccolai in regard to the Council of Revision. Why didn't you first ask me about it? To begin with, let me tell you that all your bustling about will be completely useless, because I personally will not present any petition and if the attorney should write me I probably won't even answer him. The petition was presented in June 1928, legally, according to the terms of the law, because the law permitted it. Attorney Niccolai was asked to undertake it and to be retained to plead it and he committed himself to do so. What has been done is sufficient, given the importance of the matter that, in reality, comes down to the pure exercise of a formal right, without any other foreseeable consequence that is not already contained in the exercise itself of this formal right, that is, of pure protest. This interference of yours does nothing but cast a shadow of ambiguity on this crystal clear position of mine and the others, but especially mine. Why do you refuse to understand that you are incapable, radically incapable, of taking into account my honor and my dignity in these matters, because you understand nothing, nothing at all? Mind you, I have no intention of offending you in any way, and neither do I want to cast a doubt on your sensitivity, when it is a question of everyday relations between two persons: I simply want to point out the objective impossibility for you, as an outsider, to relive the atmosphere of iron and fire that I have lived through during these last years. But nevertheless I want to convince you that this is something of enormous importance to me, in which I don't want anyone to interfere and for which I am prepared to take decisive steps, such as breaking off all relations. I beg you to consider with utter seriousness what I am writing, because I have given it much thought and I have spent several nights without sleep, for I was tormented by your postcards and yet still couldn't reply to them.

You had already caused me a great deal of distress when you mentioned to me that certain proposal that you had made to Giulia a long time ago; I made a great mistake at that time in not giving you a sharper sense of my disapproval. I allowed myself to be moved by your solicitude for me and I was loath to hurt your feelings. But now I've become fakirized, from this point of view too, and I'm even afraid that I might become hardened in another way and end up using foul language. But I believe that from now on you will be very cautious, because I am certain that you care a lot about me and that you are sorry at having wounded and grieved me so deeply. Don't be too hurt by what I have written to you; break off all contacts with Attorney Niccolai and if you so wish, repeat to him the part of this letter that concerns him. Don't send me anything, neither books nor other things that I haven't requested of you; follow this rule very strictly, without exceptions of any kind, neither those of time or place or special occasions. I'm sorry that it has been necessary for me to devote an entire letter to this subject. I hope that this time you will take proper care of yourself and no longer do so many harebrained things at the expense of your health. I've already become accustomed to the idea that you will not be coming to Turi this time, but will consider it more opportune to pay more attention to your health. Dear Tatiana, believe me that it is only because I am fond of you and cutting off all relations with you would sadden me greatly that I've been so frank and peremptory. I embrace you tenderly.

Antonio

November 18, 1929

Dearest Tania,

I've received your postcard of the sixteenth and I was very happy to get news of you after fifteen days that you haven't written to me. Dear Tatiana, I believe that Carlo has reassured you in person about my true state of mind and that he has been able to erase the impression that my last letter made on you: I only wanted to create a conviction in you, not to cause you pain, but perhaps it was impossible to obtain results without producing this other effect as well. I'm very grateful for everything that you have sent me, though I must point out that you have spent too much money; now you must no longer think that I lack for anything: I have provisions that will last at least five or six years, and that abundantly. I've also received the bulbs, but I have not yet planted them, because I think that the winter cold would freeze them; I'll put them in at the beginning of spring and I hope they will sprout unlike the dahlias that have all wilted. I've also received the books, but I beg you not to send me any more until you hear from me, because I am all stocked up, even though Carlo took quite a big pile away with him. Of the books I have mentioned to you, the Italian edition of Professor Michels's *Partiti politici e le tendenze oligarchiche della moderna democrazia* [Political parties and the oligarchic tendencies of modern democracy], which I once had is missing. If it was lost during one of my moves, let's not worry, but if it can still be found, put it aside and perhaps you can bring it to me on your first new trip; it is a large volume published in 1924 by Unione Tipografica Editrice Torinese. If they also haven't been lost put aside the Berlitz Method books for German (two small books) and for Russian (one book) and if you can manage it your copy of Goncharov's *Oblomov* in Russian (I once saw it on your desk). At present I'm only translating from German, because I don't want to overtax my memory and disperse my attention, but next year, when I'll have completed the German program I have set for myself, I'll take up Russian again in depth: *Oblomov* seems very suitable to me because I've translated a few passages from an anthology for Italian business schools and also because, since I have Lo Gatto's unabridged translation, I'll be able to check on my own work. If your edition was published before the war, as I think I remember, and maybe the date of publication is legible, I believe it won't be difficult to get it through.[1]

Just today the mail has brought two bundles of parliamentary records of the debates in the Senate. I have not yet been able to examine them because they still had to be checked. In any case their bulk has frightened me. I had written to you only to get the pages that contain the debate on the Lateran pact. If by any chance you've given Sperling bookstore orders to send me the parliamentary records all the time, do me a favor, cancel it right away because I wouldn't really know what to do with them in my present situation. If you can also cancel the orders for the debate in the Chamber of Deputies: I've read that this part will be published in a book with a preface by the Honorable Federzoni,[2] that is, in a more comfortable and manageable form.

I've seen that Giulia has not yet written after all this time. This saddens me. It cannot be only a question of a lack of time. It's been about four months since she has written to me and in the meantime I've written to her twice without receiving an answer. This causes me a certain uneasiness that I find difficult to overcome. I would not be able to write to her without first having received some news from her. I think that some of her letters must have gone astray. It is possible. It is also possible that she's wondering why I don't write to her, if she has written and her letters have indeed gone astray. Based on what I know for sure, I've written to her twice without receiving a reply, and I'm embarrassed at the thought of writing her a third time. You know, I'm getting used to the idea now that, since I am in prison, I might be entitled to some consideration. I've thought a lot about this "emotion," after having written my last letter to you. And I've laughed a bit at myself, because I remembered a sixteenth-century comedy in which among the characters there are several drunken Landskenechts[3] who argue more or less as follows: "We Lands be very lucky, we steal, beat Italians, rape Italian women, then say we drunk." And yet I've decided that mine isn't just the claim of a drunken Landsknecht and that being in prison is not precisely the same as being drunk. It doesn't create special rights toward those who are fond of us, but, for example, it explains and justifies that I don't write to Giulia if I persistently don't receive any letters from her. I do not have petty susceptibilities, but sometimes I think that if she doesn't write to me this might also depend on the fact that she no longer enjoys receiving letters and news from me: hence the uneasiness that I spoke of before. Dear Tatiana, I write these things a bit to have a laugh, but also with some melancholy. I embrace you tenderly.

Antonio

When you leave for Milan, tell me immediately. If I'm kept in suspense because I don't know where you are on the day on which I can write my letters, I end up by not writing at all and I lose my turn. You know that last time for no less than four months in a row, you wrote me every four or five days that you were about to get on a train, etc. etc.; how did you expect me to take these foolish whims seriously and not think that it was all one big fairy tale? If there should be one of these contretemps, remember that toward the middle of next month it would be a good idea to remind Sperling bookstore to renew the subscriptions to the magazines on time, otherwise the same thing will occur that took place at the beginning of this year. My dear I embrace you again.

Antonio

1. Gramsci probably means that if this book, in Russian, had been published after the war, that is, after the Bolshevik revolution, prison authorities might have routinely disallowed its use by political prisoners, regardless of its content.

2. Luigi Federzoni (1878–1967), Fascist minister of the Interior from 1924 to 1926, and president of the Senate from 1929 to 1939.

3. A reference to the period when almost all of Italy was under the direct or indirect control of Spain. It was a period marked by frequent incursions by German mercenaries.

December 2, 1929

Dearest Carlo,

Why is it that you've never sent me even one picture postcard since you left Turi? This means that for about a month now I've been without news about mother and Teresina. Do you know what you ought to do? Get one of those collections of postcards of folk costumes in Sardinia, like the ones you used to send me from Rome and then mail them one by one, writing them yourself or from time to time getting someone at home to write them. What was mother's impression about your trip? I wonder what kind of stories you told her!

The books I want you to send back to the bookstore with a letter explaining that they've been sent to me by mistake in duplicate are the following:

1. Ettore Lo Gatto, *Storia della letteratura russa*, volume 2 [History of Russian literature].

2. Méthode Toussaint-Langenscheidt, *Dictionnaire anglais-français* [English-French dictionary].

3. Ognev, *Le journal de Kostia Riabzev* [Journal of Kostia Riabzev].

In the letter I would add that in exchange for these three volumes they can send me:

1. Ettore Lo Gatto, *Storia della letteratura russa* [History of Russian literature], volume 3 (certainly by mistake they sent me a second copy of volume 2 instead of volume 3).

2. G. Salvioli, *Il capitalismo antico* [Capitalism in antiquity], ed. Laterza, Bari.

3. C. Avarna di Gualtieri, *Ruggero Settimo nel Risorgimento italiano* [Ruggero Settimo in the Italian Risorgimento] Edizione Laterza, Bari.

Wrap the package carefully so that the books won't arrive damaged, for in that case the bookstore would have the right not to accept them. Write to them on my behalf, so that no mixups will take place, more or less like this: "My brother Antonio who is a detainee in the penitentiary at T. of B. has charged me with returning to you the following books that by mistake were sent to him in duplicate—list as above. In exchange he asks you to please ship the following etc. . . ."

While you're at it, I would also ask you to send a postcard with prepaid answer to the following address: Signor Antonio Pescarzoli, the editor of *Italia letteraria*, Via della Mercede 39, Rome, along the following lines: "My brother Antonio Gramsci, a detainee in the penitentiary at Turi di Bari, a subscriber to *Italia letteraria* through the Sperling and Kupfer Bookstore of Milan, would be most grateful if you could send him the 1930 catalogues of the most important Italian and French publishing houses. As soon as you will have kindly acknowledged receipt of this card, I'll send you a few lire in stamps for the mailing of the catalogues. My brother does not know whether this kind of service falls within your task as editor of *Italia letteraria* and therefore he asks me to apologize for the inconvenience and to thank you. Regards, etc." I believe that Signor Pescarzoli will reply by accepting: at that point you may send him five or six lire in ten cent stamps.

I want you to write also to Tatiana with greetings and tell her that I wasn't able to write to her because it was your turn; tell her that I'll be glad if she will send my last letter to Giulia too.

Dear Carlo, I no longer feel like writing. Here the weather is very variable and damp and this causes me a certain discomfort accompanied by a dreadful headache. Write to me soon sending me everyone's news and embrace everyone at home.

Antonio

December 16, 1929

Dearest Tatiana,

This month you've written very very little to me: a postcard on November 28 and a short note on the twenty-ninth together with Giulia's letter. You must know though that now I too have little desire to write. I feel as though all my links with the outside world are breaking one by one. When I was in prison in Milan two letters a week were never enough for me: I was obsessed with chatting by letter. Do you remember how I used to write letter after letter? One might say that in those days all my thoughts, during the week, were concentrated on the coming Monday: what will I be able to write? how will I write this or that so that the letter will not be held back? Now I no longer know what to write, how to begin, I'm becoming completely wrapped up in myself. My attention is focused on what I read and translate. It seems to me, when I think about myself, that I have relapsed into the obsessed condition into which I had fallen during my university years, when I concentrated on one subject and it absorbed me so much that I no longer paid heed to anything and at times ran the risk of ending up under a streetcar.

You tell me that I should write Giulia a lot of little things, the details of my life. But the fact is that in my life there aren't any little things or details, there are no shaded areas. And it is good that this is the case. When prison life is full of movement, it is a very bad sign. The only area that is not like the picture that showed a black man in the dark is the cerebral one. But there are limits here too, substantive and formal. Formal because I'm in prison, and I'm limited by regulations. Substantive because what interests me often has a very relative value. Right now I'm interested in whether the language of the Niamniam, who called themselves a people of Sandeh, whereas the name Niamniam is attributed to them by their Dinka neighbors, belongs to the Western Sudanese branch, even if the territory where it is spoken is located in Eastern Sudan, between the twenty-second and the twenty-eighth degrees of eastern longitude. And thus whether it would be best to classify these languages according to geographic distribution or according to the historical process of filiation, etc. etc. This is also the reason why I'm not writing to Giulia this time either. I really don't know what to write. And I don't want to write a "proper" letter, as people say. I must still reflect on certain problems, and unless I resolve them I'm not able to write (I don't even know if I'll be able to resolve them). The fundamental problem is this: Must I think about Giulia and deal with her according to the banal psychology that is commonly attributed to the feminine world? This would be repugnant to me in the highest degree. And yet . . . How do you think one ought to interpret her letter in which she says that after my letter of July thirtieth she felt closer to me, but then precisely after that letter she let four months go by without writing to me. I myself until now have been unable to come up with a resolution of this contradiction and I doubt whether I'll ever be able to come up with it. Therefore I abstain. You tell me that you cannot decide whether you should send my last letter on to Giulia, because it might hurt her.[1] There's no doubt that it will hurt her, but I don't think that this is a good reason. On the contrary I am quite certain that she prefers to know exactly what my state of mind is. Do you believe that it is enjoyable to write these things? But I've reached the point that I had reached, as I already said, when I was at the University: in those days I never wrote letters. When I am confronted by a question that I cannot resolve, and I become convinced that I really cannot solve it, I put

298 / DECEMBER 1929

it aside and stop thinking about it. I do this, out of respect for myself and even more out of respect for others: I respect Giulia too much to consider her a sentimental petty bourgeois, what shall I say? like the protagonist of Eugene Onegin.[2] Don't you agree, dear Tatiana? In any case, send this letter to Giulia: it is still meant for her, even though indirectly. Dearest Tatiana, you see how much trouble I've been giving you in recent times? I'm really very sad about this, believe me. I embrace you tenderly.

Antonio

1. Gramsci is referring here to his letter to Tania, November 18, 1929. See letter to Giulia, December 30, 1929.
2. Tatiana Larin, the heroine of Pushkin's *Eugene Onegin*, who, after being rejected by Eugene, enters a marriage of convenience. Despite her continued love for Eugene, she rejects his subsequent passion for her in order to remain faithful to her marriage vows.

December 19, 1929

Dearest Carlo,

I've received mother's letter of December 4 and your letter of the thirteenth. Thank you for the solicitude with which you carried out my errands. Among the clothes that I had in Rome, didn't they also turn an overcoat over to you? It seems to me that it was still wearable, though no longer in its full glory. I'm talking about a winter overcoat, because another one of gabardine has already become a rag. But perhaps you did receive it and forgot to tell me about it. I no longer remember the two pairs of shoes: but I believe that they must be in very bad shape and by now quite unusable.

Of course I beg you not to give mother ideas about making a journey all the way to Turi: the very thought of such an eventuality frightens me. It seems to me that she already makes excessive use of her exceptional sturdiness by working so relentlessly at her age: by now she should be entitled to a retirement pension, if there were pensions for mothers of families. I believe that your first contact with the prison made a very deep impression on you: just imagine what an impression it would make on her. It isn't so much the long journey, with all its discomforts for an elderly woman who never traveled more than forty kilometers on the railroad and who has never crossed the sea (perhaps the trip in itself would amuse her): but it is a trip taken to visit a son in prison. It seems to me that it should be avoided at all costs. And besides, what did you tell her? I hope you didn't exaggerate in any way: in fact you yourself have seen that I'm neither downcast, nor discouraged nor depressed. My state of mind is such that even if I were sentenced to death I would continue to remain calm and even on the evening before my execution I would perhaps be studying a Chinese language lesson. Your letter and what you write me about Nannaro interested me very much, but it also surprised me. The two of you were in the war, Nannaro in particular fought in the war under exceptional conditions, as an underground mine-layer, hearing through the thin wall that separated his tunnel from the Austrian tunnel the enemies' work that was intended to hasten the explosion of his mine and so blow him up. It seems to me that under such conditions prolonged for years, and with such psychological experiences, a man should have reached the loftiest stage of stoic serenity and should have acquired such a profound conviction that man bears within himself the source of his own moral strength, that everything depends on him, on his energy, on his will, on the iron coherence of the aims that he sets for himself and the means he adopts to realize them, that he will never again despair and lapse into those vulgar, banal states of mind that are called pessimism and optimism. My state of mind synthesizes these two emotions and overcomes them: I'm a pessimist because of intelligence, but an optimist because of will.[1] In all circumstances I think first of the worst possibility in order to set in motion all the reserves of my will and be in a position to knock down the obstacle. I have never entertained any illusions and I have never suffered disappointments. I have always taken care to arm myself with an unlimited patience, not passive, inert, but animated by perseverance. Certainly today there is a very serious moral crisis, but there have been more serious ones in the past, and there is a difference between today and the past[2] . . . Therefore I'm also a bit indulgent and I beg you too to be indulgent with Nannaro who, I myself have seen it, can also be strong. Only when he is isolated does he lose his head and become discouraged. Perhaps next time I will write to him.

Dear Carlo, I've given you a full-fledged lecture, and meanwhile I forgot to urge you to give my best compliments and many good wishes to Teresina and also of course to Paolo for their new little girl.

Then I still must send general good wishes for Christmas and for all the other holidays that will follow. I will spend Christmas as best I can, a bit like the famous Mr. Chiu,[3] about whom mother used to speak to us when we were children. Embrace everyone affectionately, and especially mother.

Yours, Antonio

1. This is one of Gramsci's mottoes, customarily associated with him but that he probably borrowed from the French writer Romain Rolland (1866–1944). Rolland used the aphorism "pessimism of the intelligence, optimism of the will," in a review of Raymond Lefebvre's *Le sacrifice d'Abraham* published in *L'Humanité* (March 19, 1920): "What I especially love in Lefebvre," Rolland wrote, "is this intimate alliance—which for me makes the true man—of pessimism of the intelligence, which penetrates every illusion, and optimism of the will." Rolland was active in the campaign to secure Gramsci's release from prison in the mid 1930s. In June 1935, in Moscow, he met with Gramsci's two sons who, accompanied by Eugenia Schucht, thanked him for his efforts on Gramsci's behalf. For further information on Rolland and Gramsci, see David J. Fisher, *Romain Rolland and the Politics of Intellectual Engagement* (Berkeley: University of California Press, 1988). However, some people believe that Gramsci borrowed the aphorism "pessimism of the intelligence, optimism of the will" from Francesco Saverio Nitti, who in his turn is said to have borrowed it from the French writer Benoît Malon.

2. Gramsci was probably referring here to the crisis that followed the stock market crash of October 1929. Six lines of this letter following immediately after the word "past" were blacked out by the prison censor.

3. According to Mimma Paulesu Quercioli, Mr. Chiu was a character in some of the "Boccacesque" poems recited in Sardinian by Gramsci's mother. "In and around the town of Ales," Quercioli writes, "the surname 'Chiu' is still fairly common." Gramsci was born in Ales.

December 30, 1929

Dear Giulia,

I didn't remember to ask Tatiana, with whom I had a visit a few days ago, whether she had passed on to you my last two letters to her. I think she did, because I asked her to do so; for I wanted you to know my state of mind even at the cost of distressing you, a state that in fact has abated somewhat but hasn't completely vanished.

I've read the letter in which you described the level of Delio's development with great interest. The remarks that I'm about to make must of course be judged while keeping in mind a number of qualifying criteria: (1) that I know hardly anything about the development of the children precisely during the period in which that development presents the most typical picture of their intellectual and moral progress, that is after the age of two, when they master language with a certain precision, and when besides images and representations they begin to form logical connections; (2) that the best judgment concerning the educational orientation of children is and can only be that of those who know them intimately and can follow them during the entire developmental process, provided they are not blinded by emotion and do not therefore put aside all criteria, yielding to a pure esthetic contemplation of the child who is implicitly degraded to the status of a work of art.

Therefore, taking into account these two criteria, which in fact are only one in two coordinates, it seems to me that Delio's intellectual development, as it appears from what you write me, is very backward for his age, too infantile. When he was two years old, in Rome, he played the piano, that is, he had understood the particular diverse gradation of tonalities on the keyboard, based on the voices of animals: the chick on the right and the bear on the left, with various other animals in between. For someone who was not yet two this procedure was acceptable and normal; but at the age of five and a few months, the same procedure applied to orientation, albeit within an enormously larger space (not as large as it might seem, because the four walls of a room limit and concretize this space) is very backward and infantile. I remember with great precision that when I was less than five years old, and without ever having left the village, that is, having a very restricted concept of extensions, I knew how to find the town where I lived with the pointer, I had the idea of what an island is and I could find the principal cities of Italy on a large wall map; that is, I had a concept of perspective, of a complex space, and not only of abstract directional lines, the concept of a system of connected measures and of orientation based on the positions of the points of these connections, high-low, right-left, as absolute spatial values, outside the momentary position of my arms. I don't believe that I was exceptionally precocious, anything but. I've in general observed how "grown-ups" easily forget their childhood impressions, which at a certain age vanish in a complex of emotions or regrets or funny moments or some other distortion. And so one forgets that the child develops intellectually in a very rapid manner, absorbing from the first days after birth an extraordinary number of images that are still remembered after the early years and that guide the child during the first period of more reflective judgments, which are possible after learning how to speak. Naturally I can [only] express general opinions and impressions, because I lack specific and ample data; I am ignorant of almost everything, not to say everything, because the impressions that you have communicated to me have no connecting thread, do not show any development. But from the context of these data I've gained the impression that your conception and that of others in your family is too metaphysical, that is, it presupposes that in the child there is potentially the entire man and that one must help it develop what it already contains in a latent form, without coercion, giving free rein to the spontaneous forces of nature or something of the sort. I instead think that man as a whole is an historical formation, obtained by coercion (understood not only in its sense of brutality and external violence) and I think only this: for otherwise I would fall into a form of transcendentalism or immanentism. What is believed to be a latent force is in most cases nothing but the unformed and indistinct complex of images and sensations of the first days, the first months, the first years of life, images and sensations that are not always the more attractive ones that we would like to imagine. This way of conceiving child rearing as the unwinding of a preexistent thread had its importance when it was counterposed to the Jesuit school, that is, when it negated an even worse philosophy, but today it is just as obsolete. To renounce molding the child only means allowing its personality to develop chaotically, accepting all the motives of life from the general environment. It is strange and interesting that Freud's[1] psychoanalysis should be creating, especially in Germany (as it would seem from the magazines I read), tendencies similar to those that existed in France in the eighteenth century: and is forming a new type of "noble savage" corrupted by society, that is to say, by history. This is the source of a new, very interesting form of intellectual disarray.

Your letter made me think of all these things. Perhaps, indeed most probably, some of my comments are exaggerated or indeed unjust. To reconstruct a megatherium or a mastodon from a tiny bone was Cuvier's[2] special gift, but it may also happen that from a piece of a mouse's tail one might reconstruct a sea serpent. I embrace you affectionately.

Antonio

1. Gramsci had only a fragmentary knowledge of Freud's writings and theories, based for the most part on anthologized articles. There are passing references to Freud and psychoanalysis in the notebooks. See Notebook 3, section 3, and Notebook 15, section 74.

2. Georges Cuvier (1769–1832), French scientist. The profound significance of this reference to Cuvier is analyzed by Joseph Buttigieg in his introduction to the first volume of the Columbia University edition of the *Prison Notebooks*, pp. 42–64.

1930

January 13, 1930

Dearest Tania,

I've received your letter of the fifth with some delay, because it was marked postage due, certainly by mistake. You undoubtedly sent it from Turi, and therefore the twenty-five cents postage was correct. We'll have to put in a claim, at any rate let me tell you that if in this case the post office was wrong, in other cases it was right: you fill the postcards up too much on the side for the address, and moreover one mustn't write above the words "postcard" and perhaps not even above the state emblem. The postcard is fined forty cents and sometimes it is three days late due to the necessary paperwork.

I thank you for the news you've sent me about the family. As for my state of mind, I think that you've understood it perfectly. But I must tell you that it is difficult for anyone to understand such things perfectly, because too many elements contribute to forming them, and many of these are almost impossible to imagine; therefore it is even less possible to imagine the whole in which they combine. During these very days I have read a book, *Dal 1848 al 1861*, in which are collected letters, writings and documents regarding Silvio Spaventa,[1] a patriot from the Abruzzo, Deputy in the Neapolitan parliament in 1848, arrested after the failure of the national movement, sentenced to life imprisonment and liberated in 1859, following pressure from France and England; later on he was a minister of the Kingdom and one of the most prominent personalities of the right-wing liberal

304

party until 1876. I had the impression that in many of his letters, naturally written in the language of the times, that is, somewhat romantic and sentimental, he perfectly expresses states of mind that resemble those that I often experience. For example, in a letter of July 17, 1853, he writes to his father: "It has been two months now that I have had no news from you; more than four and perhaps even more since I have had news from my sisters; and for some time from Bertrando (his brother). Do you believe that for a man like me, who is proud of having an affectionate and very youthful heart, this deprivation does not prove to be immeasurably distressing? I do not think that I am now less loved than I ever was by my family; but misfortune habitually has two effects—it often extinguishes in the unfortunate all affection for everyone. I am not as much afraid of the first of these two effects in you as of the second in me; for, sequestered as I am here from all human and loving intercourse, the great tedium, the long imprisonment, the suspicion of having been forgotten by everyone, slowly embitters and sterilizes my heart." As I was saying, apart from the language, which reflects the sentimental climate of the period, the state of mind appears with great clarity. And, a fact that comforts me, Spaventa was certainly not a weak character, a whiner like others. He was one of the few (about 60) of the more than 600 men sentenced in 1848 who always refused to apply for clemency to the king of Naples; nor did he turn to religion, but on the contrary as he often writes, he became more and more convinced that Hegel's philosophy was the only system and the only conception of the world that was rational and worthy of the thought of those times. And do you know what will be the practical effect of this resemblance that I discovered between my states of mind and those of a political prisoner in 1848? That at this point they will seem somewhat funny, comically anachronistic. Three generations have passed and progress has been made in all fields. What was possible for the grandparents is not possible for the grandchildren (I won't say our grandparents, because my grandfather, I never told you this, was in fact a colonel in the Bourbon gendarmerie and probably was among those who arrested Spaventa, the opponent of the Bourbons and the supporter of Carlo Alberto);[2] objectively, of course, because subjectively, individual by individual, things can change.

Dear Tania, yesterday was your name day; I thought I would be able to give you my best wishes in person, instead I can send them to you in writing and you will read them only a few days from now. I hope that you feel better and that you'll be able to leave the house if the weather remains the same as today. You know how sorry I am that your journeys to Turi for a few half hour visits are so fatiguing for you and even make you ill. I'm convinced that you neglect yourself too much: I remember that Genia was pretty much like you when I met her at the sanatorium and afterward, when we had entered into a certain familiarity, I had to threaten her with a beating to make her eat: she had hidden from the doctor hundreds of eggs that she was supposed to eat and that she had instead concealed, and so on. Your mother laughed a lot when she heard the story of my threats, but she agreed with me. You too should have your ears boxed, though somewhat delicately: it seems to me that you've lost the joy of living for yourself and that you live only for others. Isn't that a mistake? And by living for yourself too, improving your health, wouldn't you live better for others, if this is what you want and this is your sole pleasure in life? I feel very tender toward you and I would like to see you strong and healthy; this too makes me bitter, knowing that you are here in Turi, like this, sickly, weak, just to give me a bit of comfort and break my isolation. Enough. This letter was supposed to be for my mother. Please do write to her so that she won't be alarmed at not receiving news from me. My dear, I embrace you.

Antonio

1. Silvio Spaventa (1822–1893), Italian patriot who supported the policies of the Turinese conservative statesman Count Camillo Benso di Cavour. See the reference to him in the introduction.

2. Charles Albert of Savoy (1798–1849), King of Piedmont-Sardinia from 1831 to 1849. It was under his rule that the relatively liberal Constitution or *Statuto* of 1848, later extended to all of united Italy, was promulgated.

January 27, 1930

Dearest Tania,

I have received your two letters and your two postcards. But I still haven't been able to form an idea about the state of your health; you give me so little news about yourself! And so I am not happy nor even tranquil.

I've read and reread your long letter.[1] I tried to convince myself that I was wrong. But I haven't succeeded. I did my very best. In any case it doesn't matter. I had examined these questions a long time ago, reexamined them, analyzed, weighed, reweighed, thinking of the possible consequences of my every attitude and my every word; and if I had decided to write it is because I have thought that not doing so would have been even worse. You believe that I have been too harsh: that's possible. But one must ask oneself whether it wasn't necessary; at times a good jolt is precisely what is needed to give new energy to someone who has lost or is about to lose volition. For the rest, I wasn't harsh by design, for pedagogical reasons. Now I think about it and draw also this consequence from it. And since this is the last time that I intend to deal with this subject permit me to point out to you that you too have been unjust with me. You have posed the question in a truly cruel and unjustified manner. I wasn't even thinking of making any comparison between the pain of someone placed on the grill and the pain of the relatives who are forced to watch him writhe. But the question being posed and the comparison having been made, it seems inhuman to me to maintain that the pain of the relative is greater and that this can therefore explain how, absorbed in this pain, they cannot think of giving a few drops of water to the man on the grill. This, dear Tatiana, is pure moral estheticism and I believe that only your haste in writing could permit such an enormity to issue from your pen. Like that other, according to which I receive greater comfort than Giulia because I get letters from my mother or my brother or you. Don't think that I haven't been offended or saddened by these enormities. And don't think that I'm dramatizing things either. I wasn't dramatizing them before. I have an ample reserve of autonomous moral strength that is independent of the external environment; but can Giulia be an "external environment" for me? So it is not a question of my needing comfort, consolation, etc.; this would all strike me as horrific. It is exactly the opposite that I would like: to be able to give a bit of strength to Giulia, who must struggle amid so many difficulties and who has been saddled with so many burdens because of our union. But I've been increasingly put in a position of not knowing anything, of being completely isolated from her life; therefore I am afraid for myself, of becoming ever more detached from her world, and of no longer understanding anything about it,

308 / JANUARY 1930

of no longer feeling anything about it. Enough. As I have said, this is the last time that I will discuss this question: otherwise there will arise such a tangle of misunderstandings that a very long, circumstantiated brief would be needed to disentangle it: and I can only write much too little. Dear Tania, be of good cheer and regain your health: this is what matters most: and be always certain that I never lose my serenity, even though I have perhaps a little now and then. I embrace you tenderly.

Antonio

Send my mother her part of the letter. My filter mesh was thrown away in Milan; I continued to make coffee anyway; it just requires a bit more time and more coffee.

1. The following excerpt from Tania's letter of January 18, 1930, to which Gramsci refers here, reveals that she did not always act solely as a devoted helper to Gramsci but also as a loving sister:

Dear, You must not believe that I was unable to understand your state of mind, but since this amounts to a really monstrous attitude on your part toward Giulia, I did not think it at all opportune even to allude to this morbid state of yours, which is very understandable given the appearance of things, but which does not correspond to the reality of the facts because calculations of time that passes between the beginning of one of your letters to Giulia and her answers, although possibly correct in a material sense, do not correspond to the time that has really elapsed between your letter and her answer. I would like you to reread that letter of hers in which she refers to the comfort she felt in having received a few lines from you that spoke of the children. This feeling of hers is sufficient to make her state of mind clear to you. If you are literally segregated from the world, Giulia has been violently and pitilessly cut off from you completely. With respect to the kind of human ties that have been maintained since your imprisonment, her situation is infinitely worse than yours. You, dear, have your mother, your brother, me; she doesn't have anyone who can communicate the real sense of your existence to her, who can convey to her the meaning of your intimate tie to each other, so that even a single allusion by you to the children you have had was enough to give her a deep sense of comfort, the sensation of the reality of your bond, of your love. . . . Perhaps, it never occurred to you that spiritually Giulia is without doubt in a situation of greater detachment from you than you are from her, in view of the fact that we can communicate with you while you are very limited in this sense.

February 10, 1930

Dearest Tania,

I've received your postcards of February 6 and 8, a short while after your letter of January 29. I'm always anxious because you don't give me precise information about the state of your health; each time you write "see you soon" and meanwhile a month and a half has gone by since you got here and fell ill. I think that Turi's extremely variable climate is not suited to your disposition and is not favorable to your recovery. It seems to me that you relapse too often into states of apathy and indecision and then try to explain this apathy, sophistically, by farfetched arguments and astounding discoveries. Before leaving you must take good care of yourself, this is not a matter for discussion, but you mustn't wallow in your present condition. It is absurd to think that life in Turi can be pleasant; perhaps this is so for a prisoner, but not for anyone whose range of choice goes beyond the dilemma of choosing between being roasted or flayed. So then energy, energy, resolve, decisiveness.

Please send a postcard to the bookstore to inform them that I have received some of the magazines I complained about last January (on the twenty-third or the twenty-fourth); I lack only Formiggini's[1] *L'Italia che scrive* [literary Italy] of December 1929 and *I problemi del lavoro* (Labor problems) of January 1929. I would like to have these issues in order to complete the collection. And while you are writing, tell them also to send me the new edition of *Cultura italiana* [Italian culture] by Giuseppe Prezzolini,[2] published by Corbaccio. As for my books that are still in Rome, I don't know what to tell you. For the time being I don't need them; I must first send home a good part of those I already have here. Besides, I only vaguely remember their titles; more than three years have passed and what's more some of them have certainly been dispersed. I do remember something, for example Graziadei's books on economics, but are they still there? In Rome Valentino told me that he had taken several of them but couldn't remember them all. I think that you might make a list and send it to me: I will tell you which ones should be sent to me in time and which are to be sent to be pulped or taken to Campo dei Fiori.

With regard to your last letter, I just want to make one indispensable correction. When I mentioned Pushkin's Tatiana I didn't for a moment think of what you thought you understood by this, which surprised me very much and in fact made me laugh. I simply had in mind an excellent caricature by the painter Dessì in which Lloyd George, dressed à la Tatiana Larina, dips his pen in the inkwell, makes a heart-shaped pout, while on the sheet of paper there is a sentence by Pushkin that I no longer recall exactly, but that in a general way corresponds with what I meant to say. So it seems to me that your imagination has gone somewhat out of control and has attributed to me banalities that can only make me laugh. Just as well, isn't it? You mustn't be offended when I write to you that you've made me laugh; I don't believe that you could be that touchy in my regard and in such an instance.

So then, become more energetic; cure your will too, do not let the southern winds fill you with languor. The bulbs have sprouted already, indeed some time back; one of the hyacinths already shows the colors of its future flower. Provided that a frost does not destroy everything. The rose has also borne new buds; it is wilder than ever, it seems a thorn bush instead of a rose, but the vegetal vigor of the thorn bush is also interesting. I embrace you affectionately.

Antonio

1. Angelo Fortunato Formiggini. When *L'Italia che scrive* was launched in 1918, Gramsci presented the new review to the readers of the Socialist newspaper *Il grido del popolo*. *Problemi del lavoro* was the organ of the pro-Fascist Associazione Nazionale Studi-Problemi, founded by Rinaldo Rigola in 1927.
2. Giuseppe Prezzolini (1882–1982), cofounder with Giovanni Papini of the review *La Voce* and a leading figure of the Florentine intellectual world prior to and during World War I. From the 1930s to the 1950s he was professor of Italian literature at Columbia University.

February 10, 1930

Dearest Giulia,

While thinking back over several things of past years, I remembered how you once said that the state bookshops not only compensate the translators of foreign books, which is obvious, but also compensate those who suggest books to be translated, if of course the suggestion is accepted. So I thought that I could suggest some of these books to you, with all the information that I can obtain, necessarily incomplete and approximate in view of my situation; it will thus be easier for me to find subjects to discuss in my letters, for writing the usual vacuities is repugnant to me and my existence does not offer many pleasant or at any rate interesting pretexts. And, incidentally, I will offer you observations on the currents of Italian intellectual life in terms of what in it is most profound and substantial.

Last year there was a new edition of a book that already was part of European culture: *Il capitalismo antico: Storia dell'economia romana* [Ancient capitalism: The history of roman economy], 204 pages, in sixteens, Laterza, Bari. The first edition appeared in 1906 in French, translated from the Italian manuscript, and it had a great success[1]; it was immediately translated into German by Karl Kautsky[2] and I believe also into Russian and other languages. The book was aimed against the tendency created by Mommsen,[3] which found all "monetary" economies "capitalistic" (a reproach that Marx addressed to Mommsen and that Salvioli critically develops and demonstrates), a tendency that today has assumed morbid proportions though the efforts of Professor Rostovtseff,[4] a Russian historian who teaches in England, and in Italy through the efforts of Professor Barbagallo[5], a disciple of Guglielmo Ferrero[6]. Salvioli was a very serious scholar (he died last year, during a lecture at the University of Naples), who accepted the theories of historical materialism, in the form they have assumed in Italy by way of Benedetto Croce's revision, that is, as a practical canon of historical study and not as a total conception of the world. The present Italian edition completely renews the preceding one, bringing it up-to-date from the scholarly point of view and stripping it of the polemical elements that were typical of 1906: in short it is a new book, because the author died before polishing it. Ask for a translator who knows Italian very well and is therefore able to understand also the syntactic distortions and the rather awkward periodic sentences. Another recent book is by Francesco Ercole,[7] at present a deputy in the Chamber: *Dal comune al principato* [From commune to principality], essays on the history of public law during the Italian Renaissance, Vallecchi, Florence, 1929, 381 pages. This is composed of four studies, which are of varying interest from the standpoint of non-Italian culture. Certainly interesting also outside Italy is the first essay, "La lotta delle classi alla fine del Medioevo" [Class struggle at the close of the middle ages], which could be published as an excellent small book or an article in an important journal. It contains a few evident examples of historical naïveté, such as satisfaction at the fact that the Ciompi movement[8] failed in Florence, thus permitting the cultural flowering of the Renaissance, but it also contains generally unknown information of great interest (its archival documents were published during the war in small publications that were almost clandestine for the uninitiated) on a number of attempts that took place in Florence between 1340 and 1350 to organize workers in the mills excluded from the craft guilds, with unusual political backlashes, etc. Ercole also belongs to Salvioli's historiographic current, to the so-called juridico-economic school, which has in part renewed the historical and traditionally academic and rhetorical or at best the purely erudite and philological doctrine.

I don't know whether these remarks can be of any use to you and whether you have the desire and the means to exploit them; in any case they have offered me the pretext to write to you about something other than the state of the weather and the state of my nervous system: these are the only things that interest me and help me to pass the time as best as I can. Why don't you write to me also about Giuliano's intellectual development and not just Delio's? I embrace you tenderly.

Antonio

1. Giuseppe Salvioli, *Le capitalisme dans le monde ancien* [Capitalism in the ancient world] (Paris: Giard et Brière, 1906).

2. Karl Kautsky (1854–1938), German Socialist thinker and neo-Marxist revisionist.

3. Theodor Mommsen (1817–1903), German historian of ancient Rome.

4. Michael Ivanovich Rostovtzeff (1870–1952), Russian historian, author of the *Social and Economic History of Ancient Rome* (Oxford: 1926).

5. Corrado Barbagallo (1877–1952), Italian positivist historian.

6. Guglielmo Ferrero (1871–1942), Italian historian of ancient Rome. He emigrated to Switzerland and actively opposed the Fascist regime.

7. Francesco Ercole (1894–1945), Italian historian who served in the 1930s as director of the National Fascist Institute of Culture.

8. The *ciompi* were Florentine textile workers who rebelled against the city's oligarchic ruling class in 1378. Their defeat paved the way for subsequent rule by an ever narrower segment of that oligarchy.

———————

February 24, 1930

Dearest Tania,

I received your letter of the sixteenth. It seems to me that you have fallen back into last year's fantasies, when you were making plan after plan about journeys up and down Italy. I think that you ought to decide once and for all to return to Milan, to stop tiring yourself out, and to achieve the best possible physical condition in order to join your family. If you persist in your old system of not making well-considered and rationally prepared decisions, I'm afraid that this year too will go by like the one before and you will still be making plans and building castles in the air. Forgive me if I sound a bit gruff, but your letter has definitely given me the impression that you are in an intellectual quagmire.[1] And how can you possibly be interested in newspaper advertisements? In my opinion the ad in the *Corriere* should under no circumstances be taken seriously; in Italy translating and writing reviews has never been a profitable occupation, and it is a job fit for students who want to scrape together a few extra lira or for government employees who want to round out their salaries or see their name printed on a piece of paper. I really don't understand why you should be interested in this sort of thing: you can resume your job in Milan, don't you think? And give up all ideas of coming to live in Bari or Taranto, or who knows where. Seriously, you ought to be more judicious and reasonable. I think that this should be your last trip to Turi. It wasn't very fortunate; well, patience, what can we do? But don't you think that it would be better for me too to know that you are in a better place than this? more at your ease, without so many petty concerns, able to take care of yourself more rationally? This seems to me more important than anything. For me too, take my word for it. I'm assailed by greater preoccupations and anxieties when you are in Turi than when you are in Milan. It seems to me that this place is also a prison for those who are not in prison, and in some ways it can not help but be that.

Did you receive the books that I gave instructions to deliver to you? I thought that after all this time you no longer had anything to read and that they might help you pass the time. You can ship them to my brother or throw them away after reading them; or you can take them with you (the book by Croce is very interesting and you could take it to give to Giulia: perhaps at some time or other she might be interested in Hegel's philosophy and in Croce's revision of it). In any case I no longer need them. (I already received Gladkov's *Cemento*[2] [Cement]; so make sure you don't send me any books I haven't asked for). Instead write to Sperling bookstore to send me *Prospettive economiche per il 1930* [Economic perspectives for 1930] by Professor Giorgio Mortara, which was just recently published and remember that I had

314 / FEBRUARY 1930

asked for a subscription to the journal *La Nuova Italia* (from the publishing house La Nuova Italia, Perugia-Venice), which replaces a journal that died last year: I still haven't received anything and so I think a reminder would be in order. Dearest Tatiana, I truly hope to see you soon, completely recovered and once more energetic and full of determination. I embrace you tenderly.

Antonio

Send my brother the part of this letter that concerns him. I received two heavily censored postcards from you yesterday, after I had already written the letter. Since I don't like to see things blotted out, I advise you to write only absolutely obvious family news. What can we do! I embrace you.

Antonio

1. In her reply to this letter, written two days later, Tania showed that she was capable of rising above Gramsci's often carping criticisms and of being frank about her own vulnerability and shortcomings. Her letter began as follows:

Dearest, I've received your letter at this very moment, I was writing to you when the mailman arrived. At the sight of your handwriting I experienced a moment of great joy, but after reading the letter I felt deep distress. Why must you consider everything that concerns me from such an unfavorable viewpoint? And I hope that you are exaggerating when you speak of an intellectual quagmire, because your opinion is certainly not meant to comfort me, while I suffer precisely from the disease of underestimating myself and, as you have justly remarked, I do not have any love at all for my life, hence all the absurd circumstances of my existence.

2. In *Cement* (1925), Fyodor V. Gladkov (1883–1958) tried to write a monumental proletarian novel about the Russian Revolution, but in doing so he raised many questions about the "monumentalism" of the Bolshevik mind.

February 24, 1930

Dearest Carlo,

I've let my two letters go by without remembering to write about a matter that, to a certain extent, interests me "intellectually" and perhaps "morally." That is, I meant to write to you to approach the Special Tribunal for the Defense of the State (the Chancellery) and ask for a copy printed on plain paper without an Internal Revenue tax stamp to present a petition to revise the sentence pronounced against me on June 4, 1928. There are no expenses for this besides the fee for the right of registration at the Chancellery, which can't be very high.

I'll tell you what I'm planning to do because you already know my opinion with regard to the result such a procedure may have. First of all I want to read the sentence. I previously thought that the sentences of the Special Tribunal, in view of its abbreviated procedure, consisted merely of the decree: instead I have seen that they are lengthy and summarize the elements of the trial in an attempt to coordinate them. Since this will be so also in my case, the formal reason for the revision will be given greater prominence by the statements of the sentence's "postulation." I will send you these elements, together with the sentence itself, and you will submit them to a reasonably well intentioned lawyer to judge them and, if advisable, prepare the petition according to the terms of the law.[1] I did not want to have any relations with Attorney Niccolai, and so I got quite angry with Tatiana when without first informing me, she turned to him for assistance. After our sentencing, Attorney Niccolai, as all lawyers will do, advised us, insidiously, to appeal, and Terracini turned to the Court of Appeals, in the absence of any other venue at that time indicated by the law of November 2, 1926, which allowed for an appeal but did not say to whom it should be addressed: therefore Niccolai was duty-bound to get in touch with Terracini, who was his client. I had nothing to do with it and could not get in contact with him. But Niccolai, who was so convinced that an appeal was justifiable in 1928, no longer was in 1929, when the venue ruling was established and an appeal actually became possible. And then there are other reasons that I won't bother to mention.

Since I'm not in a position to know what the other codefendants might have decided, I now consider myself released from any and all commitments to their previous initiatives and so I intend to study the sentence and see whether the application for a revision is legitimate. In general I believe that in my situation every recourse to legality is both a possibility and a duty, while not having any illusions, but just to be certain that I, on my part, have done everything that was legally possible to prove that I was singled out without any legal basis for it. I also want you to copy for me the articles of the military penal code of procedure on the subject of revision, so that I may have a precise picture of existing possibilities. Write and tell me what you will do and when you will do it and do not hesitate to inform me about the state of your affairs. Perhaps as far as the application is concerned (which however must be submitted by me) in order to obtain a copy of the sentence you could get together with Tatiana, if she is in Rome; so she'll be able to facilitate your request.

I embrace you together with everyone at home and I send my best wishes for Teresina's children who, as mother wrote to me, were sick. Affectionately,

Antonio

1. On the basis of a royal decree of October 3, 1929, no. 1759, concerning the review of sentences meted out by the Special Tribunal.

March 10, 1930

Dearest Tania,

I've received your letter of February 26 and the two postcards of March 3 and 7. You write that you were deeply distressed by my last letter, because I consider everything that concerns you unfavorably, and because I mentioned an "intellectual quagmire." I can see how this would displease you and I too am displeased at having to write such things to you from time to time and at having to use such emphatic expressions; but I think it is indispensable and I always want to be sincere. Do you know that I really get angry when you present me with harebrained schemes for trips left and right? Last year when you wrote me that you wanted to go to Sardinia, to Calabria, and I don't know where else, I immediately became convinced that you wouldn't even come to Turi and in fact I was right. And now that you are again giving way to these phantasmagorias about Bari, Taranto, etc., I am convinced that you are not well, that you are weak, and that you are not quite aware of your condition, that is, you do not devote all your energies to getting better, to becoming physically stronger, as you ought to. To tell the truth, nothing irritates me more than "wishful thinking" that takes the place of concrete determination; it irritates me in people with whom I am not involved emotionally and whom I consider "useless"; it dismays me in the persons with whom I'm involved and whom I do not want to and cannot judge from a utilitarian point of view but rather would like to stimulate and arouse. I've known, especially at the university, quite a few wishful thinkers and I've observed the tragicomic unfolding of their existence: one might say that I have some well-defined and delineated models in my memory, who vex me when they claim my attention due to some chain of remembrances, yes, they still irk me; and this is why when in your psychological manifestation I glimpse a pattern that resembles certain traits of those exemplary models, I become vexed and agitated and even mean and nasty with you. But you must believe that it is my affection that prompts me to reproach you just like a child, for there's really something puerile in such states of mind. In my opinion one ought always to be very practical and concrete, not dream with open eyes, but instead set for oneself modest and attainable goals and think them through together with all the conditions that alone can lead to their realization; one therefore ought to have a perfect awareness of one's limitations, even if one wishes nevertheless to expand and deepen them. All of this seems to me so obvious and banal that I almost feel as if I've given you the usual scolding of a parish priest. And besides one ought never to have too much zeal; you are too zealous with me and it seems to me that the results you have obtained are precisely the opposite of what you would wish. In many things you are a person of transcendental naïveté. When I advise you to return to Milan and not to fantasize about Bari and Taranto, believe me I know whereof I speak and I'm saying something extremely reasonable and sensible. When I make a remark that displeases you (or objectively should displease you) don't ever think that I want to hurt you; instead you should think that in the plans you have expressed there is something that deeply upsets me and that I will never be able to approve of, and you should act in accordance with this impression that will always be right.

I've received the five little Berlitz books. Why did you ever have them sent to me? Now I'll explain to you one of the psychological mechanisms that I referred to above, although in this instance the question is relatively negligible; it is only a matter of having badly spent a few dozen lire. I had written to you asking whether among my books in Rome you had found the Berlitz manuals for German and Russian. You replied that you hadn't found them, but that you had already written to the bookstore to send them to me (that is, you had written without first asking me whether in this instance I wanted them. Now, the Berlitz manuals cost approximately 25 lire each, that is, you have spent approximately 125 lire: was it worth it? Absolutely

not. I'm already much more advanced in all three languages than the
Berlitz manuals; apart from the particular arrangement of the material
that is in fact extremely elementary). If I could have had my own
books, for which money had already been spent, so much the better;
but to go and spend money again to get them, that was totally useless, it was a "luxury." So here we have an instance where, though
negligible, I become irritated and find that too much zeal is harmful.
Have you finally come to understand my way of thinking? One ought
not to do useless things, which often become harmful.

Dearest, do not be distressed by what I'm saying to you. From
your postcard of the seventh I did not understand the remark you
made about St. Francis's *Little Flowers*.[1] I believe that they can be very
interesting depending on the point of view from which the work is
read, and also on the extent of one's knowledge of the cultural history
of the time. Artistically they are very beautiful, fresh, immediate;
they express a sincere faith and an infinite love for Francis who was
considered by many to be a new incarnation of God, a reappearance
of Christ. Therefore they are more popular in Protestant than in
Catholic countries. Historically they prove what a powerful organism
the Catholic church was and still is. Francis positioned himself as the
initiator of a new Christianity, a new religion, arousing an enormous
enthusiasm similar to that of the first centuries of Christianity. The
Church did not persecute him officially, because that would have anticipated the Reformation by two centuries, but it immunized him,
disrupted his band of disciples, and reduced the new religion to a
simple monastic order at its service. If you read the *Little Flowers* as a
guide to life, you won't understand anything about them. Before the
war Luigi Luzzatti[2] happened to publish in the *Corriere della Sera* a
little flower that he considered never published before, accompanying
it with a long socioeconomic confutation, enough to make you split
your sides laughing. But today no one can think such things: not even
the Franciscan friars, whose order has been utterly changed even to
the letter and who at any rate among religious orders have lost status
compared to the Jesuits, the Dominicans, and the Augustinians, that
is, compared to the religious elements that have specialized in politics
and culture. Francis was a comet in the Catholic firmament; whereas
the ferment of development was preserved in Dominic (who produced Savonarola) and especially in Augustine from whose order

sprang first the reform and later on Jansenism. St. Francis did not go in for theological speculations; he tried to realize in practice the principles of the Gospel; his movement was popular as long as the memory of its founder lived, but already in Friar Salimbene of Parma, who lived a generation later, the Franciscans are depicted as licentious pleasure lovers. And let's not even talk about the popular literature in the vernacular: Boccaccio is there to show how the order had fallen in public esteem; all of Boccaccio's friars are Franciscans.[3]

Dearest, I've actually given you a small lesson in the history of religion. But perhaps this way you will better enjoy the *Little Flowers*. I truly hope to see you recovered and especially stronger in determination. I embrace you tenderly.

Antonio

1. The *Fioretti* are a collection of stories written by an unknown author on the life of Saint Francis of Assisi. The Italian version appeared in the mid fourteenth century. The late thirteenth century Latin original on which they were based has been lost.

2. Luigi Luzzatti (1841–1927), Italian jurist and prime minister in 1910–11. The reference is to his article "La scoperta di un nuovo Fioretto di S. Francesco" [The discovery of a new little flower of Saint Francis], in *Il Corriere della Sera* (April 6, 1915).

3. The references are to Saint Augustine and to Girolamo Savonarola, a Dominican priest who was burned at the stake in Florence in 1498 after an unsuccessful attempt to reform the city's political constitution and its morals. Among the "Franciscans" described in the *Decameron* in the way Gramsci indicates are frate Alberto (4:2) and frate Cipolla (6:10).

March 24, 1930

Dearest Tatiana,

I too was very happy to see you. A relative happiness, because I would have liked to be able to do something to effectively induce you to take care of yourself and improve your general health and I find this impossible; I understand very well that lectures via letters are useless. One would have to be near you and employ persuasive means as one does with children (and you know that I consider educational systems more efficacious with a pinch even of physical coercion if necessary). At any rate I was very glad and I really thought that you were much more run-down than you were. Now you must write to me at least every two days and let me know exactly when you will be leaving. Nothing is worse than being kept in uncertainty. And besides you must remember to send me your address in Rome and later in Milan. Remember that I must write every second Monday and if I do not have your address I lose my turn and a week, not counting the worries that would give me no peace. As you see, I'm writing only to you. In fact I beg you not to even ask me to write to Giulia, because I think that in that case I would no longer even write to you. You mustn't think that I am angry; I was four months ago and I let it all out in the letters that I wrote to you at that time. Now I've become indifferent. Even I find it hard to believe that I got into such a state. And I am sorry, but it happened and I'm the person least responsible, if one may speak of responsibilities in such matters. I've been in a crisis for more than a year (much more) and I've had some bad moments; now, as is usually the case, I've become hardened and I refuse to poison my system and suffer headaches for weeks on end. I beg you not to even hint at such matters when you write to me. Send me news, if you receive any, but do not harangue me or give me lectures. Dear Tatiana, during these years you have helped me enormously to endure prison, you have helped me to get used to the life I lead and I am very grateful to you. If anything sometimes embitters me it is the thought that perhaps I will never have the opportunity to prove to you how deeply I care for you and how grateful I am. All the same I do not want you to meddle in these matters; I really beg you with all my heart. Every hint of yours hurts me very much. By now I've become accustomed to it; let it go, don't stir things up. I think that you will always want to send me news about the children when you have any and when you see them. That's enough for me. I urge you to take care of the business with the attorney; do not neglect it. For me it especially has a psychological importance, but it has a much greater importance than you can imagine. In the letter to my mother I left a bit of space so that you can write to her that you've seen me and that I'm fairly well. I embrace you tenderly.

Antonio

Write to the bookstore that I would like to have issues no. 6068–6069 of *Lohnarbeit und Kapital* [Wage-labor and capital], Reclams Universal-Bibliothek, by Marx.

March 30, 1930

Dearest Mother,

I've received your letter of May tenth. I thank you for the news you have sent me. I no longer remember Michele Enida ———[1] but I remember very well the son of Aunt Annamaria Pitzurra who must have been my schoolmate in the elementary grades and with whom I must certainly have been good friends as a child. I'm sorry to hear about his death. You ought to get precise information before changing the money that Nannaro sends for his daughter. It seems that one Belgian lira is worth approximately two and six-tenths Italian lire; but I'm not sure. In any case write to Nannaro himself. I remember that at one time I sent you a Swiss *scudo* with which to make a small silver spoon for Mea and you wrote back that with five lire one couldn't buy a silver spoon while the Swiss *scudo* at that time was worth about thirty lire, that is, more than enough to buy a small spoon. You are not familiar with these changes in the value of currency and you might go and get yourself cheated by some scoundrel. Greetings to all. I embrace you tenderly.

Antonio

1. Last name illegible.

April 7, 1930

Dearest Tania,

I've received what you sent me. I heard that the fountain pen has been returned to you; I thought that I myself had written that fountain pens are not allowed under any circumstances but apparently I forgot to do so. On the other hand, you could have known it by the simple fact that I had sent you mine together with the watch and the small medal, all of them things regarded as valuables that aren't permitted to be kept even in storage. I also believe that the famous bag will no longer be of any use to me; to tell the truth, I can't even imagine of what use it might be in general; perhaps to go hunting for porcupines? Who knows what you were thinking about when you had it made! Of course you must have thought that you were doing something useful and convenient and therefore I thank you also for this bag, as well as for the other things that will be most useful to me.

I would be grateful if you sent me a complete list of the books that I've shipped out to you: in reconstructing it on my own I forgot some of them, because the number doesn't add up right. I would also like to have it to avoid looking for them in vain among the others. *Il diavolo al Pontelungo*[1] [The devil at Pontelungo] is quite "historical" in the sense that the experiment of the Baronata and the episode in Bologna in 1874 really took place. Like all historical novels that exist, the general framework is historical, but not the individual characters and events, one by one. What makes this novel interesting, apart from its considerable artistic qualities, is the almost complete absence of sectarian acerbity on the author's part. In Italian literature, apart from Manzoni's historical novel,[2] there exists an essentially sectarian tradition in this sort of work, which goes back to the period between 1848 and 1860; on one side stands the founder Guerrazzi,[3] on the other Bresciani,[4] the Jesuit priest. For Bresciani all patriots were scoundrels, cowards, assassins, etc., while the defenders of the throne and the altar, as one used to say in those days, were all little angels descended on earth to display miracles.[5] For Guerrazzi, obviously, the roles were reversed; the Papists were all of them dipped in the blackest coal, while the supporters of national unity and independence were all the purest heroes of legend. This tradition has been preserved until recently by the two traditional opponents in pulp serial novels; in the so-called artistic and cultivated literature the Jesuit side has held the monopoly. In *Il Diavolo al Pontelungo* Bacchelli proves to be independent, or almost; his humor rarely becomes partisan, it resides in the things themselves, rather than in the writer's extra-artistic partisanship.

Concerning the daughter of Costa and Kuliscioff there is a special novel, *The Gironda* by Virgilio Brocchi,[6] I don't know if you have read it. It isn't worth much, it is cloying, all milk and honey, along the lines of Georges Ohnet's[7] novels. It narrates, in fact, the events that lead Andreina Costa to marry the son of the Catholic industrialist Gavazzi and the succession of contacts between the two milieux,

Catholic and materialist, and how all conflicts are smoothed over: *omnia vicit amor*.[8] Virgilio Brocchi is our domestic Ohnet.

D'Herbigny's book on Soloviev[9] is very old-fashioned although it's just now been translated into Italian. However d'Herbigny is a Jesuit Monsignore of great ability; now he is at the head of the Oriental Department of the Pontifical Curia, which is working to bring back unity between Roman Catholics and the Orthodox. Also the book on *L'Action Française et le Vatican* (French action and the Vatican) is by now outdated. It is only the first volume of a series that will perhaps continue because Daudet and Maurras are indefatigable in serving up the same things in different sauces: but precisely because of this, as an exposition of principles, this book can still be interesting. I don't know whether you've been able to grasp all of the historical importance that the conflict between the Vatican and the French monarchists has for France: within certain limits it corresponds to the Italian Concordat. It is the French form of a profound reconciliation between State and Church: French Catholics as a mass organized in Catholic Action, split from the Monarchist minority, that is, they ceased to be the potential popular reserve for a legitimist coup d'état and instead tend to form a vast Catholic republican government party, which would like to absorb and certainly will absorb a considerable section of the present radical party (Herriot and Co.). This was typical in 1926, during the French parliamentary crisis: whereas Action Française announced the coup and published the names of the future ministers who were to form the provisional government that was to recall the pretender Jean IV of Orléans, the leader of the Catholics agreed to enter a republican coalition government. The livid rage of Daudet and Maurras against Cardinal Gasparri and the Papal Nunzio in Paris is due precisely to the realization of having been politically diminished by 90 percent at the very least.

Dearest, I always forget to tell you to send me a number of medicines: the neuralgia that has returned reminds me of it today. I would like to have some Bayer Aspirins and a few of Dr. Faivre's cachets against headaches. Don't send me anything for sleeping, because I have become stabilized; I sleep little, that's true (three or four hours a night), but I no longer go without sleeping for four or five nights in a row, and that is already great progress.

A few days ago I received a short letter from Carlo, who asked me to beg you to answer his letter. The poor man is very sad because he is unemployed and he is worried because, since he hasn't sent me any money for some months now, he thinks that I'm unprovided for; write and tell him that I still have money and I'll have some for several more months. Besides I'll be able to write to him myself in a few days because we'll have the special Easter letter. Dearest, I'm happy because, as you tell me, you are taking the egg cure. To me this seems of fundamental importance for you; I'm convinced, by experience, that a good part of your malaise is due to insufficient nutrition. You must try to gain at least ten kilos and go back to the way you were when you attended the university, the way you were as you look in a photograph that I remember, taken at the university clinic, I think. That's exactly what you must do. I embrace you tenderly.

Antonio

1. Riccardo Bacchelli (1891–1985), author of a cycle of historical novels entitled *Il mulino del Po* [The Mill on the Po]. His novel *Il diavolo al Pontelungo* [The devil at Pontelungo] (Milan, 1927), deals with the revolutionary anarchist-Socialist experiments initiated in Italy in the mid 1870s by the Russian anarchist Mikhail Bakunin.

2. *I promessi sposi* (*The Betrothed*), by Alessandro Manzoni (1785–1873), Italian Catholic novelist, playwright, poet, and philosopher. Manzoni's novel and his theories of language and society often engaged Gramsci's interest in prison.

3. Francesco Domenico Guerrazzi (1804–1873), whose best known historical novel is *L'assedio di Firenze* [The siege of Florence] (1836).

4. Antonio Bresciani (1798–1862), Jesuit priest and author of several novels, the best known of which is *L'Ebreo di Verona* [The Jew of Verona]. For Gramsci's analysis of "Father Bresciani and His Progeny," see Forgacs and Smith, eds., *Selections from Cultural Writings*, pp. 298–341. Lynn M. Gunzberg provides a detailed analysis of *The Jew of Verona* in *Strangers at Home: Jews in the Italian Literary Imagination* (Berkley: University of California Press, 1992), pp. 57–89.

5. The Italian for "to display miracles" reads "*a miracol mostrare*," "to show forth a miracle," taken from a line in a sonnet of chapter 26 of Dante's *Vita nuova* that pays homage to the spiritual purity of Beatrice.

6. Andreina Costa, the protagonist of Brocchi's novel, was the daughter of the freethinking Italian Socialist Andrea Costa (1851–1910) and his Russian-born companion, Anna Kuliscioff (1854–1925). Kuliscioff later became the companion of the Socialist leader Filippo Turati, with whom she cofounded the newspaper *Critica Sociale*.

7. Georges Ohnet (1848–1918), French journalist who, beginning in 1877, published a series of popular novels in the newspapers *Le Figaro* and *Revue des Deux Mondes*, under the general title *Les batailles de la vie* [The struggles of life].

8. The customary Latin quotation from Virgil is *omnia vincit amor*, love conquers all. Gramsci used the past tense *vicit*.

9. Michel D'Herbigny S. J., *Un Newman russe: Vladimir Soloviev, 1835–1900* [A Russian Newman: Vladimir Soloviev, 1835–1900] (Paris, 1911), Italian trans. 1929.

April 14, 1930

Dearest Carlo,

I've received your two letters. I'm sorry that you are so depressed and that you still haven't regained your strength. You mustn't worry about me. And you must not, as you write, feel "intimidated." This expression of yours made me laugh a bit, but about myself, however. In some of my letters I've been sententious and full of the wisest opinions in your regard in a rather comical manner. I've even managed to frighten you, as it would seem, like an old preaching friar. Perhaps it is because you are the youngest of us children and there always remains the memory of when, during the games we played at that time, you were still small while I already thought of myself as a mature person. To tell the truth I always remember you when you were a little boy and would sit on the doorstep with Teresina, holding her hand, like that time when Brisi scared you both and they even had recourse to the *scorgioli* [incantation] of the parish priest. In those days I couldn't understand why children should be so silly as to be afraid of such nonsense and I would test you to see whether I could guess your reactions. I remember that once we were coming back from Abbasanta along the Santa Lucia road: it was around one or two o'clock and the sun was very intense. I told you that we must run away because the "pebbles" were coming, and I jumped over a retaining wall: you stayed in the middle of the road screaming like a lunatic. Naturally I was being cruel without knowing it and without wanting to. I would think to myself: he is so crazy and stupid, like all children, that the word *pebbles* uttered by me with a frightened look must frighten him. So let's try. Just like that. Dear Carlo, don't worry if sometimes I still write to you as if you were four years old and I ten: these are inconsequential trifles.

You mustn't hurry with regard to the sentence of the Special Tribunal. There is no hurry. In any case you have the right to send it and there is no need for a direct petition by me. I believe that, as is the case with all offices, as soon as Tatiana shows up in person, she will be able to get a copy. Bureaucracy is never in a hurry and that is its strength. I did receive the parcel with the Casali serum: I thought that

I had written about this to you. So take heart, also for mother's sake. I embrace you.

Antonio

April 14, 1930

Dearest Mother,

I've received your letter of the seventh. I'm sorry that you're always worried about something or someone. Ah well, a mother's life must always have been like this! Don't you think? I almost feel like delivering a sermon on patience to you too, and this would be comical. Just now as I'm thinking that not even religious faith can give you tranquillity, I realize that this year I forgot to send you my good wishes for St. Joseph: I'd never forgotten about it in past years, I think, and now I'm really sorry that this year it slipped my mind. You can see that I am rapidly aging and that my head no longer works very well. Forgive me and accept my good wishes, even though they are a month late, together with those for Easter.

The children have both been sick with the usual childhood diseases, German measles and whooping cough. Now they are better and are recovering. Once more my best wishes to everyone. I embrace you affectionately.

Antonio

April 21, 1930

Dearest Tania,

On the afternoon of Easter Sunday I received your package so I was still able to eat something from it: the famous "dove," which turned out to be very intriguing because they thought it was cooked squab and they vainly looked for it in the package. I thought that in the Milanese manner you had called "dove" the round bread made with eggs, which I don't know what they might call here in Turi and that cannot properly be referred to as a "dove," because in Milan this really has the general shape of a bird with outstretched wings and something in its beak in imitation of the olive branch, I seem to remember. At any rate, whether dove or another specimen of the southern fauna, the biscuit was quite good and helped celebrate the day: and I thank you with all my heart. How did you spend these days? Were you feeling well and were you able to go out and admire the "festive populace"?[1] I hope so. For me the time went by as usual, neither good nor bad, except for the emotion that I always experience when I receive something from the outside, a pleasant and comforting emotion typical of man as "social animal," when he concretely feels that he belongs to a "voluntary" community as well as to the one to which he is forced to submit as a number in a series. Dearest, these damp and foggy days have somewhat unnerved me; I don't feel at all like writing. But I very much want to remind you of three things:

1. My brother has written to me that he has already received the verdict of the Special Tribunal; so there, you no longer have to worry about it.

2. You've written that you want to send me preparations for injections. Please don't do it and don't try to start a discussion on the subject. I am determined not to take any tonic injections while in prison and no one will change my mind. If I should receive anything, I will have it returned and I won't even mention this matter to you again.

3. Write a postcard to the Sperling bookstore, informing them that I have not received issue number twelve of last March 25 of *Rassegna della Stampa Estera* [Review of the foreign press], while just today I received the succeeding issues, thirteen and fourteen. I don't know whether a registered envelope has gone astray or the issue has been lost in some other way; at any rate I would like them to get it for me and send it.

My dearest, I thank you again and I embrace you tenderly.

Antonio

If you feel like it, write to my mother that I've received the things she has sent me and I very much enjoyed the Sardinian bread, though by the time it arrived it was so hard that it made my gums bleed: but its flavor had not suffered at all.

1. The quotation marks no doubt serve to mimic the rhetoric used by Fascist journalists when talking about the people's participation in festivities organized by the regime.

May 5, 1930

Dearest Tania,

I must first of all offer my compliments: it seems to me that I've found you in much better health compared to previous occasions. However, I hope that these compliments will not lead you again to neglect the general condition of your life; for a few months at least you should eat three eggs a day, besides your regular meals, and try to recover completely.

Please write my brother, putting what follows in the letter: (1) I've received his registered letter of the end of April with 150 lire; as of May 1, taking account also of these 150 lire, I had approximately 400 lire at my disposal; (2) I've received a copy of the sentence of the Special Tribunal and the abstract of the articles of the Military Penal Code; this abstract is no use at all to me. Carlo has obviously misunderstood. I had asked for a copy of the articles or article of the Code of Military Penal *Procedure* that refers to the *revision*. I have not been sentenced on the basis of the Military Penal Code, but on the basis of ordinary penal law in accordance with military procedure in time of war; the procedure alone is military, not the articles referring to the crime. On the other hand, there is no point in losing time and patience over this, because the question interests me hardly at all; (3) I already possess the special law; (4) I no longer want any catalogues; tell him to forget about it; (5) Just today I received the volume from the Hoepli Antiquarian Collection Series,[1] I'm thankful, but I warn everybody not to send me any more books of this kind, which are of no use whatsoever in prison; they just make me regret that I didn't follow the impulses of my youth and didn't become a peaceful bookworm who feeds on printed paper and produces dissertations on the use of the imperfect in Sicco Polenton.[2] Last year in November I told Carlo to send me a couple of light summer undershirts; now he asks me whether by any chance you have already thought of getting them for me. I really need these undershirts, because even in summer I have to wear something against my skin to protect me from colds and the three that I have are in shreds. You decide what is to be done or write something to Carlo.

Dear Tatiana, I received your two letters after the visit. You'll see that I will know how to behave. I've perfectly understood what I must do. It won't be difficult. Besides, I am more and more aware that my language is becoming completely incomprehensible: so I must have recourse to the dictionary, where there is an ample stock of the fossils of universal knowledge: and furthermore I've been a journalist for fifteen years and know the rudiments of the trade. I beg you to acknowledge my good will and to avoid touching these particular keys in the future. On the other hand, I'm less of a dried-up fig than I myself tended to think I was. I embrace you tenderly.

Antonio

1. Raffaello Bertieri, *Editori e stampatori italiani del Quattrocento* [Italian publishers and printmakers of the fifteenth century] (Milan: Hoepli, 1929).
2. Paduan humanist of the early fifteenth century.

May 5, 1930

Dearest Giulia,

During a recent visit[1] Tatiana drew a rather dark picture of your state of mind and of your health. In a previous letter she had informed me of the illnesses contracted by both Delio and Giuliano. However, it seemed to me that Tatiana herself is not too well informed and only indirectly and I do not know what I should think. The time when you assured me that you would never conceal anything from me regarding your health and the development of the children seems frightfully remote. It is clear that your opinion has changed and there certainly must be some reason for this change even though I am unable to imagine what it is. I think that you must be really very ill, must be very tired. But why won't you let me know something, why increase the feeling of impotence that is already produced in me due to the many limitations of will and freedom to which I have been condemned by the Special Tribunal for Defense of the State?[2] If Tatiana had not been in Italy and hadn't kept me informed off and on I don't know what I would have done, perhaps I would have had recourse to the consulate. I think that you must make a great effort and tell me with great sincerity and frankness about your condition and

that of the children, without hiding anything at all from me; I'm reduced to such a state that I prefer to receive bad news rather than no
news at all, for this leads me to think of the worst. I wait. I embrace
you.

Antonio

1. In December 1929 Tania had moved to Turi, where she remained until July 1930;
during this period she was often ill and bed-ridden, but visited Gramsci as often as possible.
2. This becomes a persistent and ever more obsessive theme of Gramsci's letters to and
about his wife. My essay in *The Italian Quarterly* gives a brief analysis of it.

May 19, 1930

Dearest Tatiana,

I received your letters and postcards. Your curious conception of
my situation in prison has again made me smile. I don't know
whether you've read the works of Hegel, who wrote "The criminal
has a *right* to his punishment."[1] You more or less imagine me as someone who insistently lays claim to his right to suffer, to be martyred,
to not be defrauded of even a second or a nuance of his punishment.
I supposedly am a new Gandhi, who wants to bear witness to the
torments of the Indian people before the gods of heaven and hell, a
new Jeremiah or Elijah or I don't know what prophet of Israel who
descends into the square to eat foul things, to offer himself as a sacrifice to the god of vengeance, etc. etc. I don't know where you got
this notion of me, which is very naive in terms of your personal relations and quite unfair in terms of your relations with me, unfair and
thoughtless. I have told you that I am eminently practical; I think that
you don't understand what I mean to say by this expression, because
you don't make the slightest effort to put yourself in my situation
(therefore I must probably appear to you as a play actor or something
similar). My practicality consists in this: in knowing that if you bang
your head against the wall, it is your head that will crack and not the
wall. Very elementary, as you see, and yet very difficult to understand
for those who have never thought of banging their heads against the
wall, but have heard it said that it is enough to say open sesame! for
the wall to open. Your attitude is unconsciously cruel; you see someone bound (actually you don't see him tied up and you cannot conjure

up what his shackles are) who doesn't want to move because he can't move. You think that he doesn't move because he doesn't want to (you don't see that, since he did try to move, the shackles have cut into his flesh) and so there you go, urging him on with fiery darts. And what do you achieve? You make him writhe and you add stinging burns to the shackles that are already making him bleed. I'm quite certain that this horrifying picture worthy of a cheap novel about the Spanish Inquisition will not convince you and that you will continue; and since burning pustules are also purely metaphorical, what will happen is that I will continue to follow my "practice" of not trying to tear down the walls by battering them with my head (which already hurts me too much to engage in this sort of sport) and that I will put aside problems for whose solution I lack the indispensable elements. This is my strength, my only strength, and it is precisely this strength that you are trying to take from me. On the other hand it is a strength that one unfortunately cannot give to others; one can lose it, one cannot give it away as a gift or transmit it. I think that you have not given sufficient thought to my case and are unable to break it down into its various elements. I'm subject to various prison regimes: there is the prison regime constituted by the four walls, the bars on the window, the spy hole on the door, etc. etc.; this had already been taken into account by me and as a subordinate probability, because the primary probability from 1921 to November 1926 was not prison but losing my life. What had not been included in my evaluation was the other prison, which is added to the first and is constituted by being cut off not only from social life but also from family life etc. etc.

I could estimate the blows of my adversaries whom I was fighting, I could not foresee that blows would also come at me from other sides, from where I would least suspect them (metaphorical blows, of course, but the code also divides crimes into acts and omissions; that is, omissions too are faults or blows).[2] That's all. But what about me, you will say. It's true, you are very kind, and I'm very fond of you. But these are not matters where one person can replace another and what's more, the matter is very very complicated and difficult to explain completely (also because of the walls that are not metaphorical).[3] If the truth be told, I am not very sentimental and it isn't sentimental matters that torment me. It's not that I am insensitive (I don't want to pose as a cynic or a blasé person); but in fact emotional matters concern me too, I live them, combined with other elements (ideological, philosophical, political, etc.) so that I couldn't say where emotion ends and where instead one of the other elements begins, perhaps I couldn't even say precisely which of these elements is involved, so much have they became united in an inseparable whole and in a single life. Perhaps this is a strength; perhaps it is also a weakness, because it leads one to analyze other people in the same manner and therefore perhaps to draw erroneous conclusions. But I won't continue, because I'm writing a dissertation and it seems to me that it is better not to write anything than to write dissertations.

Dearest Tatiana, don't worry about the undershirts; the ones I have allow me to wait for the others you will send me. Do not send me the thermos or send it to me only after the warden's office assures you that it will be given to me; if I have to keep it in storage, I might as well not have it. Signora Pina definitely lives at Via Montebello 7, I don't believe that she'll be coming here for the time being, in fact I know she won't. I'll send you a few more books and two tattered shirts. Write to my mother, give her my greetings and assure her that I am fairly well. I embrace you tenderly.

Antonio

1. In the *Philosophy of Right* (1821).
2. Gramsci enjoys some wordplay here with the words *colpe* (faults or guilt) and *colpi* (blows).
3. In a 1991 essay on Gramsci's relationship with the PCI and the Comintern during the prison years, Giuseppe Vacca cites this letter, together with a remark by Apollon Schucht in a letter to Tania, June 6, 1930, as rather convincing, although still inconclusive, evidence that political censorship by Soviet authorities of Giulia's letters to Gramsci helps to explain their vague, inhibited character. In *Antigone e il prigioniero*, p. 65, Aldo Natoli cites Apollon Schucht's letter of June 6, 1930 (transcribed by Tania for Gramsci), as proof of Soviet censorship: "One can see that neither you nor Antonio has understood me," wrote Apollon. "I did not say that Giulia doesn't write because she is ill, I said that she writes only rarely because it is very painful for her to do so under the conditions in which she is compelled to do it." See letter to Tania, January 13, 1931, n. 2; see also Spriano, *Antonio Gramsci and the Party*, p. 58.

May 24, 1930

Dearest Mother,

I received your letter of the eleventh and a postcard from Teresina. I've been very sorry about the trouble that has befallen Mario, also for you, since you never manage to have a quiet life. I hope that the news that you will have received in the meantime has kept improving and that Mario, with his strong constitution, will quickly be able to overcome the crisis and recover properly. Send him my best wishes. I do not need to insist that you keep me informed of all the news that you have already received and that you will receive.

Carlo has not yet written to me and therefore I know nothing about his new job and his departure from Ghilarza; also on these subjects I beg you to be more openhanded with news and not to think that I already know everything because Carlo might have written to me. I haven't received any letters from Carlo for more than four months, to my great disappointment, because it seemed to me that I had explained matters to him quite clearly.

And so you didn't answer me with regard to the dictionary that I had meant for Edmea. Why? I asked you about it three or four times. Do you know what I suspect? That Carlo, sick and tired of having to drag around all those cumbersome books, has tossed them out along the way. Actually it wouldn't be such a great disaster, but I would like to know something about it in order to know how to act in the future. In short, it seems to me that if Mea has received the dictionary she too ought to write something to me, all the more so since by now she must have progressed in her studies and know how to write nicely and even draw with a certain grace.

Dearest mother, I want to leave a bit of space for Tatiana to add a few lines. I embrace you affectionately, with many good wishes to all.

Antonio

May 30, 1930

Dearest Carlo,

I've received your insured letter of the twenty-eighth with the 100 lire and I thank you cordially. The abstract of the military code that you sent me some time ago is of no use to me for the simple reason that I wasn't sentenced on the basis of articles of the military penal code but on articles of the Zanardelli[1] penal code under military procedure. That is, the pretrial investigation and the entire judicial process has been conducted according to military procedure in time of war and therefore the petition for revision must also be made in accordance with the precedents and modalities of this same procedure. Therefore I have no use for an abstract from the military penal code but I need one from the code of military penal procedure and specifically the articles or article in which are pinpointed precisely the instances where a petition for revision is permissible together with the instructions on how it must be drawn up. Actually this abstract is not indispensable for me. If I had felt like it, I could certainly have already compiled (as I shall do) a memorandum for the attorney containing a list of the motives that in my opinion would justify a revision. The attorney could then have a selection made,[2] ———— those elements that are not valid legally and utilizing those that are contemplated by the military procedure. This is what I will definitely do as soon as I get rid of my headache that has been tormenting me for more than a month. As Tatiana has written to you, I think, you can forget about the catalogue and about Pescarzoli.[3] I have received a book on the *Stampatori del 400* [Print makers of the fifteenth century]. I am sure that you've understood that if lately I haven't written to you directly, but have delegated Tatiana to pass on information from me, I did so only in order to be able to write more to Tatiana, who is still at Turi, leading a monk's life, isolated from the entire world, without distractions or interests to occupy her. Tell this also to mother. I embrace you affectionately.

Antonio

1. Giuseppe Zanardelli (1826–1903), Italian liberal prime minister from 1901 to 1903, who championed the idea of punishment for crimes after the fact, against the widespread notion in Italy of restrictive preventive measures.
2. Illegible words.
3. Antonio Pescarzoli. See letter to Tania, January 29, 1929.

————————————

June 2, 1930

Dearest Tatiana,

I've received the undershirts you sent and I thank you. I don't have any more worn-out linens to send you besides the two shirts that you have received; these two got torn just in the last few weeks; they were cobweb thin but without tatters, as you yourself can ascertain by looking at them. So don't wait for anything; your talent as a mender will not have an object on which to express itself, at least this time.

I've also received your two letters of May 24 and 31. You are greatly mistaken if you believe that I "should bear with you because you have decided not to hide anything from me," or when you write that "your sincerity forces you to be cruel by not hiding the truth from me." I would say instead that you've been much more cruel by waiting three years before writing me about certain things.[1] But I won't reproach you: I've given up trying to understand anything, because I'm convinced that, for one reason or another, I will never manage to have sufficient information to understand anything. Your father's postcards, which you transcribed for me, have indeed persuaded me of this.

Dearest, I want to write to you about a question that will make you angry or will make you laugh. While leafing through the *Petite Larousse*, I remembered a rather curious problem. As a child I was an indefatigable hunter of lizards and snakes, which I fed to a beautiful falcon I had domesticated. During these hunts in the fields of my village (Ghilarza) three or four times I happened upon an animal very similar to the common snake (grass snake), only it had four tiny legs, two close to the head and two very far from these, close to the tail (if you can call it that). The animal was sixty to seventy centimeters long, very thick in relation to its length, its thickness corresponds to that of a grass snake one meter twenty or one meter fifty long. The little legs were not very much help to it, because it escaped by slithering very slowly. In my village this reptile is called *scurzone*, which means shortened (*curzu* means short), and the name must certainly refer to the fact that it looks like a shortened grass snake (mind you, there also exists the *orbettino*,[2] whose short length is accompanied by a proportionate slimness of body). In Santu Lussurgiu where I attended the last three classes of gymnasium, I asked the natural history professor (who really was an old local engineer) what the Italian name was for *scurzone*. He laughed and told me that it was an imaginary animal, like the asp[3] or basilisk,[4] and that he did not know of any animal similar to the one I was describing. The boys of Santu Lussurgiu explained that in their town the *scurzone* was in fact the basilisk, and that the animal I described was called *coloru* (Latin *coluber*), while the grass snake was called *colora* with a feminine ending, but the professor said that these were all peasant superstitions and that grass snakes with legs don't exist. You know how angry a boy can get at being told he is wrong when he knows instead that he is right or even at being made fun of as guilty of superstition, when a question of reality is at stake; I think that it is due to this reaction against authority put at the service of self-assured ignorance that I still remember the episode. Besides, in my home town I had never heard talk about the maleficent qualities of the basilisk—*scurzone*, which in other towns however was feared and surrounded by legends. Now in fact in the *Larousse* in the reptile table I saw a saurian, the *seps*,[5] which in fact is a grass snake with four small legs (the *Larousse* says it lives in Spain and in southern France, that it belongs to the family of the *scincides* whose typical representative is the *scinque* (perhaps the green lizard?) The illustration of the *seps* does not look very much like the *scurzone* from my town: the *seps* is a regular grass snake, thin, long, well-proportioned, and its little legs are harmoniously attached to its body; the *scurzone* instead is a repulsive animal: its head is very large, not small like that of the grass snake; its "tail" is very conic; the two front legs are too close to the head, and they are too far from the legs in the back; the paws are whitish, sickly, like those of the *proteo* (newt)[6] and they give one an impression of monstrosity, of abnormality. The entire animal, which lives in damp places (I always saw it after turning over large stones) makes a disagreeable impression, not like the lizard and the grass snake, which apart from man's general repugnance for reptiles, are actually elegant and graceful. I would now like to know from your vast knowledge of natural history, whether this animal has an Italian name and whether it is known that in Sardinia there exists this species that should be of the same family as the French *seps*. It is possible that the legend of the basilisk stood in the way of the search for this animal in Sardinia; the Santu Lussurgiu professor was not stupid, just the opposite, and he was also quite scholarly; he had collections of minerals, etc., and yet he did not believe that the *scurzone* existed as a very pedestrian reality, without poisonous breath and incendiary eyes. This animal is certainly not very common: I did not see it more than a dozen times and always under boulders, while I've seen grass snakes by the thousands and without any need to move stones.

Dear Tatiana, don't be too angry because of these digressions of mine. I embrace you tenderly.

Antonio

1. This is a reference to the reluctance on Tania's part fully to inform Gramsci of the seriousness of Julca's mental and emotional problems.

2. The *orbettino* (anguis fragilis) is a small, harmless reptile with a cylindrical, tailless body.

3. *Aspide* is a generic term designating "poisonous snakes."

4. The *basilisco* is a term used for an imaginary animal, a legendary monster dating back to the Middle Ages. It was believed to have the power to kill with its breath, or just by looking at its victim.

5. The *seps* is a reptile found commonly in Sardinia and Sicily. Its body is about thirty-five to forty centimeters long, half of which is formed by its tail.

6. The *proteo* is not a reptile, but an amphibian with a pinkish white color.

June 16, 1930

Dearest Tatiana,

I just had a visit with my brother and this has given a zigzag course to my thoughts.[1] It has truly been something extraordinarily new, for which I wasn't in the least prepared; I would not have thought that I would see my brother again in Turi. This has made me very happy, also because I've been much closer to Gennaro than to the rest of the family. Meanwhile, however, I don't know what to write to you. I'll have to be content with odds and ends. I heard from Gennaro that you're eating very little: he was struck by this and he mentioned it of his own accord (there was no malice at all on my part and I didn't even question him on the subject: so his opinion carries weight: you eat so little that it immediately leaps to the eye and this is very serious). You've got to change and take care of yourself, before you have the right to preach to me.

One thing in your last card that made me laugh a lot is your statement that you know how much importance I attach to receiving good wishes for my name day. I don't know who revealed this secret to you that I kept carefully hidden in the most intimate recesses of my most profound subconscious; so hidden and so secret that at the age of six I was no longer aware of harboring it (I received presents for my name day only until the age of six). I'm afraid that you might discover who knows what other hidden wounds: perhaps that of becoming a Trappist monk or of joining the Society of Jesus (I shall reveal to you a single secret desire that has always tormented me, that I have never been able to satisfy and that perhaps, alas, I never will satisfy: that of eating a mixed fry of babirussa[2] and rhinoceros kidneys and brains!).

Dear Tatiana, in any case I thank you for the good wishes, with the simple reminder that the St. Anthony who protects me is not the one in June but the one in January[3] accompanied by the European species of babirussa (unfortunately the babirussa lives on the Molucca islands and is therefore hard to procure, especially in the form of fresh brains and kidneys).

I would like you to ask Sperling bookstore to send me two small books: (1) Benedetto Croce, *Alessandro Manzoni*, Laterza, Bari; (2) Albert Mathiez, *La révolution française*, volume 3, *La terreur*, Armand Colin series, Paris (tell them that I want only this third volume, since I already have the first two).

Dearest Tatiana, I thank you very much for the news you've sent me. I embrace you tenderly.

Antonio

Let me know exactly when you are leaving Turi.

1. This letter alluding to Gennaro's conversation with Gramsci at the Turi prison on June 16, 1930, has been the subject of much controversy. The problem lies in determining what Gramsci is referring to when he writes of the "zig-zag" in his thoughts as a result of his talk with his brother. The generally accepted interpretation is that Gennaro, although not a Communist party member, had been entrusted by the PCI leadership in Paris with the task of informing Gramsci of the recent expulsions of three Party members—Pietro Tresso, Sergio Ravazzoli, and Alfonso Leonetti—for their Trotskyism and for having rejected the left turn taken by the Communist International (CI) in 1930. Since available documentary evidence and personal testimony lead to the conclusion that Gramsci was strongly opposed to the new sectarian leftism of the CI, and that in fact he had begun to espouse the idea of a Constituent Assembly and to revise his thinking in the direction of closer collaboration with non-Communist anti-Fascist parties and movements, the zig-zag may allude to tensions in his relationship with the PCI. Many years later, in the early 1960s, Gennaro told Giuseppe Fiori, Gramsci's biographer, that when he returned to Paris in 1930 he told PCI leaders that Gramsci had approved of the new Party line and of the expulsions. He had lied, Gennaro said, in order to protect Gramsci from condemnation and even expulsion. On the other hand, a Communist fellow prisoner, Bruno Tosin, recalls that Gramsci did go along with the expulsion of the three dissidents, but only if it could be shown that they had violated Party norms and Party discipline, not because of their ideological deviation. Paolo Spriano reports evidence to substantiate still another point of view: that Gramsci did not express any opinion one way or the other about the expulsions in his talk with Gennaro. This is what Luigi Longo recalled about the incident, which is supported by the fact that in a letter of August 27, 1930, to Giuseppe Berti, Palmiro Togliatti made no mention of a position taken by Gramsci on the matter. (Spriano, *Antonio Gramsci and the Party*, pp. 57–58)

2. A large, hoglike quadruped.

3. See letter to Tania, March 26, 1927, n. 1.

June 30, 1930

Dearest Mother,

I haven't received news from you for more than a month now. How come neither letters nor postcards; Carlo has given a sign of life only with . . . cigarettes, which however are no substitute for a letter.

Were you happy about Nannaro's visit? I can imagine your and Edmea's joy. Isn't it true that Nannaro has remained marvelously young? I was astonished by it: I had the impression of seeing him again exactly the same as he was nine years ago.

You will have received copious news about me from him, who on the other hand had also seen Mario and must therefore have been able to reassure you about his condition too. Nothing new.

Write to me as soon as possible and at length and describe your impressions about the many new things that have happened to you. I embrace you tenderly.

Antonio

July 14, 1930

Dearest Tatiana,

I received your two letters, the letters from Giulia, and the photograph. However you haven't told me anything about your trip. Did you stop in Bari? Did you consult the eye doctor and what did he say? All these things interest me very much: I really hope that you will decide to take serious care of your health, but I don't put much stock in it. What you need is a real "slave driver" who would force you to nourish yourself properly, even by resorting to coercive measures and physical means (a few taps on the ears, etc.), but I don't see how this can be accomplished: perhaps only I would be able to carry out this task efficiently, combining a correct dose of ruthlessness and affectionate persuasion. You really ought to make a solemn commitment to me (accompanied by your word of honor) that every morning you will eat three egg yolks with sugar in your hot coffee and in each of your letters assure me that you have respected this commitment. Will you do this? This seems ridiculous, and yet I believe that perhaps it could be a very serious thing.

During these last days there has been a small piece of real news. I've received the communication that my sentence has been shortened by one year four months and five days: therefore the total sentence has been shortened to nineteen whole years and the day of release shifted from May 25, 1947 to January 20, 1946. In the communication a reference was made to a declaratory judgment by the Special Tribunal dated May 1930, following the decree of January 1 or 2 that involves the measure adopted on the occasion of the crown prince's marriage. As you see, this is really something new, because by now the persuasion had struck root that the January decree did not apply to those sentenced by the Special Tribunal: instead the reduction has been granted and I, like many others, did not receive a year, but in fact a year, four months and five days. How can all this be explained? I explain it as follows: in the sentences handed down because of the alleged crimes committed before the special law and therefore judged under the old Zanardelli code, the charges are several: I had six charges that involved a total of thirty-one years and eight months counting both reclusion and detention, reduced by juridical consolidation to twenty years, four months and five days. I think that the tribunal has applied the one year remission decree to three or four or perhaps five charges, thus revising the calculation of the judicial consolidation so that we now have a subtraction of sixteen months and five days. I'm writing you all this because I'm very curious to know whether my hypothesis is correct and to which charges the remission was applied. Would you please find out? As soon as you feel better, you could go to the tribunal's chancellery and ask for this clarification: I don't know if there is another way. Perhaps you could ask Piero.

Please get the bookstore to send me this book: P. Louis Rivière, *L'après guerre: Dix ans d'histoire (1919–1929)* [After the war: Ten years of history (1919–1929)] Paris, Ch. Lavauzelle & Co. You must definitely inform me if you decide to have the three daily egg yolks in coffee (they must really be three, because often enough you won't eat anything else all day). I'll also get Gennaro to tell you about the eggs; perhaps at the beginning of next week he will be going to Rome. I embrace you affectionately.

Antonio

July 14, 1930

Dearest Giulia,

Let me introduce this letter with a small calculation of . . . epistolary accounting. During the first two weeks of July I've received four letters from you, one dated December 24, 1929, one February 5, 1930 and two very recent ones written in June; previously I had received a letter in December 1929 dated November 15 and before that another letter from June. This means that between July 1929 and July 1930, one year, I had received only one letter from you. These simple factual observations lie at the basis of a whole psychological superstructure that I certainly will refrain from describing: certainly this year did not pass without leaving many marks on me. During this time I've often remembered a strange fellow I met during the war, who had a certain odd talent because he managed to invent a small mechanical horse that moved its legs and walked like a real horse: he seriously wanted me to subject myself in company with him to this exercise that was meant to make us invulnerable: we were to shoot methodically at ourselves with pistols, going inch by inch over our skin, loading the cartridge by degrees and going from minimal doses to normal doses. I made sure not to accept and so I was not able to immunize my skin physically; but during these last months I've acquired the conviction that I've immunized my, so to speak, moral or emotional or psychological skin; I've been a bit obsessed, true enough, but since then I have fallen into a state of complete obtuseness and insensitivity, which still continues to some extent. I'm glad that I've received your four letters and the photograph, but they have left me with the impression that you have gone through a serious crisis and that you have not yet overcome it: your photograph has also left me with this impression. You mentioned the small photograph in which I thought you had a "warlike" expression, well, this reminds me of the photograph with the "sweet and mild" expression but with the addition of something new, I don't know whether sorrowful or resigned. This upsets me. Perhaps, true enough, it would take little to change all this, but this "little" is incredibly difficult and a great deal: it would take a caress on your brow. And yet I am convinced, and despite the impressions that I have received this conviction has been reinforced, that you do not know yourself and the reserves of energy you bear within you and that your crises of weakness and depression are precisely due to this. Therefore I think that you should write me more often: not only for me (naturally I too would be very happy, don't you agree?) but also for yourself. It seems to me that you are distressed because you write so little and so on, tormenting yourself on an ever-growing scale. You should write me more often and with greater boldness. What you write about the children is interesting and typical (you are very good at choosing the traits that might please me) but it does not give me the idea of a development, of a progressive enrichment of their small lives as men being formed, of the formation in them of an embryonic conception of the world. My reference to the atlas had only this meaning and was not at all pedantic, even though I believe that with children, until their personality has reached a certain stage of development, a bit of pedantry is necessary and indispensable. It usually happens, at least where I come from, that on the contrary pedantry is exercised later on, just when it is harmful, between the ages of 12 and 16, except when people don't even bother; but this results in "outlaw" children. This letter is a bit disheveled, under the impression of your many recent letters. I want you to really feel as if I were embracing you very tightly together with Delio and Giuliano and with a smile were caressing your brow.

Antonio

July 28, 1930

Dearest Tania,

I have not been able to inform Gennaro about what you wrote to me, because your postcard was given to me after the visit. In this connection: you will do well to keep in mind on what day I will be able to write to you; from now on I will always have to limit myself to one letter a month and you must take care to write me about things that require an answer so that I won't have to put off the answer for a month. Gennaro wants me to write sometimes to him too and I will be able to do so only by devoting to him half a page of the letter that I write home.[1]

I'm happy to hear that you are resolved to eat properly: the entire state of your health rests on this. You must really promise to do what I have recommended, without quibbling about the eggs being too heavy or what not. You are always searching for something perfect and naturally you end up by doing nothing: it is a typical form of abulia that consists in setting oneself iron-bound aims that then never find the "perfection" through which they can be realized. It is very distressing that you were not able to take advantage of Piero's trip[2] and travel in his company, but I'm afraid that you will have to pass up other fine opportunities if you don't recover sufficiently to travel without risks. I don't know why you worry about customs, visas, etc. These are all trifles, because all you need is a traveling bag and a small suitcase holding things you need for the trip itself: the luggage is sealed at the border of departure and travels with you to the border of arrival without any trouble beyond that of handing the ticket stub to the porter[3] at the end of the line for the transfer from one train to another: in this way you will go through customs with only what you carry personally, and this does not require a great effort, because the customs officials can only ask to see whether you have any jewels. I write all this to you to convince you that your only problem is your health and nothing else: everything depends on your good will and on your perseverance; but unless you start once and for all, you'll never be ready or have the proper attitude. Do you understand? No quibbling, no extraneous reasons or difficulties, etc. etc. You yourself are the alpha and omega of your own life and of your freedom of movement. Dearest, you really must be good and not keep me forever plagued by remorse and feeling that because of me you cannot do as you please. I embrace you tenderly.

Antonio

Send my mother the part that concerns her.

1. As of this date, none of Gramsci's letters to Gennaro have been found. Their dispersion was due, no doubt, to the fact that Gennaro led an adventurous and at times vagabond life.

2. In August and September 1930, Sraffa made a trip to the Soviet Union, during which he was able to meet with Giulia, who at that time was under treatment at a sanatorium in the Crimea.

3. Gramsci uses the German word *träger*.

July 28, 1930

Dearest Mother,

I like the two small photographs that Nannaro brought me very much: even though technically they are not very successful, they succeed in giving a reasonably direct impression of your physiognomy and your expression. It seems to me that, despite your years and all the rest, you have remained quite young and strong: you must have few white hairs and your expression is very vivacious though a bit, how shall I say? . . . matronly. I bet that you'll be able to see your great grand-children and see them quite grown-up: we'll really have to take a large photograph, on some day in the future, which will include all of our generations and you at the center, keeping order. Mea has grown a lot, but she is still very . . . *spabaiada*.[1] Nannaro, from what you wrote to him, had thought that his daughter was who knows what monster of wisdom and genius. And because of this he has gone to the opposite extreme and has forgotten that the child is still only nine or ten years old. But he does have a point, especially when he observes that at that age we were more mature and more developed intellectually. This strikes me too. It seems to me that Mea is too childish for her age, even for her age, that she has no other ambitions than cutting a pretty figure outwardly and has no inner life, that she has no emotional needs that aren't chiefly sensual (vanity, etc.). Perhaps you spoiled her too much or haven't forced her to discipline herself. It is true that I and Nannaro and the others were not forced to discipline ourselves, but we disciplined ourselves. I remember that at Mea's age I would have died of shame if I made so many spelling errors; do you remember how I used to read until late at night and how many subterfuges I had recourse to in order to obtain books. And Teresina too was like that, though she too was a girl like Mea and certainly was even prettier physically. I would like to know what Mea has read until now: I would say, from what she writes, that she can't be reading anything but her school books. In short, you must try to accustom her to work with discipline and somewhat restrict her "social" life: less successes of vanity and greater seriousness in matters of substance. Get Mea to write to me and ask her to tell me about her life, etc. Kisses to everyone. I embrace you tenderly.

Antonio

1. "Clumsy," in Sardinian.

August 11, 1930

Dearest Tatiana,

You write that you have already spoken about the application that I decided to present some time ago, that I've had to postpone and recently I haven't felt like writing because I was literally brutalized from lack of sleep and the heat; it means that I will make a "great" effort during these coming days and write it. I still haven't regained my balance, although for a few nights I have slept a bit: I'm overcome by a kind of psychic aphasia that manifests itself in the impossibility of focusing my attention, in the difficulty of connecting concepts, and even the difficulty of finding the actual words and of remembering the most common things from one minute to the next. It is nothing serious: I know what is involved, because I've already had such crises on other occasions in an even worse form.

On the twenty-second of June, my brother Gennaro wrote me a letter from Namur while he was still en route, then nothing more. I find it hard to believe that he didn't write to me at some other time and I doubt that the letter was lost. Do you have his address and can you write to him? You ought to inform him of what happened and also tell him that his letter from Namur was abundantly censored, so that he'll know how to behave.

I'm sorry that you went to live with old Isaac[1]: that environment is too depressed and depressing. I hope that you won't lose the bit of willpower that you seem to have regained and that you will continue the intensive egg cure. Do you know that I had to laugh at your remark that you are "always hungry"? You talk about it as if it were an illness and not a sign of good health. This is a point of view that the Neapolitans have humorously embodied in the figure of Monsignor Perrelli[2] and the care he took of his horses to cure them of the disease of hunger. But at least Monsignor Perrelli was trying to cure his horses and did not apply the regime of abstinence to himself! You instead apparently have not yet learned that by eating one stops being hungry: such a way of dealing with oneself is truly astounding. You should increase your daily menu and besides the three egg yolks "force on yourself" some other regular comestible: but that would really be an exaggeration and besides I wouldn't know what to recommend because I don't know how you have organized your life, whether you eat at home, whether you're boarding, etc. Let me know, please. I at least want to exert all possible moral pressure, because it seems to me that I'm responsible to your mother for the state of your health.

Do you know that they have published a continuation of Father Brown's adventures? The book has been published by Alpes of Milan and is entitled *La saggezza di Padre Brown*[3] [The wisdom of Father Brown]; I'm telling you because, I think, you had liked the first volume very much and if in the first Father Brown was naive while in the second he is wise one wonders what progress has been made in his capacity for induction and psychological introspection. Dear Tania, I embrace you tenderly.

Antonio

1. Isaac Schreider. See letter to Tania, January 7, 1927, n. 3.
2. The reference is to the Neapolitan Catholic prelate Filippo Perelli (1707–1789), known by the name Monsignor Perelli to the people of Naples, who made him into a legendary figure around whom turned many humorous anecdotes. One such anecdote described his attempts to cure his horse of excessive hunger by imposing on it a rigorous diet. The diet was so rigorous that the horse died of malnutrition. Monsignor Perelli is mentioned again in letter to Tania, August 10, 1931. (*Dizionario Enciclopedico Italiano*, vol. 9, p. 268).
3. By Gilbert K. Chesterton (1874–1936), British poet, essayist, and novelist. See letter to Tania, October 6, 1930, for Gramsci's acute comments on the differences between Chesterton and Arthur Conan Doyle as crime-fiction writers.

August 11, 1930

Dearest Giulia,

I really don't feel in the mood to write you a letter, but I just want to say hello to you. Tania has written that you've already gone to the rest home; I hope that you'll regain your strength and will quickly be once again in a condition to resume your activity. Let me know what is or what might be the precise meaning for the children of realizing that they are a year older. I don't know what form you give to this birth date and what stimulating and energizing strength one might derive from it in a practical way. In truth I know nothing at all about the entire educational system and it would interest me very much. Tania has written that our friend Piero was going to bring some presents for Delio: tell me something about this. Do you remember the celluloid ball half filled with water and floating swans that Delio used to have in Rome? It was a present from Piero, but I remember that Delio was particularly interested in opening it, that is, in destroying it as a toy, which seems to prove that it wasn't really suited to its purpose. Write me about your rest cure and about a lot of other things. I embrace you.

Antonio

August 25, 1930

Dearest Carlo,[1]

I received your insured letter with the 250 lire and a little while ago I received your letter of the twenty-third: a few days ago a letter came from mother and Mea. As I have written to Tatiana, I got a letter, postmarked Namur,[2] dated July 22, from Nannaro and then nothing: I would simply like you to inform him of this in case he did write and his letter went astray. As for Mea, I don't think you are right. Since the matter is important and could decide the girl's entire future, I'll set down a few more observations. Of course, I did take into account the environment in which she lives, but environment does not justify anything: it seems to me that all of life is a struggle to adapt to the environment but also and especially to dominate it and not let it crush you. At home all of you are first of all Mea's environment, then there are her friends, the school, and then the entire town with its Corroncus, its aunts Tane and Juanna Culamantigu, etc. etc. From which parts of this environment will Mea receive the impetus that molds her habits, her ways of thinking, her moral judgments? If you abstain from intervening and guiding her by using the authority that comes with fondness and family coexistence, by putting pressure on her in an affectionate and loving but nevertheless stern and inflexibly firm manner, what will undoubtedly happen is that Mea's spiritual formation will be the mechanical result of the chance influence of all the stimuli of this environment: that is, Aunt Tana as well as Corroncu, Uncle Salomone and Uncle Juanni Bobbai, etc., will contribute to Mea's upbringing. (I mention these names as symbols because I imagine that if these personages have died, other equivalent ones must exist.) A mistake that is usually made in bringing up children seems to me to be this (you can think about yourself and then decide whether I'm right): one does not make the distinction that in the lives of children there are two very clearcut phases, before and after puberty. Before puberty the child's personality has not yet formed and it is easier to guide its life and make it acquire specific habits of order, discipline, and work: after puberty the personality develops impetuously and all outside intervention becomes odious, tyrannical, insufferable. Now it so happens that parents feel responsibility toward their children precisely during this second period, when it is too late: then of course the stick and violence enter the scene and yield very few results indeed. Why not instead take an interest in the child during the first period? It doesn't seem much, but sitting at a desk five to eight hours a day is an important habit that can be inculcated without unpleasantness until the age of fourteen, but it is no longer possible afterward. I think for women it is the same, and perhaps worse, because puberty for them is a much more serious and complex crisis than for men: with modern life and the relative freedom of girls, the question has become even more serious. I am under the impression that the older generation has renounced educating the young generation, and that the latter are making the same mistake; the clamorous failure of the old generations is being reproduced in exactly the same way in the generation that now seems to be dominant. Give some thought to what I have written and reflect on whether it isn't necessary to educate the educator.[3]

As regards the applications that have to be made for the books by Trotsky, it is perhaps better that you take care of the procedure. This is how the matter should be presented. I would like to be granted permission to read: (1) some books by Trotsky written after his expulsion from Russia, that is, his autobiography, translated also into Italian and published by Mondadori,[4] and also these two: *La révolution défigurée* (The revolution betrayed) and *Vers le capitalisme ou vers le socialisme* [Toward capitalism or toward socialism], (I already have these two, but an authorization is required for them to be released to me.; (2) the book by Fülöp Miller, *Il volto del bolscevismo* [The face of bolshevism], translated into Italian with a preface by Curzio Malaparte, the present director of *La Stampa* of Turin and a well-known Fascist from the earliest days; (3) the following books that I already own and that for reasons that I cannot discuss will not be granted without authorization: (1) Mino Maccari, *Il trastullo di strapaese* [The plaything of Strapaese]. This is a book of Fascist lyrics: Maccari was the leader of the Fascists in Colle Valdelsa and is now chief editor of *La Stampa*); (2) Giuseppe Prezzolini, *Mi pare* [It seems to me]. This is a collection of articles on fashion, bookstores, etc.): the book was published in Florence by Arturo Marpicati, at present secretary and chancellor at the Academy of Italy; Prezzolini is the director of the Italian Section of the Institute of Intellectual Cooperation and his immediate superior is none other than the honorable Rocco, Minister of Justice; (3) Maurice Muret, *Le crépuscule des nations blanches* [The twilight of the white nations] (Muret is a Swiss writer, very friendly to Italy: he writes many columns on Italian literature in French and Swiss newspapers and magazines: the book deals with the colonial question); (4) Petronius Arbiter, *Satyricon* (this is one of the masterpieces of Latin literature: I took a two-year course on this book at the university and I still remember long parts of it by heart: it contains some obscenities, like all Latin and Greek books, but I do not collect obscene books; (5) Krassnoff,[5] *Dall'aquila imperiale alla bandiera rossa* [From the imperial eagle to the red flag] (this is a novel by the former Cossack general Krassnoff, now a Czarist émigré in Berlin: it is published by Salani side by side with the novels of Carolina Invernizio; (6) Heinrich Mann, *Le sujet* [The subject], (this is a German novel of the time of Wilhelm II); (7) Jack London, *Le memorie d'un bevitore* [John Barleycorn] (I don't know it but it must be an adventure novel dealing with sailors and miners in Alaska); (8) Oscar Wilde, *Il fantasma di Canterville*, etc. [The Canterville ghost] etc. (these are three humorous stories against spiritualism and English ghost stories). Let me know what you are going to do. Embrace everyone at home. Cordially.

Antonio

1. This letter was held by the prison warden at Turi in order to prevent Carlo from carrying out the request made by Gramsci. On the basis of prison regulations, Gramsci was able to have the letter sent to the Ministry of Justice, which confirmed that the books mentioned were forbidden, "given the political material they deal with." Gramsci then decided to send a letter of appeal directly to Mussolini, dated September 30, 1930, which appears in this volume in its chronological place. The appeal received a positive response in November, as can be seen in letter to Tania, December 1, 1930.

2. A town and provincial capital in Belgium.

3. This phrase is taken from the third of Marx's *Theses on Fuerbach*. See also letter to Teresina, May 4, 1931.

4. Leon Trotsky, *La mia vita: Tentativo di autobiografia* [My life: An attempt at an autobiography], Italian trans. Ervino Pocar (Milan: Mondadori, 1930). Trotsky had been expelled from the Soviet Union in February 1929. For an analysis of the intellectual and political connections between Trotsky and Gramsci, and a fairly extensive bibliography on the subject, see my essay "The Gramsci-Trotsky Question (1922–1932)," in *Social Text*, 11 (Winter 1984/85): 65–95.

5. The usual spelling is Krasnov.

September 22, 1930

Dearest Mother,

I duly received Carlo's insured letter some time back with the two hundred lire. I'm not sick and have not had any illnesses. The lack of letters has been due to other causes. I did not receive the letter from Nannaro that Carlo had announced. I truly hope that, as Carlo writes me, you will finally be able to be treated thoroughly: you know, I always think that you rely too much on your past sturdiness, when you were almost never sick, and that therefore you are not too diligent in following the doctor's advice and you neglect yourself. Carlo and Grazietta should force you to take care of yourself and not allow you to tire yourself out, even if they have to tie you to a chair. But Grazietta does not seem to be very firm and Carlo is also probably easily mollified. And so you perhaps continue to stand in front of the stove and then perhaps go out into the courtyard even though you are overheated, etc., etc. Oh! Peppina Marcias, you would really need a son like me at your side to see to it that you follow your treatments properly and to prevent you from running left and right like a ferret. Dearest mother, write to me or have someone else to write to me about your health. Kisses for everyone at home and many affectionate embraces for you.

Antonio

September 22, 1930

Dearest Tatiana,

I've received your package and Giulia's letters and the photograph of your father. The over-stockings fit more or less when it comes to size (perhaps they are a bit too large) but they are not very useful, they began to wear out from the very first day. If you want to send me some made of cloth, as you write, make sure of the color: they must be white or at least the color white must be predominant, otherwise they're not permitted. As for the medicines, I've begun to take the Uroclasio and the Benzofosfan: I have the impression that the Uroclasio has already helped me somewhat against my expulsive gingivitis (this is the name of the illness and not "explosive gingivitis" as I once told you): even though all my teeth continue to move and by now only two of them fit together (one upper and one lower, canines), so that I cannot chew anything, but at least they don't hurt and my gums don't burn so much; however, I have not yet noticed any benefit where my headache is concerned, but according to the instructions the cure still has a long way to go. I'm putting the other medicines aside for the time being; I don't want to fill my stomach with so very many disparate things and to tell the truth I don't know the purpose of some of them because I don't have the instructions. I've almost finished the Benzofosfan.

I don't think that your father's photograph came out very well: it does not render his peculiar and most personal expression. It's true that he no longer has a full beard and that somewhat changes the general physiognomy that I remember, but nevertheless it seems to me that much else is missing. Perhaps he shortened his beard because when Delio was in his crib in 1925 he used to tear at it with great vigor; you know I used to watch this scene for a long time: your father would bend over the boy to get him to play and he would clutch his beard to lift himself up, while your father laughed wholeheartedly even though he must have felt considerable pain.

Yesterday I was given the Pushkin translation: it's quite a while since I read such silly rubbish: this is a true case of literary teratology; it didn't even succeed in being amusing since the stupidity is so monotonous. But it will be useful to me anyway to help me to understand the original better. Please write to the bookstore to tell them I haven't received the August issue of the magazine *Gerarchia* and that I want to have it. And I also want to receive the two volumes of the *Racconti biografici* (Autobiographical stories) by Leo Tolstoy, recently published by Slavia. If you have the time you yourself should go to the Littorio bookstore that must be somewhere in midtown and get them to send me a sample issue of the review *Bibliografia Fascista*: perhaps you'll have to buy it and get them to send it by paying for the postage: perhaps some other bookstore might also take care of this service.

Dearest Tatiana, you mustn't worry and especially you mustn't think that you might have displeased me: in order to think this, you would also have to think that I'm not only a disgraceful egoist, but actually a boor. I feel fairly well. Next time I'll make sure to try to write the entire letter to Giulia. I embrace you tenderly.

Antonio

Perhaps it would be a good idea for you to send me some writing paper and envelopes for the letters, because I think that my stock is finished or about to be finished.

September 30, 1930

Petition addressed to His Excellency the Head of the Government, forwarded on September 30, 1930.

What is happening to me is curious and strange enough for me to feel impelled to turn to Your Excellency since I have in vain performed all the intermediary petitions. In June of 1928 the chaplain of the Judiciary Prison in Rome confiscated from me the small book of verses by Mino Maccari, a well-known Fascist writer, *Il trastullo di strapaese* (publisher Vallecchi, Florence). I made a protest to the Military Advocate of the Special Tribunal for the Defense of the State, and Commendatore Isgrò, during one of his visits to the prison, not only gave orders to return the confiscated book, but advised me and other defendants of the same trial who had complained about similar seizures to protest and to have recourse to higher authorities if in the penitentiaries to which we would be assigned, we would be refused access to scientific and classical books, and he specified that only books of political agitation were forbidden. In the penitentiary of Turi di Bari where I am at present confined, the Maccari book has once more been seized together with the following: Giuseppe Prezzolini, *Mi pare* [It seems to me]. (A collection of short topical articles published in 1925 by Arturo Marpicati); Oscar Wilde, *Il fantasma di Canterville* and two other humorous short stories; H. Mann, *Le sujet* [The subject], published by Kra (a novel about Kaiser Wilhelm's Germany); Petronious Arbiter, *Satyricon*; J. London, *Le memorie d'un bevitore*; Krasnov, *Dall'aquila imperiale alla bandiera rossa* (this is a novel by the Cossack General K., a Czarist émigré in Berlin, published by Salani in Florence); Maurice Muret, *Le crépuscule des nations blanches*, 1925. These are anondyne and insignificant books, true enough, but for me who must still serve fifteen years in prison it is an important matter of principle: to know exactly which books I can read. Since, according to a communication from the Director of the Prison, the Ministry of Justice also deems that it is not permissible to read Mino Maccari's verses or the other books listed above, I turn to Your Excellency and ask you to give instructions that I be permitted to do so. At the same time, I would request that you be kind enough to give instructions that I be permitted to read Fülöp Miller's book, *Il volto del bolscevismo*, with a preface by Curzio Malaparte, published by Libreria d'Italia, in Milan and also Leon Trotsky's autobiography issued by Mondadori. Thank you and regards.

October 6, 1930

Dearest Tania,

I was happy with Carlo's visit. He told me that you have recovered quite well. But I would like to have more information about the state of your health. Thank you for everything that you sent me. I've not yet been given the two books: the *Bibliografia Fascista* and Chesterton's short stories that I'll read with pleasure for two reasons: first because I imagine that they will be at least as interesting as the first series and second because I will try to reconstruct the impression they must have made on you. I confess that the latter will be my greatest pleasure. I recall exactly your state of mind when reading the first series: you had a happy capacity to receive impressions that were most immediate and least complicated by cultural residues. You didn't even realize that Chesterton has written a most delicate caricature of detective stories rather than detective stories per se. Father Brown is a Catholic who pokes fun at the mechanical thought processes of the Protestants and the book is basically an apologia of the Roman Church as against the Anglican Church. Sherlock Holmes is the "Protestant" detective who finds the end of the criminal skein by starting from the outside, relying on science, on experimental method, on induction. Father Brown is the Catholic priest who through the refined psychological experiences offered by confession and by the persistent activity of the fathers' moral casuistry, though not neglecting science and experimentation, but relying especially on deduction and introspection, totally defeats Sherlock Holmes, makes him look like a pretentious little boy, shows up his narrowness and pettiness. Moreover, Chesterton is a great artist while Conan Doyle was a mediocre writer, even though he was knighted for literary merit; thus in Chesterton there is a stylistic gap between the content, the detective story plot, and the form, and therefore a subtle irony with regard to the subject being dealt with, which renders these stories so delicious. Don't you agree? I remember that you used to read these stories as though they were accounts of real events, and you became involved to the point of expressing a sincere admiration for Father Brown and for his marvelous acumen in such a naive way that I was extraordinarily amused. But you mustn't be offended, because this amusement contained a touch of envy of your capacity for fresh and unspoiled impressionism, so to speak. To tell the truth, I don't feel very much like writing: my brain cells have evaporated. I embrace you affectionately.

Antonio

October 6, 1930

Dearest Giulia,

I received two letters from you: one of the sixteenth of August and the other, a later one, I think of September. I would have liked to write to you at length, but it is impossible for me because, at certain moments, I cannot piece together my memories and the impressions that I experience in reading your letters. Unfortunately, however, I can only write on specific days and hours that are not set by myself and that sometimes coincide with moments of nervous depression. I was very pleased by what you wrote to me: that having reread my letters of 1928 and 1929 you were struck by the similarity of our thoughts. But I would like to know under what circumstances and in relation to what subjects you were particularly struck by this similarity. Our correspondence lacks precisely an effective and concrete "correspondence": we have never been able to initiate a "dialogue": our letters are a series of monologues that do not always manage to find a point of accord even along general lines; if to this we add the time element, which causes us to forget what was written previously, the impression of pure " monologue" is reinforced. Don't you agree? I remember a short Scandinavian folk tale: three giants live in Scandinavia far from one another like great mountains. After thousands of years of silence, the first giant shouts to the other two: "I hear a herd of cows bellowing!" Three hundred years later, the second giant answers: "I heard the bellowing too!" And after another 300 years the third giant announces: "If you go on this way, making such a racket, I'll leave!" Well! I'm really not in the mood to write, there's a scirocco wind that gives me the sensation of being drunk. My dear, I embrace you tenderly together with our children.

Antonio

October 20, 1930

Dearest Tatiana,

I've received the photographs and all your comments and observations were not able to improve them; they are very bad and it seems to me that your comments put everything in a false light. I believe that what you write about the state of Giulia's health is not correct and that it is indeed dangerous or at least unadvisable to pose the matter in these terms; it seems to me that your conversations with Signorina Nilde have contributed to misleading you. It is evident that Giulia suffers from nervous exhaustion and from cerebral anemia that

tends to become chronic because she does not want to or does not
know how to take care of herself. Giulia is imperceptibly falling into
the same state in which Genia had fallen in 1919, that is, she refuses
to understand how a particular rhythm of work is possible only if the
organism is replenished and by following a certain way of life and
that at any rate what was at least explicable in 1919 is only absurd
romanticism in 1930. The serious aspect of the matter consists, it
seems to me, in the fact that it appears to be insoluble: what in fact
can we do, you and I? A few sermons, general warnings, which will
be fruitless. In my opinion, in situations of this kind, the only remedy
consists in a correct blend of persuasive and coercive measures, but
this is precisely the point: who will be able to exercise this necessary
coercion? In any case I believe that your approach is mistaken and
that if you want to intervene you must abandon it. I say this seriously,
because I'm well aware of how things stand, since I have examined
them carefully. I will write Giulia a long letter that of necessity will
take the form of a "dissertation," even though this form is odious: I
fail to see what else I could do. On the other hand, we are not dealing
with an individual phenomenon, regrettably it is widespread and
tends to spread even further, as we can gather from scientific publications dealing with the new methods of work introduced by America. I don't know whether you follow this literature. It is also interesting from the pathological point of view and interesting too are the
measures taken by the American industrialists themselves, like Ford
for example.[1] He has a corps of inspectors who check on the private
lives of the workers and impose on them a certain regimen: they control even the food, sleeping arrangements, the room size, the hours
of rest, and even their most intimate affairs; whoever won't go along
is fired and no longer has the six dollars minimum daily salary. Ford
pays a minimum of six dollars, but he wants people who know how
to work and are always in a condition to work, that is, who know
how to coordinate work with their life regimen. We Europeans are
still too bohemian, we believe that we can do a certain kind of work
and live as we please, like bohemians: naturally, machinism crushes
us and I mean machinism in a general sense, as scientific organization
that encompasses also intellectual work. We are too romantic in an
absurd way and not wanting to be petit bourgeois we fall into the
most typical form of petit bourgeoisism that is precisely bohemian-

ism. And so I have already begun a dissertation with you. I embrace you tenderly.

Antonio

1. For Gramsci's analysis of "Americanism and Fordism," see Hoare and Smith, eds., *Selections from the Prison Notebooks*, pp. 277–318, and Forgacs, ed., *A Gramsci Reader*, pp. 275–299.

October 20, 1930

Dearest Carlo,

From one of Tatiana's letters I think I understand that you went back to Sardinia from Milan. Why didn't you write me about it? In all this time I've only received a short note from mother: obviously she is still very weak. She asks me for news about the children and Giulia: I believe that you yourself have given her this news. She didn't even write me two lines; get her to write me a few letters at greater length. My health remains the same. Greetings and kisses to all at home; an affectionate embrace for mother. Cordially

Antonio

November 4, 1930

Dearest Tatiana,

I was happy to hear from your last letter that you agree with me in regard to the state of Giulia's health. It is always best, in such matters, that an identical moral pressure be applied from the outside; considering the scant effectiveness that moral pressure can have in such matters, let it at least be uniform and in accord so that it won't be completely useless! You are surprised that in Rome I didn't side with you in trying to get Giulia to adopt a way of life that was materially less fatiguing as regards the demands of her work. Your surprise is correct and I ought to justify myself. But that is not possible today: my justification would perhaps appear grotesque or at least comical or perhaps even simply romantic.

My health remains the same and my greatest effort is devoted to maintaining at least the present stabilization. The whole problem is insomnia, which being due only partially to organic causes and in good part to causes that are external, mechanical, more or less inherent in prison life, cannot be defeated by therapeutic measures but only palliated.[1] I have drawn up statistics for the month of October: only two nights did I sleep five hours, for nine whole nights I did not sleep at all, on the other nights I slept less than five hours, in variable amounts, which adds up to a general average of less than two hours per night. I myself wonder sometimes at having so much endurance and at not experiencing a general breakdown. I regularly take the Benzofosfan (which is almost finished) and the Uroclasio, and in the evening I take Sedobrol. I take them, I repeat, to try to maintain at least the present level of my physical condition.

I always forget to write that among the books given to Carlo there was a brand new uncut copy of the *Discorsi* [*Speeches*] given by the Head of the Government in 1929; two copies of this book had been sent to me by mistake and we should send it back to the Sperling bookstore, asking for another book of the same price in exchange. I don't know whether those books are already in Sardinia or are still in Rome. If they are still in Rome please see to the shipment yourself or if they are in Sardinia tell Carlo, who still hasn't written to me after his trip to Turi. I also asked you to inform the Sperling bookstore that I hadn't received the August issue of the *Gerarchia*[2] magazine and you had informed me that you had done so. You'll have to try again because besides the month of August I'm now lacking September and October; on top of this, it's more than a month since I received *Italia Letteraria* (the last one I received is the September 21 issue). I beg you to send a registered postcard so that we can be sure that they receive it. I did not read Ford's book about the Jews,[3] but I know his point of view from other fundamental books of his: the struggle against the Jews is the sharpest aspect of his struggle against the plutocracy that has repeatedly tried to take over his industrial system through financial pressure and also through the activities of the labor unions. Who knows how much greater Ford's hatred has now grown following the crises of the New York Stock Exchange that have slowed down the construction of automobiles! All the optimism of his industrial vision has been destroyed with a single blow and it will be difficult to revive it. My dear, I embrace you tenderly.

Antonio

1. See Gramsci's letter of September 1, 1932, to the warden of Turi prison protesting the noise made by the prison guards who, night after night, slammed the doors leading from other corridors and from the infirmary into the section of the prison where Gramsci's corner cell was located, thereby causing his "insomnia."

2. *Gerarchia*, one of the principal cultural organs of the Fascist party, was founded by Mussolini in 1922 and appeared regularly until its demise in July 1943.

3. Gramsci was referring to the Italian translation: Henry Ford, *L'ebreo internazionale* [The international Jew] (Milan: Sonzogno, 1928), a collection of articles that had appeared in the *Dearborn Independent*.

November 4, 1930

Dearest Giulia,

I don't know whether you're still in Soci and whether this letter must be forwarded to you, and whether you have already returned from your rest.[1] Therefore I will not again administer to you a long letter in the manner of Doctor Grillo,[2] which I had already thought out in its entire structure as an academic treatise. We'll leave it for next time. Meanwhile I warn you that "all is revealed," that there no longer exist any mysteries for me, that I have in fact been minutely informed about the true state of your health. This, to tell the truth, was what in Italy is called "the mystery of evident things" in the sense that I had understood that you were quite ill or were at least going through a psychic crisis that must have had a physiological basis; I would have been a very poor "man of letters" if I hadn't understood this from reading your letters, which, after a first reading, which I will call disinterested, and in which my only guide is my affection for you, were then reread, so to speak, by the literary and psychoanalytic "critic."[3] For me the literary (linguistic) expression is a relationship between form and content: this analysis demonstrates to me or helps me understand whether between form and content there is complete adherence or whether there are cracks, veilings, pentimenti, disguises, etc. One can of course make mistakes, especially if one wants to deduce too much, but if one has common sense one can understand a lot, at least the general state of mind. I write all this to you to let you know that at this point you can and must write to me with great frankness. I've received some photographs of our children, very bad technically but nevertheless very interesting for me. I embrace you affectionately.

Antonio

1. See letter to Tania, July 28, 1930, n. 2.

2. A reference to the game "Guess it if you can," based on the figure of the "wise" cricket (*grillo* in Italian), who would be placed at the center of a circle of numbers. The number toward which the cricket pointed its leg was regarded as the one able to reveal secrets about future events. The remote origins of the game are believed to be a poem published in Lucca in 1519 concerning a "Master Grillo," a peasant who became a doctor and fortune-teller (*Dizionario Enciclopedico Italiano*, 5: 606).

3. Gramsci derived this notion of two moments or phases in the reading process, one emotionally involved, the other detached and critical, from Francesco De Sanctis.

November 17, 1930

Dearest Tatiana,

I've received your postcard of November 10 and the letter of the thirteenth. I'll try to answer your questions in order. (1) For the time being you mustn't send me any books. Put the ones you have aside and wait for me to tell you to ship them. I first want to get rid of all the old magazines that have accumulated over four years: before sending them away I go through them and take notes on the subjects that interest me most and naturally this takes up a good part of my day, because the scholarly notes are accompanied by references, comments, etc. I've focused on three or four principal subjects, one of them being the cosmopolitan role played by Italian intellectuals until the end of the eighteenth century, which in turn is split into several sections: the Renaissance and Machiavelli, etc. If I had the possibility of consulting the necessary material I believe that there is a really interesting book to be written that does not yet exist; I say book, meaning only the introduction to a number of monographs, because the subject presents itself differently in different epochs and in my opinion one would have to go back to the times of the Roman empire. Meanwhile I write notes, also because reading the relatively little that I have brings back to mind my old readings of the past. Besides, this is not a completely new thing for me, because ten years ago I wrote an essay on the language question according to Manzoni,[1] and that required a certain research into the organization of Italian culture, from the time when the written language (the so-called medieval Latin, that is, the Latin written from 400 AD until 1300) became completely detached from the language spoken by the people, which, Roman centralization having come to an end, was fragmented into numberless dialects. This medieval Latin was followed by vulgar Latin, which was again submerged by humanistic Latin, giving rise to an erudite language, vulgar in its lexicon but not in its phonology and even less in its syntax, which was reproduced from Latin: thus there continued to exist a double language, the popular or dialectal one and the erudite, that is, the language of intellectuals and the cultivated classes. Manzoni himself, in rewriting *The Betrothed* and in his treatises on the Italian language, actually only took into account a single aspect of the language, the lexicon, and not the syntax that is in fact the essential part of any language, so much so that English, though it contains more than 60 percent of Latin or neo-Latin words, is a Germanic language, whereas Roumanian, though it contains more than 60 percent of Slavic words, is a neo-Latin language. As you see, this subject interests me so much that I've let it carry me away. (2) For the magazines: I haven't much use for *Bibliografia Fascista* because the bibliographic magazines that I receive are compiled by the same writers and the books reviewed are the same. You write to me about an English magazine: perhaps it would be a good idea to send me a sample copy through the Sperling bookstore. You could also get them to send me a sample issue of the weekly supplement to the *Manchester Guardian* and to the *Times*, which I saw in the prison in Rome: I believe, however, that the literary prose of these magazines is still too difficult for me. And furthermore I have no great desire to study languages. (3) I didn't understand what you wrote to me with regard to a "jacket" that Carlo is supposed to have mentioned to me, (. . . .)[2] From what I remember of what Carlo told me, this is supposed to be a knitted or woolen undershirt for the winter. You call it a "jacket" and in prison we are only allowed the regulation jacket. I had already told Carlo that I have enough knitted undershirts to last me several years, and not only simple undershirts: I have four if not five sweaters and two of them I haven't even touched yet. What's the point of sending me more objects of the same kind even if of a better form? or simply different? So that the moths can eat them (. . . .)[3]

You were too quick to write to Sperling bookstore about the subscription to the magazines: too much zeal, because in two months they'll have plenty of time to forget the request. I do receive *Secolo Illustrato* regularly. I absolutely don't want *Emporium*: I already have enough slippers. Don't be angry with me. I embrace you tenderly.

Antonio

I've received the Sedobrol and the over-stockings. Thank you. Send the other half page to my sister Teresina Gramsci-Paulesu.

1. Here Gramsci was probably referring to an essay he wrote under the tutelage of his professor of linguistics at the University of Turin, Matteo Bartoli.
2. Several censored words.
3. Several censored words.

———————

November 17, 1930

Dearest Teresina,

I've received your letter of the eleventh with a photograph of your children. They are very appealing and pretty and they are also sturdy and healthy, I would say. I'm really astonished at how much more robust Franco has become; some time ago you sent me a photograph of him in which he appeared thin and puny, now he looks clearly strong, quick, and very vivacious. I'm really happy about it and I would be grateful if you would send a copy of the same photograph to Tatiana who will send it to Giulia: I sent her some of the other photographs (which had turned out very bad technically) and she wrote me that Delio and Giuliano took a great interest in them and asked many questions.

I've been very worried because I haven't received any news from mother for more than a month: Carlo hasn't written to me since his trip to Turi (or at least I did not receive his letter); as for Nannaro, despite all his promises, he has never written to me (in his case, however, it is likely that his letters did not arrive). You really ought to make up your mind to write to me a bit more often and especially give me news of your children. This interests me very much. Your reference to Franco, who writes "long letters in his own fashion" that amuse you, pleases me: it means that he has imagination, that he has something to say, and that he makes an effort to give expression to the things that swirl around in his head. Who knows if he will resemble us two: do you remember how fanatical we were about reading and writing? It seems to me that you too, around the age of ten, having run out of books, read all the Codices. On the contrary Mimì does not seem very imaginative to me: she has the astonished expression of one who is too busy admiring the world to have any time to fantasize on her own. It seems to me that the little one is most of all happy at being protected by the two older ones and therefore being able to trust without qualms the camera and its *moro cabbanu*[1] apparatus. It even seems to me that she has a certain air of defiance, holding her head at a forty-five degree angle. Of course a photograph freezes a very restless movement of life and it is possible to misinterpret a single attitude even if it is very dramatic, as in the photograph of your children. Write to me also about mother and about the real condition of her health. Overcome your apathy and listlessness and don't allow yourself to be overwhelmed by the monotonous environment of the office and its clients and by their silly, tedious chatter. You must become vivacious as in the past (not in the physical sense, for in that sense you've never been vivacious, it seems to me, but in the intellectual sense) so that you can properly guide the children outside school and not leave them to their own devices, as too often happens especially in so-called proper families. I embrace you affectionately.

Antonio

1. "Black cape," in Sardinian.

December 1, 1930

Dearest Tatiana,

I've received the package with the medicines and the other small things that you sent me. The over-stockings you sent me are perfect, but I'm afraid that the shoes will get the best of them too; in any event I will no longer use up a pair of socks a week. I don't think that there is any point in your sending me more tonics such as Benzofosfan or painkillers such as the last one you sent me: I'm convinced that they don't help me at all. I'll tell you what you can send me if I need anything.

Carlo still hasn't written to me since his trip to Turi, I don't know why, though I can guess. Right now I don't need money: I have 870 lire that will last me for several months. For a few months now we are no longer allowed to receive cigarettes; we can however receive loose tobacco. I had reminded Carlo that when I was in prison in Rome I received from him or from you a pack of Turkish tobacco, which was very good, since it was similar to the Italian Macedonia tobacco of old, when they were not yet mixing it with American tobacco: it cost, as I remember, four twenty a pack and now it can't cost much more, because the price of foreign tobacco hasn't gone up much. If you feel like taking care of this, you could try to find it again; but send me just a little of it, so that in case of a mistake there won't be a great loss; I can only smoke light tobacco of the Macedonia type.

I would be glad if in some bookstore in Rome you could find the October issue of the magazine *La Nuova Italia* directed by Professor Luigi Russo[1] and if you could send it to Giulia. In it is published a letter that talks about the courteous debate that took place at the International Congress of Philosophers recently held in Oxford[2] between Benedetto Croce and Lunacharsky with regard to the question of whether there exists or there can exist an esthetic doctrine of historical materialism. This letter is perhaps by Croce himself, or at least by one of his disciples, and it is strange.

It seems that Croce answered a dissertation by Lunacharsky, adopting a certain paternal tone, part protective and part humorous banter, to the congress's great amusement. From the letter it also appears that Lunacharsky did not know that Croce has given a lot of thought to historical materialism, has written much about it, and is in any case deeply versed in the entire subject, and this seems strange to me, because Croce's books are translated into Russian and Lunacharsky knows Italian very well.

From this letter it also appears that Croce's position on historical materialism has completely changed from what it was until a few years ago. Now Croce maintains, no less, that historical materialism marks a return to the old . . . medieval theologism, to pre-Kantian and pre-Cartesian philosophy. A most extraordinary thing that makes one suspect that he too, despite his Olympian serenity, is beginning to doze off too often, more often than happened to Homer. I don't know if he will write a special account of this subject: it would be very interesting and I think that it would not be difficult to answer him, drawing the necessary and sufficient arguments from his own works. I believe that Croce has had recourse to a very transparent polemical sleight of hand and that his opinion, rather than a philosophic-historical opinion, is only an act of will, that is, it has a practical purpose. That many so-called theoreticians of historical materialism might have fallen into a philosophical position similar to medieval theologism and might have made of "economic structure" a sort of "unknown god" can perhaps be proven; but what would it mean? It would be as though one were trying to judge the religion of the Pope and the Jesuits and were to talk about the superstitions of the peasants of Bergamo. Croce's position on historical materialism seems to me similar to the position of Renaissance men on the Lutheran Reform: "Where Luther enters, civilization disappears," said Erasmus, and yet the historians and Croce himself today recognize that Luther and the Reformation stand at the beginning of all of modern philosophy and civilization, Croce's philosophy included. The men of the Renaissance did not understand that a great movement of moral and intellectual renewal, inasmuch as it was embodied by the vast popular masses, as happened with Lutheranism, would at first assume coarse and even superstitious forms and that this was inevitable due to the very fact that the German people, and not a small aristocracy of great intellectuals, was the protagonist and the standard-bearer of the Reformation. If Giulia can do it, she ought to let me know whether the Croce-Lunarcharsky polemic will give rise to intellectual manifestations of some importance.

As you remember, some time ago I submitted a request to the Head of the Government to be allowed to read certain books that have been withheld and besides those two other books that I did not yet have and wanted permission to buy, that is: Fülop-Miller, *Il volto del bolshevismo* [The face of Bolshevism], with a preface by Curzio Malaparte, Bompiani, Milan; and Leon Trotsky, *Mia vita* [My life], Mondadori, Milan (I'm not sure whether Trotsky's book has this title or something similar). The answer has arrived and it is favorable so I ask you to please write to the bookstore and have them sent to me. I would also like to receive these other books: (1) Benedetto Croce, *Eternità e storicità della filosofia* [Eternity and historicity of philosophy], Biblioteca editrice, Rieti; (2) Henri De Man, *La gioia nel lavoro* [The joy of work], Laterza, Bari; (3) Biagio Riguzzi, *Sindacalismo e riformismo nel Parmese* [Trade unionism and reformism in the region of Parma], Laterza, Bari. With regard to my request to the Head of the

Government you would perhaps do well to tell Carlo not to make further requests, in case he is planning to; I would say that things turned out pretty well.

Dearest, I must hand in this letter. I embrace you very tenderly.

Antonio

The lines—the last on the preceding page and the first on this page—have been crossed out by me. If you write to Carlo tell him that I'm unhappy that he has not written to me for so long and that he has not sent me news about mother's health.

Let me congratulate you warmly on the way you put together the over-stockings: you did a wonderful piece of work and it must have cost you a great effort because the fabric is very heavy and must be hard to sew. I thank you with all my heart.

Antonio

1. In his many books and essays on Italian literature, Luigi Russo (1892–1961) played an important part in reintegrating the Crocean concept of art as intuition into a historically grounded critical methodology. His essay "Il Dante del Vossler, e l'unità poetica della *Divina commedia*," in *Studi Danteschi*, 12 (1927): 5–29, influenced Gramsci's way of reading canto 10 of the *Inferno*.

2. Gramsci's reference is to the seventh international philosophical congress held in Oxford from September 1–5, 1930. The letter was published in *La Nuova Italia* (October 10–20, 1930): 431–432. Anatoli Lunacharsky (1875–1933), Russian playwright and Bolshevik revolutionary, headed the Soviet People's Commissariat of the Enlightenment (*Narkompros*) from 1917 to 1929.

December 15, 1930

Dearest Mother,

I don't understand what is happening. It is three months now that Carlo hasn't written to me. Your last note arrived approximately two months ago. About a month and a half ago I received a letter from Teresina, which I answered, without getting a reply (I wrote to Teresina four weeks ago, exactly). I really can't find an explanation for this systematic silence: why not interrupt it at least with a postcard now and then? Tatiana tells me that she has received a letter from Carlo who apologizes for not writing more often, pointing to his tremendous workload as an excuse. This seems to me an insufficient justification; it can explain why a person doesn't write long letters, but it does not explain absolute silence. A picture postcard can be written in a second.

I wonder whether Carlo has had some difficulties because of me and whether he doesn't want to or doesn't know how to explain to me that he is in a disconcerted or hesitant state of mind. I would therefore beg him to reassure me or get someone else to reassure me, perhaps by asking Mea to write me a letter. And in the same way I would like to have more frequent news about your health. Have you regained your strength? If you haven't got the strength to write me ask someone else to write me a postcard and then add only your signature; for me it will be enough. Dearest mother, this is the fifth Christmas that I spend deprived of freedom and the fourth that I spend in prison. Truly my condition as a detainee in which I spent the Christmas of 1926 in Ustica was still a kind of paradise of personal freedom compared to my condition as a prisoner. But you mustn't believe that my serenity has left me. I'm four years older, I have many white hairs, I've lost my teeth, I no longer laugh with gusto as I used to, but I believe that I have become wiser and that I have enriched my experience of men and of things. When all is said and done, I have not lost my taste for life; everything still interests me and I'm certain that, even though I can no longer *zaccurrare sa fae arrostia*,[1] I still would not mind seeing others *zaccurrare*. So I haven't really become old, don't you agree? We become old when we begin to fear death and when we feel displeasure at seeing others do what we can no longer do. In this sense I am sure that you have not become old either, despite your age. I'm sure that you've made up your mind to live a long time, to be able to see us all together again and to be able to get to know your grand-children: as long as we want to live, as long as we have a taste for life and we still want to attain some goal, we succeed in withstanding all misfortunes and all illnesses. But you must understand that it is also necessary to husband one's strength and not insist on making too many demands on oneself when one is no longer a youngster. Now I actually remember that Teresina in her letter mentioned a bit mischievously that you insist on doing too much and that you do not want to give up your supremacy when it comes to housework. You must on the contrary give it up and rest. Dearest mother, I send you so many good wishes for the holidays, above all to be cheerful and untroubled. Many good wishes and greetings to everyone at home. I embrace you tenderly.

Antonio

1. "To munch roasted beans," in Sardinian. By the end of 1930, Gramsci had lost most of his teeth.

December 15, 1930

Dearest Tatiana,

Yes, yes, I did receive Zangwill's book[1] a long time ago and I always forgot to tell you. It is a very interesting book, but I already knew it; nevertheless I was glad to reread it.

The magazines *Pegaso* and *Les Nouvelles Littéraires* have always arrived regularly and do interest me: you can confirm the subscription with the Sperling bookstore, but I think that you have already confirmed all current subscriptions and therefore a specific confirmation is not needed; isn't that so? As for the application for revision, since it has already been submitted by one of the persons sentenced, there is no need for me to submit it. The individual elements are useful for the appeal, not for the revision, in which the only justification required is proof of technical error or of conflict with other sentences by the same tribunal, etc., that is, elements of a technical, judicial nature that only a lawyer can determine. I don't know which lawyer Umberto has appointed to deal with his petition, if it is accepted; to tell the truth, I don't even know what the procedure for the petitions for revision is, whether it is a deliberation in chambers or whether the lawyer is allowed to present the reasons for the petition before the council that hands down the judgment. At any rate, for our sort of trial, which was exquisitely political, the petition too will be accepted or rejected for political and not for formal juridical reasons and therefore the request by one person is sufficient. It's a matter of seeing whether in the petition all of the juridical points have been set forth by Umberto, and this I doubt, since at the trial the lawyers, from a professional point of view, were of an astounding inadequacy (I say inadequacy not to use a harsher term). They did not inform us of an essential fact, that is, that in another trial that preceded ours, the trial of the Florentine Serafino Masieri & Co. there had been an acquittal for the crime of inciting to civil war.[2] In our trial, however, it appeared that Masieri had committed this crime and we were sentenced to fifteen years imprisonment as "instigators" of a crime whose executant was acquitted! This too is no great matter, because, as I told you, it was a political trial, as the military prosecutor said and as the sentence repeats, we were sentenced for "mere danger," because we could have committed all the crimes contemplated by the code: that we had or hadn't committed them was a secondary matter. So forget about the problem of the petition; it was important that it should be presented, that is, that it should become part of the records of the Special Tribunal and that we had carried out all the actions granted by the law to protest the sentence; I don't believe that anyone had the least hope for an actual revision, I at least never thought of it and even less do I think of it today.

Dear Tatiana, I still don't want to write to Giulia; I first want to receive a letter from her and have news about her health directly from her. In any case I think that you should continue to send her all my letters, also the ones that are written to you personally. If you are sending her this one as well, she'll read about my wish, which expresses a real psychological need that I cannot suppress. Perhaps it is because my entire intellectual formation has been of a polemical order; even thinking "disinterestedly" is difficult for me, that is, studying for study's sake. Only occasionally, but rarely, does it happen that I lose myself in a specific order of reflections and find, so to speak, in the things themselves enough interest to devote myself to their analysis. Ordinarily, I need to set out from a dialogical or dialectical standpoint, otherwise I don't experience any intellectual stimulation. As I once told you, I don't like to cast stones into the darkness; I want to feel a concrete interlocutor or adversary; in my family relations too I wish to carry on dialogues, otherwise it would seem to me that I'm writing a novel in epistolary form, who knows what, that I'm turning out bad literature. Of course I would be interested to know what Delio thinks about his trip, what impressions he has gathered from it, etc. I no longer feel up to asking Giulia to urge Delio to tell me some story. I did this once; I wrote Delio a letter, perhaps you remember, but nothing came of it.

I can't think why the fact that I'm in prison has been hidden from Delio, without considering that he might find out about it indirectly, that is, in the most unpleasant form for a child, who will begin to doubt the truthfulness of his educators and will begin to think on his account and to live a life apart. At least this is what happened to me when I was a child: I remember it perfectly.[3] This element in Delio's life does not lead me to write to him directly: I think that any educational orientation, even the worst, is still better than interferences between two conflicting systems. Since I know about Delio's great nervous sensitivity and I know hardly anything about his real life and his intellectual development (I don't even know whether he has begun to read and write) I hesitate to take initiatives where he's concerned, precisely because I think that I might cause interferences of contradictory emotional stimuli that might be harmful. What is your opinion on this? Therefore it would be necessary to urge Giulia to write to me with more method or perhaps to suggest to me what I should write, and she should also be persuaded that in the final analysis it is neither right nor useful to hide from the children the fact that I am in prison. It is possible that at first the information may provoke unpleasant reactions, but the way in which they are given this information must be chosen thoughtfully. I think that it is appropriate to treat children as already reasonable beings with whom one speaks seriously also about the most serious things; this makes a very deep impression on them, strengthens their character, but it especially prevents the child's formation from being left to chance impressions from the environment and to the mechanical nature of chance encounters. It is really strange how grown-ups forget that they've been children and do not take their own experiences into account; as far as I'm concerned, I remember how all discoveries of the subterfuges resorted to in order to hide things that might distress me, offended me and led me to withdraw into myself and live a life apart; when I was about ten years old, I had become a real torment for my mother, for I had become so fanatical about frankness and truth in our mutual relationship that I made scenes and caused uproars.

I received the two packets of tobacco, which is good, but too strong. I thank you, but we better forget about it. I would like you to check whether the December issue of the magazine *Educazione Fascista* contains the recent speech by Senator Giovanni Gentile at the Fascist Cultural Institute. You can find this magazine at the Littorio bookstore and perhaps the sales clerk will be able to tell you whether the speech has been published in some other magazine (perhaps in *Bibliografia Fascista* which is also edited by Gentile). In any case, I would be grateful if you could arrange for me to receive a sample issue of *Educazione Fascista*, so that I can see how it is put together now and whether it is worth subscribing to: the December issue, which contains the year's summary, is the best sample. Dearest, I send you my best wishes for the holidays and I embrace you tenderly.

Antonio

1. Israel Zangwill, *Giuseppe il sognatore* [Joseph the dreamer] (Milan: Delta, 1929).
2. See letter to Tania, July 14, 1929.
3. See letter to Giulia, July 27, 1931, on this same theme. Gramsci's sons were apparently not told about his imprisonment by members of the Schucht family until circumstances forced them to do so. In his introduction to Tatiana Schucht, *Lettere ai familiari*, p. xv, Giuliano Gramsci says that "I learned that my father was in prison just a short time before his death. The truth was revealed to me by a neighbor." And in a letter to Gramsci of October 2, 1930, Tania told him that his sons "do not know that you are in prison and when Delio learned of it from another child at the kindergarten he was very affected by it: later they persuaded him that it wasn't true." (Natoli, *Antigone*, pp. 228–29).

December 29, 1930

Dearest Tatiana,

I've received the six photographs and I like them very much. I don't think there is any need to enlarge them, because in their details they are very clear and sharp. Don't you agree? Unless you want to have copies of them for yourself; in that case tell me and I'll return them to you. But on another occasion it would be a good idea to delay sending them to me; believe me when I tell you that I've become completely unaccustomed to haste; I've learned to wait and to be patient. The photographs are all significant and interesting; the children are attractive and charming in general and the *nianie*[1] look serious. Did you notice how Delio, in terms of physiognomy, is so different from the others? One can immediately see that he belongs to another race; in the other children, even in their personal characteristics (and indeed it is remarkable how prominent these characteristics are), one notices a certain general resemblance in the structure of the head and face that distinguishes them from Delio.

I've received from the Sperling bookstore the books I've ordered through you. However I haven't received *Gerarchia* for six months and

I don't understand why. I don't think that this time too they will say that it has stopped publication, as they did in 1928 for *Critica Fascista*: do you remember? I therefore beg you to continue with your complaints: I'm missing the issues from August on, that is, the second semester of 1930. Of the English publications I only need the weekly supplements of the *Times* but the supplement of the *Manchester Guardian* specializes too much in the cotton industry and related subjects and besides reading English I find still costs me too much effort, so the supplement to the *Times* is quite enough.

You haven't told me anything about your health. You tell me that you wrote your last letter while in bed, but you do not add any details. And in the same way you no longer have told me anything about the regime you are following. And yet you really ought to resolve to get as strong as possible if this year you positively want to undertake the journey to see your family again. Believe me, this is necessary; you must go on a body-strengthening diet and observe it scrupulously, otherwise with what right can you reproach or advise Giulia and Genia? You too resemble them in taking such little care to eat properly, though your form of romanticism is different from theirs. Dearest, I'm not in the mood to go on writing; I'm in a semistupor. I embrace you tenderly.

Antonio

Send the other half of the page, but to my sister Grazietta, not to Teresina like the last time.

1. *Nianie* means "babysitters," or "nursemaids," in Russian.

December 29, 1930

Dearest Grazietta,

I received your letter together with Mea's note. On Christmas day the package arrived. Tell mother that everything was just so and that nothing had spoiled; also the bread was still really fresh and I've eaten it with great relish: I could taste the flavor of the very good Sardinian durum wheat. And in the same way I've enjoyed eating *sa panischedda*,[1] I think that it is fifteen or sixteen years since I last ate it. The news about mother's health has greatly distressed me, I'm sure that you will be very patient with her: if you think about it, she would certainly deserve much more than patience, because she has worked for us all of her life, sacrificing herself in unimaginable ways; if she had been a different woman who knows to what disastrous end we would have come even as children; perhaps none of us would be alive today, don't you agree?

I had seen Father Soggiu's[2] photograph in two illustrated magazines, but I hadn't recognized him, indeed I hadn't even thought that it dealt with him; although under one of the photographs it said that he was born in Norbello. I looked at him again after your letter and even under that large Franciscan beard I was able to make out the lineaments of his brothers' features, especially of his brother Gino. And he hadn't even aged, just the opposite; and yet he had become a friar at least twenty-five years ago and after getting his university degree. He was truly a good man and he must have been a very good friar, I don't doubt it for a moment. And so the people of Ghilarza will have another local martyr, after Palmerio, indeed more deservedly, because Palmerio only had the "merit" of having undertaken a journey to Jerusalem. But I do think that if a Buddhist monk came to Ghilarza from China and preached in order to get them to abandon the religion of Christ for that of Buddha, the people of Ghilarza would certainly murder him just as the Chinese have done with Father Soggiu.

I really hope that Carlo will make up his mind to write to me; an attack of nerves does not justify such a long silence. I would also like to know if Nannaro has written to you that he has written to me. After his departure from Turi he sent me a telegram from Switzerland and a letter from Namur, en route to his place of residence, and I don't know where that is. I would like to know whether he has ever written to me after that and if his letters have gone astray. Thank Mea for her note; I was happy that she wrote to me, but I'm sorry to see that she still writes like a little girl in the third grade (and she must be attending the fifth, if I'm not mistaken). It is a real shame, because in the Ghilarza schools our family enjoyed a certain reputation; this Mea must really have been born in Pirri[3] and her cradle must have been deafened by the frogs in the ponds that must have turned her too into a frog's brain: she knows how to croak, but she doesn't know how to think and reflect. Pull her ears for me and tell her that she must go on writing to me every so often to show me that her spelling has improved. Dear Grazietta, you too must write me sometimes. I embrace you affectionately, together with mother and the entire family (including the maid, if she'll permit it).

Antonio

1. *Sa panischedda*, a Sardinian candy made with nuts, almonds, and cooked grape juice.

2. Giovanni Soggiu (1883–1930), Sardinian priest and an acquaintance of the Gramsci family, who was killed by bandits on November 22, 1930, while on missionary duty in China.

3. A town near Cagliari surrounded by swamps that were partly reclaimed after World War II.